Educational Input, Resource Allocation and Returns to Human Capital

Weifang Min

Educational Input, Resource Allocation and Returns to Human Capital

Analysis of Education and Human Resources Issues in China

中国财经出版传媒集团
经济科学出版社
Economic Science Press

Springer

Weifang Min
Graduate School of Education
Peking University
Beijing, China

Translated by
Lijuan Zhang
School of Economics
Shandong University
Jinan, China

This book is sponsored by the Chinese Fund for the Humanities and Social Sciences

ISBN 978-981-96-4686-9 ISBN 978-981-96-4687-6 (eBook)
https://doi.org/10.1007/978-981-96-4687-6

Jointly published with Economic Science Press
The print edition is not for sale in Chinese Mainland. Customers from Chinese Mainland please order the print book from: Economic Science Press.
ISBN of the Co-Publisher's edition: 978-750-58-8196-9

Translation from the Chinese Simplified language edition: "教育投入, 资源配置与人力资本收益" by Weifang Min, © Economic Science Press 2009. Published by Economic Science Press. All Rights Reserved.

This Springer imprint is published by the registered company Springer Nature Singapore Pte Ltd.
The registered company address is: 152 Beach Road, #21-01/04 Gateway East, Singapore 189721, Singapore

Preface

The Communist Party of China had set grand goals at its 16th National Congress in 2002 to build a moderately prosperous society in all respects and accelerate the country's modernization. To achieve these goals, there was an urgent need to review and update China's educational and human resource development strategies, so that the world's largest, richest and most valuable human resources can be fully tapped in a way that will provide continuous human resources and intellectual support to the efforts to build a prosperous society. Following the publication of the book, *Stride from a Country of Tremendous Population to a Country of Profound Human Resources*, the Ministry of Education approved a research project on China's education and human resources as a major research project in the field of philosophy and social sciences, to pursue further study in this area. The project was completed by a team of researchers mainly from Peking University, with Professor Min Weifang as the project leader.

The research took place in two phases. In the first phase, from January 2004 to June 2005, research focused on theoretical studies and cases in relevant countries. The research team also conducted empirical research based on macro data at both the country and provincial levels. All the research results are included in a published book named *China Education and Human Resource Development Report (2005–2006)*. During the second phase, from July 2005 to January 2007, the team focused on empirical research based on micro-data for families and individuals, and conducted some theoretical research as well as comparative studies of cases in different countries.

The research team focused on China's education itself in the first phase, including the philosophies for educational development, demand and supply for education, education and training system and mechanism, educational development index, etc. The second phase focused on the relationship between human capital and education, with emphasis on the cost and investment of education, the benefits of education and training, and the fairness and effectiveness of education. The two phases each has its own focus, but both were trying to define essential issues relating to China's education and human capital. The research was conducted in a much coordinated manner with well-planned steps, to form a complete and comprehensive research system. This book is a collection of the research results from the second phase.

The book was planned, coordinated and edited by Professors Min Weifang, Ding Xiaohao, Yue Changjun, and Guo Jianru. The authors for each chapter include Min Weifang, Yue Changjun, and Guo Jianru (Chapter 1); Ding Xiaohao and Xue Haiping (Chapter 2); He Feng and Yan Fengqiao (Chapter 3); Bao Wei (Chapter 4); Yue Changjun (Chapter 5); Ding Yanqing and Mun Chiu Tsang (Chapter 6); Guo Jianru (Chapter 7); Ding Xiaohao (Chapter 8); Li Ying and Ding Xiaohao (Chapter 9); Fan Aiai and Ding Xiaohao (Chapter 10); Hong Xiaoying and Li Wenli (Chapter 11); Chen Xiaoyu (Chapter 12); Li Fengliang and Ding Xiaohao (Chapter 13); Yue Changjun (Chapter 14); Guo Congbin and Min Weifang (Chapter 15).

An international symposium was held on this topic while the research project was in progress, and it was attended by domestic and foreign experts and scholars from the following universities and institutions: Columbia University in the United States, University of Toronto in Canada, University of Kassel in Germany, University of Tokyo in Japan, Bar-Ilan University in Israel, The Chinese University of Hong Kong, Indian National Institute of Education Planning and Management, World Bank, Ford Foundation, Ministry of Education of the People's Republic of China, China Education Television, China Education Research and Development Center, Shanghai Academy of Educational Sciences, Chinese Academy of Social Sciences, Chinese Academy of Sciences, Peking University, Tsinghua University, Beijing Normal University, Huazhong University of Science and Technology, Xi'an Jiaotong University, and Southwest University. In addition, more than a dozen Chinese and foreign scholars were invited to give lectures at Peking University. We would like to express our deep gratitude to all the experts and scholars for the guidance and advice they have offered.

Many doctoral and master students from the Department of Educational Economics and Management at the Graduate School of Education of Peking University also participated in different ways in the research.

As this book is formed on the basis of work conducted by a number of scholars under a major research project, the writing style of the chapters may not be very consistent. And errors and omissions may still exist in the book due to the authors' limitations. Comments and suggestions from readers are therefore very welcome.

Beijing, China Weifang Min

Main Members of the Research Group

According to the stroke order of Chinese surnames

Ding Xiaohao
Ding Yanqing
Wen Dongmao
Wang Rong
Li Wenli
Chen Xiaoyu
Yue Changjun
Guo Jianru
Yan Fengqiao

Contents

Chapter 1
Introduction

This book is compiled on the basis of the final project report on *Education and Human Resources Issues in China*, a key philosophy and social sciences research project sponsored by the Ministry of Education of the People's Republic of China. The first phase research results were incorporated into the *China Education and Human Resources Development Report* (*2005–2006*). This book examines the development of China's education, often in the context of country comparisons on similar issues. The study covers current educational demand, philosophies for educational development, means of delivery, educational financing, and post compulsory education training. An education development index has been developed using education data from different provinces. In the second phase of the project, a questionnaire survey was conducted for data collection, which the research team used for more detailed empirical studies from multiple angles on China's education and human resource issues. On this basis, the researchers have provided policy recommendations which they believe are feasible.

1.1 Current State and Challenges in China's Education and Human Resources Development

1.1.1 Significance of Education and Human Resources Development

The twenty-first century is an era of the knowledge economy in which human capital has become one of the most important sources of economic growth. It is also an era of globalization in which competition among countries becomes more intense than ever before. China today is a country that is increasingly integrated with the global economy. In 2006, China's foreign trade reached US$1760.7 billion, direct foreign

W. Min, *Educational Input, Resource Allocation and Returns to Human Capital*,
https://doi.org/10.1007/978-981-96-4687-6_1

investment was US$63 billion, and foreign exchange reserves reached US$1066.3 billion. In order to maintain a strong momentum for long-term growth amid fierce international competition and build up its strengths in different areas, China must transform its economic growth pattern. Instead of growth solely driven by investment and exports, China needs to rely more on knowledge and technology. Its vast human resources need to be turned into powerful human capital. Fundamentally, China's growth will be determined by the level of its educational development. As education helps improve individual productivity, increase personal income, and stimulate economic growth, it is regarded by many countries and international institutions as an important tool to narrow the income gap between rich and poor. It is fair to say that education is becoming more and more important as the knowledge economy flourishes and globalization continues to expand. In China, education is not only a source of economic growth, but also a cornerstone for the development of a harmonious society.

1.1.1.1 Education as a Source of Economic Growth

According to the new economic growth theory, human capital is considered a more important production factor than physical capital and natural resources. Education is the dominant form of human capital investment, and plays a vital role in knowledge diffusion, technological progress, and economic growth. Education is an input to economic growth in the sense that it provides the human capital that helps improve labor productivity. The experiences of Organization for Economic Co-operation and Development (OECD) countries prove that increased human capital can improve labor productivity and promote technological advancement. From 1990 to 2000, increased labor productivity contributed at least half of the growth of the per capita GDP in most OECD countries (OECD 2004). Another study on 24 OECD countries, based on their 1950–1990 data, shows that there is a significant positive correlation between the level of formal education and labor productivity, with the exception of a few countries (Wolff 2000).

The close relationship between education and economic development is also manifested in regional development in China. In 2006, among the 31 provinces, autonomous regions, and municipalities directly under the central government, Shanghai ranked the top with the highest per capita GDP of RMB51474, 9.2 times more than RMB5052 in Guizhou. A simple linear regression analysis was done in this study using regional per capita GDP in 2005 as the dependent variable and the mean years of schooling (MYS) of employees as the explanatory variable. It shows that there is a significant positive relationship between the MYS and the per capita GDP. The goodness of fit reaches 0.5062, indicating that human capital is the reason for 50.62% of the regional difference in the per capita GDP. The regression result shows that when the MYS of employees extends by one year, the per capita GDP increases by about RMB5463 (see Fig. 1.1). Although a more sophisticated model is needed to accurately measure the marginal impact of education on per capita GDP,

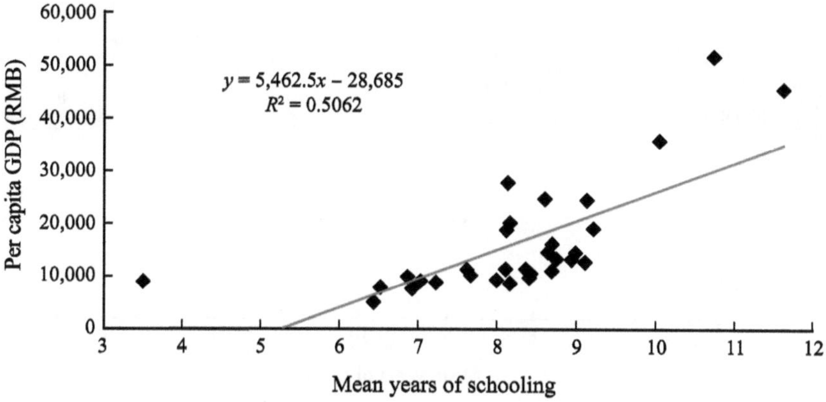

Fig. 1.1 Per capita GDP and MYS of employees across China in 2005

the above simple linear regression model is sufficient to show the significant positive relationship between education and economic growth.

1.1.1.2 Education as a Cornerstone for the Development of a Harmonious Society

China has been one of the fastest-growing economies in the world since 1978. According to data published by the National Bureau of Statistics (NBS), China's real GDP from 1978 to 2004 grew at an average annual rate of 9.4%, doubling every 7.7 years. Its real per capita GDP had an average annual growth rate of 8.1%, doubling every 8.9 years. Along with rapid economic development, issues have emerged and caused difficulties for the country as it works to achieve its goal for a moderately prosperous and harmonious society. The most prominent problem is inequitable income distribution, mainly reflected in the gap between urban and rural residents and the gap within urban residents. Among the issues, sectoral income difference is particularly outstanding. In 2006, workers in information and communication, computer services and software development industry earned the highest annual income of RMB40,588 on average, which was 3.9 times more than that of their counterparts in agriculture, forestry, animal husbandry and fishery sector, who earned only an annual income of RMB8309, the lowest of all sectors.

While there are multiple reasons for the income difference among different sectors, imbalanced human capital distribution is a major influencing factor. In a simple linear regression analysis, which employs the average wage of all industries in 2005 as the dependent variable, and the MYS as the explanatory variable, it can be seen that there is a significant positive relationship between the MYS and average wage of an industry. The goodness of fit reaches 0.4853, indicating that human capital variation can explain 48.53% of the income difference among industries. The regression result also shows that for each additional year of the MYS, the average annual wage of an

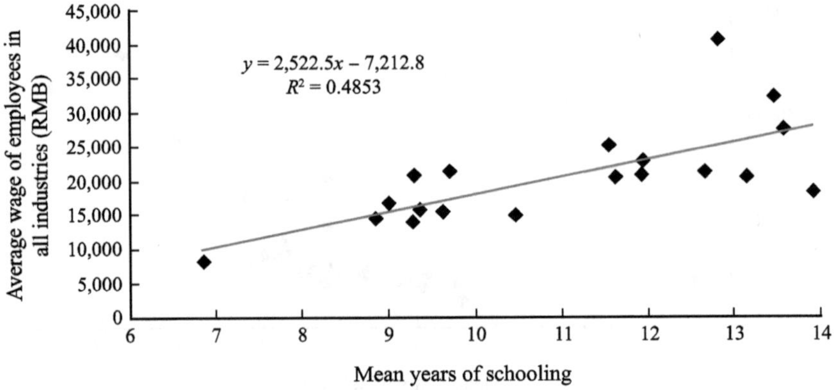

Fig. 1.2 Average annual wage and MYS in all industries in 2005

industry increases by about RMB2523 (see Fig. 1.2). Given the notable impact education could have on income, a general improvement of education would be of great significance in raising the income of the vulnerable groups and ameliorating social inequality. Therefore, education has become the cornerstone for the development of a harmonious society in China.

1.1.2 Current State and Challenges

China is a country with massive human resources, but it still has much to improve in its educational and human resource development, with the average education level of its residents remaining relatively low overall. The educational background of workers in different regions and industries varies greatly, and such difference results in income gaps. The overall low-level and imbalanced development of education poses a challenge not only to sustained economic growth, but also to the country's efforts to build a harmonious society.

Based on a census of 1% of the population conducted by the NBS in 2005, the research team found that the educational level of China's labor force is generally low. By the end of 2005, a total of 758.25 million people were employed in China. A high percentage of them (44.1%) received middle school education, followed by 29.2% who only went to primary school. Only 12.1% of the people employed attended high school and 6.8% received college or higher education. The MYS is therefore 8.2 years.[1] Nationwide, more than 80% of the employed population received education up to middle school. In contrast, urban workers are better educated. In 2005, the employed population in urban areas reached 273.31 million, accounting for 36%

[1] For the purpose of MYS, schooling is defined as 0 for those who have never been to school, 6 for those who attended primary school, 12 for those who completed middle school, 15 for education up to high school, 16 for junior college, and 19 for undergraduate or graduate studies.

of the total workforce in the country. Among them, 43.3% received middle school education, 21.1% attended high school, and 15.3% had college academic credentials or higher, making an MYS of 9.6 years.

Regional differences in MYS are quite significant[2] (also based on the 1% national census done by the NBS in 2005). Beijing, Shanghai, and Tianjin have the best-educated workers, with an MYS of 11.6, 10.7, and 10.0 years respectively. The proportion of workers who received college education or above reached 30.9%, 21.9%, and 14.8% respectively. In contrast, Tibet, Guizhou and Yunnan have a much less educated workforce, with an MYS of 3.5, 6.4 and 6.5 years respectively. Only 0.9% of the workers in Tibet have attended college, followed by 4.5% in Guizhou and 3.9% in Yunnan. In these six regions, the range of MYS (i.e., the maximum minus the minimum) is 8.1 years, while the range of percentage of workers with college education or above is 30%.

Sectoral difference in education is significant as well (also based on the 1% national census done by the NBS in 2005). Of the 20 sectors sampled, education, technology, and finance have the best-educated workforce, with an MYS of 13.9, 13.6 and 13.4 years respectively. 64.9% of the employees in the education sector have received college education, followed by 57.7% in technology and 55.1% in finance. In contrast, workers in agriculture, forestry, animal husbandry and fishery have the lowest level of education, with an MYS of only 6.9 years, and those who have received college education account for 0.2% only. The range of MYS in these sectors is 7.0 years, while the percentage range is 64.7% for those with college degrees. Of the 20 sectors sampled, agriculture, forestry, animal husbandry and fishery are the only ones that have an MYS lower than the national level of 8.2 years. If the employed population in urban areas is taken as a separate category, the numbers are more or less the same. People in education, technology, and finance sectors are better educated, with an MYS of 14.2, 13.7, and 13.6 years respectively. Those who have received college education or above account for 71.0%, 59.7%, and 57.6% respectively. Agriculture, forestry, animal husbandry and fishery, on the other hand, have a less educated workforce with an MYS of 7.3 years. Those who have received college education account for a mere 0.7%. The range of MYS is 6.9 years, while the percentage range is 70.3% for those who have received college education or above.

The lagging income increase for rural residents and the existence of vulnerable groups in urban areas have become the most prominent challenges to the building of a harmonious society in China. Education plays an important role in rural poverty alleviation and improving the overall status of urban vulnerable groups. It should be noted that China's arable land area is quite limited on a per capita basis, implying that if the rural population does not decrease, it would be hard for farmers to achieve a considerable income increase, even if advanced agricultural technologies are used, efficient forms of farming are adopted and preferential tax policies are offered. In order to reduce the agricultural population, education and training opportunities must be made available to farmers, so that more of them are able to find jobs in

[2] The word "region" is used herein for short to refer to the province, autonomous region or municipality directly under the central government (the same below).

non-agricultural sectors. The workers in agriculture, forestry, animal husbandry and fishery sectors are poorly educated. In 2005, only 4.9% of them received high school education or above, marking an MYS of 6.9 years. Such human capital structure will keep China from advancing urbanization and improving income for rural workforce and urban migrant workers. Statistics have shown that urban employed population in 2005 accounted for 36.0% of China's total employment, up from 32.8% in 2001 (Year 2001–2005 was also known as the 10th Five-year Plan period), having grown at an annual average rate of only 0.8% (see Table 1.1). At this rate, China will still have about 25% of its population working in rural areas four decades later. In order to accelerate urbanization, it is important to continue efforts to improve education and training of rural laborers, ensure that rural children can complete the nine-year compulsory education, and encourage more of them to pursue secondary and higher vocational education or regular university education.

The above analysis shows that education and human resources development, at the macro level, has become the key to China's economic growth and the building of a harmonious society. At the micro level, education is intrinsically consistent with employment quality, and thereby with income level. Generally speaking, those who are better educated are more productive, and they would be more likely to find better-paying jobs, and therefore have better income. It can be said that the level of education and the equity of education opportunities not only have economic implications, i.e., on the growth of individual income and national economy, but also have an immediate impact on social equity. To review the education and human resources issues in China with all their complexities, the research will examine, from the perspectives of efficiency and equity, the whole process of education from its input to the returns to human capital.

1.2 Research Questions and Framework

1.2.1 Analytical Questions

The whole process of education and human resources development includes educational input, resource allocation and access to educational opportunities, allocation of human resources in labor market, and conversion of human resources into returns on human capital. The issues of equity and efficiency at each link of this process is to be discussed in the following paragraphs.

1.2.1.1 Educational Cost and Resource Input

The input of educational resources directly affects the development of education. After entering the new era, China faces new challenges in its educational input. These challenges exist in two stages of education:

Table 1.1 Employment in urban and rural areas at year-end (2001–2005)

Year	Employed population (million)	Employment-to-population ratio (%)	Urban employed population (million)	Urban-to-total employment ratio (%)	Rural employed population (million)	Rural-to-total employment ratio (%)
2001	730.25	57.2	239.40	32.8	490.85	67.2
2002	737.40	57.4	247.80	33.6	489.60	66.4
2003	744.32	57.6	256.39	34.4	487.93	65.6
2004	752.00	57.9	264.76	35.2	487.24	64.8
2005	758.25	58.0	273.31	36.0	484.94	64.0

- Stage of compulsory education: The new safeguards mechanism of the rural compulsory education funds was implemented in the western region in the spring of 2006, and then extended to the rural areas in the central and eastern regions in the spring of 2007, which have effectively eased the financial burden of compulsory education on rural families. In the meantime, the burden of compulsory education on urban families started to draw people's attention. Is compulsory education a burden on urban families? How much do they spend on children's compulsory education? Are there notable differences in the spending on compulsory education between public and private schools?
- Stage of higher education: As higher education is being popularized, China has seen its higher education system diversified, i.e., different types of higher education institutions (HEIs) collect and invest educational resources through various channels, so as to deal with the impact from popularization of higher education. When facing a new landscape in the development of education, what kind of input responsibility should the government assume to alleviate the burden of compulsory education on families and popularize higher education? By learning from international experiences and considering the national financial strength and the demand for education, what will be a reasonable scale of government spending on public education? All these problems are worthy of analysis and exploration.

1.2.1.2 Equity in Resource Allocation and Educational Opportunities

In a society that values harmony and equality, the equity of educational opportunities means that individuals are able to receive basic education regardless of the socio-economic conditions of their families, which requires the government to prioritize equity in public educational resources allocation. In recent years, China has mainly universalized compulsory education, vigorously developed high school and secondary vocational education, and popularized higher education, which has greatly increased educational opportunities at each stage of education. However, the equity of educational resource allocation, the equity of educational process and outcome are increasingly concerned by all sectors of society.

In the stage of compulsory education, the equity of educational resource allocation is mainly manifested as equalization. Inequity has been a long-standing issue in China's economic and social development, due to unbalanced regional development and large urban–rural income gap. In such a context, different regions and even the urban and rural areas within the same region encounter inequity in educational resource allocation. Is there is a big gap in educational resources input between regions or between urban and rural areas in the same region? In compulsory education, whether the inequity of resource allocation is mainly caused by the imbalance between regions or that between urban and rural areas in the same region needs to be carefully examined. The geographic distribution of primary and secondary schools for compulsory education in rural areas directly affects the efficiency of educational resource allocation. China has been solving the phenomenon of "every village running a school", which was initiated since the mid-1990s to popularize the compulsory education in rural areas, so as to raise the efficiency of using educational resources, thereby motivating many places to adjust the geographic distribution of local primary and secondary schools. The adjustment in geographic distribution of rural primary and secondary schools not only concerns the efficiency of resource allocation, but relates to the issues of cost sharing and education equity. For this reason, a comprehensive understanding of the adjustment has drawn widespread concern. In urban areas, the imbalance in educational resources input has given rise to a hot topic of school choice. In the process of choosing schools, which groups are beneficiaries? What groups will see their interests infringed? How to safeguard the interests of disadvantaged groups? All of these questions need to be thoroughly investigated.

In the stage of higher education, the equity of educational resource allocation is mainly manifested in the access to HEIs: For children from families of different social strata, are there any differences in their entrance opportunities, field of study in college, post-graduation profession and work units? How could the socio-economic status of families affect the equity of the educational process, and how does this influence come about? Can the government-led fiscal policy for higher education reduce the inequality of entrance opportunities? How to properly design a fiscal policy for higher education? All of these issues need to be further explored.

1.2.1.3 Allocation of Educational and Human Resources

The situation of labor market depends on the process in which labor supply matches with demand. Although China has entered the stage of popularizing higher education, quite a number of high school graduates are worried about getting a job after failure in the college entrance examination. In order to mitigate the negative impact of popularized higher education on people with lower education level, China has implemented supportive policies to vigorously develop secondary vocational education, and the enrollment rate and number of students of secondary vocational schools have greatly increased. However, in the labor market, whether the secondary vocational school graduates are more competitive than the high school graduates is an issue in need of further study.

The allocation of human resources is a dynamic process. The people who have already got a job may keep flowing throughout their careers. There could be inter-regional, inter-industry, inter-department, inter-profession, and inter-position flow. Does the level of education affect one's job mobility? Does job mobility affect one's income improvement? Besides, in modern society, the vast majority of jobs are provided by bureaucratic organizations, thus stimulating lots of job seekers to pursue positions with relatively higher job autonomy. While they are looking for such jobs, to what extent does the educational level affect the outcome of job hunting? It is also an issue of concern.

1.2.1.4 Returns to Education and Human Capital

The returns to education are not only reflected in the job hunting of the unemployed in labor market, and the search for better jobs by the employed, but also in the improvement of labor productivity and income. Increasing income is a powerful driving force for most people to receive education. In the last decade, China has seen remarkable development in both basic education and higher education, which is largely motivated by the returns to education. How much are these returns? How will the rate of returns change in the future? Is there any room for further increase in such returns? These issues are directly related to the sustainable development of education in China.

The main reason why enterprises prefer to hire better-educated employees and organize on-the-job training for them is that they believe education and training could improve labor productivity. However, the myth of human capital is being tested from time to time in reality. In China, how much education plays a role in improving labor productivity and personal income? What are the factors that affect training? And to what extent could training increase the income of employees? These issues are in need of empirical study.

In China's labor market there are gender differences in multiple income levels, competence differences among individuals, and income difference among varied social strata. Better education can improve the livelihood of disadvantaged groups and increase their income, such effect is exactly what the society and the general public expect from education. The research team has made a special analysis on this topic.

1.2.2 Block Diagram for Research

Based on the above discussion of the issues related to education and human resources development, the research team has drawn a block diagram for detailed analysis (see Fig. 1.3).

In Fig. 1.3, the left part depicts the education process, with the upper left corner showing the cost sharing and input in education. Education does have a cost, which is necessary to sustain the development of education and ensure that education meets the needs of individual citizens, the government and society. The education system should have different types and levels to meet the general needs of mass public and the special or additional needs of certain groups. Different types and levels of education have divergent forms of cost sharing. In general, education input consists of two parts: (1) Household expenditures on education. (2) Fiscal expenditure on public education. Such division of responsibility for education input involves both efficiency and equity.

The lower left corner of Fig. 1.3 shows the allocation of education resources and the distribution of education opportunities, which are also associated with efficiency and equity. Any unreasonable allocation of education resources may affect

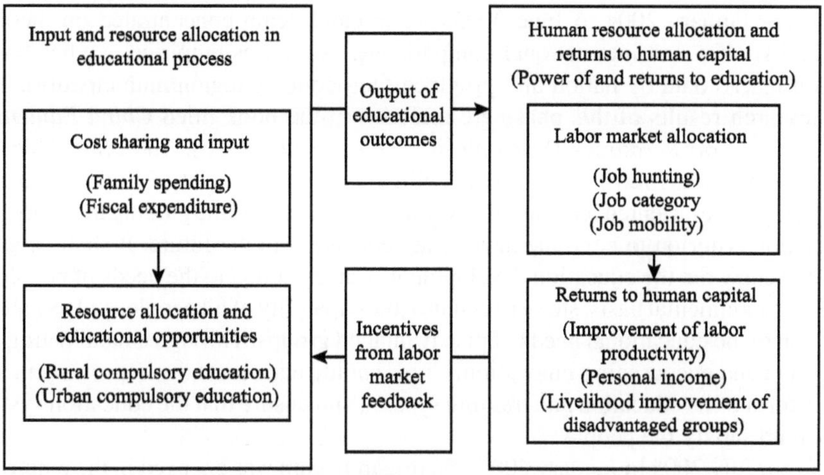

Fig. 1.3 Block diagram for analyzing "education input, resource allocation and returns on human capital"

the efficiency of education resources and equity of education opportunities. Take the rural compulsory education for example, if the geographic distribution of schools is too scattered, it may waste education resources, and deprive rural students of the same educational facilities and conditions as those in urban schools, thus resulting in inequity of education opportunities.

The right part of Fig. 1.3 shows the allocation of human resources in labor market and returns to human capital. The effect of education in labor market is manifested in the following scenarios: the better-educated persons find jobs more quickly than others, enjoy higher job autonomy, and may attempt upward mobility to seek higher-paid jobs.

The lower right corner of Fig. 1.3 illustrates returns to human capital, which are the end result of the educational process and the source of more educational demand. The motivation of individual/family input in education is expectation of higher income, while the reason for government spending on education is expectation of higher labor productivity and improved social welfare. They are premises for the returns to education (including training).

1.3 Research Process and Methodology

1.3.1 Research Process and Ideas

The research team divided its work from January 2004 to January 2007 into two phases:

1. From January 2004 to June 2005: the research team concentrated on theoretical studies and international comparisons, as well as empirical studies based on macro data by nation and province (autonomous region/municipality). The research results of this phase are included in the book titled *China Education and Human Resources Development Report* (*2005–2006*). The central idea of this book is as follows: "In order to build a harmonious society, China should take the 'people-oriented' education development concept as the guiding ideology and action criterion to continue developing education in the future. It shall develop and carry out the education development strategy suited to the needs of people as the fundamental basis, strive to enhance the capability of all people, and pay attention to the educational needs of disadvantaged groups. Through emancipating the mind and encouraging innovation, China should accelerate the improvement and reform of its education and training system, and ensure that the education system could satisfy the people".[3]
2. From July 2005 to January 2007: the research team was engaged in the empirical studies based on the micro-survey of households and individuals. The research in this phase focused on human resources issues and their links to education, the returns to education and training, education costs and inputs, as well as efficiency and equity of education.

The two phases of research are closely around the core issues of China's education and human resources. Each of them has its own focus, yet they are connected and consistent enough to constitute an integrated research framework. In terms of methodology, the research team insists on combining theory and practice, theoretical and empirical research, international comparison and Chinese characteristics, macro-data and micro-survey, static analysis and dynamic comparison.

1.3.2 Description of Sampling Survey Data

In order to comprehensively learn about the education and training status of Chinese urban residents, and the impact of education level on their employment and financial conditions, which will be basis for decision-making of education and other competent departments, the "China Education and Human Resources" Research Team, which was sponsored by the Institute of Economics of Education of Peking University, joined with the Urban Economic Survey Team of the NBS in April 2005 to investigate education and employment of Chinese urban residents in 2004. They surveyed 10,000 urban households in 12 provinces, including Beijing, Shanxi, Liaoning, Heilongjiang, Zhejiang, Anhui, Hubei, Guangdong, Sichuan, Guizhou, Shaanxi and Gansu. The content of this door-to-door survey covers the basic information of households and individuals, the status of education and training, household expenditures on education, work experience and income of major family members.

[3] Min Weifang (2006) *China Education and Human Resources Development Report* (*2005–2006*), Beijing: Peking University Press.

The survey questions are organized into four parts: basic situation of family; basic situation of family members and parents of different households; education status of the head of a household, his/her spouse and children; and work experience of the head of household and his/her spouse. (1) Basic situation of family: family size, total family income and expenditure, housing status, financial assets, ownership of computer and automobile, etc. (2) Basic situation of family members and parents of different households: gender, age, ethnicity, education level, type of household (*hukou*) registration, employment status, and income of all family members, parents of the head of a household and of his/her spouse. (3) Information about education: educational level, type, cost of schooling, educational subsidy, grades at school, and years of schooling. (4) Information about work experience: work unit, workload, salary, job satisfaction and job changes, as well as on-the-job training of the head of a household and his/her spouse. This questionnaire survey collected 752 variables.

The research team surveyed the basic situation and education status of over 67,000 people (head of household, his/her spouse and children, and his/her parents in different households) in 10,000 sample households, including the education status and spending of 6000 students and training status of more than 2000 employees. This research team also collected information on income, employment and education of all 68,000 respondents in 12 sample provinces, which was collected by the NBS through door-to-door surveys.

In addition to the survey data mentioned above, this book also employs the household survey data and other survey data (2004) collected by the NBS Urban Economic Survey Team. The data sources are explained in detail in the corresponding chapters.

1.4 Content of Research and Major Conclusions

This book emphasizes empirical research. Guided by theories and based on survey data, the research team has come to lots of valuable conclusions and findings. Corresponding to the four parts illustrated in Fig. 1.3, conclusions and findings are summarized as follows.

1.4.1 Education Costs and Returns

In terms of basic education, Ding Xiaohao et al. observed in the urban household surveys that families with children receiving compulsory education only fall to the group with relatively worse economic conditions. On the one hand, these families bear a heavy burden to support more family members, both their per capita disposable income and per capita expenditure are quite low. On the other hand, these families have to spend a considerable portion of their income on children's education (Chapter 2, "Urban Household Expenditures for Compulsory Education"). The studies of He Feng et al. showed that no matter it is compulsory education, high school or higher education, different types of school have a significant impact on the scale and structure of educational expenditure. For example, the total educational expenditure for private schools is greatly higher than that of public schools, so is the necessary expenditure (Chapter 3, "Public and Private Education Choices and Household Expenditures on Education").

According to Bao Wei, in the face of the popularization of higher education, there are significant differences between the universities administered by the central government and those run at the local level in terms of fund input and financing: the HELs operated at the local level are less capable of scientific research and fund-raising, most of their fund-raising channels are limited to expanding enrollment scale and increasing tuition and fees; they usually borrow from banks to fill in the funding gap, especially the gap in capital construction (Chapter 4, "Education Financing in the Context of Higher Education Expansion").

Regarding the responsibility and ability of the Chinese government in undertaking the public education expenditure, Yue Changjun has, through international comparison, predicted China's education development fund during the 11th Five-year Plan period (2006 to 2010) based on both supply and demand. (1) In the aspect of supply: If only considering the level of economic development, Yue Changjun found that the international average of the proportion of public education expenditure to GDP shall reach 4.37% to accord with China's economic development level in 2010. If the fiscal capacity and fiscal allocation structure are also considered, such proportion shall be 4.11%. (2) In the aspect of demand: If only considering the current situation and future development goals of China's education, the ratio of fiscal expenditure on public education to GDP shall reach 3.99% in 2010. If only the perspective of international comparison is considered, the international average of such ratio shall reach 4.49% to accord with China's education development goals in 2010 (Chapter 5, "Multi-Country Comparison of Public Education Expenditures").

1.4.2 Equity in Educational Resource Allocation and Educational Opportunities

In reference to the statistical statements on county-level educational finance released by the Ministry of Education, Ding Yanqing and Mun Chiu Tsang studied the imbalanced resource allocation in rural compulsory education across China from 1997 to 2000. Their conclusions are as follows: (1) In 2000, the educational expenditure per primary school student had an adjusted extremes ratio of 5.64 times, while such a ratio for middle school students was 7.51 times. (2) Inequality in educational expenditure per student mainly referred to the intra-provincial inequality. (3) The intra-provincial inequality was mainly due to inequality between counties, and only slightly influenced by urban–rural differences. (4) Although the inter-provincial inequality only occupied a relatively small share, it showed a tendency to expand (Chapter 6, "Inequality in Resources Allocation for Compulsory Education"). The locations of rural primary and secondary schools directly affect the equity and efficiency of educational resource allocation. From the perspective of sociology, Guo Jianru proposed a preliminary analytical framework for understanding the process in which the geographic distribution of China's rural primary and secondary schools are adjusted (Chapter 7, "Adjustment in Geographic Distribution of Rural Primary and Secondary Schools").

Along with the popularization of higher education, the Chinese people increasingly desire to receive higher education, and pay more attention to equal access to it. When studying the overall participation rate of higher education, Ding Xiaohao noticed that while the degree of inequality declines in terms of quantity, it keeps deteriorating in terms of quality (Chapter 8, "Research on Equal Access to Higher Education").

1.4.3 Allocation of Education and Human Resources

Li Ying and Ding Xiaohao studied the overall unemployment time of urban young people with middle school education and above. By employing the life table method, they figured out the unemployment rate of groups with different levels of education at different time points. The results showed that the level of education significantly affects the unemployment time of young people, while the investment in human capital contributes to youth employment and helps graduates to save time on job hunting (Chapter 9, "Survival Analysis Based on Unemployment Duration after Graduation and Education Level"). When discussing the topic "education and job autonomy", Fan Ai-ai and Ding Xiaohao found that the higher the educational level, the greater one's job autonomy (Chapter 10, "Education and Job Autonomy"). Hong Xiaoying, Li Wenli (Chapter 11, "Education, Job Mobility and Income") explored the relationship between education, job mobility and income, and held that higher educational level explains greater job mobility, and job mobility will bring about higher income accordingly.

1.4.4 Education and Returns to Human Capital

1.4.4.1 Returns to Human Capital

Chen Xiaoyu made a quantitative estimation of the rate of returns to all levels of education in China, and depicted its dynamic variation trend. In his studies, Chen observed that since 1990, China has seen the returns to education maintain an upward trend and reach 11.7% in 2004; and the marginal returns to education have reached or even exceeded the international average level, marking that China's education has entered the high-yield stage. However, the private education cost is quite high in China, causing the private rate of returns to education (calculated in combination with educational cost) to remain low. Since the government and society have started paying attention to the issue of educational costs, it is expected that the rapid increase in private educational costs could be curbed. Coupled with growing private returns to education, China will see the private rate of returns to education keep increasing in the future (Chapter 12, "Return on Education for Urban Residents"). Li Fengliang and Ding Xiaohao examined the role of education in improving labor productivity, pointing out the positive correlation between education and income in China's labor market. In addition to signal role, they also found that education is attracting increasing attention in economic realm for its effect on improving labor productivity, and its value is manifested in income (Chapter 13, "The Role of Education in Promoting Labor Productivity").

1.4.4.2 The Role of Education in Improving Gender Discrimination, the Situation of Low-Income Earners and Social Stratification

In his studies on the impact of education on income of different groups, Yue Changjun found that those coming from the "low-income group" realize relatively higher returns on education, or the input into education for this group yields a relatively higher benefit (Chapter 14, "The Impact of Education on Income of Different Groups"). According to Guo Congbin et al., the intergenerational income transmission is quite evident among the Chinese urban residents, i.e., most young people earn the same level of income as their fathers. With the advancement of marketization, education will keep improving the intergenerational income mobility, weaken the persistence of unfair income distribution between generations, and promote income equity as a whole (Chapter 15, "Urban Residents' Education and Intergenerational Income Mobility").

References

OECD. (2004). Education at a Glance: OECD Indicators.

Wolff, E. (2000). Human Capital Investment and Economic Growth: Exploring the Cross-Country Evidence. *Structural Change and Economic Dynamics*, *11*(4), 433–472.

Part I
Cost of Education and Its Financing

Part I includes four chapters, which focus on the cost of education and its financing urban household expenditures on education and the supply and demand of public education funds in China. Chapter 2, "Urban Household Expenditures for Compulsory Education", contains an empirical analysis of educational expenditures by urban households, based on data from the National Bureau of Statistics 1997–2000 Urban Household Survey. Chapter 3, "Public and Private Education Choices and Household Expenditures on Education", is another empirical analysis on the impact of the choice of schools or universities on educational expenditure and its structure, respectively for compulsory education, high school, and university education. Chapter 4, "Education Financing in the Context of Higher Education Expansion", further examines the disparities in funding between universities administered by the central government and those run at the local level. Chapter 5, "Multi-Country Comparison of Public Education Expenditures", looks at supply and demand of education and uses statistics and quantitative regression methods to forecast China's educational expenditures during the 11th Five-year Plan period (2006–2010).

Chapter 2
Urban Household Expenditures for Compulsory Education

Since the beginning of the economic reform, the income gap has been widening (Li 2000), which led to the differentiation of demand for education. The middle and high-income groups, in particular, have had a strong demand for high-quality education. Thus, an issue to be studied in the research on urban compulsory education financing would be building a fair compulsory education system while making sure that individualized needs for education are also met. This chapter analyzes the family financial burden for education by looking at urban households' compulsory educational expenditures and their changes over time. This will help further understand the affordability of education for urban residents and provide some useful ideas for reforms in urban compulsory education financing.

2.1 Existing Research on Compulsory Education Financing

In the past twenty years, the imbalance in the allocation of resources for compulsory education has attracted the attention of many scholars. Researchers such as Wang Shanmai et al. (2003) believe that financial resources for compulsory education in China have been distributed in a seriously unequal manner, as evidenced in the inequality between regions, between urban and rural areas, and between residents. Wang Rong (2003.) examined the resources for different groups of schools and used a multi-level regression analysis method in her research to look into the unbalanced fund distribution in compulsory education. She found that there are serious disparities in resource allocation among various types of schools at the county level. Yuan Liansheng (2001) pointed out that a huge gap exists in terms of available resources between key schools and non-key schools even in the same city or the same district under the same budget. Du Yuhong (2000) has conducted research on different provinces, and provided a systematic analysis of the changes over time in educational funding at all levels in different regions. This study pointed out that

W. Min, *Educational Input, Resource Allocation and Returns to Human Capital*,
https://doi.org/10.1007/978-981-96-4687-6_2

between 1988 and 1996, there was a bigger gap between provinces in primary and middle school students' expenditures. In order to address the imbalance in the allocation of compulsory education resources, Wang Shanmai (2002) proposed setting up a separate dedicated budget for compulsory education as a feasible solution to the issue. He suggests that a model be established at the county level for allocating resources for compulsory education through a dedicated budget, based on identified needs, and he has also provided a description of such a model. Other researchers such as Zhong Yuping and Lei Wanpeng (2002), Mun Chiu Tsang and Ding Yanqing (2003) have also proposed that a consistent and dedicated government budget allocation for compulsory education could be a solution to the unbalanced resources allocation for compulsory education in the country. A review of existing research shows that Chinese scholars have mostly focused their research on unbalanced allocation of compulsory education resources between urban and rural areas, between regions, and between schools. There are very few empirical studies done using samples to look at urban households in different income classes for their expenditures for compulsory education.

In fact, national policies and academic research have, for a long time, all focused on rural compulsory education finances. In contrast, much less attention has been given to compulsory education finances in urban areas. While it is important to ensure adequacy of financing for compulsory education in the rural areas, unbalanced allocation of educational resources remains a challenge in the urban areas. Compulsory education financing in the urban areas has the following characteristics: First, after the reform of the basic education management system in 1985, compulsory education financing became the responsibility of local governments (mainly county or municipal governments). Therefore, educational financing, to a large extent, is correlated to the financial capability of the local governments. Second, urban compulsory education is financed through multiple channels, in order to make up for the shortage of government funding. Family funding has therefore become an important part of compulsory education financing. Urban households need to pay for the following expenses for their children's education: (1) miscellaneous fees, including textbooks and other expenses; (2) additional costs for selecting better schools outside the school district; (3) fees for extracurricular tutoring, such as after-school interest classes, tutoring for specific subjects, etc., for the purpose of enhancing the education their children could receive. These characteristics, on the one hand, have led to serious imbalance in the distribution of educational resources in compulsory education, which is mainly reflected in three aspects: (1) unbalanced resource availability between urban and rural areas; (2) unbalanced resources between regions and between different schools in the same region; and (3) inequality between different income groups and among people in different social strata in terms of availability of educational resources. On the other hand, this unbalanced resource allocation has in turn exacerbated the disparities in education expenditures among households.

Table 2.1 Distribution of urban households in different categories (Unit: %)

Year	Number of households	Households without children in school	Households with children in compulsory education only	Households with high school students only	Households with technical school students only	Households with college students only	Others
1997	4600	44.3	38.7	10.5	2.2	2.5	1.9
1998	4598	45.7	37.4	10.3	2.0	3.2	1.5
1999	4897	45.4	35.8	11.4	2.4	3.9	1.2
2000	4894	48.8	32.3	10.7	2.3	4.9	1.0

2.2 Urban Household Financial Burden for Compulsory Education

2.2.1 Data Source and Its Description

The samples used in this study are from the National Bureau Statistics 1997, 1998, 1999, and 2000 Urban Household Surveys. These samples cover information over four years about households in 7 provinces, involving background information such as the number of people per household, occupation, sectors involved, educational background, and detailed information about income and expenditures. For the purpose of data analysis, income and expenditure data from 1997, 1998, and 1999 were adjusted based on prices in the year 2000. Table 2.1 shows the distribution of households in different categories based on their need for education.

2.2.2 Comparison of Urban Household Income and Expenditure

The annual income and expenditure of urban households in different categories are shown in Table 2.2.

An important observation from Table 2.2 is that the disposable income and actual expenditures of families with students, on a per capita basis, are significantly lower than those without students. Taking a family with only compulsory school students as an example, their per capita disposable income is RMB661 lower than that of families without school students (accounting for about 24% of the average income of families without school students). Their per capita actual expenditure is also RMB573 lower (approximately 21% of the average expenditure of families without school students). This can be explained by the fact that the dependency ratio of households with school students (dependency ratio = the number of household members with no income/

Table 2.2 Annual income and expenditure of urban households in different categories (Unit: RMB)

Year	Income and expenditures	Households without children in school	Households with children in compulsory education only	Households with high school students only	Households with technical school students only	Households with college students only
1997	Per capita disposable income	2338.1	1799.8	1859.8	1831.8	2191.8
	Per capita actual expenditure	2221.2	1770.6	1870.3	1700.7	2241.5
	Per capita educational expenditure	42.3	105.7	146.0	123.7	165.7
1998	Per capita disposable income	2593.0	1963.8	2050.2	1925.2	2551.1
	Per capita actual expenditure	2528.7	1974.1	2191.3	2061.6	2620.2
	Per capita educational expenditure	55.4	132.7	200.5	130.1	180.2
1999	Per capita disposable income	2905.9	2225.6	2226.4	2195.3	2599.2
	Per capita actual expenditure	2843.4	2262.1	2357.9	2110.5	2591.3
	Per capita educational expenditure	67.4	148.7	254.4	142.3	211.0
2000	Per capita disposable income	3202.2	2404.8	2547.1	2399.3	2915.6
	Per capital actual expenditure	3115.9	2410.4	2742.4	2405.7	2935.1
	Per capita educational expenditure	78.2	167.1	298.3	195.3	316.7

the number of household members with income) is significantly higher than that of families without children in school (see Table 2.3).

Moreover, families with children in compulsory education generally have slightly lower disposable income and spend less than households with school children in other categories. It is probably because that parents of these families are generally younger (see Table 2.4), with less work experience (see Table 2.5), and therefore, have lower income and less expenditure.

Table 2.3 Dependency ratio of households in different categories

Year	Households without children in school	Households with children in compulsory education only	Households with high school students only	Households with technical school students only	Households with college students only	Others
1997	0.19	0.57	0.56	0.58	0.51	1.13
1998	0.19	0.60	0.57	0.57	0.54	1.26
1999	0.19	0.62	0.57	0.62	0.52	1.28
2000	0.23	0.65	0.61	0.60	0.54	1.40

Table 2.4 Ages of heads of household (Unit: Year)

Year	Households with children in compulsory education only	Households with high school students only	Households with technical school students only	Households with college students only
1997	39.52	46.56	46.89	50.40
1998	39.72	46.51	46.79	49.67
1999	39.71	46.06	46.95	49.85
2000	39.76	45.73	46.65	49.38

Table 2.5 Work experience of heads of household (Unit: Year)

Year	Households with children in compulsory education only	Households with high school students only	Households with technical school students only	Households with college students only
1997	19.52	25.01	25.69	24.25
1998	19.56	25.12	24.00	22.74
1999	19.38	24.85	24.71	24.47
2000	18.94	24.08	23.27	25.30

2.2.3 *Urban Household Financial Burden for Education*

The financial burdens of urban households in different categories is shown in Table 2.6.

Table 2.6 could also be illustrated by Fig. 2.1.

Figure 2.2 shows an increase over time in financial burdens for education for families in all categories. Taking compulsory education students as an example, their spending ratio to income rose from 5.97% in 1997 to 6.93% in 2000, an increase of 0.96%. The average annual growth rate is 5.28%.

Table 2.6 Ratio of per capita educational expenditure to per capita disposable income for households in different categories

Year	Households without children in school	Households with children in compulsory education only	Households with high school students only	Households with technical school students only	Households with college students only
1997	0.019	0.060	0.078	0.073	0.074
1998	0.022	0.067	0.092	0.063	0.069
1999	0.024	0.066	0.108	0.067	0.081
2000	0.025	0.069	0.109	0.081	0.108

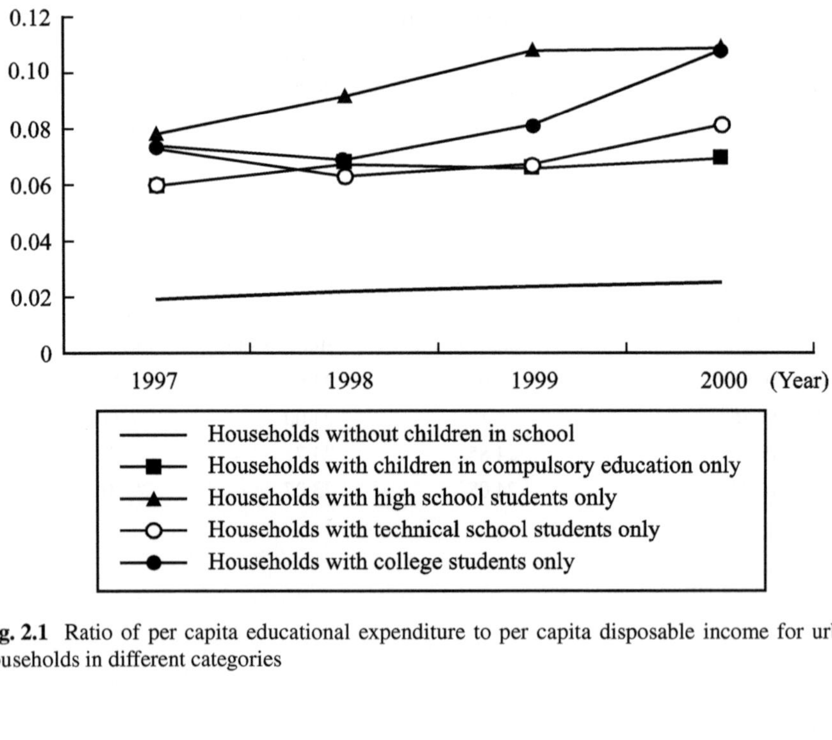

Fig. 2.1 Ratio of per capita educational expenditure to per capita disposable income for urban households in different categories

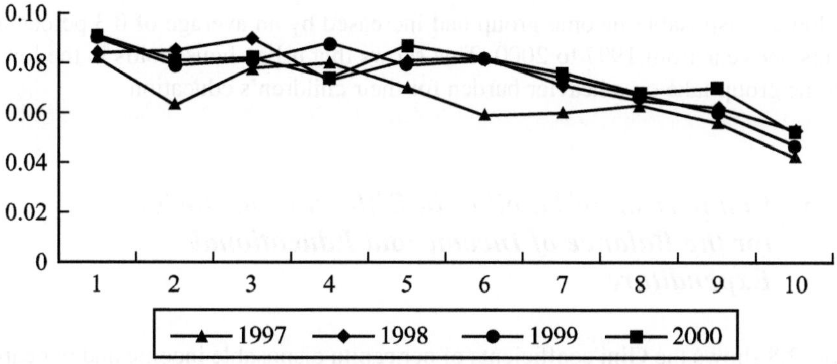

Fig. 2.2 Ratio of per capita education expenditure to per capita disposable income

2.2.4 *Educational Expenditure of Families with Children in Compulsory Education Only*

Urban households with children in compulsory education only are divided into 10 groups based on their per capita disposable income. Table 2.7 shows the average ratio of per capita education expenditure to the per capita disposable income in each group:

The content of the Table 2.7 can also be expressed in Fig. 2.2.

We have two findings from Fig. 2.2: (1) In spite of changes in different years, the ratio of educational expenditure overall is in a declining trend. It is important to note, however, that the group with the lowest disposable income has the highest ratio of educational expenditure to their per capita disposable income, whereas such ratio is the lowest for the group with the highest disposable income. Take the year 2000 as an example, the per capita educational expenditure of the lowest income group accounted for 9.1% of their per capita disposable income, the highest among all groups. The per capita educational expenditure of the highest income group, however, accounted for only 5.2%, the lowest of all groups. That is a 4 percentage-point difference between the two. This shows that as per capita disposable income increases, the proportion of per capita educational expenditure declines, with the highest ratio of spending for the lowest income group, and the lowest for the top income group. (2) If we look at the changes over time, the ratio of per capita educational expenditure in

Table 2.7 Ratio of per capita education expenditure to per capita disposable income in each group

Year	1	2	3	4	5	6	7	8	9	10
1997	0.082	0.063	0.078	0.080	0.070	0.059	0.060	0.063	0.056	0.042
1998	0.084	0.085	0.090	0.073	0.081	0.082	0.071	0.065	0.062	0.053
1999	0.090	0.079	0.081	0.088	0.079	0.081	0.074	0.067	0.060	0.047
2000	0.091	0.081	0.082	0.074	0.087	0.082	0.076	0.068	0.070	0.052

the lowest disposable income group had increased by an average of 0.3 percentage points per year from 1997 to 2000. This shows that urban households in the lowest income group take on a heavier burden for their children's education.

2.2.5 *Comparison of Families in Different Categories for the Balance of Income and Educational Expenditure*

Table 2.8 shows the Gini coefficients of per capita disposable income and per capita educational expenditure of urban households in all categories.

It can be seen from Table 2.8 that households in all categories have a Gini coefficient of per capita educational expenditure that is generally greater than the Gini coefficient of per capita disposable income. The data shows that compared with the level of per capita income, there is more disparity in household educational expenditure.

Table 2.8 Gini coefficients of per capita disposable income and per capita educational expenditure of urban households in all categories

Households	Gini coefficient	1997	1998	1999	2000
All	Per capita disposable income	0.35	0.36	0.35	0.36
	Per capita educational expenditure	0.65	0.66	0.65	0.68
Households with children in compulsory education only	Per capita disposable income	0.32	0.32	0.32	0.33
	Per capita educational expenditure	0.49	0.50	0.49	0.51
Households with high school students only	Per capita disposable income	0.32	0.52	0.29	0.31
	Per capita educational expenditure	0.54	0.54	0.55	0.55
Households with technical school students only	Per capita disposable income	0.32	0.25	0.32	0.33
	Per capita educational expenditure	0.60	0.59	0.61	0.60
Households with college students only	Per capita disposable income	0.34	0.34	0.32	0.32
	Per capita educational expenditure	0.57	0.55	0.56	0.58

2.2.6 *Structure of Educational Expenditures for Families with Children in Compulsory Education Only*

Based on the original data, which contains information on expenditures on textbooks, reference books, tuition and miscellaneous fees, childcare, adult education, and other expenditures, this analysis focuses on three kinds of expenditures related to components of compulsory education, i.e., textbooks and reference books, fees and miscellaneous expenses, and other related educational expenditures.

In order to look into the extent of the differences in educational expenditures for families with only compulsory education students, we calculated the coefficient of variation for expenditures in different categories for these families (see Table 2.9).

The above analysis shows that the coefficient of variation for "other educational expenditures" is much higher than that of "miscellaneous fees" and "textbooks and reference books". This shows that other educational expenses are an important reason for the imbalance of education expenditures in urban households with only compulsory education students. As the criteria for data collection were not clearly defined, it is impossible to know exactly what expenses are included in "other educational expenditures", but it could very well include fees for extracurricular study sessions, or hiring tutors, by an educated guess. These costs are the major reasons for the differences in educational expenditures.

Based on the per capita disposable income, families with only compulsory education students are divided into 10 groups, and Table 2.10 shows the ratio of "other educational expenditures" to total education expenditure for each group.

The contents of Table 2.10 can better reflect the trend by the curve in Fig. 2.3.

Table 2.9 Coefficient of variation for expenditures in different categories for families with children in compulsory education only

Year	Expenditures for education	Miscellaneous fees	Textbooks and reference books	Other educational expenditures
1997	0.122	0.148	0.148	0.312
1998	0.129	0.154	0.146	0.416
1999	0.109	0.119	0.146	0.346
2000	0.122	0.144	0.151	0.361

Table 2.10 Ratio of other expenditures to total education expenditures for each group

Year	1	2	3	4	5	6	7	8	9	10
1997	0.094	0.097	0.113	0.096	0.124	0.167	0.157	0.165	0.157	0.137
1998	0.066	0.119	0.163	0.122	0.173	0.169	0.161	0.179	0.247	0.114
1999	0.103	0.101	0.139	0.217	0.160	0.243	0.156	0.176	0.192	0.125
2000	0.074	0.082	0.132	0.143	0.138	0.167	0.228	0.218	0.304	0.219

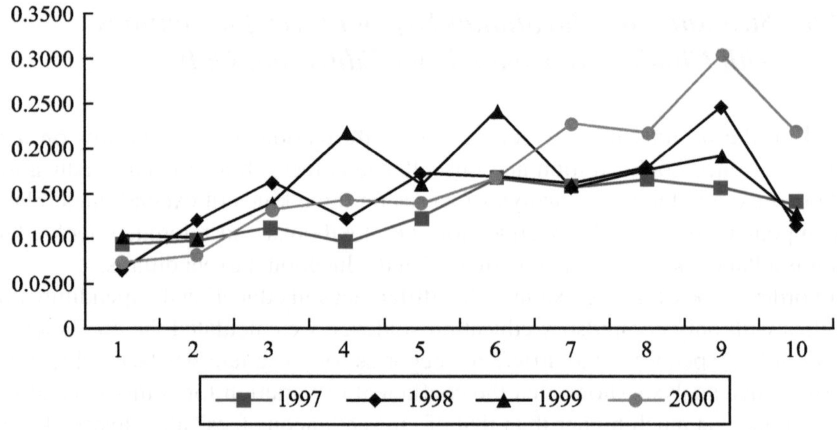

Fig. 2.3 Ratio of other expenditures to total education expenditures for each group

Table 2.10 indicates that the proportion of "other educational expenditures" as part of the total education expenditures tends to increase along with an increase in income, especially in 2000. It further proves that a family's financial status, to some extent, determines the level of its educational investment. In other words, it has a direct bearing on a family's "other educational expenditures", besides textbooks and fees and miscellaneous expenses. This single category of expenditures is the major reason for the disparities in education expenditures between families.

2.3 Factors Contributing to Financial Burden for Compulsory Education

Educational expenditures may be affected by a number of factors, such as per capita disposable income, parents' educational level, parents' occupation and the sectors or industries they are in, the level of education received by the children, duration of schooling, etc. This section, therefore, attempts to establish a regression equation between these factors and household education expenditure. As the father or mother of the student is usually the head of the household, the following analysis will use variables referred to as that of the head of the household. The samples used for the analysis are of urban households that have children in compulsory education only.

$$Y = \beta_0 + \beta_1 X_1 + \beta_2 X_2 + \beta_3 X_3 + \sum \lambda_j z_j + \sum \lambda_k h_k + \sum r_i t_i + \mu \tag{2.1}$$

Y: Per capita educational expenditure as a percentage of per capita disposable income.

X_1: Disposable income per capita.

X_2: The education level of the head of the household. The original data listed 7 types of education: four-year college (and more advanced degrees), technical college, high school, middle school, primary school and others. The corresponding number of years of schooling for each category is set as 16 years, 15 years, 12 years, 12 years, 9 years, 5.5 years, and 2 years respectively.

X_3: Dummy variable of level of education received by the children. In this analysis, families with primary school students are used as the benchmark, against which, families with children in middle school are compared. The coefficient β_3 represents the difference between the two types of families in terms of per capita educational expenditures. The positive (or negative) regression coefficient indicates that the family with children in middle school only has higher (or lower) per capita educational expenditure or its educational expenditure accounts for a higher (or lower) ratio of the family's actual per capita expenditures as compared with families with children in primary school only.

z_j: Job dummy variable (1 for job, represented as j, and 0 for others). For jobs performed by heads of household, 8 occupations are listed for the purpose of this study: professional and technical personnel; government officials and business leaders; office workers; business staff; service workers; farmers and fishermen; factory and transportation workers (referred to as "workers" in this study); and others. In this analysis, "worker" is set as the basis of comparison for all other occupations.

h_k: Industry (or sector) dummy variables (1 for industry, represented as k, and 0 others). There are 16 industries or sectors identified for heads of household, and they are put into three groups based on the possible level of income that can be generated: "high-income", "middle-income" and "low-income" industries (Yue 2004). "High-income industries" include electricity, gas and water, scientific research and comprehensive technical services, finance and insurance, and real estate. "middle-income industries" consist of transportation and storage, post and telecommunications, health, sports, and social welfare, education, culture and art, radio, film and television, government agencies, political parties, and social organizations. "Low-income industries" refer to agriculture, forestry, animal husbandry and fishery (in cities/towns), construction, geological survey, water conservancy management, social services, mining, wholesale and retail, catering, manufacturing, and other industries. "Low-income industries" are used as the benchmark industry for comparison in this study.

t_i: Year dummy variables (1 for year, represented as i, and 0 for others). 1997 is set as the base year for comparison with other years.

The calculation shows that the collinearity test values of the equation are all less than 10, which indicates that collinearity between independent variables in the equation is not a serious issue. The adjusted equation R^2 is 0.05. The overall significance level of the equation is 0.000, which is better than the 0.01 standard set in the significance level test. Table 2.11 shows the independent variables whose coefficients in the equation have passed the significance level test.

The above analysis shows that, with other variables remaining constant, the following observations could be drawn:

Table 2.11 Independent variables and coefficients have passed significance level test

Independent variables	Coefficient	Coefficient significance
1998	0.010	0.000
1999	0.012	0.000
2000	0.016	0.000
Per capita disposable income	−0.000007	0.000
Service workers	−0.01	0.031
Undefined other workers	0.042	0.000
Middle income industries	−0.008	0.001
Households with children in middle school only	0.029	0.000

1. The ratio of per capita educational expenditure to per capita disposable income in 1998, 1999, and 2000 was 0.01, 0.012, and 0.016 higher than that of 1997, respectively. This indicates a year-on-year increase in the financial burden for urban households with children in compulsory education only.
2. For every RMB1 increase in per capita disposable income, the percentage of per capita educational expenditure as opposed to per capita disposable income will slightly drop by 0.000007, indicating that an increase in income will help lower the financial burden of urban households that have children in compulsory education only.
3. Compared with heads of households whose occupations are "workers", "service workers" households are 0.01 lower in their educational financial burden. Households in "other undefined sectors", however, have a financial burden that is 0.042 higher.
4. Compared with households in low-income industries, the educational expenditure to income ratio of those in middle-income industries is 0.008 lower. For households in the high-income industries, they, too, have a lower educational expenditure to income ratio, in spite of the fact that they may fail the significance level test. The above analysis shows that families in low-income industries, in general, bear a financial burden for compulsory education that is higher than that of families in middle-income and high-income industries.
5. Compared with families with children in primary school, households with middle school students have an educational expenditure ratio that is 0.029 higher, indicating that their financial burden is heavier than families with children in primary school.

2.4 Conclusions and Policy Implications

This chapter discussed the current status and changes in the compulsory education expenditures of urban households. The main conclusions are:

1. More than half of urban households have children in school. Those with children in compulsory education, in particular, constitute an economically disadvantaged group. These families have relatively lower per capita disposable income and expenditure due to the need for dependent support. In addition, a considerable part of their limited expenditure will have to be used for their children's education. Although their financial situation may improve when their children eventually graduate from school and begin to work, such a financial burden will last for at least 9 years, up to 16 years or even more. Therefore, it is important to keep in mind such a group of urban households as fiscal policies are developed for education in urban areas and efforts are made to reduce poverty and improve the well-being of the people.
2. The educational financial burden of urban households with compulsory school students is increasing year by year, and the educational financial burden of low-income families is much higher than that of high-income families.
3. There is a large gap between families with children in compulsory education in terms of their educational expenditures, and this gap tends to widen over time.
4. A possible and important reason for the difference in educational expenditures of families with children in compulsory education in urban areas is that high-income families spend much more in choosing schools, putting their children in extracurricular interest classes, or hiring tutors. Due to limited data availability, there is no knowledge of the composition of the household expenditures on education, especially the expenses for after-school activities, and therefore a thorough analysis is not possible. However, experience tells us that this type of expenditure is becoming an important and even a major part of a family's educational expenditure. The author will use more appropriate data for detailed analysis in future research.
5. The regression analysis shows that household income, the level of education of the children, parents' occupation, and the industries they are in are factors that determine the financial burden of an urban household for their children's compulsory education. Specifically, the financial burden decreases with the increase in family income. Heads of households in low-income industries have heavier financial burdens than families in middle-income or high-income industries, and families with children in middle school have a heavier financial burden than those with children in primary school.

These conclusions may have the following policy implications:

1. Families with children in compulsory education have lower incomes, and a heavier financial burden for education, which is increasing year by year. This is therefore an issue that needs more attention from the government, which may consider providing more financial support for compulsory education. Fees and miscellaneous expenses constitute a major part of urban households' expenditures for compulsory education and are the main reason for families' financial burden for education, especially for low-income families. Given the sound

economic development and improved fiscal conditions in the country, the government should take steps over time to reduce or eliminate all fees for compulsory education so that it becomes truly free education. Such measures will go a long way to help reduce the financial burden of urban families for compulsory education.

2. The financial burden of urban households for compulsory education decreases with the increase in family income, and the financial burden of low-income families is much heavier than that of high-income families. In order to reduce such burdens for low-income families, it is important to put in place an effective system of support to help poor families with their children's education. As municipal governments are usually in a stronger fiscal position, measures could be taken by these governments to reduce or exempt fees for children from low-income families before the fees for compulsory education are abolished across the board. Further support in the form of subsidies could also be offered to families in very difficult financial situations.
3. A possible important reason for the disparities in the expenditure on compulsory education is the fact that families tend to spend more on school selection, extracurricular tuition classes, and hiring tutors as their income increases. This has to some extent shown that compulsory education, as it is now, is not in a position to meet the strong demand for quality education. Excessive disparities in expenditures for compulsory education may lead to a gap in education between children from different income groups in terms of quantity and quality. As compulsory education is supposed to be the basic form of education to be provided to all, the government should make sure that it is made available to all citizens in a fair and just manner. Therefore, efforts should be made by the government to help weak schools with their capacity building and therefore narrow the differences in quality of education, which will then disincentivize parents from choosing better schools for their children.

References

Du, Y. (2000). *Imbalance in Educational Development*. Beijing Normal University Press.

Li, S. (2000). *An Empirical Analysis on Income Distribution in China*. Social Sciences Academic Press (China).

Mun, C. T. & Ding Y. (2003). Financial Challenges in Compulsory Education and Intergovernmental Education Grants, *Peking University Education Review*, *1*(1), 84–94.

Wang, R. (2003). Inequity in School Finance in China. *China Economic Quarterly*, *2*.

Wang, S. (2002). *Concept of the Reform of China's Compulsory Education Financial System*. China Education Daily, March 12, Second Page. https://www.edu.cn/zhong_guo_jiao_yu/ji_chu/zong_he/ji_chu_zhuan_ti/pu_jiu_jiao_yu/200603/t20060323_25477_2.shtml.

Wang, S., Yuan, L., & Liu, Z. (2003). Progress, Problems and Countermeasures of China's Public Educational Finance System Reform. *Journal of Beijing Normal University (Social Sciences)*, *6*.

Yuan, L. (2001). Discussion on the Inequity in China's Compulsory Education Finance. *Education & Economy*, *4*.

Yue, C. (2004). The Relations Among Industrial Monopoly, Income, and the Industrial Choice of Employment for College Graduates. *Peking University Education Review, 3.*

Zhong, Y., & Lei, W. (2002). China's Basic Education Finance Policy from the Perspective of Equity. *Education & Economy, 1.*

Chapter 3
Public and Private Education Choices and Household Expenditures on Education

Since the reform and opening up, China has achieved remarkable economic growth and social progress, which enabled ongoing improvements in overall national strength and standard of living. As the country looked beyond basic necessities for its people and sought moderate prosperity, consumer spending underwent profound structural changes, as reflected by the declining share of income spent on food and more sophisticated needs for education, culture, and entertainment.

The following is a discussion on the three basic factors that underpin this study: demand, supply, and pricing mechanism: As their income grew, Chinese parents started to develop higher expectations for the quantity and quality of the education received by their children, hence the ongoing increase in their spending on education. Meanwhile, the provision of educational services shifted fundamentally. A sizable market for such services emerged over time, thanks to governmental policies to encourage the founding of private schools, which mobilized resources from outside the public sector. Current market-based services are supplied by private schools, different types of academic tutoring programs for low or high-performing students, and paid extracurricular learning activities offered by public schools or other institutions.

The compulsory and non-compulsory stages of education are examined separately in this study, for each possesses a different set of realities in terms of the public education offered, the education market, and personal spending on education, which is a result of the varying roles assumed by the government during these two stages. Compulsory education is essentially a public good that is primarily funded by the state, which explains the predominant role of public schools in its provision. The uneven levels of development among schools, however, make it difficult for the public system to completely satisfy people's demand for high-quality services. In response to the resulting "excess demand for education," various private institutions and activities have been created. As for non-compulsory education, which begins at the upper secondary level, public schools are allowed to expand their enrollment

W. Min, *Educational Input, Resource Allocation and Returns to Human Capital*,
https://doi.org/10.1007/978-981-96-4687-6_3

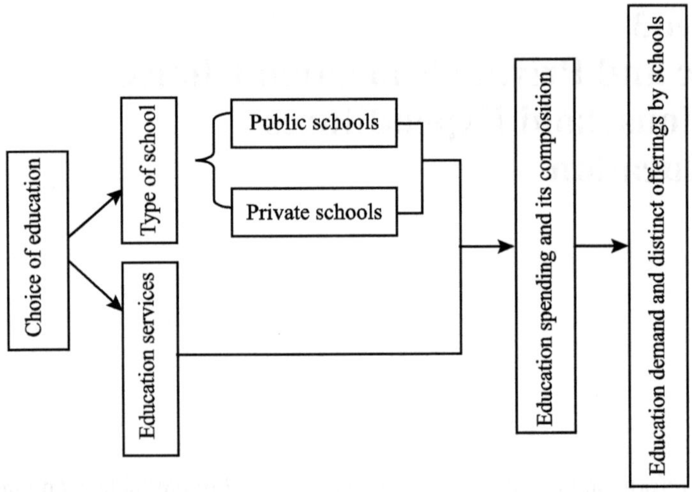

Fig. 3.1. Conceptual framework adopted in this chapter

to include less qualified candidates, while private providers are also allowed more room for development.

Pricing mechanism also plays a role in the education market. Public and private schools differ in their methods and sources of funding, which may be why their students spend differently on education and make varying choices about the services to receive.

This chapter focuses on how such choices impact household expenditures on education. The term "choice of education" is used to refer to the selection of an educational service and its provider. This includes choosing the type of school (public or private) and other services received outside of schools, such as extracurricular learning and training activities, home tutoring, etc. Because of these choices, students differ in the amount and composition of their education spending. Studying such differences and the factors affecting them may reveal insights into how families make their choices of education and the costs they incur. This is conducive to further understanding the distinct offerings and practices of China's public and private schools, which also allows for a discussion about some of the characteristics of the education market that has taken shape in the country. Figure 3.1 is an illustration of the analysis above.

This chapter examines the differences between public and private school students in their spending on education using data from Chinese Urban Household Education and Employment *Survey—2005* by the Institute of Economics of Education at Peking University. These differences are not only represented by the amount of spending, but also by its composition. This chapter investigates how both are affected by the type of school chosen, examining each of the three distinct stages of education—compulsory, upper secondary, and higher education—on its own, with individual students and their families as the unit of analysis. The current operational practices, offerings, and objectives of public and private schools in China are then discussed based on the findings of the investigation.

There are three main steps in the study:

(1) Comparison of household expenditures on education between public and private school students, examining the differences in the amount and composition of the spending and the factors that may affect it; (2) comparative and statistical analyses of the factors that affect students' education spending, using double logarithmic regression models built with proper independent variables; this step seeks to find out whether the chosen type of school has a significant effect on the amount and composition of students' education spending, and exactly how significant if it does; and (3) characterization of the students enrolled in public and private schools and profiling of their different needs for educational services, based on the comparative analysis of the influencing factors and composition of their education spending; this enables a further discussion on how the two types of schools differ in their main purpose and objectives, considering the realities in China.

3.1 Literature Review and Theoretical Framework

3.1.1 Review of Previous Empirical Research

3.1.1.1 Review of Empirical Studies in Other Countries on Direct Private Spending on Education

Foreign researchers in education economics investigating this subject mostly focused on how parents invested in the human capital of their children. The majority of their studies were conducted between the late 1970s and late 1980s, the most representative being the work by Becker (1976, 1978, 1986, 1994) and Taubman (1989).

1. Parental Income and Children's Schooling

In their 1977 study, Robert Hauser and Thomas Daymont analyzed data of US high school graduates using a single logarithmic model. They chose years of schooling completed as the dependent variable and parental income, parents' education, and father's occupation as the independent variables, plus a dummy variable for farm background. Their analysis reported that the coefficient on parental income was 0.0056, i.e. for every unit of increase in parental income, the children's years of schooling increased by 2%.

In his 1982 study on a model for analyzing parental allocation of resources, Behrman assumed that the parental utility function was determined by parental consumption and the children's expected lifetime earnings, whereas the children's earnings depended on their own endowments and the investments in their human capital. The study used age of respondent, parental age and education, family income, and religion as variables for family background. The results showed that the correlation between family income and children's years of schooling was significant at the 0.05 level, while the correlation between family income and children's income was significant at the 0.1 level.

A 1986 paper by Taubman and Behrman reported coefficients on parental earnings of 0.013 for male offspring and 0.017 for females in the years of schooling equation that controlled for birth order, father's and mother's age at birth (and the square of each), parents' education, father's religion, and number of siblings. The difference between the sexes did not have any statistically significant effect.

2. Family Size and Children's Opportunity for Schooling

In their 1989 study on family resources, family sizes, and children's attainment of higher education, Behrman, Pollak, and Taubman (1989) focused on equal access and concluded that family size might have led to inequality of access to education. Because of the inverse relationship between parental spending on the education of each child and the number of children, those living in households with more siblings had, on average, worse access to education and less future earnings. The researchers believe that parents with fewer children substituted quality for quantity, where quality was measured by the average parental spending on the education of each child.

3. Commentary on Previous Studies in Other Countries

Foreign researchers were mainly interested in the relationship between investment in human capital and its returns. In their analyses, the researchers developed multiple linear regression models, single logarithmic models, or double logarithmic models, where children's years of schooling and/or earnings enabled by education were selected as operational substitution variables to represent how parents invested in the human capital of their children. Factors potentially affecting these investments, including family financial status, parental occupation, parental income, family size, and birth order were chosen as explanatory variables. Despite their varying emphases, these studies have proven that factors like financial status and parental occupation and income have a significant impact on a family's human capital investments in its children.

3.1.1.2 Review of Empirical Studies in China on Direct Private Spending on Education

Most of the empirical work on household expenditures on education done by Chinese researchers in education economics happened after 2000. Their research, which examined different stages of education relevant to their respective objectives, mainly focused on the factors that affected private spending on education and the scale of the effects. The most representative of these studies are described below.

In his 1999 empirical study, Ye Wenzhen analyzed the education spending data of primary and secondary school students in the city of Xiamen using a multiple regression model. The study discussed the factors that determined the children's spending on education and examined the composition of such spending. Three sets of determining factors were listed: (1) explanatory variables denoting the children's demographics, including gender, age, and only child or not, all of which were found to be directly proportional to spending on education; (2) explanatory variables associated with family resources, including family income, family size, and age of mother at her first marriage, where all except family size had positive effect on the children's education spending; (3) explanatory variables representing the personal backgrounds of the parents, including parental educational attainment and job level, which affected education spending in different ways.

Li Hongwei (2000) characterized current investments by urban households in China using data samples collected in 1999 by the Urban Socioeconomic Survey Department of the National Bureau of Statistics from 150,000 urban households across 30 provinces, autonomous regions, and municipalities. The study found that household expenditures on education was directly proportional to income and children's educational attainment.

In his 2005 study on high school students' spending on tutoring services, Lei Wanpeng (2005) used general linear regression to analyze the factors affecting the differences in this type of spending, and logistic regression to examine those that might determine whether tutoring services were used. Annual family income, students' location, urban or rural household, and existing family human capital were chosen as independent variables. The study found that family income and mother's educational attainment had a significant impact on whether high school students received tutoring, while annual family income and whether the household was urban or rural affected the spending on tutoring services significantly.

Having focused on family backgrounds, especially factors related to financial status, all of the studies above found that household income had a significant positive effect on what families spent on their children's education.

None of the Chinese and foreign studies described above treated type of school (public or private) as a main influencing factor for examination, and none contained any structural analysis of private spending on education. Deriving inspiration from the models and variables employed by the work preceding it, this study further explores the factors that may affect private education spending. It centers on the effect of the chosen type of school and presents a comparative analysis of the differences between public and private school students in the amount and composition of their spending on education.

3.1.1.3 Studies on the Roles of the Public and Private Sectors in Education Provision

In their recent work on the different roles of public and private providers of education and the demand related to them, foreign researchers discussed the division of responsibility for education provision between the public and private sectors by studying the reasons behind the rise of private schools. The most notable example is Estelle James, who conducted a comparative study on the scale of private education at the secondary level in developed and developing countries (James 1987, 1993). She discovered that limited public spending was the key explanation for the larger scale of private secondary education in developing countries, while in developed countries, private secondary schools existed mainly because of the so-called "differentiated demand" driven by cultural—especially religious—considerations. In her study, James developed a utility function for the parents' choice of education for their children: when public and private schools were perfect substitutes, people would choose private schools as a second-best option if public ones offered limited capacity and private education generated more benefits than costs; when public and private schools were imperfect substitutes, people developed differential preferences for the educational products and services provided by private schools due to their various religious, linguistic, and ethnic backgrounds, hence the "differentiated demand" for private education; different preferences for quality of educational services also influenced the development of private education, as low-quality public education allowed high-quality private schools to grow by catering to families that demanded better quality and were able to afford it.

Existing studies often adopted the national perspective in their discussions on the macro-level drivers and factors behind the rise of private education within a certain country or region. No previous literature has offered a micro-level view of the pricing mechanism of educational services, where the distinct practices and offerings of public and private schools were examined through a quantitative and structural comparison of their students' spending on education.

3.1.2 *Theoretical Framework and Hypotheses*

3.1.2.1 Theoretical Framework and Research Design

The chapter builds on the foundation formed by the theories and empirical research on family human capital investment and the roles of the public and private sectors in education provision.

Originating from the theory of human capital investment, the theories and models for family human capital investment focus on a number of key issues: how family background factors—including parents' accumulated human capital and family financial profile—impact the human capital investments in children; how parents' decisions about the education of their children are affected by the choice of school type, quality of instruction provided by the school, number of children and their gender, etc.

Inquiry into the roles of the public and private sectors in education provision, meanwhile, seeks to explain the reasons behind the rise of private education. It also aims to identify which defined types of education demand are served by public schools, which by private ones, and what varying services they each provide to satisfy that demand. Each stage of education and each social group may be associated with a distinct mix of demand for educational services, while government policy and public funding differ for private education and for each stage of schooling. These differences are possible focal points for exploring the drivers behind the rise of private education, especially those created by private demand.

Based on the two-part theoretical foundation described above, this chapter first examines how family income and choice of school type affect the amount and composition of students' spending on education. It then combines the observations with a review of the different types of education demand to enable a discussion on the differences between the public and private schools in their distinct offerings and objectives.

3.1.2.2 Hypotheses

This chapter makes the following assumptions, which are based on current theories and previous research, in combination with the realities of China's education:

1. Compulsory Education

Hypothesis 1:
In compulsory education, the chosen type of school has a significant effect on the student's education spending and its composition.

Hypothesis 1.1:
The chosen type of school has a significant effect on students' total education spending; private school students spend considerably more than their public school peers.

Hypothesis 1.2:
The chosen type of school has a significant effect on the composition of students' total spending on education; the essential spending of private school students is a lot larger than that of public school students, whereas for extended spending the opposite is true.[1]

2. Upper Secondary Education

Hypothesis 2:
The chosen type of school has a significant effect on the amount and composition of the total education spending of high school students.

Hypothesis 2.1:
The chosen type of school has a significant effect on students' total education spending; private high school students spend considerably more than their public high school peers.

[1] The operational definitions for essential and extended spending are given in later paragraphs.

Hypothesis 2.2:
The chosen type of school has a significant effect on the composition of students' total spending on education; the essential spending of private high school students is considerably larger than that of public school students, whereas for extended spending there is no significant difference between the two types of schools.

3. Higher Education

Hypothesis 3:
The chosen type of school has a significant effect on the total education spending of college students; students attending private institutions spend considerably more than their peers in public institutions; significant differences also exist for learning and living expenses.

3.1.3 Operational Definitions of Key Concepts

This chapter involves the following sets of key concepts. Their operational definitions are described below to enable a more targeted discussion.

3.1.3.1 Types of Schools

There are two types of schools: public and private. The term "public school" is used in its general sense; "private schools" include schools owned and run independently by non-governmental entities and hybrid ones that are "privately owned with public funding support" or "publicly owned with private funding support."

3.1.3.2 Categories of Education Spending

To simplify the analysis, the education spending of students in compulsory and upper secondary education is divided into two categories: essential spending and extended spending, which is in line with the content of the questionnaires and the objectives of this study. Here, essential spending refers to the amount that must be paid in order for the student to get enrolled and stay in school; extended spending includes the additional expenses paid for improving academic performance or satisfying the needs for diversified services. More specifically:

Essential spending = tuition and fees + boarding + books, stationery and learning materials (including photocopying and printing), etc. + out-of-pocket spending when living on campus (meals) + uniforms + travel expenses needed for schooling + contributions (school selection fees);

Extended spending = extracurricular programs (enrichment classes, tutoring classes, etc.): tuition and expenses for the necessary books, stationery, or tools + home tutoring fees + other expenses.

Student spending during higher education changes fundamentally compared with the previous stages. Consumer behavior and composition of spending become completely different, since college students enjoy greater freedom in their personal spending decisions and a wider range of choices for boarding, living expenses, and travel. This study thus divides the spending of college students into learning and living expenses, or more specifically:

Learning expenses = tuition + books, stationery, learning materials (including photocopying and printing), etc. + extracurricular programs (enrichment classes, tutoring classes, etc.): tuition and expenses for the necessary books, stationery, or tools + home tutoring fees;

Living expenses = boarding + out-of-pocket spending when living on campus (meals) + uniforms + travel expenses needed for schooling + other expenses.

3.1.3.3 Types of Education Demand

This chapter divides education demand into two categories: excess demand and differentiated demand.

Excess demand: this refers to the demand from those who are unable to gain desired access to a public school because of the inadequate capacity of the public system, which is a result of limited state funding for education. This is consistent with James' definition of "excess demand" (James 1987).

Differentiated demand: in this chapter, the term refers to the demand for high-quality and diversified services, which the existing public system cannot offer. This type of demand also drives certain groups of people to turn to private providers for education. This is mostly consistent with James' definition of "differentiated demand," which is demand created by "differential preferences about quality" (James 1987).

3.2 Education Expenditures for Public and Private School Students in Compulsory Education

3.2.1 Family Backgrounds of Students in Compulsory Education

Family background factors include total family income, total household spending, father's and mother's educational attainment, number of children, etc., each of which—and total family income in particular-affects the amount and composition of children's education spending to a certain extent. This study used a sample consisting of 2456 students in compulsory education. 2329 among them attended a public school and 127 went to a private one. All of the students came from urban households. Table 3.1 presents the descriptive statistics on their family backgrounds.

Table 3.1 also contains data on family financial status, showing that the average annual family income of private school students is nearly 30% higher than that of public school students. The former was RMB38,629.37 and the latter, RMB29,976.28, which was RMB8653.09 lower. Independent samples t-test revealed that the differences in annual family income and spending between the two groups were significant at the 0.05 level, proof that private school students' family financial status was much better than public school students'. This indicates that urban private schools offering compulsory education accepted on average more students from families with better financial means. Because of how private schools operated, their students spent more than those in the public system, meaning the students' families must have a stronger ability to pay. On the other hand, thanks to their objectives and service quality, private schools in compulsory education did possess distinct advantages that helped them attract and serve students from wealthier families with particular needs.

The following sections examine whether the chosen type of school has a significant effect on students' education spending.

Table 3.1 Family backgrounds of students in compulsory education (2005)

Item	Public schools		Private schools	
	Means	Standard deviations	Means	Standard deviations
Annual household income (RMB)	29,976.28	24,454.86	38,629.37	25,925.98
Annual household spending (RMB)	23,869.49	24,446.60	28,228.94	20,847.03
Market value of currently owned residential property (RMB)	137,465.43	145,565.96	159,333.33	136,476.85
Number of computers owned	0.68	0.56	0.76	0.54
Number of private cars owned	0.14	0.35	0.16	0.37
Number of children	1.13	0.66	1.09	0.36
Father's average years of schooling	11.76	3.07	12.17	3.10
Mother's average years of schooling	11.22	2.91	11.31	2.89

3.2.2 *Breakdown of Students' Spending in Public and Private Schools of Compulsory Education*

Following the categorization of education spending and the operational definitions provided in Sect. 3.2, this chapter divides the spending of students in compulsory education into two categories: essential spending and extended spending. Table 3.2 presents the data on these two categories, including the specific items within each category and their share of total spending on education.

Table 3.2 shows that, in compulsory education, the average total spending of private school students was RMB6143.06, which was RMB3462.3, or 2.3 times higher than what public school students spent in total RMB2680.76. Zooming in on the components, one finds that the key difference lies with essential spending. The average essential spending was RMB5295.57 for private school students and

Table 3.2 Breakdown of students' spending in public/private schools of compulsory education (2005)

Item	Public schools			Private schools		
	Means (RMB)	Standard deviations (RMB)	Share of total spending (%)	Means (RMB)	Standard deviations (RMB)	Share of total spending (%)
Essential spending						
Tuition	583.99	952.16	21.78	2226.13	2885.07	36.24
Boarding	32.96	249.77	1.23	130.39	377.51	2.12
Books, stationery, and learning materials	280.61	334.56	10.47	354.84	366.96	5.78
Out-of-pocket spending when living on campus (meals)	282.80	630.85	10.55	690.12	1135.01	11.23
Uniforms	73.92	112.03	2.76	98.61	139.86	1.61
Travel expenses needed for schooling	80.61	193.94	3.01	150.91	278.08	2.46
Contributions (school selection fees)	388.36	1995.87	14.49	1644.57	3865.47	26.77
Subtotal	1723.24	2710.53	64.28	5295.57	5134.46	86.20
Extended spending						
Extracurricular learning*	650.80	1032.46	24.28	554.68	917.83	9.03
Home tutoring fees	157.15	675.72	5.86	118.68	471.61	1.93
Other expenses	149.57	501.81	5.58	174.13	380.70	2.83
Subtotal	957.52	1411.89	35.72	847.49	1106.42	13.80
Total education spending	2680.76	3207.17	100	6143.06	8036.30	100

Note This refers to the item called "extracurricular programs (enrichment classes, tutoring classes, etc.): tuition and expenses for the necessary books, stationery, or tools" in the questionnaires

RMB1723.24 for public school students. The former was RMB3572.33, or 3.07 times higher than the latter. On each of the specific items within this category—tuition, boarding, books, stationery, and learning materials (including photocopying and printing), out-of-pocket spending when living on campus (meals), uniforms, travel expenses needed for schooling, and contributions (school selection fees)—private school students spent more than their public school peers. Take tuition, for example, private school students needed to pay RMB2226.13, which was 3.81 times higher than the RMB583.99 that public school students spent. The difference between the two was RMB1642.14, accounting for 46% of the total difference in essential spending. As for contributions (school selection fees), private school students paid on average RMB1644.57 and public school students RMB388.36, 4.23 times smaller than the former. The difference here was RMB1256.21, or 35.2% of the total gap in essential spending.

Turning to extended spending, Table 3.2 shows that the average spending by private school students on this category was lower than those attending a public school, with the former spending RMB847.49, or 88.5% of what the latter paid, which was RMB957.52. The difference between the two was RMB110. In the item "extracurricular programs (enrichment classes, tutoring classes, etc.): tuition and expenses for the necessary books, stationery, or tools," private school students spent an average of RMB554.68, or 85.23% of the amount their public school peers did, which was RMB650.80. The former paid RMB96.12 less than the latter; in home tutoring, private school students spent RMB118.68, or 75.52% of what public school students paid, which was RMB157.15 which was RMB38.47 bigger than the former; for other expenses, private school students paid slightly more than those going to a public school.

Composition-wise, essential and extended spending accounted for 64.3% and 35.7%, respectively, of the total spending of public school students, whereas the corresponding percentages for private school students were 86.2% and 13.8%. This indicates that public schools were not as effective in meeting the diversified demand of students' families as their private sector counterparts. Calculations have also shown that the education spending of households with public school students was equal to 8.9% of their annual household income and 11.2% of their annual household spending. For private school students, the two ratios stood at 15.9% and 21.8%. These percentages show that urban households spent a sizable share of their annual income on their children's education. This was especially true for families that sent their children to a private school, who have higher education spending to total income ratios, despite being financially more capable.

From the data in Table 3.2 and the descriptive analysis above we may conclude:

1. The total education spending of private school students is higher than that of public school students.
2. The essential spending of private school students is higher than that of their public school peers.
3. The extended spending of private school students is lower than that of public school students.

The following examines whether the chosen school type has a significant impact on the students' education spending and whether the three conclusions above are true.

3.2.3 Comparison of Students' Total Spending in Public and Private Schools of Compulsory Education

The following analysis uses a double logarithmic regression model to examine whether the total education spending of students is significantly affected by the type of school chosen or the student's total family income.

The model uses total education spending as the explained variable, and total family income and type of school as the explanatory variables; the control variables include father's years of schooling, mother's years of schooling, whether there are siblings or not, gender, whether the school is the first choice, parental assessment of the child's academic performance, parental assessment of the overall quality provided by the child's school, and parental satisfaction with the child's school. Among these variables, total family income, father's years of schooling, and mother's years of schooling are ratio variables; parental assessment of the child's academic performance, parental assessment of the overall quality provided by the child's school, and parental satisfaction with the child's school are ordinal variables with a 5-point scale in the questionnaires used by this study, which may be processed as interval variables by approximation[2]; binary variables, including type of school, whether there are siblings, gender, and whether the school is the first choice, are processed as dummy variables.

The double logarithmic model is expressed as:

$$\begin{aligned}\ln E_1 = \alpha_1 + \beta_{11}\ln X_{11} + \beta_{12}X_{12} + \beta_{13}X_{13} + \beta_{14}X_{14} + \beta_{15}X_{15} + \beta_{16}X_{16} + \beta_{17}X_{17} \\ + \beta_{18}X_{18} + \beta_{19}X_{19} + \beta_{110}X_{110} + \varepsilon_1 \end{aligned} \tag{3.1}$$

where E_1: total education spending of the student;

X_{11}: annual income of the student's household;

X_{12}: type of school, a dummy variable that takes the value 0 when the student attends a public school, and the value 1 when the student attends a private one;

X_{13}: father's years of schooling;

X_{14}: mother's years of schooling;

[2] Author's note: In the questionnaires, parental assessment of the overall quality of the child's school is an ordinal variable with a 4-point scale, where 1 denotes the highest quality as assessed by the parents. This chapter, on the other hand, uses parental assessment of the child's academic performance as the substitution variable for student endowments, focusing on whether it has a significant positive or negative effect on education spending. Therefore, processing it by approximation as interval data has no impact on the results of this study. This is why it is still treated as ratio data in the regression model. This note applies to the rest of this chapter.

X_{15}: parental assessment of the child's academic performance, on a scale of 1 to 5, 1 being the best performance;

X_{16}: parental assessment of the overall quality provided by the child's school, on a scale of 1 to 4, 1 being the best quality;

X_{17}: parental satisfaction with the child's school, on a scale of 1 to 5, 1 being the most satisfied;

X_{18}: whether the child's school is the first choice, a dummy variable that takes the value 0 when it is not the first choice, and the value 1 when it is;

X_{19}: whether the child has any siblings, a dummy variable that takes the value 0 when there are no siblings, and the value 1 when there are;

X_{110}: gender, a dummy variable, 0 for female and 1 for male;

ε_1: other factors that are not considered in this study but may affect the student's education spending.

The main factors examined by this chapter are the financial status of the family (measured as annual family income) and the chosen type of school. The hypothesis is that the financial status of the family has a positive effect on the education spending for the children, so does the chosen type of school when private ones are favored.

A regression was run using Model (3.1) in the statistical analysis software SPSS 12.0. Its results are presented in Table 3.3.

The resulting regression equation is as follows:

$$\begin{aligned} \ln E_1 = 3.259 + 0.434 \ln X_{11} + 0.744X_{12} + 0.03X_{14} - 0.138X_{16} - 0.085X_{18} \\ - 0.143X_{19} - 0.094X_{110} \end{aligned} \tag{3.2}$$

Generally speaking, family financial status is the main factor affecting how parents invest in the human capital of their children, the more total income a family has, the better its financial status is, leading to more human capital investments in the children, as represented first and foremost by increased spending on their education. The model uses the natural logarithms of total education spending and annual family income. In economic terms, the regression coefficient of 0.434 can be interpreted as the income elasticity of total education spending, i.e., for 1% of increase in annual family income, the parents may spend 0.434% more on their children's education. The chosen type of school affects the actual amount of financial resources needed: the total spending of private school students is higher than that of their public school peers.

Table 3.3 Double logarithmic regression analysis of students' total spending in compulsory education (2005)

Variable	Unstandardized coefficients		Standardized coefficients	t-value	*p*-value
	B	Standard deviations	Beta		
Constant	3.259	0.279		11.662	0.000
Natural logarithm of annual family income	0.434	0.027	0.328	15.888	0.000
Type of school	0.744	0.075	0.187	9.962	0.000
Father's years of schooling	−0.009	0.007	−0.031	−1.303	0.193
Mother's years of schooling	0.030	0.007	0.098	4.055	0.000
Academic performance	0.000	0.023	0.000	−0.013	0.990
Quality of school	−0.138	0.024	−0.126	−5.662	0.000
Satisfaction with school	0.028	0.026	0.023	1.054	0.292
First choice or not	−0.085	0.042	−0.040	−2.035	0.042
Presence of siblings	−0.143	0.058	−0.047	−2.462	0.014
Gende	−0.094	0.033	−0.053	−2.831	0.005

Note Fitting coefficient for the model $R = 0.463^{a}$, $R^2 = 0.214$, adjusted $R^2 = 0.211$

3.2.4 Comparison of the Composition of Students' Spending in Public and Private Schools of Compulsory Education

3.2.4.1 Comparison of Students' Essential Spending in Public and Private Schools of Compulsory Education

A double logarithmic regression model is used for this part of the study, with essential spending as the explained variable, annual family income and type of school as the explanatory variables, and the rest as control variables. The model is expressed as follows:

$$\ln E_{b1} = \alpha_{b1} + \beta_{b11} \ln X_{11} + \beta_{b12}X_{12} + \beta_{b13}X_{13} + \beta_{b14}X_{14} + \beta_{b15}X_{15} + \beta_{b16}X_{16} + \beta_{b17}X_{17} + \beta_{b18}X_{18} + \beta_{b19}X_{19} + \beta_{b110}X_{110} + \varepsilon_{b1} \quad (3.3)$$

where E_{b1}: the essential spending of the student;

X_{11} to X_{110}: the same variables that were used in Model (3.1), with the same definitions; no dedicated explanation is repeated here.

ε_{b1}: other factors not considered in this study but may affect the student's essential spending.

A regression was run using Model (3.3) in the statistical analysis software SPSS 12.0. Its results are presented in Table 3.4.

The resulting regression equation is as follows:

$$\ln E_{b1} = 1.959 + 0.569 \ln X_{11} + 0.708X_{12} - 0.045X_{13} + 0.023X_{14} \quad (3.4)$$

The equation indicates that family financial status still has a significant effect. The more total income a family has and the better its financial status is, the more the parents tend to pay for the necessary education of their children. The chosen type of school is another factor that affects students' essential spending significantly. Choosing a private institution means considerably higher necessary expenses than going with the public system, not least since parents need to pay more just to secure their children's enrollment in a private school.

Table 3.4 Double logarithmic regression analysis of students' essential spending in compulsory education (2005)

Variable	Unstandardized coefficients		Standardized coefficients	t-value	*p*-value
	B	Standard deviations	Beta		
Constant	1.959	0.990		1.980	0.049
Natural logarithm of annual family income	0.569	0.097	0.385	5.857	0.000
Type of school	0.708	0.198	0.216	3.583	0.000
Father's years of schooling	−0.045	0.025	−0.126	−1.749	0.082
Mother's years of schooling	0.023	0.025	0.065	0.884	0.077
Academic performance	0.032	0.077	0.026	0.413	0.680
Quality of school	−0.040	0.088	−0.034	−0.454	0.650
Satisfaction with school	−0.129	0.090	−0.104	−1.439	0.152
First choice or not	−0.086	0.137	−0.041	−0.629	0.530
Presence of siblings	−0.014	0.207	−0.004	−0.066	0.948
Gender	−0.147	0.114	−0.077	−1.289	0.199

Note Fitting coefficient for the model $R = 0.421^{a}$, $R^2 = 0.177$, adjusted $R^2 = 0.174$

3.2.4.2 Comparison of Students' Extended Spending in Public and Private Schools of Compulsory Education

A double logarithmic regression model is used for this part of the study, with extended spending as the explained variable, total family income and type of school as the explanatory variables, and the rest as control variables:

$$\ln E_{k1} = \alpha_{b1} + \beta_{k11} \ln X_{11} + \beta_{k12}X_{12} + \beta_{k13}X_{13} + \beta_{k14}X_{14} + \beta_{k15}X_{15} + \beta_{k16}X_{16} + \beta_{k17}X_{17} + \beta_{k18}X_{18} + \beta_{k19}X_{19} + \beta_{k110}X_{110} + \varepsilon_{k1} \quad (3.5)$$

where E_{k1}: the extended spending for the student;

X_{11} to X_{110}: the same variables that were used in Model (3.1) and Model (3.3), with the same definitions; no dedicated explanation is repeated here;

ε_{k1}: other factors that are not considered in this study but may affect the student's extended spending.

A regression was run using Model (3.5) in the statistical analysis software SPSS 12.0. Its results are presented in Table 3.5.

Table 3.5 Double logarithmic regression analysis of students' extended spending in compulsory education (2005)

Variable	Unstandardized coefficients		Standardized coefficients	t-value	*p*-value
	B	Standard deviations	Beta		
Constant	−1.917	1.228		−1.560	0.120
Natural logarithm of annual family income	0.764	0.120	0.388	6.362	0.000
Type of school	−0.623	0.300	−0.119	−2.079	0.039
Father's years of schooling	−0.011	0.030	−0.025	−0.361	0.718
Mother's years of schooling	0.058	0.033	0.118	1.737	0.084
Academic performance	0.042	0.098	0.025	0.424	0.672
Quality of school	−0.045	0.106	−0.029	−0.421	0.674
Satisfaction with school	0.076	0.115	0.044	0.664	0.507
First choice or not	0.081	0.180	0.028	0.450	0.653
Presence of siblings	−0.201	0.243	−0.047	−0.828	0.408
Gender	−0.035	0.145	−0.014	−0.240	0.810

Note Fitting coefficient for the model $R = 0.459^{a}$, $R^2 = 0.210$, adjusted $R^2 = 0.179$

The resulting regression equation:

$$\ln E_{k1} = 0.764 \ln X_{11} - 0.623X_{12} + 0.058X_{14} \tag{3.6}$$

Annual family income has a significant positive effect on the student's extended spending, which has an income elasticity of 0.764. The chosen type of school is another factor that impacts the extended spending category significantly, with the statistics showing that public school students spent considerably more on this category than their private school peers. It seems that after sending their children to a public school, parents often ended up paying more for various extended items, including the tuition and books, stationery, or tools for extracurricular programs (enrichment, tutoring classes), home tutoring, and other expenses.

A comparison of Eq. (3.4) and Eq. (3.6), meanwhile, shows extended spending having a greater income elasticity than essential spending (0.764 > 0.569), which means the former is affected more significantly by family financial status than the latter. This may have been determined by the different composition and characteristics of the two categories of education spending. The public good nature of compulsory education makes it necessary to ensure fairness by regulating the rates of essential expenses with national policies and having them monitored by education authorities and the general public. As for the extended educational services, parents and students have the freedom to choose any option they can afford.

In addition, the absolute value of the regression coefficient for the dummy variable "type of school" is greater in Eq. (3.4) than in Eq. (3.6) (0.708 > 0.623). This means that the increase in essential spending due to choosing a private school is larger than the decrease in extended spending resulting from the same decision, which can be a structural explanation of the higher total spending of private school students.

3.2.5 *Analysis of the Types of Demand Served by Public and Private Schools in Compulsory Education*

Based on the comparative analysis of the factors affecting the amount and composition of students' education spending, one may conclude that the chosen type of school has a significant effect on education spending and its composition. The choice between public and private schools leads to differences in how much the students spend on their education and in the specific components of such spending. The analysis above and its conclusion thus provide empirical support for Hypothesis 1 of the study, i.e., the chosen school type has a significant impact on the student's education spending and its composition. Private school students spend considerably more in total than public school students; in terms of the components of their spending, private school students spend significantly more than their public school peers on essential items, while the opposite is true for extended spending. Hypotheses 1, 1.1, and 1.2 are thus supported by the results of an empirical study.

Further investigation into the wide structural differences in students' spending in public and private schools of compulsory education helps characterize the offerings of the two kinds of schools in urban China and identify the types and features of their educational services, which allows for a better characterization of the educational demands of urban residents. Today, China offers 9-year compulsory education through a complete national system that relies on public schools. Because of the public good nature of this stage of education, the idea that compulsory education should be funded by the government is widely agreed on and implemented. In the meantime, however, demand for high-quality and diversified educational services still exists, which cannot be entirely satisfied by the public system. This demand is becoming ever more dynamic, thanks to socioeconomic progress and increasing living standards. The development of private schools is an active response to such unmet demand in compulsory education. Private schools grew fast precisely because they have addressed people's need for diversified options. They play an important role in providing parents and students with choices and in closing the supply gap for high-quality and diversified educational services. One of the questions in its survey allowed this study to obtain data on the parents' assessment of the overall quality of their children's school. An independent samples t test on the data found that private schools received higher scores for overall quality than public ones, indicating that the quality of service provided by the former is significantly better than the latter,[3] which may be the reflection of the quality advantage associated with urban private schools of compulsory education.

Empirical research found that in urban areas, private school students spend significantly more than public school students on the essential category, as their parents need to pay more for them to enroll in a private school and enjoy the services it provides; on the other hand, private school students spend a lot less on extended items than their public school peers, as the parents of the latter need to pay more after enrollment for extracurricular education to help improve the students' academic performance or access diversified services. By opting for a private school, students are choosing education resources and services dissimilar to those offered by the public sector, whereas public school students are paying extra for higher quality and more diversity in the services they receive, on top of the resources and services already provided by their schools. This is how the choice of school types leads to different compositions of spending on education.

Focusing on the composition of urban households' spending on their children's education, this section has presented an empirical analysis on how public and private school students spend differently in compulsory education. The conclusion is as follows: in terms of their offerings and objectives, private schools of compulsory education in urban China today are aimed more at satisfying the residents' needs for high-quality resources and diversified services, i.e., these schools are addressing

[3] Parental assessment of the overall quality of the children's school is a 4-point ordinal variable in the survey, on a scale of 1 to 4, 1 being the best quality. Independent samples *t*-test shows that at the significance level of 0.1, private schools do better in the assessment of overall quality than public schools.

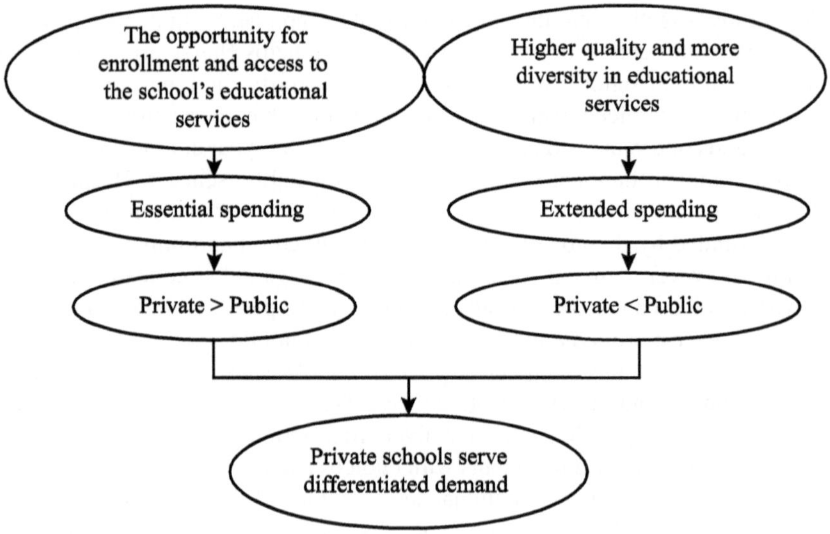

Fig. 3.2 Private schools and the existing types of demand in compulsory education

the differentiated demand for education. Figure 3.2 is a structural illustration of this conclusion.

3.3 Education Expenditures for Public and Private High School Students

3.3.1 Family Backgrounds of Students in High School

This chapter uses a sample consisting of 1035 high school students from urban areas in China. 964 of them attended a public high school and 71 went to a private one. Table 3.6 presents the descriptive statistics on their family backgrounds. On average, families that sent their children to a private high school had slightly better financial means than those who chose the public system. Independent samples t-test did not find any significant difference in the financial status of these two types of households, meaning that these private high school students did not enjoy significantly better family financial resources than their public school peers.

Upper secondary education is optional in China, and the public system has not yet grown to a scale that can accommodate all of the demand for this stage of education. In addition, many public high schools enjoy stronger reputation and advantages such as better faculty and quality of instruction, which may be impossible for their private counterparts to replicate in the short term. Under these circumstances, people

Table 3.6 Family backgrounds of students in high school (2005)

Item	Public schools		Private schools	
	Means	Standard deviations	Means	Standard deviations
Annual household income (RMB)	31,287.85	41,388.77	33,339.96	22,739.81
Annual household spending (RMB)	24,648.38	27,149.40	27,014.51	16,389.90
Market value of currently owned residential property (RMB)	151,416.41	162,974.58	179,735.85	147,569.56
Number of computers owned	0.72	0.51	0.79	0.47
Number of private cars owned	0.10	0.31	0.12	0.33
Number of children	1.17	0.54	1.20	0.44
Father's average years of schooling	11.02	2.69	10.83	2.70
Mother's average years of schooling	10.60	2.56	10.25	2.91

who choose private high schools do so in order to gain access to upper secondary education, which requires them to spend more.

This means the choice of school types will lead to different amounts and compositions of spending. The following subsections seek to examine whether the decision about the type of school has a significant effect on students' spending, and if yes then to what extent.

3.3.2 *Breakdown of Students' Spending in Public and Private High Schools*

Following the categorization of education spending and the operational definitions provided above, this part divides the spending of high school students into two categories: essential spending and extended spending. Table 3.7 presents the data on these two categories, including the specific items within each category and their share of total spending on education.

Table 3.7 shows that the average total education spending of private high school students was RMB9125.66, which was RMB3394.36, or 1.59 times higher than what public high school students spent in total of RMB5731.30. The average essential spending was RMB8090.17 for private high school students and RMB4845.41 for public high school students. The former was RMB3244.76, or 1.67 times higher than the latter. Within this category, average high school tuition was RMB3351.76 for

Table 3.7 Breakdown of students' spending in public and private high schools (2005)

Item	Public schools			Private schools		
	Means (RMB)	Standard deviations (RMB)	Share of total spending (%)	Means (RMB)	Standard deviations (RMB)	Share of total spending (%)
Essential spending						
Tuition	1774.22	1582.61	30.96	3351.76	2822.57	36.73
Boarding	172.19	425.61	3.00	329.86	489.77	3.61
Books, stationery, and learning materials	528.77	548.83	9.23	523.89	661.14	5.74
Out-of-pocket spending when living on campus (meals)	939.65	2268.65	16.40	1694.65	1905.02	18.57
Uniforms	108.94	231.93	1.90	105.59	169.95	1.16
Travel expenses	181.95	346.69	3.17	166.11	242.88	1.82
Contributions (school selection fees)	1139.69	4060.90	19.89	1918.31	5369.18	21.02
Subtotal	4845.41	5360.61	84.54	8090.17	6763.92	88.65
Extended spending						
Extracurricular learning*	416.19	1287.67	7.26	416.39	869.01	4.56
Home tutoring	261.66	833.20	4.57	247.46	720.72	2.71
Other expenses	208.03	594.32	3.63	371.63	824.64	4.07
Subtotal	885.89	1685.31	15.46	1035.49	1375.43	11.35
Total education spending	5731.30	5718.02	100	9125.66	7225.47	100

Note *This refers to the item called "extracurricular programs (enrichment classes, tutoring classes, etc.): tuition and expenses for the necessary books, stationery, or tools" in the questionnaires

private schools and RMB1774.22 for public ones, so the former was RMB1577.54, or 1.89 times higher than the latter; for out-of-pocket spending when living on campus (meals), private school students paid an average of RMB1694.65, RMB755, or 1.92 times higher than the RMB939.65 paid by public school students. Spending on books, stationery, and learning materials (including photocopying and printing), cost of school uniforms, and schooling-related travel expenses were similar for the two types of schools.

Turning to extended spending, Table 3.7 indicates no obvious difference between the average amount spent by private high school students and that by public school students. In particular, when only the tuition and necessary books, stationery, or tools for extracurricular programs (enrichment/tutoring classes) and home tutoring expenses are considered, the average spending was basically the same for public and private school students.

Composition-wise, the necessary and extended spending for public high school students accounted for 84.5% and 15.5% of the total spending per student, while the corresponding percentages for private school students were 88.6% and 11.4%.

This means that private high school students had higher essential spending both in terms of the absolute amount and the percentage. Calculations have also been made to shed light on the financial burden undertaken by families. For those who chose public schools, education spending was 18.3% of their annual family income, while the percentage for private school students' families was 27.4%. Both were rather high, but the latter was higher than the former by 9.1 percentage points.

From the data in Table 3.7 and the descriptive analysis above we may conclude:

1. The total education spending of private high school students is higher than that of public school students.
2. The essential spending of private high school students is higher than that of their public school peers.
3. No significant difference exists between the extended spending of public and private high school students.

The following sections examine whether the three conclusions above are true and whether the chosen school type has a significant impact on the students' education spending.

3.3.3 Comparison of Students' Total Spending in Public and Private High Schools

The following analysis uses a double logarithmic regression model to examine the total education spending of high school students. It also seeks to understand what factors affect the total spending and the extent of their effect.

The model uses total education spending as the explained variable, and total family income and type of school as the explanatory variables; the control variables include: father's years of schooling, mother's years of schooling, whether there are siblings or not, gender, whether the school is the first choice, parental assessment of the child's academic performance, parental assessment of the overall quality provided by the child's school, and parental satisfaction with the child's school. The resulting equation is as follows:

$$\begin{aligned}\ln E_2 = {} & \alpha_2 + \beta_{21}\ln X_{21} + \beta_{22}X_{22} + \beta_{23}X_{23} + \beta_{24}X_{24} + \beta_{25}X_{25} + \beta_{26}X_{26} + \beta_{27}X_{27} \\ & + \beta_{28}X_{28} + \beta_{29}X_{29} + \beta_{210}X_{210} + \varepsilon_2 \qquad (3.7)\end{aligned}$$

where E_2: total education spending of the student;

X_{21}: annual income of the student's household;

X_{22}: type of school, a dummy variable that takes the value 0 when the student attends a public school, and the value 1 when the student attends a private one;

X_{23}: father's years of schooling;

X_{24}: mother's years of schooling;

X_{25}: parental assessment of the child's academic performance, on a scale of 1 to 5, 1 being the best performance;

X_{26}: parental assessment of the overall quality provided by the child's school, on a scale of 1 to 4, 1 being the best quality;

X_{27}: parental satisfaction with the child's school, on a scale of 1 to 5, 1 being the most satisfied;

X_{28}: whether the child's school is the first choice, a dummy variable that takes the value 0 when it is not the first choice, and the value 1 when it is;

X_{29}: whether the child has any siblings, a dummy variable that takes the value 0 when there are no siblings, and the value 1 when there are;

X_{210}: gender, a dummy variable, 0 for female and 1 for male;

ε_2: other factors that are not considered in this study but may affect the student's education spending.

A regression was run using Model (3.7) in the statistical analysis software SPSS 12.0. Its results are presented in Table 3.8.

The equation derived from the regression results in the Table 3.8 is as follows:

Table 3.8 Double logarithmic regression analysis of students' total education spending in high school (2005)

Variable	Unstandardized coefficients		Standardized coefficients	t-value	*p*-value
	B	Standard deviations	Beta		
Constant	4.927	0.404		12.197	0.000
Natural logarithm of annual family income	0.350	0.040	0.287	8.778	0.000
Type of school	0.478	0.088	0.161	5.413	0.000
Father's years of schooling	−0.001	0.010	−0.005	−0.128	0.898
Mother's years of schooling	0.013	0.010	0.045	1.287	0.198
Academic performance	0.038	0.031	0.038	1.226	0.221
Quality of school	−0.135	0.032	−0.159	−4.201	0.000
Satisfaction with school	0.027	0.035	0.028	0.776	0.438
First choice or not	−0.121	0.053	−0.073	−2.302	0.022
Presence of siblings	−0.164	0.064	−0.077	−2.559	0.011
Gender	−0.052	0.044	−0.035	−1.170	0.242

Note Fitting coefficient for the model $R = 0.396^a$, $R^2 = 0.157$, adjusted $R^2 = 0.149$

$$\ln E_2 = 4.927 + 0.35 \ln X_{21} + 0.478X_{22} - 0.135X_{26} - 0.121X_{28} - 0.164X_{29} \tag{3.8}$$

The coefficients of the explanatory variables in Eq. (3.8) show that family financial status has a significant positive effect on the student's total education spending. Families with higher annual income tend to invest more in their children's education, and the income elasticity of their total spending here is 0.35. The chosen type of school is the other factor that has a significant effect, as choosing a private high school entails higher expenses than attending a public school.

3.3.4 Comparison of the Composition of Students' Spending in Public and Private High Schools

3.3.4.1 Comparison of Students' Essential Spending in Public and Private High Schools

This analysis of the essential spending of high school students uses the same double logarithmic regression models as the previous section, with essential spending as the explained variable, annual family income and chosen school type as the explanatory variables, and all other factors as the control variables. The equation is as follows:

$$\begin{aligned}\ln E_{b2} = {} & \alpha_{b2} + \beta_{b21} \ln X_{21} + \beta_{b22}X_{22} + \beta_{b23}X_{23} + \beta_{b24}X_{24} + \beta_{b25}X_{25} + \beta_{b26}X_{26} \\ & + \beta_{b27}X_{27} + \beta_{b28}X_{28} + \beta_{b29}X_{29} + \beta_{b210}X_{210} + \varepsilon_{b2}\end{aligned} \tag{3.9}$$

where E_{b2}: the essential spending of the high school student;

X_{21} to X_{210}: the same variables that were used in Model (3.7), with the same definitions; no dedicated explanation is repeated here;

ε_{b2}: other factors that are not considered in this study but may affect the student's education spending.

A regression was run using Model (3.9) in the statistical analysis software SPSS 12.0. Its results are presented in Table 3.9. The regression equation is as follows:

$$\ln E_{b2} = 5.184 + 0.31 \ln X_{21} + 0.542X_{22} + 0.06625X_{25} - 0.125X_{26} - 0.122X_{28} \tag{3.10}$$

Equation (3.10) indicates that family financial status has a significant positive effect on the essential spending of high school students. The other factor that affects essential spending significantly is the chosen type of school. In order to enroll in a private school and enjoy the education services it provides, the parents and students have to pay a higher amount than those who chose the public system.

Table 3.9 Double logarithmic regression analysis of students' essential spending in high school (2005)

Variable	Unstandardized coefficients		Standardized coefficients	t-value	*p*-value
	B	Standard deviations	Beta		
Constant	5.184	0.447		11.585	0.000
Natural logarithm of annual family income	0.310	0.044	0.235	7.016	0.000
Type of school	0.542	0.098	0.169	5.544	0.000
Father's years of schooling	0.000	0.011	0.001	0.027	0.978
Mother's years of schooling	0.005	0.011	0.015	0.427	0.669
Academic performance	0.066	0.034	0.062	1.944	0.052
Quality of school	−0.125	0.036	−0.136	−3.510	0.000
Satisfaction with school	−0.017	0.038	−0.017	−0.449	0.653
First choice or not	−0.122	0.058	−0.068	−2.087	0.037
Presence of siblings	−0.080	0.071	−0.035	−1.135	0.257
Gender	−0.005	0.049	−0.003	−0.096	0.924

Note Fitting coefficient for the model $R = 0.340^{a}$, $R^2 = 0.116$, adjusted $R^2 = 0.107$

3.3.4.2 Comparison of Students' Extended Spending in Public and Private High Schools

Similar to the analysis of essential spending above, another double logarithmic regression model—Model (3.11)—is used to examine the extended spending of high school students:

$$\ln E_{k2} = \alpha_{k2} + \beta_{k21} \ln X_{21} + \beta_{k22}X_{22} + \beta_{k23}X_{23} + \beta_{k24}X_{24} + \beta_{k25}X_{25} + \beta_{k26}X_{26} + \beta_{k27}X_{27} + \beta_{k28}X_{28} + \beta_{k29}X_{29} + \beta_{k210}X_{210} + \varepsilon_{k2} \tag{3.11}$$

where E_{k2}: the extended spending of the student;

X_{21} to X_{210}: the same variables that were used in Model (3.7) and Model (3.9), with the same definitions; no dedicated explanation is repeated here;

ε_{k2}: other factors that are not considered in this study but may affect the student's extended spending.

A regression was run using Model (3.11) in the statistical analysis software SPSS 12.0. Its results are presented in Table 3.10.

The resulting equation is as follows:

Table 3.10 Double logarithmic regression analysis of students' extended spending in high school (2005)

Variable	Unstandardized coefficients		Standardized coefficients	t-value	*p*-value
	B	Standard deviations	Beta		
Constant	0.820	0.827		0.991	0.322
Natural logarithm of annual family income	0.535	0.082	0.268	6.550	0.000
Type of school	0.097	0.174	0.021	0.557	0.577
Father's years of schooling	0.004	0.020	0.008	0.181	0.856
Mother's years of schooling	0.040	0.021	0.085	1.940	0.053
Academic performance	−0.114	0.062	−0.072	−1.838	0.066
Quality of school	−0.029	0.065	−0.021	−0.443	0.658
Satisfaction with school	0.112	0.070	0.072	1.587	0.113
First choice or not	−0.013	0.105	−0.005	−0.121	0.903
Presence of siblings	−0.450	0.133	−0.127	−3.386	0.001
Gender	−0.161	0.089	−0.067	−1.810	0.071

Note Fitting coefficient for the model $R = 0.417^{a}$, $R^2 = 0.174$, adjusted $R^2 = 0.150$

$$\ln E_{k2} = 0.535 \ln X_{21} + 0.04X_{24} - 0.114X_{25} - 0.45X_{29} - 0.161X_{210} \qquad (3.12)$$

Equation (3.12) shows that family financial status has a significant positive effect on the extended spending of high school students. This may be why it has a higher income elasticity: for every unit of increase in family income, extended spending increases by a factor of 0.535. The regression indicates that, unlike the factors affecting essential spending, the chosen type of school has no significant effect on the extended category, since public and private high school students have no significant difference in their extended spending.

A comparison of Eq. (3.10) and Eq. (3.12) also shows that the extended spending of high school students has a higher income elasticity than their essential spending (0.535 > 0.310), meaning that any change in family income will likely affect extended spending more than it does essential spending—a reflection of the different goals that parents may have in mind when they pay for these expenses. Essential spending covers enrollment and other necessary expenses on campus. Most of its specific items, including tuition, boarding, and contribution, are heavily regulated by the government, hence the smaller shifts of essential spending resulting from changes in family income. Extended spending, on the other hand, covers educational services and expenses over which parents and students have the freedom of choice.

3.3.5 *Analysis of the Types of Demand Served by Public and Private High Schools*

This chapter has conducted a comparative analysis of the composition and influencing factors of students' education spending in urban high schools. The results show that the chosen type of school has a significant effect on the spending and its mix of components, which differ between the students of public and private schools. Hypothesis 2 of the study has been tested by the analysis above: the choice between public and private high schools does affect students' education spending and its composition significantly, with private school students having considerably higher total spending; as for the main components, private school students spend significantly more than their public school peers on essential items, while no obvious difference is found for the extended category. Hypotheses 2, 2.1, and 2.2 are thus supported by the results of an empirical study.

Since the composition of education spending differs significantly between public and private high school students in urban areas, investigating the different factors that affect the essential and extended components of spending may help explain the varying operational practices adopted by the two types of schools and reveal the actual current state of high school education in China.

The upper secondary stage of education represents a period of transition. It is at once the more advanced stage following compulsory education and the necessary preparatory phase leading to higher education. Since the successful implementation of universal 9-year compulsory education in the late 1990s, China has shifted its focus in education development from this previous goal to expanding higher education. The country immediately started popularizing college education—a change that had undeniable impacts on the development of high school education. Certain more developed regions are indeed moving towards universal upper secondary education, a goal that has already been achieved in the most developed cities, but at the national level, the existing high school education system still does not completely satisfy the existing demand. In particular, the country as a whole is experiencing a shortage of general high school education.

Upper secondary education is non-compulsory and optional. As China's economy grows and its people become better educated in general, the bars for knowledge and skills are also rising in the country's labor market, leading to strong demand for education beyond the compulsory stage. Hence the growing needs—both in terms of quantity and quality—for high school learning. Since public funding is limited, expanding access to upper secondary education depends on the development of private schools.

However, because of the existing system of college entrance exams (*gaokao*), private schools have been facing relentless pressure from their public competitors since day one. The public high school system has attracted most of the better prospective students, thanks to its long history of operation, massive pool of skilled teachers, robust infrastructure, and high quality of instruction. As late entrants, private high schools struggle to compete with public schools in a number of areas while still charging higher fees, which may be the reason why parents and students generally lean towards the public system. Only a handful of reputable private schools offering high-quality services are able to compete with public schools for incoming candidates and achieve similar college enrollment rates. Generally speaking, private schools are weaker competitors who mainly target the part of demand that the public system cannot satisfy due to its limited capacity. Meanwhile, those private schools with better quality are meeting the needs of students who come from wealthier families but fail to enter any top-tier public school due to their clearly inadequate academic performance.

The empirical analysis above has found that in upper secondary education, the essential spending of private school students is significantly higher than that of public school students, i.e., the families that send their children to a private school need to pay more for enrollment and the various services offered by the school; once enrolled, the students of the two types of schools do not spend very differently on extended items for improving academic performance or obtaining more diversified services—in other words, the chosen type of school does not have a significant effect on extended spending. The analysis of the parental assessment of overall quality offered by the chosen school through an independent samples t-test has found no significant difference in the quality offered by public and private high schools.

The examination of the factors affecting the composition of spending for high school students reveals that the chosen type of school is indeed a factor with significant impact. Combining the results of the empirical research above with the current realities of high school education in China, one may conclude that, in terms of their overall offerings and objectives, private high schools in urban areas are mainly targeting the excess demand for upper secondary education, i.e., the part of demand that cannot be satisfied by a public system with limited capacity. Figure 3.3 is a structural illustration of this conclusion:

3.4 Education Expenditures for Public and Private College Students

3.4.1 Family Backgrounds of Students in Higher Education

This chapter uses a higher education sample consisting of 948 students in total, among which 856 attended a public college and 92 went to a private one. All of the students came from urban households. Table 3.11 presents the descriptive statistics on their family backgrounds.

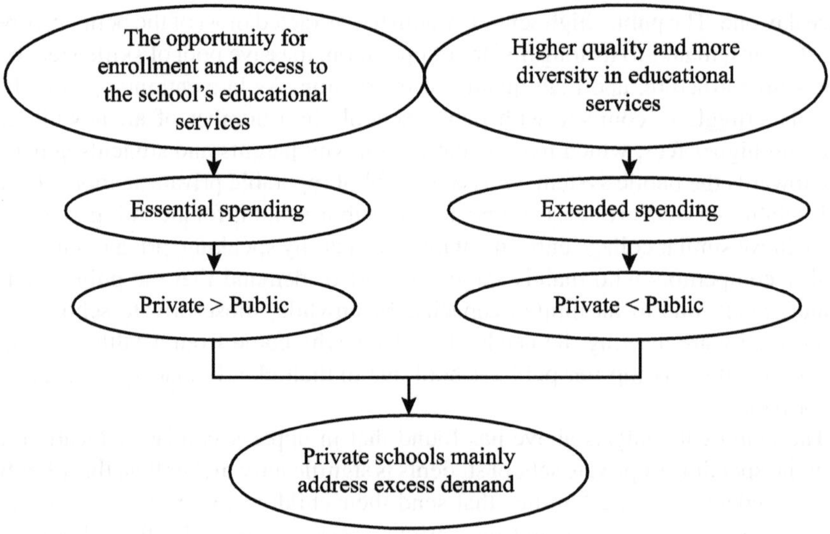

Fig. 3.3 Private high schools and the existing types of demand

Table 3.11 Family backgrounds of students in higher education (2005)

Item	Public schools		Private schools	
	Means	Standard deviations	Means	Standard deviations
Annual household income (RMB)	30,648.89	20,096.25	38,040.82	24,526.20
Annual household spending (RMB)	26,306.26	19,775.13	32,095.32	18,560.90
Market value of currently owned residential property (RMB)	145,620.32	143,123.50	204,450.26	202,760.63
Number of computers owned	0.82	0.56	0.93	0.40
Number of private cars owned	0.10	0.33	0.18	0.39
Number of children	1.23	1.08	1.10	0.39
Father's average years of schooling	11.09	2.78	10.47	2.42
Mother's average years of schooling	10.56	2.68	10.36	2.82

The data presented by Table 3.11 shows that, on average, the family financial status of students who attended a private college was better than those who went to a public one. Average family income was RMB38,040.82 for private college students and RMB30,648. 89 for public college students. The former was RMB7391.93 or 24% higher than the latter. Average family annual spending was RMB32,095.32 for private college students and RMB26,306.26 for public college students. The former is RMB5789.06 or 1.22 times higher than the latter. Independent samples *t*-test revealed that, in such items as annual income, total annual spending, market value of currently owned residential property, and number of computers owned, the differences between the families of public and private college students were significant at the 0.05 level. This means that in urban areas, students who attend a private college tended to have considerably better family financial status than those going to a public institution. Private higher education in China has a short history and a small scale. It is typically chosen by families who have a strong demand for college education and more financial resources to spare. When their children fail to enroll in any public college, they have to pay more for choosing a private institution instead.

The following sections examine whether the chosen type of school has a significant effect on students' education spending.

3.4.2 *Breakdown of Students' Spending in Public and Private Colleges*

Following the definitions of education spending described earlier, this section divides the spending for students of higher education into two categories—learning expenses and living expenses. Table 3.12 presents the data on these two categories, including the specific items within each category and their share of total spending on education.

As shown in Table 3.12, the students' average total spending was RMB15,430.12 for private colleges and RMB11,534.46 for public ones. Private college students paid RMB3895.66, or 1.4 times more than their peers in public colleges. The average learning expenses were RMB8566.09 for private colleges and RMB6214.26 for public ones. The former was RMB2351.83 higher, or 1.38 times the latter. The differences existed mainly in tuition and books, stationery, and learning materials, as students of private colleges paid on average RMB2334.86 and RMB117.54 more for these items. Students of public colleges paid slightly more for extracurricular learning and home tutoring, while none of the private college students in the sample spent anything on home tutoring. As for living expenses, the average spending per student was RMB6864.03 for private colleges and RMB5320.20 for public ones; the former was 1.29 times the latter. Students of private colleges spent more on every specific item within this category, except uniforms, which showed basically no difference between the two groups. For students of private colleges, 55.5% of their total spending covered learning expenses and 44.5% went to living expenses. The

Table 3.12 Breakdown of the spending of college students (2005)

Item	Public colleges			Private colleges		
	Means (RMB)	Standard deviations (RMB)	Share of total spending (%)	Means (RMB)	Standard deviations (RMB)	Share of total spending (%)
Learning expenses						
Tuition	5352.50	5812.34	46.40	7687.36	7822.37	49.82
Books, stationery, and learning materials	601.84	862.35	5.22	719.38	1146.72	4.66
Extracurricular learning*	222.11	856.26	1.93	159.34	540.98	1.03
Home tutoring	37.80	459.03	0.33	0	0	0
Subtotal	6214.26	6128.78	53.88	8566.09	7976.69	55.52
Living expenses						
Boarding	1015.28	2117.77	8.80	1425.60	3128.11	9.24
Out-of-pocket spending of living on campus(meals)	3513.01	3277.74	30.46	4139.56	3162.80	26.83
Uniforms	79.94	277.49	0.69	69.45	178.73	0.45
Travel expenses	340.80	511.87	2.95	734.19	1605.87	4.76
Other expenses	371.17	1020.63	3.22	495.23	1120.57	3.21
Subtotal	5320.20	5504.50	46.12	6864.03	7210.02	44.48
Total education spending	11,534.46	10,438.49	100	15,430.12	14,457.84	100

Note * This refers to the item called "extracurricular programs (enrichment classes, tutoring classes, etc.): tuition and expenses for the necessary books, stationery, or tools" in the questionnaires

corresponding percentages for students of public colleges were 53.9% and 46.1%, respectively. This structural view shows that the learning expenses of private college students were higher both in terms of the average amount and percentage of total spending on education.

The descriptive statistics above lead to the following observations: per-student total education spending of private colleges was higher than that of public ones; more specifically, private college students spend more on both components—learning expenses and living expenses. The following sections examine whether the conclusions above are true and whether the chosen school type has a significant impact on students' education spending.

3.4.3 Comparison of Students' Total Spending in Public and Private Colleges

The following section uses a double logarithmic regression model to explore whether the type of institution chosen by students and their parents has a significant effect on the amount and composition of spending on education.

The model uses total education spending as the explained variable, total family income and type of institution as the explanatory variables, and father's years of schooling, mother's years of schooling, presence of siblings, gender, application for student loan, location of the student's household, and the nature of the higher education program as the control variables. Among these variables, total family income, father's years of schooling, and mother's years of schooling are interval variables; type of institution, presence of siblings, gender, student loan, location of the student's household, and the nature of the higher education program are treated as dummy variables in the model.

The double logarithmic model is expressed as:

$$\ln E_3 = \alpha_3 + \beta_{31} \ln X_{31} + \beta_{32}X_{32} + \beta_{33}X_{33} + \beta_{34}X_{34} + \beta_{35}X_{35} + \beta_{36}X_{36} + \beta_{37}X_{37} + \beta_{38}X_{38} + \beta_{39}X_{39} + \beta_{310}X_{310} + \beta_{311}X_{311} + \varepsilon_3 \quad (3.13)$$

where E_3: total education spending of the student;

X_{31}: annual income of the student's household;

X_{32}: type of institution, a dummy variable that takes the value 0 when the student attends a public institution, and the value 1 when the student attends a private one;

X_{33}: father's years of schooling;

X_{34}: mother's years of schooling;

X_{35}: whether the child has any siblings, a dummy variable that takes the value 0 when there are no siblings, and the value 1 when there are;

X_{36}: gender, a dummy variable, 0 for female and 1 for male;

X_{37}: whether a student loan has been applied for, a dummy variable that takes the value 0 when there is no loan, and the value 1 when there is;

X_{38}: whether the student attends a vocational college, a dummy variable that takes the value 1 if yes and the value 0 if no; enrollment at a technical college is the baseline;

X_{39}: whether the student attends an undergraduate degree program, a dummy variable that takes the value 1 if yes and the value 0 if no; enrollment at a technical college is the baseline;

X_{310}: whether the student comes from the Eastern region, a dummy variable that takes the value 1 if yes and the value 0 if no; students from the Western region are considered the baseline;

X_{311}: whether the student comes from the Central region, a dummy variable that takes the value 1 if yes and the value 0 if no; students from the Western region are considered the baseline;

ε_3: other factors that are not considered in this study but may affect the student's total education spending.

This part focuses on family financial status (measured as annual family income) and the chosen type of institution as the main factors affecting the spending of college students. Other variables that may have a certain degree of effect on students' spending are treated as control variables.

A regression was run using Model (3.13) in the statistical analysis software SPSS 12.0. Its results are presented in Table 3.13. The regression equation is as follows:

$$\ln E_3 = 6.836 + 0.156 \ln X_{31} + 0.297X_{32} + 0.231X_{37} + 0.128X_{38} + 0.533X310 + 0.825X_{311} \quad (3.14)$$

This shows that both factors still have a significant effect on the total spending of students in higher education. The more a family earns, the more the parents will spend on their children's education. Increase in family income has a positive effect on private spending on higher education, which has an income elasticity of 0.156, based on the regression analysis. When the type of institution is concerned, those who attend a private college spend significantly more in total than those going to a public one.

Table 3.13 Double logarithmic regression analysis of students' total spending in college (2005)

Variable	Unstandardized coefficients		Standardized coefficients	t-value	*p*-value
	B	Standard deviations	Beta		
Constant	6.836	0.348		19.648	0.000
Natural logarithm of annual family income	0.156	0.034	0.167	4.531	0.000
Type of school	0.297	0.059	0.161	4.998	0.000
Father's years of schooling	0.004	0.007	0.020	0.549	0.583
Mother's years of schooling	−0.002	0.008	−0.010	−0.285	0.776
Presence of siblings	−0.049	0.054	−0.029	−0.904	0.366
Gender	0.031	0.034	0.028	0.891	0.373
Applied for a loan or not	0.231	0.107	0.069	2.156	0.031
From Eastern region or not	0.128	0.044	0.110	2.919	0.004
From Central region or not	−0.010	0.042	−0.009	−0.240	0.810
Attends a vocational college	0.533	0.143	0.465	3.731	0.000
Attend undergraduate	0.825	0.142	0.725	5.827	0.000

Note Fitting coefficient for the model $R = 0.421^a$, $R^2 = 0.177$, adjusted $R^2 = 0.167$

3.4.4 Comparison of the Composition of Students' Spending in Public and Private Colleges

3.4.4.1 Comparison of Students' Learning Expenses in Public and Private Colleges

A double logarithmic regression model is used for this part of the study, with learning expenses as the explained variable, annual family income and type of college as the explanatory variables, and all others as the control variables.

$$\ln E_{j3} = \alpha_{j3} + \beta_{j31} \ln X_{31} + \beta_{j32}X_{32} + \beta_{j33}X_{33} + \beta_{j34}X_{34} + \beta_{j35}X_{35} + \beta_{j36}X_{36} + \beta_{j37}X_{37} + \beta_{j38}X_{38} + \beta_{j39}X_{39} + \beta_{j310}X_{310} + \beta_{j311}X_{311} + \varepsilon_{j3} \quad (3.15)$$

where E_{j3}: learning expenses of the student;

X_{31} to X_{311}: the same variables that were used in Model (3.13), with the same definitions; no dedicated explanation is repeated here;

ε_{j3}: other factors that are not considered in this study but may affect the student's learning expenses.

A regression was run using Model (3.15) in the statistical analysis software SPSS 12.0. Its results are presented in Table 3.14.

The resulting regression equation on the learning expenses for college students is as follows:

$$\ln E_{j3} = 6.908 + 0.099 \ln X_{31} + 0.305X_{32} + 0.219X_{38} + 0.385X_{310} + 0.593X_{311} \quad (3.16)$$

The Eq. (3.16) shows that annual family income has a significant positive effect on the education spending of college students, for which the results of the regression indicate an income elasticity of 0.099. Students of private colleges spend significantly more than those of public colleges, with tuition being the biggest contributor to the difference. Calculations based on the data in Table 3.12 show that the share of tuition in total education spending is 86.1% for students of public colleges and as high as 89.7% for those of private colleges. The learning expenses in private colleges are higher both in terms of its absolute amount and its share of total spending.

3.4.4.2 Comparison of Students' Living Expenses in Public and Private Colleges

A double logarithmic regression model is used for this part of the study, with living expenses as the explained variable, annual family income and chosen type of college as the explanatory variables, and all others as control variables. The regression model is expressed as follows:

Table 3.14 Double logarithmic regression analysis of students' learning expenses in college (2005)

Variable	Unstandardized coefficients		Standardized coefficients	t-value	p-value
	B	Standard deviations	Beta		
Constant	6.908	0.424		16.275	0.000
Natural logarithm of annual family income	0.099	0.042	0.092	2.367	0.018
Type of school	0.305	0.072	0.143	4.216	0.000
Father's years of schooling	0.009	0.009	0.040	1.034	0.301
Mother's years of schooling	−0.008	0.009	−0.030	−0.799	0.424
Presence of siblings	0.093	0.067	0.047	1.395	0.164
Gender	0.002	0.042	0.002	0.050	0.960
Applied for a loan or not	0.129	0.131	0.033	0.987	0.324
From eastern region or not	0.219	0.054	0.162	4.081	0.000
From central region or not	0.057	0.052	0.041	1.103	0.271
Attends a vocational college	0.385	0.174	0.289	2.213	0.027
Attends an undergraduate program	0.593	0.173	0.449	3.437	0.001

Note Fitting coefficient for the model $R = 0.307^{a}$, $R^2 = 0.094$, adjusted $R^2 = 0.083$

$$\ln E_{s3} = \alpha_{s3} + \beta_{s31} \ln X_{31} + \beta_{s32} X_{32} + \beta_{s33} X_{33} + \beta_{s34} X_{34} + \beta_{s35} X_{35} + \beta_{s36} X36 + \beta_{s37} X_{37} + \beta_{s38} X_{38+} \beta_{s39} X_{39} + \beta_{s310} X_{310} + \beta_{s311} X_{311} + \varepsilon_{s3} \quad (3.17)$$

where E_{s3}: the learning expenses of the student;

X_{31} to X_{311}: the same variables that were used in Model (3.13), with the same definitions; no dedicated explanation is repeated here;

ε_{s3}: other factors that are not considered in this study but may affect the student's living expenses.

A regression was run using Model (3.17) in the statistical analysis software SPSS 12.0. Its results are presented in Table 3.15, and the regression equation is as follows:

$$\ln E_{s3} = 5.151 + 0.191 \ln X_{31} + 0.299 X_{32} - 0.201 X_{35} + 0.387 X_{37} + 0.902 X310 + 1.318 X_{311} \quad (3.18)$$

Equation (3.18) shows that annual family income has a significant positive effect on the living expenses of college students, the income elasticity of which is 0.191. The

Table 3.15 Double logarithmic regression analysis of students' living expenses in college (2005)

Variable	Unstandardized coefficients		Standardized coefficients	t-value	*p*-value
	B	Standard deviations	Beta		
Constant	5.151	0.568		9.072	0.000
Natural logarithm of annual family income	0.191	0.056	0.131	3.400	0.001
Type of school	0.299	0.096	0.104	3.108	0.002
Father's years of schooling	0.006	0.012	0.018	0.481	0.631
Mother's years of schooling	0.000	0.013	0.000	−0.010	0.992
Presence of siblings	−0.201	0.090	−0.074	−2.225	0.026
Gender	0.078	0.056	0.045	1.386	0.166
Applied for a loan or not	0.387	0.174	0.074	2.230	0.026
From Eastern region or not	0.000	0.072	0.000	−0.003	0.998
From Central region or not	−0.059	0.069	−0.031	−0.854	0.393
Attends a vocational college	0.902	0.232	0.499	3.895	0.000
Attends an undergraduate program	1.318	0.229	0.735	5.745	0.000

Note Fitting coefficient for the model $R = 0.355^a$, $R^2 = 0.126$, adjusted $R^2 = 0.114$

type of institution has a significant effect on the living expenses of college students. Private college students spend more than their public college peers in this category.

Limited by the range of survey and other data-related reasons, this study was not able to provide a detailed breakdown of college students' spending with separate views of quantitative and a qualitative metrics, which could offer adequate empirical evidence for identifying the types of demand associated with private higher education.

3.5 Conclusions and Policy Recommendations

3.5.1 Conclusions

This chapter has examined how the choice between public and private schools affects students' education spending and its composition during each of the three education stages in China, building on previous empirical research on how parents invested in the human capital of their children, as well as theories and studies on the roles of the public and private sectors in providing education. The key findings of this chapter include:

1. In compulsory education, the type of school chosen affects students' spending significantly, in that it has: (a) a significant effect on the total education spending of students, where those attending a private school pay considerably more than their public school peers; (b) a significant effect on the composition of education spending, where private school students spend a lot more on essential items and considerably less on extended items, compared with their public school peers.

   Choosing a private school requires the student's family to possess adequate financial resources, since its total cost—and essential expenses in particular—can be much higher than that of public ones. Thus, family financial status has a significant positive effect on the education spending of students. On average, families that sent their children to private schools have better financial means than those who chose a public school.

   These observations on how the chosen type of school affects the composition of education spending lead to the conclusion that, currently in China, private schools in compulsory education are targeting people's "differentiated demand," i.e., their need for high-quality, diversified educational services.
2. The chosen type of school also has a significant effect on the education spending of students during the upper secondary stage, in that it has: (a) a significant effect on the total education spending of students, as private high school students pay considerably more than their peers in public school; (b) a significant effect on the composition of the spending, as private high school students spend significantly more on essential items, while no obvious difference has been found in extended spending.

   Private schools require significantly higher total education spending than their public competitors, and family financial status has a significant positive effect on total spending. On average, private school students come from families wealthier than those of public school students.

   Analysis of how the chosen school type affects the composition of students' education spending indicates that, in general, private high schools in urban areas mainly address the "excess demand" for upper secondary education, which the public system cannot completely satisfy.
3. In higher education, the chosen type of institution still has significant effects on the amount and composition of students' spending, as those who attend a private college spend considerably more in total; significant differences have been observed in both learning and living expenses—the two components of total spending during this stage—and students of private colleges spend more on both categories.

   People will need to pay more if they seek higher education and choose to attend a private college because of their own failure to enroll in a public one. Family financial status is a factor that impacts private education spending significantly.

Annual family income has a considerable effect on the total spending, learning expenses, and living expenses of students.

3.5.2 Policy Recommendations

The following policy recommendations are offered based on the results of the empirical study above:

1. The development of private education produces practical benefits. The government should continue to encourage it on every level and provide stronger support. Results of the empirical study show that, in urban areas, private primary and middle schools are an important way to address people's demand for services with distinct features in compulsory education; as for upper secondary and higher education, private providers are an effective solution for resolving the supply shortage and improving overall educational attainment in the country.
2. In urban areas, private schools of compulsory education have already developed their own advantages and distinct features, gaining a solid foothold in the market. They will want to stay committed to offering these features, which will allow them to better address the demand for quality and diversity in educational services; on the other hand, private high schools and colleges must redouble their efforts to improve overall quality; the government needs to ensure a conducive external environment for the development of private institutions and provide guidance and oversight for the evaluation of quality.
3. Public investment in education should be increased. Children's education spending has become one of the main sources of financial burden for urban households. As China transforms into a moderately prosperous society, more public funding should be allocated to education and ensure there are adequate resources to invest in its development.

3.5.3 Suggestions for Future Research

1. This chapter only included samples from urban areas. It did not examine the education spending of children in rural households, hence the relevance of these conclusions to areas outside cities may be limited. If data on how rural families spend on their children's education can be obtained, the conclusions may carry more explanatory power.
2. Due to limitations on the setup of the study, the clarity of the categorization of education spending can be further improved. The item "other expenses" under extended spending, for example, is not clearly defined. Because of the design of the questionnaire and the different consumer behaviors and spending components of college students, this study does not include a data-based analysis of the various types of demand for education in college. It is therefore incomplete.

3. Education spending is one of the main ways for parents to invest in the human capital of their children. Due to limitations on its setup, this chapter has not measured or examined the returns on these investments, which could have allowed for a cost–benefit analysis of household expenditures on education.
4. The data from the samples are cross-sectional with a wide range of variation between observed values, which may be why none of the regression equations provides a clearly good fit. This affects the explanatory power of the regression models.

References

Becker, G. (1978). *The Economic Approach to Human Behavior*. The University of Chicago Press.

Becker, G., & Tomes, N. (1976). Child Endowments and the Quantity and Quality of Children. *The Journal of Political Economy, 84*(4), S143–S162.

Becker, G., & Tomes, N. (1986). Human Capital and the Rise and Fall of Families. *Journal of Labor Economics, 4*(3), S1–S39.

Becker, G., & Tomes, N. (1994). *Human Capital, A Theoretical and Empirical Analysis, with Special Reference to Education* (3rd ed., Chapter X: Human Capital and the Rise and Fall of Families). The University of Chicago Press.

Behrman, J., Pollak, R., & Taubman, P. (1989). Family Resources, Family Size, and Access to Financing for College Education. *The Journal of Political Economy, 97*(2), 398–419.

James, E. (1987). The Public/Private Division of Responsibility for Education: An International Comparison. *Economics of Education Review, 6*(1), 1–14.

James, E. (1993). Why Do Different Countries Choose a Different Public-Private Mix of Educational Services. *The Journal of Human Resources, 28*(3), 571–592.

Lei, W. (2003). An Empirical Study on Educational Expenditures of Chinese Rural Households: 1985–1999. *Theory and Practice of Education, 7*, 38–42.

Lei, W. (2005). Expenditure on Private Tutoring for High School Students: Determinants and Policy Implications. *Education & Economy, 1*, 39–42.

Li, H. (2000). An Empirical Study on Educational Consumption of Chinese Urban Households. *Education & Economy, 4*, 1–7.

Taubman, P. (1989). Role of Parental Income in Educational Attainment. *The American Economic Review, 79*(2), 57–61. Papers and Proceedings of the Hundred and First Annual Meeting of the American Economic Association.

Chapter 4
Education Financing in the Context of Higher Education Expansion

The financing system of higher education in many countries is falling into the vortex of two trends. One is the degradation and change of bureaucratic resource allocation, and the other is higher efficiency brought about by marketization. As a result, financing mechanisms for higher education have become more and more diversified. Since 1999, China's higher education has experienced rapid enrollment expansion. What impact has the enrollment expansion brought to the higher education financing system? How will the enrollment expansion affect the behavior of higher education institutions and the quality of higher education? Focusing on the funding mechanism of higher education, this chapter analyzes the current state and challenges facing China's higher education financing in the context of higher education expansion.

The structure of this chapter is as follows. The first section reviews the relevant literatures, compare different stages of higher education development, and analyze the characteristics of higher education financing after the enrollment expansion from a macro perspective. The second section analyzes the differences in financing strategies between "universities affiliated with central government agencies" and local higher education institutions after the enrollment expansion. The third section summarizes the future challenges facing China's higher education financing system.

W. Min, *Educational Input, Resource Allocation and Returns to Human Capital*,
https://doi.org/10.1007/978-981-96-4687-6_4

4.1 Changes in China's Higher Education Financing in the Context of an Enrollment Expansion

4.1.1 Types of Higher Education Financing

The higher education financing reflects the characteristics of a country's social and economic development, the development stages of higher education institutions (HEIs), as well as the attitude of the government and society towards higher education. According to the current situation of education financing in various countries, Ziderman and Albrecht (1995) divided the higher education financing mechanisms into three types. The first is government dominance, that is, the government provides financial support to HEIs directly, and also provides financial aid or tuition reduction and exemption to students, as indirect funding to HEIs. The second is cost recovery, which means that colleges and universities charge tuition fees for education and services provided. The third is revenue diversification, that is, HEIs have diversified revenue sources such as government funding, tuition paid by students, and donations from individuals and groups, etc. US colleges and universities can be seen as a model of this type. Ziderman's classification provides a broad overview of the current state of higher education financing.

However, the changes in financing systems are not limited to changes in fund providers. Changes in the decision-making system and rules of fund allocation are also important perspectives of higher education financing systems. Gareth Williams (1982) divided the decision-making system of higher education fund allocation into three models.

- Financing under Bureaucratic Control. Higher education is funded by off-campus institutions (i.e., the government). In this model, funds are allocated to various institutions in accordance with clearly defined standards. The power is in the hands of government departments or administrative officials, and political power is transformed into rules or standards for fund allocation.
- Financing under Collegial Controls. HEIs have independent financing sources, such as land, funds, property or donations, and fund allocation is jointly determined by the colleagues (faculty) with equal authorization within a HEI. This is a self-regulation model based on the power decentralization between disciplines and peers.
- Market Model. HEIs raise funds by providing consumers with various services, such as teaching, research, social services, etc. In this model, consumers' intention has a strong influence on fund allocation.

In subsequent research, Gareth Williams (1995) put forward three fund allocation models corresponding to these three decision-making models: an input-base allocation model with designated use of funds, a package appropriation model, and a performance-based model by which funds are allocated according to several outcome indicators. Using the two dimensions of "government-led vs. market-led" fund allocation and the multi-level relationship in the funding source structure, Masakazu

Table 4.1 Types of higher education financing

Type	Government-led (g)	Market-led (m)
I: Two-party relationship	(I g) government → university	(I m) university ← students
II: Three-party relationship	(II g) government → university ↑ students	(II m) university ← students ↑ enterprises
III: Four-party relationship	(III g) enterprises ↓ government → university ↑ students	(III m) government ↓ university ← students ↑ enterprises

Source Yano (2003)

Yano (2003) formed a multi-level government-led and market-led financing framework shown in Table 4.1. He emphasized that the marketization of higher education has two connotations, the "external marketization" and the "internal marketization". "External marketization" refers to the financing model of HEIs transforming from government-led to market-led. "Internal marketization" means the financing model of HEIs goes beyond the relationship between HEIs and the government, and transforms into multi-level financing, building II g three-party and III g four-party relationships, through tuition collection and even fundraising from enterprises.

4.1.2 Development Stages of China's Higher Education Financing

Since the reform and opening up, China's economy has achieved a historic take-off and China has become a key engine for the world's economic growth. With the transition from a planned economy to a market economy and the continuous expansion of university autonomy, the previous government monopoly model has gradually degraded, and more diversified higher education funding mechanisms have emerged. This part will review the development of China's higher education funding mechanism from four dimensions: the guiding principles, the funding sources, the setting of tuition criteria, and the government funding allocation model. By comparing different stages, we will try to summarize the characteristics and trends in China's higher education financing in the context of enrollment expansion.

4.1.2.1 1978–1985: Type I g

After the founding of the People's Republic of China in 1949, China began to restore its national economy. At the same time, the Chinese government restored the higher education system, and formed a preliminary higher education administration system under the planned economy. Correspondingly, for a long period of time, China's higher education has followed the guiding principle of "funded by the organizers". That is, as the main funding source, the government provided operating funds to HEIs, while HEIs did not collect tuition from students. Since the reform and opening-up policy was launched, the proportion of HEIs' self-raised revenue had gradually expanded. The sources of self-raised revenue mainly included scientific research funding commissions, World Bank loans, individual and corporate donations, and various social services, such as personnel training, scientific and technological consulting, commercialization of scientific and technological achievements, etc. (Guo 2004). However, according to the data released by the government,[1] in 1985, the above-mentioned self-raised revenue only accounted for 8.5% of the total revenue of HEIs, while the proportion of government funding was as high as 91.5%. Therefore, the government still remained the core grantor at this stage.

In 1980, China's government finance began to implement the system of "revenue and expenditure division between the central and local governments, financial responsibility contracts at various levels". As a result, higher education funding became financial responsibility for both the central and local governments, with tiered responsibilities. This system of financial responsibility sharing among different levels of government not only strengthened the local governments' responsibility in supporting higher education, but also expanded their autonomy in the financial administration of higher education institutions. It has achieved remarkable results in mobilizing local governments' enthusiasm to invest in higher education and promoting higher education to contribute to regional social and economic development.

During this period, the government mainly adopted the "basic funds + development needs" incremental funding method. Specifically, when the government ratified next year's funding for HEIs, it first took the funding of the previous year as the basis, then took into account the financial capacity of the government and the development needs of HEIs, and increased the development coefficient accordingly. This funding method guaranteed the stability of higher education funding, but it could not motivate HEIs to effectively control costs and improve the efficiency of fund use. These drawbacks are due to the lack of incentive mechanisms and reasonable cost analysis. (Guan and Wei 1995).

[1] Educational Statistics Yearbook of China (1985), Beijing: People's Education Press.

4.1.2.2 1985–1998: Type II g

With China's economic and political reform and opening up, its higher education system, which relied solely on government appropriation, unified student enrollment, and unified graduate job assignment, became clearly incompatible with the new situation. The call for reform grew louder both from the higher education community and the entire society. In 1985, the Central Committee of the Communist Party of China (CPC) made the Decision on the Reform of the Educational System, stating that "the key to the current reform of the higher education system is to eliminate the government's excessive control over the higher education institutions, and to expand higher education institutions' autonomy, under the guidance of the unified education principles and plans." The Decision also put forward the idea of raising education funds through diverse channels. In 1993, the CPC Central Committee and the State Council passed the Program of China's Educational Reform and Development. The Program clearly stated that, "gradually establish a system of raising education funds through multiple channels, mainly based on government financial appropriation, supplemented by collecting taxes and administrative charges for education, collecting tuition and fees from students in non-compulsory education, generating revenue from school-run enterprises and social donations, as well as establishing education-themed foundations." In 1998, the Higher Education Law of the People's Republic of China was adopted by the 9th CPC National People's Congress, which clearly stipulates: "The state establishes a system based on financial appropriations, supplemented by other multi-channel financing of education funds."

The Decision on the Reform of the Educational System in 1985 also affirmed the model of HEIs recruiting tuition paying students and employer sponsored students, and pointed out that HEIs "may recruit a small number of tuition paying students in addition to the total planned enrollment set by the state, and such students should pay a certain amount of tuition". In 1989, the State Education Commission, the State Price Bureau, and the Ministry of Finance jointly issued Regulations on HEIs Charging Tuition, Fees and Accommodation, announcing that "regular students enrolled under the national plan (except normal university students) will be charged for tuition, fees and accommodation." In the same year, most colleges and universities began to charge tuition ranging from RMB100 to RMB300 per year. In 1997, the government further improved the higher education fee collection system, adjusted charge standards, and uniformly implemented it throughout the country. This series of measures affirmed a cost-sharing and recovery system in higher education financing (Fan 2005). It meant that since 1985, China's higher education financing system has abandoned the long-standing guiding principle of "funded by the organizers" and transformed into "funded by beneficiaries", so the government and higher education consumers share the cost. The funding model transformation from the traditional two-party relationship (I g type) to three-party relationship (II g type) can be interpreted as a transition from the government-dominant to the cost recovery type proposed by Ziderman. However, in 1998, the proportion of state financial appropriation in the total revenue of HEIs was still as high as 65%, while the proportion of tuition and fee revenue was only 13%. In other words, even though the proportion of government funding had declined, the government remains the core provider of China's higher education financing.

In the same period, the allocation model of higher education funds has also undergone a fundamental change. In 1986, the former State Education Commission and the Ministry of Finance jointly promulgated the Implementation Measures for the Financial Management Reform of Higher Education Institutions. The annual budget approval method for higher education funds has been changed from the original "basic funds + development needs" appropriation to "comprehensive quota + special subsidies" method. The comprehensive quota was calculated by multiplying the number of students in school by the per capita expenditures, which were determined by the HEI's level, type and location. The special subsidies were separately approved and distributed according to the government policy and HEIs' special needs. This simple budget appropriation method improved the transparency and fairness of funding appropriations, and reduced political and arbitrary interference from decision-making departments. However, this funding model has obvious limitations in improving the efficiency of higher education fund use.

In 1994, the state began to implement a tax-sharing system, which consolidated the original financial responsibility sharing mechanism between the central and local governments. As a result, the responsibilities of governments at all levels in education investment have been further strengthened and clarified.

4.1.2.3 1998–2005: Type III g

In 1999, China's higher education experienced a leapfrog expansion, with the total enrollment of colleges and universities reaching 1.68 million, an increase of 47% over the previous year. The enrollment growth rate dropped in the following years, and remained at 20%. In just seven years, the number of undergraduate and junior college students rose from 3.4 million in 1998 to 15.61 million in 2005, an increase of 3.6 times. During this period, the government continued to follow the principle of "funded by beneficiaries" for higher education and rapidly increased the tuition burden of students and their families. According to calculations,[2] the average tuition and fees paid by college students were RMB25 in 1990, and reached RMB2145 in 1998. After the enrollment expansion, per-student tuition and fees increased to RMB4857 in 2004 (see Fig. 4.1). In 2002, the proportion of tuition expenditure in rural and urban per capita net revenue reached 177.6% and 80% respectively (Li 2004). Judging from this, the current tuition level has largely exceeded the general public's ability to pay, and there was little room for tuition increase. In 2004, tuition received accounted for 32% of the total revenue of colleges and universities, and tuition has become the second main source of funding after government appropriation, which accounted for 47% (see Fig. 4.2). In 2007, the government experimented

[2] The calculation is based on the total tuition and fees of HEIs in the *China Educational Finance Statistical Yearbook* of each year and the number of undergraduate and junior college students in the same year.

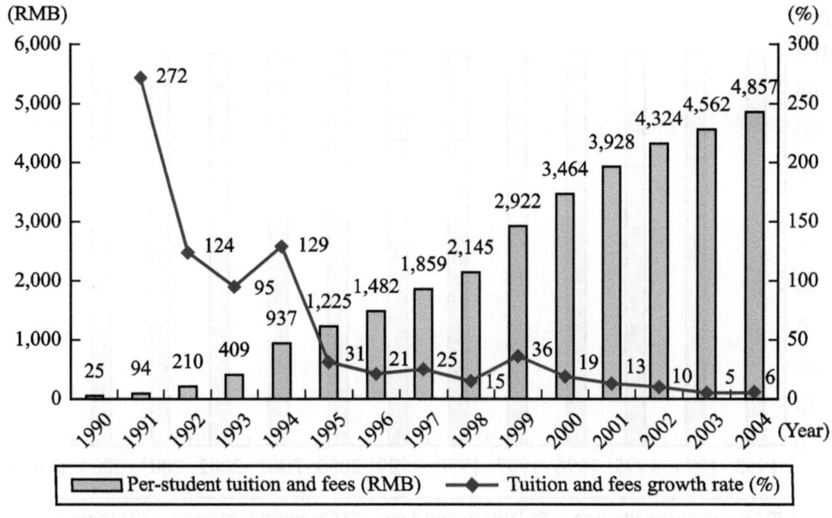

Fig. 4.1 Changes in per-student tuition and fees (1990–2004) (*Source China Educational Finance Statistical Yearbook and Educational Statistical Yearbook of China* in each year)

with the reform of postgraduate education funding mechanisms in 10 universities including Peking University and Tsinghua University.[3] With the continuous expansion of postgraduate enrollment, whether charging postgraduate students tuition and fees will become a new growth point for university funding in the future is still an issue worth attention and discussion.

In addition to tuition revenue rise, another notable trend in the funding mechanism in this period is the rise of university bank loans. In 1998, the total amount of bank loans for universities that directly affiliated with the Ministry of Education was only RMB500 million. At the end of 2002, the total amount of loans reached RMB8.8 billion, rose to RMB14.1 billion in 2003, and reached RMB23.7 billion[4] by the end of 2004. The average loan amount for HEIs was RMB320 million by the end of 2004 with an average annual growth rate of 76% from 1998 to 2004. To summarize, the higher education financing system in the mid-1990s has diverted from the long-term dependence on a single source of funds with government funding as the main source. In the late 1990s, the emergence and popularization of bank loans further diversified and marketized China's higher education funding system. After government funding, tuition and fees, bank loans have become the third main channel for China's HEIs to raise funds. In this sense, after the enrollment expansion, the funding model of China's HEIs had transformed into the four-party relationship (Type III g). However, unlike

[3] 10 Universities Including Peking University, Tsinghua University, etc. Starting to Implement a Postgraduate Fee System in 2007, *Beijing Evening News*, July 11, 2006.

[4] The data for 2003–2004 comes from Zheng E's Thoughts on Preventing University Loan Risks [J]. *Journal of Beijing Normal University* (Social Science Edition), Issue 5 (Total Issue 191) of 2005, pp. 117–121. The data for 1998 and 2002 are from Zhang Qinglan, Analysis and Suggestions on University Loans [J]. *Finance and Accounting* (Academic), Issue 9 of 2004, pp. 94–96.

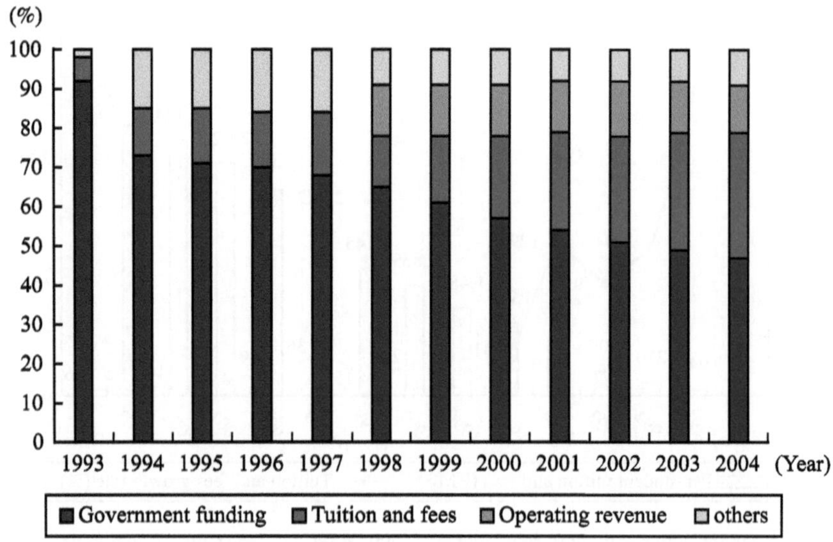

Fig. 4.2 Changes in the revenue structure of China's HEIs (1993–2004). *Note* Government funds include operating funds, scientific research funds and infrastructure funds (*Source China Educational Finance Stastical Yearbook* in each year)

Masakazu Yano's (2003) definition, it was not enterprises but financial institutions that emerged as the third core providers of China's higher education funding.

The role of financial institutions in China's higher education funding is not limited to loan providers. They also play an important role in China's student loan system. In order to promote equal access to higher education, the government started to build a national student loan system since 1999 as an indirect channel of higher education funds. However, due to limited government financial resources, most student loans were provided by financial institutions. To be precise, the current student loans can be regarded as microloans provided to students from families with financial difficulties on the basis of financial discounts and risk compensation. Since 1999, a total of 3.952 million students have applied for student loans nationwide, and 2.405 million have been approved by banks. The total amount of loan applications has reached RMB30.56 billion, and the amount of loans approved by banks has reached RMB20.14 billion (Ministry of Education 2006).

From the perspective of the way the government allocates funds, the Ministry of Finance approved the budget of the central government departments with a method of "basic expenditure budget + project expenditure budget" in 2002. The basic expenditure budget is the annual basic expenditure plan to ensure the normal operation and daily tasks. The project expenditure budget is the annual project expenditure plan for special tasks. Accordingly, the education authorities' funding for HEIs was also reformed (Fan and Ma 2004). During this period, another important measure of government resource allocation was that HEIs as well as government agencies uniformly implemented the centralized treasury payment system under the framework of the national fiscal system reform. This system centralized all the fiscal funds within a unified treasury system, and implemented whole-process management and supervision over fiscal funds. This financial supervision system was not only conducive to the standardization of financial funds appropriation and management, but also conducive to improving the accuracy of college budget preparation and execution. However, in view of the fact that HEIs are independent legal entities that run schools independently according to the law, will the implementation of this system limit the autonomy of HEIs in running schools? Is it in line with the financial characteristics of HEIs with multi-level management systems and diversified funding channels? Will it reduce the efficiency of HEIs financial operations? These issues need further analysis.

We have sorted out the changes in China's higher education financing system from four dimensions: policy principles, funding sources, tuition standards, and government funding methods. Table 4.2 summarizes the characteristics of different development stages. It shows clearly that, in order to meet the growing demand for higher education and expand the total supply of higher education opportunities, the government followed the principle of beneficiary funding under the condition of limited financial capacity, taking government funding as main resource, expanded the operational autonomy of HEIs, and strived to build a diversified funding system. After the enrollment expansion, the government has accelerated the process of promoting the diversification of funding sources, which to some extent also reflects the continuous deepening marketization of higher education.

Table 4.2 Changes in China's higher education financing system

Period	Principle	Funding sources	Tuition standard	Government funding method
1978–1985 (Type I g)	Organizer funding	Government	Free of charge	Base funds + development needs (1955–1985)
1985–1998 (Type II g)	Beneficiary funding	Central and local government, students	Paid higher education, rising tuition	Comprehensive quota + special subsidies
1998–2005 (Type III g)		Central and local government, students, financial institutions	Tuition and fees rising close to the limit, postgraduate fees trial	Basic expenditure budget + project expenditure budget

4.2 Financing: Limited Sources of Funding in a Seemingly Diverse Financing Structure

Can the concept of building a diversified financing mechanism be implemented in reality? We will try to answer this question by analyzing the revenue structure and financing strategies of different types of HEIs in China.

4.2.1 Changes in HEIs' Funding Structure After the Enrollment Expansion

Figure 4.2 shows the trend of China's higher education funding structure from 1993 to 2004, which presents the following characteristics.

First, as the traditional main source of operating funds for HEIs, the total amount of government funding has kept growing from RMB15.46 billion in 1993 to RMB94.3 billion in 2004, an increase of five times. However, its proportion in HEIs revenue has dropped sharply from 92 to 47%. This means that the increase in government funding has been much slower than the expansion of higher education. The government funding was no longer the core funding source for China's HEIs. In addition, within the government funding, scientific research funds and operating funds have increased significantly, while the proportion of infrastructure funds has declined sharply. In 1998, infrastructure funds accounted for 11.9% of the total revenue of HEIs, while in 2004 the proportion was only 4.5%. With the enrollment expansion and the increasing demand for infrastructure such as school buildings, the increase in infrastructure funding gaps has put tremendous pressure on HEIs' financial management, which is an important reason for emerging and growing university loans in those years. Another crisis hidden behind the declined proportion of government funds is the decrease in per-student funds for college students. From Table 4.3, it can be found that after the enrollment expansion, the per-student expenditure began to decline since 2000. In 2004, both the per-student budgetary education funds and operating funds fell below the level of 1996.

Second, from the perspective of self-raised revenue, the most noticeable trend is the sharp increase in the proportion of tuition and fees, which was 6.1% in 1993 but reached 16% in 1997 when the tuition fee collection policy was fully implemented. In 2004, the proportion of tuition and fees further rose to 32%. In sharp contrast, the revenue from college-run enterprises, social services, and fundraising activities, which were once regarded as the most potential sources of HEIs' incremental revenue, has been growing much slower than expected. In 2004, the proportion of revenue from school-run enterprises, donations and fundraising remained no more than 1%.

The above analysis shows that although the government has put forward the goal of building a diversified fundraising mechanism with government funding as the main

Table 4.3 Changes in per capita public funds for college students (comparable prices in 1978; Unit: RMB)

Year	Per-student public funds	Per-student operating funds
1992	1961	3846
1993	1979	3577
1994	1663	4067
1995	1998	4647
1996	2405	5500
1997	2788	6345
1998	2916	6830
1999	3004	7303
2000	2910	7280
2001	2595	6769
2002	2473	6228
2003	2324	5704
2004	2212	5344

Source Calculated based on data from the *Statistical Bulletin on Education Spending* and *China Statistical Yearbook*

source, in reality, this model has not been effectively implemented. After the enrollment expansion, China's higher education funding system has presented an essentially single pattern with a diversified surface. The dominant role of the government has been gradually diminished, while the importance of individuals (the educated persons and their families) has been increasing. China's HEIs have tried to raise funds through multiple channels such as research projects, technology transfers, equipment leasing, education foundations, social donations and capital interest, but such funding sources have not shown the desired effect. It looks like the financing model of higher education has successfully transformed from type I g to III g, while the third main source of funding is not enterprises, but financial institutions such as banks that provide loans to HEIs or students. All the loans are actually endorsed by the government. Therefore, under the premise that HEIs have not established effective cooperative relations with society, individuals and enterprises, whether China's diversified fundraising model can provide a stable and sustainable funding system for HEIs is still worthy of attention and consideration.

4.2.2 Funding Strategies of Different Types of HEIs

The above analysis takes higher education as a whole and analyzes the changing trend of its revenue structure since the 1990s. However, is this changing trend common to all types of colleges and universities? This part will further analyze the differences in funding strategies between "HEIs affiliated with central government agencies"

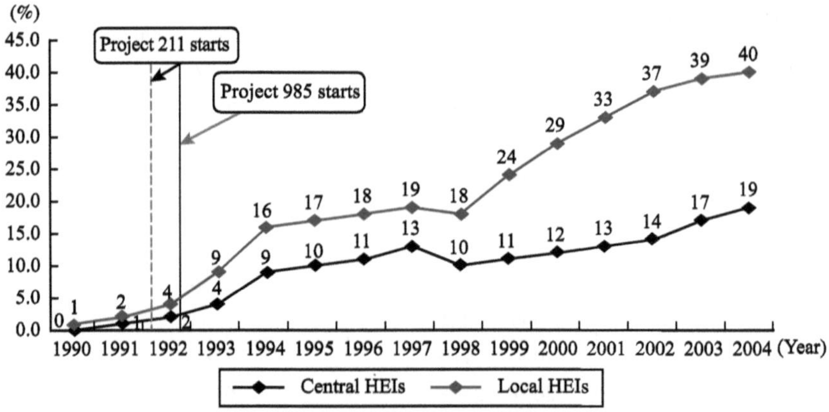

Fig. 4.3 The ratio of tuition and fees to the revenue of central and local HEIs (1990–2004) (*Source China Educational Finance Statistical Yearbook* in each year)

(hereinafter referred to as "central HEIs")[5] and "locally affiliated HEIs" (hereinafter referred to as "local-HEIs").[6]

Figure 4.3 shows the changes in the proportion of tuition and fees in the revenue of central and local institutions from 1990 to 2004.

When analyzing the difference in the tuition and fees ratios of the two types of HEIs, we can regard 1992 and 1998 as two watershed years, and divide the 14 years into three stages. 1990–1992 is the first stage. During this period, the difference in the ratio of tuition and fees between central and local HEIs was extremely small, around 2 percentage points. From 1992 to 1998, the difference began to increase to less than 10 percentage points. However, in the third period (1999–2004), the difference showed a further widening trend. In 2004, the ratio of tuition and fees of national institutions was 19%, and that of local institutions was 40%, so the difference increased to 21 percentage points.

Does the difference in the ratio of tuition and fees revenue between central and local HEIs mean that the revenue structure of these two types of HEIs has fundamentally changed? Why did the proportion of tuition and fees revenue of the central HEIs maintain within a certain range despite the continuous enrollment expansion and tuition rise? Such questions are closely linked to the preferential investment mechanism of China's higher education financing. In fact, how to effectively use limited financial resources is a challenge for all governments in the world. The Chinese

[5] "HEIs affiliated with central government agencies" refer to a group of national universities under directly jurisdiction of the constituent departments of the State Council and its directly affiliated institutions, such as the Ministry of Education, Ministry of Industry and Information Technology, and other departments of the State Council. For more information, please visit https://daxue.eol.cn/bushu.shtml.

[6] "Locally affiliated HEIs" refer to ordinary colleges and universities affiliated with various provinces, autonomous regions, and municipalities directly, most of which rely on local finance to provide public funds.

government has chosen to invest limited funds in a very small number of key HEIs, that is, a public finance titled investment mechanism that provides major funding to key HEIs represented by institutions affiliated with central government agencies. In the 1990s, China's state finance increased its investment in special funds for higher education. Since the founding of the People's Republic of China, the two largest key education projects in China's higher education history are the "211 Project" launched in 1992 and the "985 Project" launched in 1999. Based on the principle of "efficiency first", the 211 Project aimed to invest in China's top 100 universities and a number of key disciplinary areas. Most of the 100 universities that were designated as 211 Project universities are affiliated with government agencies. The universities that were included in the 985 Project universities are also the top ones including Peking University and Tsinghua University. Besides, the Action Plan for Education Rejuvenation for the twenty-first century issued by the Ministry of Education in 1999 also involved some special funds for higher education, such as high-tech industrialization in HEIs and high-level creative talent projects. These special funds were also concentrated in central HEIs. With this, we can conjecture that the special funds have further strengthened the preferential investment mechanism of higher education, and further widened the funding gap between central and local HEIs. In particular, the 211 Project and the 985 Project have both resulted in significant differences in the revenue structure of the two types of institutions.

Table 4.4 shows the revenue structure of central and local HEIs in 2004. In terms of scale, the total revenue of central HEIs exceeded RMB73.6 billion in 2004, the average school revenue reaching RMB660 million. In contrast, the total revenue of local HEIs was RMB126.41 billion, and the average school revenue was RMB78.032 million, accounting for only 11.8% of that of central HEIs. From the perspective of the revenue structure, the two types of institutions showed significant differences in government funding, scientific research funds appropriation, tuition and fees, and other operating revenue. Specifically, government funding was still the most important revenue source for central HEIs, accounting for 51.7%, while the proportion of government funding in local HEIs has dropped to 44.5%, meaning that over half of the revenue of local institutions was self-raised. The total amount of scientific research funds allocated to the 111 central HEIs is 4.8 times that of the 1620 local HEIs. For local colleges and universities, tuition and fees have become the most important source of revenue, with a proportion of 40.1%, nearly 20 percentage points higher than that of central HEIs. It is worth noting that within the operating revenue of central HEIs, other operating revenue was close to tuition and fees, with a proportion gap of only 1 percentage point.

From Table 4.4, we can conclude that the two types of HEIs have adopted different funding strategies after enrollment expansion. Specifically, the central HEIs' funding strategies include the following.

- Strive to obtain scientific research funds and special education funds from the central government's scientific research funds for building key disciplines and improving scientific research competitiveness.

Table 4.4 Revenue structure of central and local HEIs (Year 2004)

Item	Central HEIs		Local HEIs	
	Amount (RMB million)	Proportion (%)	Amount (RMB million)	Proportion (%)
I Government funding on education	38,044.318	51.7	56,257.136	44.5
I-1 Budgetary operating funds	33,719.367	45.8	50,335.653	39.8
I-1-1 Education operating funds	25,325.524	34.4	45,256.027	35.8
I-1-2 Scientific research funds	5994.597	8.1	1232.458	1.0
I-1-3 Other operating funds	2399.246	3.3	3847.168	3.0
I-2 Investment in infrastructure	4280.954	5.8	4762.845	3.8
I-3 Education surcharge	43.997	0.1	1158.638	0.9
II Non-government funding on education	35,558.265	48.3	70,155.596	55.5
II-1 Operating revenue	27,459.297	37.3	61,492.507	48.6
II-1-1 Tuition and fees	14,105.667	19.2	50,663.546	40.1
II-1-2 Other operating revenue	13,353.630	18.1	10,828.961	8.6
II-2 Revenue from school-run enterprises or social services used for education	916.481	1.2	1283.394	1.0
II-3 Donations and fundraising	1212.369	1.6	942.028	0.7
II-4 Other revenue	5970.118	8.1	6439.667	5.1
Total	**73,602.583**	**100.0**	**126,412.732**	**100.0**

Source China Educational Finance Statistical Yearbook

- Give full play to its research advantages and increase financial support from enterprises and other social sectors through channels such as technology transfer, consulting services, and joint research projects.
- Expand the enrollment scale of part-time non-regular students by offering various non-academic training programs to increase funding revenue.

In contrast, a considerable part of China's local HEIs were facing serious financial difficulties after the enrollment expansion due to insufficient government funding and disadvantages in raising funds by themselves. The preferential investment mechanism has led to a huge government funding gap between the two types of HEIs. According to data released by the government,[7] in early 2000s, local governments' per-student budgetary expenditures for HEIs have been dropping, which was insufficient to maintain the operation of local colleges and universities, not to mention

[7] According to the Statistical Bulletin on Education Spending issued by the Ministry of Education, the National Bureau of Statistics and the Ministry of Finance each year, local governments' per-student budgetary operating expenditure was RMB7309.58 in 2000, RMB6816.23 in 2001, RMB6177.96 in 2002, and RMB5772.58 in 2003.

capital investment. Regrettably, in the comprehensive evaluation of colleges and universities carried out, the Ministry of Education did not formulate different evaluation standards according to the differences in the educational orientation and funding among different types of HEIs, but adopted a unified evaluation index for both central and local HEIs (Hong and Hu 2006). The rigid constraint index that did not match the financial capacity of local HEIs has forced them to generate more revenue for infrastructure investment. However, due to the lack of research capabilities and fund-raising channels, their funding strategies were concentrated on the following two aspects: (1) expand the scale of enrollment and increase the revenue from tuition and fees; (2) fill the funding gap through bank loans, especially to make up for the lack of infrastructure funds.

4.3 Challenges and Pressure on China's Higher Education Financing

How to alleviate the financial pressure of higher education is a severe challenge faced by all the countries in the world today, but the pressure that China bears now exceeds that of any other country. On the one hand, the Chinese government needs to expand college enrollment to meet the fast-growing demand for higher education and the needs of socio-economic development. On the other hand, China needs to improve the teaching quality of colleges and universities. After years of hard work and exploration, the Chinese government has built a diversified higher education funding system with a cost-sharing model as well as loans from the financial market. This diversified funding system has effectively mobilized social resources, made good use of private funds, and realized the scale expansion of higher education with limited government financial resources. It has also improved the financial autonomy and operational efficiency of HEIs. However, the preferential investment mechanism has also brought challenges to the sustainable development of the higher education funding system and equal access to higher education.

4.3.1 Challenges to China's Higher Education Financing After the Enrollment Expansion

The continuous expansion of college enrollment since 1999 has posed various severe challenges to China's original education financing and administration system which is suitable for a relatively small-scale elite higher education system. These challenges can be summarized into the following three aspects.

The first challenge is the widening of the "three gaps" in higher education funding. The above analysis has shown the increasing funding gap between central and local HEIs. It needs to be emphasized that the funding gap is not limited to different types of institutions. As the gap in economic development between regions widens and the difference in funding capabilities in different disciplines within an institution increases, the funding gap between HEIs in different regions and between different disciplines or departments within an institution has also widened. The disparity in funding will directly hurt the fairness of China's higher education, leading to further deterioration of unbalanced education quality between regions.

The second challenge is the simplification of higher education funding mechanisms. Since 1999, the tuition and fees of colleges and universities are constantly rising, the level of tuition fees has reached the limit of students' or their families' ability to pay, so there is little room to raise tuition and fees. In addition to government financial appropriation, tuition and fees, and bank loans, whether colleges and universities can tap new and effective funding channels is the key to whether China's higher education can maintain sustainable and stable development in the future.

The third challenge is the rising risk of financial operation in colleges and universities. At present, the revenue of China's HEIs, especially local universities, is overly dependent on tuition and fees, which inevitably increases the instability of their operations. At the same time, the blind lending of some colleges and universities has also greatly expanded the financial risks. The existence and rise of such risks will, to a large extent, lead to short-sighted behaviors in decision-making and constrict the sustainable and stable development of colleges and universities.

4.3.2 Issues that China's Higher Education Financing Must Deal with in the Future

As the government's core funding for HEIs has been relatively reduced, the operational autonomy of HEIs and market pressures they are facing continue to increase. How will the government help colleges and universities avoid financial risks, ensure the balanced quality of higher education and the sustainable development of colleges and universities while ensuring that the development of HEIs stays consistent with the public interest? To address these policy challenges, it is necessary to respond to a series of issues in improving the future higher education financing system.

The core problem is how to define the different responsibilities between the government and universities in the higher education financing mechanism. To a large extent, the diversification of higher education financing mechanism means complication of a college's objectives and financing environment. We can tentatively construct a theoretical analysis framework based on the goals, targets, and principles of higher education investment (see Fig. 4.4).

First of all, in order to ensure and build the basic capabilities of higher education, colleges and universities must have a stable source of funds to ensure their sustainable development. According to different investment targets, such funds can be divided into two categories, basic operating funds (Quadrant 1) directly paid to HEIs and financial aid paid to students with financial difficulties (Quadrant 2). The former

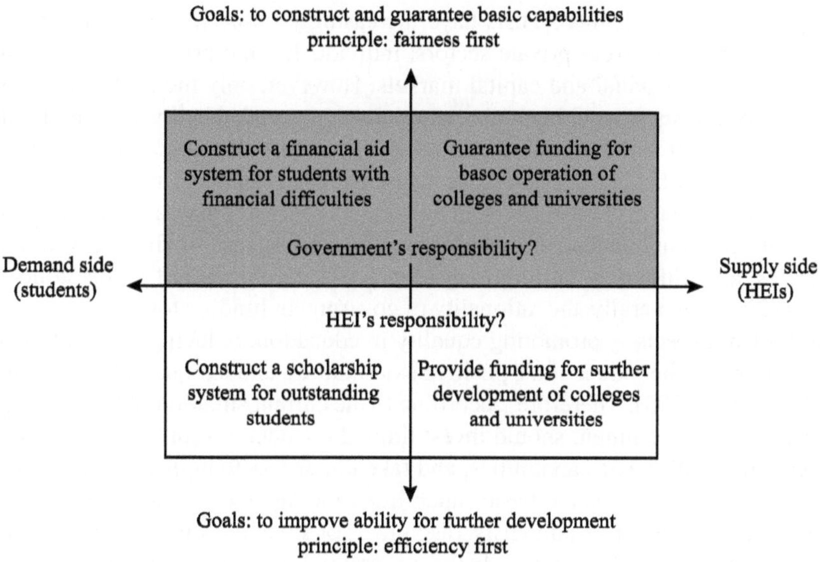

Fig. 4.4 The financial responsibilities of government and HEIs in a cost sharing system

focuses on the supply side of higher education, and is a direct funding to HEIs that ensures basic operations of HEIs' core functions, such as infrastructure maintenance, teaching and research, etc. The latter focuses on the demand side, and is a form of indirect financial support to HEIs. By narrowing the gap in students' ability to pay for higher education, the financial aid system can improve learning and living conditions for students with financial difficulties and better guarantee their learning rights. By complementing each other, and "supporting the disadvantaged group", these two types of funds will promote fair access and equal quality of higher education. To reduce the funding gap between HEIs and different student groups, these two types of funding should follow the principle of fairness first.

Second, to advance the competitiveness and quality of higher education, HEIs must have sufficient funds to enhance their own unique advantages in a specific teaching or research field. Here the funds can also be divided into two categories according to different investment targets. One is incentive funding (Quadrant 4) directly allocated to HEIs with advantages in specific teaching and research projects. The other focuses on incentive scholarships (Quadrant 3) delivered to students with outstanding learning or research achievements. The principle behind these two types of funds is "rewarding the excellent group" to improve higher education's overall efficiency, and to maximize its contribution to social and economic development.

In the above funding mechanism, what roles should the government and HEIs play respectively? There is no simple answer to this question. In reality, the role of the government and HEIs is often restrained and influenced by various factors such as the level of social and economic development, the government's financial capacity, and HEIs' fund-raising capability. With the continuous acceleration of marketization of higher education, China's HEIs have increasingly raised funds through market-oriented mechanism from private sectors, individuals, enterprises, social organizations, and even financial and capital markets. However, only the central HEIs with leading advantages in teaching and research have succeeded in diversifying funding sources. Local HEIs are at great disadvantage in almost all sources, and funds from the financial market, i.e., loans, have caused greater financial risks. Further, the current preferential investment system will lead to excessive association of academic goals with economic incentives, resulting in the convergence of HEIs' development strategies, and ultimately hurting long-term goals and fairness of higher education (OECD 2004). Generally, the rationality of government funding for higher education includes five aspects— promoting equality in education, reducing waste of talents, sharing risks, higher education's positive externalities, and national interests (Eicher and Chevallier 1993). Therefore, according to the current situation of China's higher education, the government should invest limited financial resources in constructing higher education's basic capabilities, and take fair access to higher education as the primary goal. On the basis of basic capabilities and fair access, the government can preferentially invest in certain HEIs, disciplines or student groups, so as to improve overall capabilities and efficiency. In the preferential funding part, the autonomy and initiative of HEIs should be brought into full play. Those HEIs with advantages in teaching or research should attract more private funds and social resources, as well as expand cooperation with enterprises.

In addition to clarifying the different responsibilities of the government and HEIs, there are many other issues worth consideration in further improving China's higher education funding system. To name a few, how to narrow the funding gap between different HEIs and among different regions, how to build a financial risk control mechanism for HEIs, how to supervise HEIs and ensure the rational and normative use of funds and establish an accountability system without hurting the autonomy of HEIs, how to help HEIs develop a fourth effective source of funds besides government appropriation, tuition and fees, and financial loans, such as policy loans or bonds.

With the decrease in the proportion of government funding in HEIs' revenue, the role of government as the "owner and core appropriator" of HEIs formed under the more centralized higher education system in the last century, has been gradually replaced by the "partners" and "consumers" (OECD 2004). In this case, building a reasonable and effective higher education funding mechanism is a shared responsibility of the government and HEIs. In building institutional governance and financial management systems, HEIs have to clarify their strategic goals and positioning, understand the changes in higher education supply and demand, calculate the economic costs of various activities, and improve its efficiency of fund use while exploring more funding channels. In addition, HEIs need to improve risk management by establishing a system for financial risk assessment, crisis warning and response system.Through the financing mechanism of higher education, we can clearly see the challenges currently facing China's higher education financing. Higher education financing is an institutional system formed by different stakeholders including the government, HEIs, and diverse social groups. Looking to the future, scholars have great responsibilities in providing suggestions on how to cope with various challenges and pressures, how to conduct reasonable and systematic analysis of higher education financing issues and the impact mechanisms behind them from a comprehensive perspective, and how to promote dialogue and understanding between different stakeholder groups.

References

Eicher, J., & Chevallier, T. (1993). Rethinking the Finance of Post-Compulsory Education, *International Journal of Educational Research, 19*(5), 445–519.

Fan, L. (2005). Fifty Years of Reform of China's Higher Education Charging System. *Forum on Contemporary Education, 1.*

Fan, W., & Ma, L. (editors). (2004). *Quality Evaluation and Funding in International Higher Education.* Educational Science Publishing House.

Guan, F., & Wei, X. (1995).Research on Higher Education Funding Models. *Educational Research,* 2.

Guo, H. (2004).Trends of the Sources of Higher Education Funding in China in the 1990s. *Economics of Education Research (Peking University), 3.*

Hong, L., & Hu W. (2006). Evaluation Indicators and Educational Investment: The Development of Local Public Universities. *Jiangsu Higher Education, 4,* 69–71.

Li, W. (2004). An Analysis of Diversified Sources of Higher Education Funding in China. *Economics of Education Research (Peking University), 3.*

Ministry of Education of China. (2006). *Introduction to China's Policy System for Funding College Students from Poor Families.* 16th News Release Conference. http://www.xszz.cee.edu.cn/index.php/shows/22/1190.html.

OECD. (2004). *On the Edge: Securing a Sustainable Future for Higher Education.* IMHE-HEFCE Conference, 8–9 January, Paris.

Williams, G. (1982). The Economic Approach. Clark, B., Ed. *Perspectives on Higher Education: Eight Disciplinary and Comparative Views.* Papers Presented at the Summer Seminar (University of California, Los Angeles, California). ERIC Number: ED267683.

Williams, G. (1995). The "Marketisation" of Higher Education: Reforms and Potential Reforms in Higher Education Finance. *Emerging Patterns of Social Demand and University Reform: Through a Glass Darkly,* 170–193. International Association of Universities and Pergamon-Elsevier Science.

Yano, M. (2003). Diversification and Governance of University Financing. *Comprehensive Research on Funding and Financial Management of National Universities.*

Ziderman, A., & Albrecht, D. (1995). *Financing Universities in Developing Countries* (1st ed.). Routledge.

Chapter 5
Multi-Country Comparison of Public Education Expenditures

The development of human society in the twenty-first century has entered the era of the knowledge economy. Manifested in knowledge and technology competition, the increasingly fierce competition between countries is essentially human capital competition. The key to effective human capital development and knowledge and technology advancement lies in education. Since China's reform and opening up, the Chinese government has paid great attention to the prominent role of education in promoting economic development and the building of a harmonious society. Concepts such as "powering the country through education" and "prioritizing education development" have been successively put forward and implemented in the education development plannings.

In February 1993, the State Council issued the Outline for China's Education Reform and Development, which clearly stated: "Gradually increase the proportion of national fiscal expenditure on education in GDP, reaching 4% by the end of the twentieth century." However, the proportion did not reach 4% in 2000, only 2.58%. Although the ratio rose to 2.90% in 2002, it is still far from the 4% target. China has made great progress since the reform and opening up, but its education has not achieved its goals in terms of scale, quality, or structure.

In March 2006, the State Council promulgated the 11th Five-Year Plan for National Economic and Social Development. The Plan states that "to ensure that the growth rate of fiscal education expenditure is significantly higher than the growth rate of regular fiscal revenue, and gradually increase national fiscal expenditure on education until it accounts for 4% of GDP." This goal is exactly the same as that in the Outline for China's Education Reform and Development. Will the goals that were not achieved in 2000 be achieved by 2010? Will the government be able to provide sufficient financial support? In accordance with the education development goals in the 11th Five-year Plan, what is the estimated total amount of education funding? From a practical perspective, is the demanded proportion of fiscal education funding in GDP consistent with the proposed 4% target?

W. Min, *Educational Input, Resource Allocation and Returns to Human Capital*,
https://doi.org/10.1007/978-981-96-4687-6_5

In order to answer the above questions, this chapter will estimate the proportion of fiscal education expenditure in GDP by international comparison, both from the supply side and demand side. On the supply side, we will use an econometric regression model to estimate the ratio of fiscal education expenditure to GDP and to predict the government's ability to finance education, based on factors such as the level of economic development, fiscal revenue, and the proportion of education in fiscal expenditure. On the demand side, we will estimate the required proportion of fiscal education expenditure to GDP using statistical data, based on the education development goals.

5.1 Prediction of China's Public Education Funding Supply in the 11th Five-Year Plan Period

5.1.1 An Outline of the World's Public Education Expenditures

5.1.1.1 Overall Trends in Public Education Expenditures

Human capital theories have been fully developed since the early 1960s. Many governments around the world believe that education can promote long-term, sustainable and rapid economic development by improving the overall labor quality and increasing labor productivity. Therefore, most governments have increased investments in education. Throughout the 1960s, the public expenditures on education as a percentage of GDP (hereinafter referred to as "public expenditure ratio") increased rapidly, and the growth rates of developed and developing countries reached 40% and 42% respectively (Carnoy 2000). The worldwide economic depression caused by the oil crisis in the 1970s led to a significant decline in the growth rate of the public expenditure ratio. In the 1980s, the ratio even slightly declined (Carnoy 2000).

In July 2006, the World Bank divided the world's economies into four income groups based on the gross national income (GNI) per capita in 2005: low income (US$875 or less), lower-middle income (US$876–US$3465), upper-middle income (US$3466–US$10,725), and high income (US$10,726 and more). Table 5.1 shows the public expenditure ratios of countries with different income levels from 1975 to 2002. The results show that: (a) The trend of changes in high-income countries is obvious. From 1975 to 1990, the ratio of public expenditure showed a significant downward trend, and after 1990 a significant upward trend. Since 1975, the ratio has been fluctuating around 5.3%. (b) The overall trend in upper-middle income countries is basically the same as that of high-income countries. Since 1975, the ratio has been fluctuating around 4.3%. (c) The public education investment in lower-middle income countries fluctuated frequently and there is no obvious pattern to follow. Since 1975, the ratio has been fluctuating around 3.6%. (d) The ratio in low-income countries has also fluctuated frequently, fluctuating around 3.2% since 1975.

Table 5.1 The public education expenditure ratios of countries at different income levels (Unit: %)

Country category	1975	1980	1985	1990	1995	2000	2001	2002
High income	5.59	5.45	5.10	4.95	5.15	5.25	5.42	5.73
Upper-middle income	4.48	4.23	4.39	3.78	4.84	3.95	4.49	4.64
Lower-middle income	3.49	3.23	3.20	4.04	4.29	4.30	3.53	3.53
Low income		3.11	2.76	3.22	3.52	3.17		

Source World Development Indicators Database of the World Bank

5.1.1.2 The Relationship Between the Public Education Expenditure and the Level of Economic Development

There is a significant positive correlation between public education investment and the level of economic development. The higher the level of economic development of a country, the higher its public investment in education. The statistical results in Table 5.2 show that whether calculated by the arithmetic mean or the median, the public expenditure ratio is the highest in the high income countries, followed by the upper-middle income, then the lower-middle income, and the last low income countries. The same pattern is shown in the level of government fiscal revenue. The higher the level of economic development, the higher the proportion of fiscal revenue to GDP, and the more abundant resources the government has to invest in education. Economic strength is also reflected in the goals of educational development. The higher the level of economic development of a country, the more expected years of education per capita.

The above statistical results reflect the significant impact of economic development on education investment. The international average is a widely used standard to make an international comparison of the public expenditure ratio. However, simply comparing the public spending ratio between countries with different levels of economic development is not sufficient. Therefore, the following discussion will apply an econometric regression method to calculate the public expenditure ratio in various countries, with control variables such as the economic development level, fiscal revenue, fiscal expenditure structure, education development level, and population growth rate.

5.1.2 Econometric Regression of Public Education Investment

The public education expenditure ratio is an important indicator of a government's "efforts" on education. But how large should this ratio be? In theory, there is no unified understanding or standard, and in practice, the ratio varies from country to

Table 5.2 Comparison of public education expenditure indicators in countries with different income levels (2000–2004 average)

Item	Country category	Public education expenditure as a percentage of GDP (%)	GDP per capita (US$)	Fiscal revenue as a percentage of GDP (%)	Public education expenditure as a percentage of fiscal expenditure (%)	Expected years of education per capita (years)	Population growth rate (%)
Arithmetic average	High income	4.8	19,217	32.8	12.5	15.6	0.8
	Upper-middle income	4.7	4330	26.8	16.9	13.4	0.7
	Lower-middle income	4.3	1504	19.5	17.6	12.0	1.3
	Low income	3.9	420	17.2	17.5	8.1	2.1
Median	High income	4.8	21,154	36.2	12.1	15.8	0.6
	Upper-middle income	4.6	4528	26.4	17.8	13.1	1.0
	Lower-middle income	4.2	1391	17.1	17.4	12.0	1.5
	Low income	3.3	346	12.4	15.6	8.8	2.1

Note The above statistics only include countries with a population of more than 10 million
Source World Development Indicators Database of the World Bank

country. Scholars generally use the method of international comparison. Internationally, a country's "public education expenditure as a percentage of its gross domestic product (GDP) or gross national product (GNP)" is usually used as an indicator of the country's public education investment level. Therefore, the following study will use the ratio of public education expenditure to GDP as an indicator to conduct an international comparison of public education investment, analyze the relative status of China's current public education spending ratio, as well as its trend and growth potential during the 11th Five-year Plan period.

Education has a huge contribution to a country's economic development. At the same time, the development of education is constrained by a country's level of economic development. Chinese scholars have been paying attention to the international comparative study on the public expenditure ratio since the 1980s. Using GDP per capita as an indicator of a country's level of economic development, Chen Liangkun et al. (1988) tried to find the international average of education investment ratios compatible with different levels of economic development. Their study used data from 38 countries to conduct an empirical analysis of the public expenditure ratio in each country from 1961 to 1979. Later, they conducted another study using the data of 40 countries from 1980 to 1985 (Chen et al. 1992), and proposed that by 2000, China's appropriate fiscal education investment would reach 4% of GDP that year.

Yue Changjun (2003) used the same econometric regression model and method as Chen (1988, 1992) in an empirical analysis using relevant data from 54 countries from 1986 to 1997. The results showed that by 2010, China's GNP per capita would reach about US$1600, while the corresponding international average of the public expenditure ratio would be about 4.04%. By 2020, China's GNP per capita would exceed US$3000, and the corresponding international average level of the public spending ratio would be about 4.3%. Liu and Yuan (2006) used relevant data of 57 countries in 2001 and estimated that by 2010, China's public expenditure ratio would be close to 4%.

5.1.2.1 The Regression Models

The ratio of public education expenditure to GDP varies greatly from country to country, and is affected by both supply and demand factors. On the supply side, countries with higher per capita income have a greater proportion of public expenditure on education. Within high-income countries, the public spending expenditure ratio varies with the ratio of government fiscal revenue to GDP. Countries with a higher fiscal revenue ratio have more financial resources and are more likely to invest more in education. In addition, the fiscal expenditure structure of different countries is also quite different, causing the proportion of education expenditure in total fiscal expenditure to be significantly different. On the demand side, the educational development goals of a country affect the scale and proportion of public spending on education. Indicators such as enrollment rates at all levels of education and years of education per capita reflect the efforts of governments in education. In addition, countries with fast-growing school-age populations have a larger demand for education investments.

In this chapter, we use the following three variables to measure a country's financial capacity in educational input: GDP per capita, the proportion of fiscal revenue to GDP, and the proportion of public education expenditures in government fiscal expenditure. Two variables, expected years of education per capita and the population growth rate, are used to measure a country's demand for education. Although the public expenditure ratio generally rises with economic development, its growth rate tends to decline. Therefore, the logarithmic GDP per capita is used.

The model is as follows:

$$\begin{aligned} edugdp_{jt} &= \beta_0 + \beta_1 \ln gdppc_{jt} + \beta_2 revgdp_{jt} + \beta_3 edugov_{jt} \\ &\quad + \beta_4 syear_{jt} + \beta_5 gpop_{jt} + u_{jt} \end{aligned}$$

The explained variable *edugdp* represents the ratio of public education expenditure to GDP, i.e., the public expenditure ratio. The explanatory variable *gdppc* represents the GDP per capita (in logarithmic form), *revgdp* is the ratio of fiscal revenue to GDP, *edugov* is the ratio of public education expenditure to government fiscal expenditure, *syear* is the expected years of education per capita, *gpop* is the population growth rate, and *u* represents the random disturbance term.

The first three explanatory variables represent a country's potential educational funding supply capacity, whose coefficients are expected to be positive. The latter two explanatory variables represent a country's demand for public education funding, and the coefficients are also expected to be positive.

Using the regression results, we can calculate the conditional expected value of the explained variable. That is, given the value of each explanatory variable, the international average level of the public expenditure ratio.

5.1.2.2 Data Description

The data used in this chapter comes from UNESCO's World Education Indicators, the World Bank's World Development Indicators Database, *China Statistical Yearbook*, and *China Educational Finance Statistical Yearbook*. When the data of the same year are inconsistent in various yearbooks, the data of the most recent yearbook are adopted.

The names, meanings, and data sources of variables included in the model are summarized in Table 5.3. The time span is from 2000 to 2004. The GDP per capita in each year is calculated at constant prices in US$2000.

The purpose of this chapter is to compare public education expenditure in China with other countries. To facilitate a reasonable international comparison, we select countries with a population of more than 10 million, which also have larger economies and more sophisticated industrial structures, based on the 2005 demographic data released by the World Bank in 2006. In this database, a total of 76 countries have a population of more than 10 million, of which 20 countries are excluded from the sample due to serious lack of data. Therefore, there are 56 countries included in the sample. Among them, there are 14 high income countries, 11 upper-middle income countries, 14 lower-middle income countries, and 17 low income countries (see Table 5.4).

Table 5.3 Variable names, meanings and data sources used in regression

Variable name	Variable meaning	Data source
edugdp	Public education expenditure as a percentage of GDP	UNESCO
gdppc	GDP per capita	World Bank
revgdp	Government revenue as a percentage of GDP	World Bank
edugov	Public education expenditure as a percentage of government fiscal expenditure	World Bank
syear	Expected years of education per capita	World Bank
gpop	Population growth rate	World Bank

Table 5.4 The 56 selected sample countries

Country category	Number of countries	Name of countries
High income	14	Australia, Belgium, Germany, France, Republic of Korea, Netherlands, Canada, the United States, Portugal, Japan, Spain, Greece, Italy, the United Kingdom
Upper-middle income	11	Argentina, Poland, Russia, Czech Republic, Romania, Malaysia, Mexico, South Africa, Turkiye, Hungary, Chile
Lower-middle income	14	Angola, Brazil, Ecuador, Philippines, Colombia, Kazakhstan, Cameroon, Peru, Morocco, Thailand, Tunisia, Ukraine, Iran, Indonesia
Low income	17	Ethiopia, Pakistan, Cambodia, Zimbabwe, Côte d'Ivoire, Kenya, Madagascar, Malawi, Bangladesh, Nepal, Niger, Nigeria, Senegal, Uganda, Yemen, India, Zambia

Note In 2005, there were 11 countries with a population of more than 100 million. Except for China, the remaining countries in descending order of population are: India, the United States, Indonesia, Brazil, Pakistan, Russia, Bangladesh, Nigeria, Japan, and Mexico

5.1.2.3 Regression Results

Since the sample is mixed with both time-series and cross-section data, it is necessary to examine the influence of time factors on the regression results. Due to missing data, the sample is not a complete panel data, so it is impossible to determine whether to use a fixed effects model, a random effects model, or an OLS model passing the Hausman test. We used the OLS regression method, introducing time dummy variables to test the influence of time. The regression results showed that the coefficients of all the time dummy variables are insignificant at the 10% statistical level. Therefore, there is no need to introduce time dummy variables in the regression.

Since the regression model contains five explanatory variables, we used condition number and variance inflation factor for multicollinearity test and found that multicollinearity does exist in the regression that includes all the explanatory variables. Therefore, we gradually increased the variables for regression.

First, we start by only examining the impact of GDP per capita on the public education expenditure ratio. The model is as follows:

$$edugdp_{jt} = \beta_0 + \beta_1 \ln gdppc_{jt} + u_{jt} \tag{5.1}$$

Second, we comprehensively examine the supply capacity of a country's public education investment. On the basis of Model (5.1), the ratio of fiscal revenue to GDP and the ratio of education expenditure to total fiscal expenditure are introduced. GDP per capita measures the overall level of economic development of a country. The ratio of fiscal revenue to GDP represents the relative financial resources available to the government, while the ratio of education expenditure to total fiscal expenditure represents the government's allocation of public finances. Although there may be a high correlation between the three explanatory variables, the model does not show serious multicollinearity in econometric tests, indicating that the three explanatory variables can be introduced into the model at the same time. The model is as follows:

$$edugdp_{jt} = \beta_0 + \beta_1 \ln gdppc_{jt} + \beta_2 revgdp_{jt} + \beta_3 edugov_{jt} + u_{jt} \tag{5.2}$$

Third, we focus on the impact of demand factors on public education expenditures and introduce the other two variables: expected years of education per capita and the population growth rate. A test shows that there is strong multicollinearity between these two explanatory variables. In addition, we find that there is strong multicollinearity between these two variables and the first three variables that represent supply factors. Therefore, in order to examine the impact of demand factors, we only retain the expected years of education per capita as a proxy variable, which reflects a government's goals on educational development. The model is as follows:

$$edugdp_{jt} = \beta_0 + \beta_4 syear_{jt} + u_{jt} \tag{5.3}$$

The OLS method is used to estimate coefficients and carry out the measurement tests. The regression results are shown in Table 5.5. In the three regression results, the statistical significance level of the regression model and all the regression coefficients reached 1%, indicating that these explanatory variables have a significant impact on the explained variables. Since the sample is not a single time series and contains cross-sectional data, the R-squared (R^2) is not large. The R-squared value of Model (5.1) and Model (5.3) are both 0.10, and that of Model (5.2) is the highest, reaching 0.44.

Table 5.5 Regression results (explained variable: *edugdp*)

Variable	Regression model (5.1)		Regression model (5.2)		Regression model (5.3)	
	Regression coefficient	t value	Regression coefficient	t value	Regression coefficient	t value
Intercept term	1.789***	3.330	−2.859***	−2.882	2.906***	6.304
gdppc	0.339***	4.946	0.457***	5.013		
revgdp			0.03627***	2.815		
edugov			0.182***	6.616		
syear					0.128***	3.651
gpop						
Sample size	204		76		204	
Adjusted R^2	0.10		0.44		0.10	

Note ***, **, and * indicate statistical significance of 1%, 5%, and 10%, respectively

5.1.2.4 Comparison with Previous Studies

Model (5.1) is completely consistent with the models of Chen et al. (1992) and Yue (2003), which adopted the same regression method. The only difference is that an explanatory variable used in this study is GDP per capita instead of GNP per capita. Since there is little difference between GDP per capita and GNP per capita, we can still compare the regression results. The regression coefficient with the data from 1980 to 1985 is 0.84 (Chen et al. 1992), while the one using the data from 1986 to 1997 is 0.41 (Yue 2003). The regression coefficient of the 2000–2004 data used in this chapter is 0.339. Over time, the effect of the level of economic development on the public expenditure ratio has diminished. This is because the GDP per capita of countries has continuously increased over time, but the public expenditure ratio cannot increase indefinitely, and will gradually converge to a certain level.

5.1.3 International Comparison of Public Education Expenditures

5.1.3.1 A Detailed Comparison with Eight Selected Countries

We selected eight representative countries for a further comparative analysis, with the United States and Germany representing high income countries, Russia and Mexico representing upper-middle income countries, the Philippines and Indonesia representing lower-middle income countries, and India and Bangladesh representing low income countries. Substituting the GDP per capita, the ratio of fiscal revenue to GDP, and the ratio of education expenditure to total fiscal expenditure of the eight countries from 2000 to 2004 into Model (5.2), the corresponding international average of the public expenditure ratio can be obtained and compared with the ratio of each country (see Table 5.6).

The United States and Germany's public expenditure on education as a percentage of GDP is roughly the same as the corresponding international average. In 2001, the public expenditure ratio of the United States was 5.75%, and the corresponding international average level was 5.78%, a difference of only 0.03 percentage points. The public expenditure ratio of Germany in 2000 and 2001 was 4.53% and 4.57%, and the corresponding international average levels were 4.63% and 4.58%, with a difference of only 0.10 percentage points and 0.01 percentage points respectively. The economies of high income countries are relatively more mature, and their public expenditure ratios are not only high, but also stable.

Russia and Mexico are both upper-middle income countries, but their public expenditure on education as a percentage of GDP showed quite different features. Russia's public expenditure ratio was basically the same as the corresponding international average. In 2002, the ratio was 3.84%, 0.14 percentage points higher than the international average. In 2003, it was 3.68%, 0.19 percentage points lower than

Table 5.6 Public education expenditure comparison: international average vs country data (2000–2004)

Country	Indicator	2000	2001	2002	2003	2004
The United States	GDP per capita (US$)	34,599	34,484	34,759	35,521	36,655
	Proportion of fiscal revenue in GDP (%)		20.43	18.12	17.34	17.17
	Proportion of education expenditure in total fiscal expenditure (%)		17.15			
	International average estimated by model (%)		5.78			
	The actual public spending ratio (%)		5.75	5.71	5.86	
Germany	GDP per capita (US$)	23,114	23,354	23,342	23,332	23,705
	Proportion of fiscal revenue in GDP (%)	30.34	29.61	29.51	29.67	28.62
	Proportion of education expenditure in total fiscal expenditure (%)	9.87	9.72			
	International average estimated by model (%)	4.63	4.58			
	The actual public spending ratio (%)	4.53	4.57	4.77		
Russia	GDP per capita (US$)	1775	1870	1968	2122	2286
	Proportion of fiscal revenue in GDP (%)			31.76	27.51	27.29
	Proportion of education expenditure in total fiscal expenditure (%)	10.65	11.48	10.66	12.25	
	International average estimated by model (%)			3.70	3.87	
	The actual public spending ratio (%)	2.94	3.11	3.84	3.68	
Mexico	GDP per capita (US$)	5935	5842	5806	5803	5968
	Proportion of fiscal revenue in GDP (%)	14.74				
	Proportion of education expenditure in total fiscal expenditure (%)	23.62	24.32			
	International average estimated by model (%)	5.95				
	The actual public spending ratio (%)	4.86	5.16	5.30	5.79	
Philippines	GDP per capita (US$)	1002	1000	1024	1041	1085

(continued)

Table 5.6 (continued)

Country	Indicator	2000	2001	2002	2003	2004
	Proportion of fiscal revenue in GDP (%)	15.16	15.26	14.36	14.90	14.81
	Proportion of education expenditure in total fiscal expenditure (%)	13.95	14.03	17.79	17.22	
	International average estimated by model (%)	3.39	3.40	4.07	3.99	
	The actual public spending ratio (%)	3.49	3.20	3.18	3.22	
Indonesia	GDP per capita (US$)	800.0	819.8	844.3	873.7	906.2
	Proportion of fiscal revenue in GDP (%)		18.28	17.06	17.05	18.31
	Proportion of education expenditure in total fiscal expenditure (%)		9.60	9.03		
	International average estimated by model (%)		2.62	2.48		
	The actual public spending ratio (%)	1.24	1.36	1.06	0.94	
India	GDP per capita (US$)	450.2	465.8	477.4	510.8	538.3
	Proportion of fiscal revenue in GDP (%)	11.99	11.25	11.73	11.94	12.58
	Proportion of education expenditure in total fiscal expenditure (%)	12.71			10.74	
	International average estimated by model (%)	2.68			2.38	
	The actual public spending ratio (%)	4.12			3.26	
Bangladesh	GDP per capita (US$)	353.1	364.6	373.4	385.6	402.1
	Proportion of fiscal revenue in GDP (%)		9.83	10.21	10.10	9.97
	Proportion of education expenditure in total fiscal expenditure (%)	14.99	15.70	15.76	15.50	
	International average estimated by model (%)		3.05	3.09	3.05	
	The actual public spending ratio (%)	2.47	2.55	2.32	2.38	2.25

Note Blank spaces indicate missing data

the international average. Mexico's public spending ratio was significantly lower than the corresponding international average. In 2000, the actual ratio was 4.86%, 1.09 percentage points lower than the corresponding international average. However, from 2001 to 2003, the actual ratio rose rapidly, reaching 5.79% in 2003, approaching the corresponding international average.

Both the Philippines and Indonesia are lower-middle income countries, and their public expenditure on education as a percentage of GDP is generally lower than the corresponding international average. The actual ratio of the Philippines in 2000 was 3.49%, 0.10 percentage points higher than the corresponding international average. However, from 2001 to 2003, the ratio dropped to about 3.20%, significantly lower than the corresponding international average. The annual difference reached 0.77 percentage points in 2003. The public expenditure ratio of Indonesia was significantly lower than the corresponding international average. In 2001 and 2002, the actual ratio was only 1.36% and 1.06%, respectively, 1.26 and 1.42 percentage points lower than the corresponding international average levels.

India and Bangladesh are both low income countries, yet their public education expenditure ratios showed different characteristics. India's ratio was significantly higher than the corresponding international average. In 2000, the ratio was 4.12%, 1.44 percentage points higher than the corresponding international average. In 2003, the actual ratio was 3.26%, 0.88 percentage points higher than the corresponding international average. The public expenditure ratio of Bangladesh was significantly lower than the corresponding international average. From 2001 to 2003, the ratio was 0.50, 0.77, and 0.67 percentage points lower than the corresponding international average.

Due to data limitations, the analysis has to exclude four countries with a population over 100 million, such as Japan, Brazil, Pakistan, and Nigeria, and includes another six countries with the same level of population size, including the United States, Russia, Mexico, Indonesia, India and Bangladesh. It can be said that it is difficult for countries with particularly large populations to raise their public education expenditure ratio to a very high level. Among the eight countries in Table 5.6, only India had a significantly higher public expenditure ratio than the corresponding international average. As the most populous country in the world, India has attached great importance to public education investment over years, which has promoted the rapid accumulation of human resources, and the role of education in promoting economic development is gradually emerging.

5.1.3.2 China's Public Education Expenditures

Substituting China's GDP per capita from 2000 to 2005 into Eq. (5.1), the corresponding "international average 1" of the public expenditure ratio can be obtained. Substituting China's GDP per capita, the ratio of fiscal revenue to GDP, and the ratio of education expenditure to total fiscal expenditure from 2000 to 2003 into regression result (5.2), the corresponding "international average 2" of the public expenditure ratio can be obtained (see Table 5.7). The last two rows of Table 5.7 are the actual public expenditure ratio in China, in which the last row is the result based on the adjusted GDP.

If the economic development level is the only factor considered, the international average of public expenditure ratio corresponding to China's GDP per capita from 2000 to 2005 would have risen from 4.11% to 4.25%. However, for a given level of economic development, the relative financial resources available to a country and the share of government public finance allocated to education would also differ. Therefore, when considering the ratio of fiscal revenue to GDP and the ratio of education expenditure to fiscal expenditure, the international average ratio corresponding to China's per capita GDP could have risen from 3.78% in 2000 to 3.88% in 2003. Since China's ratio of fiscal revenue to GDP and education expenditure to fiscal expenditure are both relatively low, it is not sufficient to only consider per capita GDP when conducting international comparative analysis, otherwise there will be overestimated results.

Even if calculated according to Model (5.2), the actual level of China's education expenditure-to-GDP ratio is still significantly lower than the international average. From 2000 to 2003, the difference was 0.88, 0.69, 0.52 and 0.58 percentage points respectively. If calculated according to the adjusted GDP, the difference became 1.20, 1.09, 0.98 and 1.04 percentage points respectively.

Table 5.7 Comparison of the international average and actual level of china's public education expenditure

Item	2000	2001	2002	2003	2004	2005
GDP per capita (US$)	949	1021	1106	1209	1323	1436
Proportion of fiscal revenue in GDP (%)	16.0	17.2	18.3	18.1	17.8	
Proportion of education expenditure in total fiscal expenditure (%)	16.1	16.2	15.8	15.6		
International average 1 estimated by Model (5.1) (%)	4.11	4.14	4.16	4.20	4.23	4.25
International average 2 estimated by Model (5.2) (%)	3.78	3.88	3.88	3.88		
China's actual ratio 1 (%)	2.90	3.19	3.36	3.30		
China's actual ratio 2 (%)	2.58	2.79	2.90	2.84		

Note (1) China's *public expenditure ratio refers to the ratio of fiscal education expenditure to GDP;* (2) *The ratio of fiscal revenue to GDP is the data adjusted by the National Bureau of Statistics in January 2006;* (3) *The international average 1 and 2 were estimated according to the econometric regression Model* (5.1) *and Model* (5.2) *respectively;* (4) China's *actual ratio 1 is calculated with the unadjusted GDP, while* China's *actual ratio 2 was calculated with the adjusted GDP*
Source GDP per capita data comes from the World Development Indicators Database of the World Bank; the ratio of fiscal revenue to GDP, the ratio of education expenditure to total fiscal expenditure, and China's actual ratios are all from the *China Statistical Yearbook*; China's GDP adjustment coefficient comes from the National Bureau of Statistics

5.1.4 China's Financial Capacity on Public Education Investment

Using the above regression results, we can predict China's capacity for public expenditure on education during the 11th Five-year Plan period.

Before using the regression model to make predictions, each explanatory variable must be estimated first. For GDP per capita, the actual value in 2005 was US$1436 (calculated at constant prices in 2000). Assuming that the average annual growth rate of GDP per capita is 7.18% (equivalent to doubling in ten years), the GDP per capita during the 11th Five-year Plan period would increase from US$1539 in 2006 to US$2031 in 2010. Due to the large fluctuations in China's economic growth rate in early 2000s, the ratio of fiscal revenue to GDP and the ratio of education expenditure to total fiscal expenditure have also fluctuated greatly. GDP has grown rapidly since 2002, but the proportion of fiscal revenue in GDP and the proportion of education expenditure in fiscal expenditure have both declined. Therefore, these two proportions are not easy to estimate. The median average of the two proportions in lower-middle income countries with a population of more than 10 million from 2000 to 2004 were 17.1% and 17.4%, respectively. The latest data of these two proportions of China were 17.8% (2004) and 15.6% (2003) respectively, both of which were close to the international average. Therefore, we assume that during the 11th Five-year Plan period these two proportions will remain 17.8% and 15.6% respectively.

With the assumptions above, we can estimate the Chinese government's potential public education spending using Model (5.1) and Model (5.2).

Model (5.1) only considers the level of economic development. Substituting China's GDP per capita in each year during the 11th Five-year Plan period into model (5.1), the international average of the public expenditure ratio corresponding to China's economic development level is obtained. It is 4.28% in 2006 and would rise to 4.37% in 2010 (see Table 5.8).

Model (5.2) takes into account all the indicators assumed above. Substituting GDP per capita, the proportion of fiscal revenue in GDP, and the proportion of education expenditure in fiscal expenditure in each year of China's 11th Five-year Plan period into model (5.2), we get the international average of the public expenditure ratio, 3.98% in 2006, and would rise to 4.11% in 2010.

Table 5.8 Trend of China's GDP per capita and the corresponding international average level of the public expenditure ratio (2006–2010)

Item	2006	2007	2008	2009	2010
GDP per capita (USD in 2000)	1539	1649	1768	1895	2031
Proportion of fiscal revenue in GDP (%)	17.8	17.8	17.8	17.8	17.8
Education expenditure as a proportion of total fiscal expenditure (%)	15.6	15.6	15.6	15.6	15.6
International average 1 (%)	4.28	4.30	4.32	4.35	4.37
International average 2 (%)	3.98	4.01	4.04	4.07	4.11

5.2 Prediction of China's Public Education Funding Demand in the 11th Five-Year Plan Period

5.2.1 Estimation with Statistical Data

The demand for education funding, especially the demand for government education funding, is determined to a large extent by policies. Such policies may include educational development goals, the fiscal education expenditure as a percentage of total education expenditure, and the proportion of education expenditure to total fiscal expenditure. The following part analyzes and predicts the education expenditure in 2010 based on the educational development goals and China's current education funding situation.

A commonly used method for estimating education funding demand is to determine a relatively reasonable amount of investment per student at all levels of education and multiply that by the corresponding number of students at each level. However, theoretically there is no common understanding or unified standard on the reasonable amount of investment per student, and in practice the situation varies from country to country. The method of international comparison is generally used in research. A commonly used measure for international comparison is the per-student expenditure index. The per-student expenditure index is the ratio of per-student expenditure at corresponding level of education to per capita GDP. This indicator reflects how many students a country can support with its per capita GDP for the students to complete one year of study. We will use this indicator, based on the results of international comparison and China's actual conditions, to analyze the amount of investment per student for education at all levels in China. When analyzing the demand for government education funding, the most important parameter is the ratio of government funding amount to the total education funding amount.

The steps of the estimation are as follows.

First, calculate the per-student expenditure index.

The index of expenditure per student can be calculated by dividing the education expenditure per student by the GDP per capita. The changing trend of the per-student expenditure index for education at all levels from 1999 to 2004 is as follows: (1) The per-student expenditure index at primary school level has shown an upward trend, rising from 9.5% in 1999 to 12.6% in 2004. (2) The change of the per-student expenditure index at middle school level is not significant, basically stable at around 16%. (3) The per-student expenditure index at high school level has shown a gradual decline, from 40.4% in 1999 to 34.6% in 2004. (4) The per-student expenditure index of higher education has shown a significant downward trend, from 208.9% in 1999 to 120.8% in 2004. The corresponding international average levels of the index for primary school, middle school, high school and higher education were 19%, 24%, 29%, and 44% respectively (Wang et al. 2003). As China's per-student expenditure indexes at primary and middle school levels were lower than the international average, we expect an increase in them during the 11th Five-year Plan period, reaching 15% and 20% respectively. With the per-student expenditure indexes of China's high school and higher education higher than the international average, we expect them to maintain the current level of 40% and 120% respectively during the 11th Five-year Plan period (see Table 5.9).

Second, calculate the number of students in school.

According to the school-age population data in the book *Stride From A Country If Temendous Population to a Country of Profound Human Resources*, the gross enrollment rate for primary schools is calculated at 100%. The gross enrollment rate of middle school is 98% according to the goal in the 11th Five-year Plan. Based on the above data, the estimated number of students enrolled in primary and middle schools were 97.97 million and 52.84 million respectively. In addition, according to the 11th Five-year Plan, the number of students enrolled in regular high schools and colleges and universities in 2010 should be 24.1 million and 21.3 million respectively.

Third, calculate the total demand for education funding.

The total demand for education funding in ordinary schools is equal to the per-student funding index for all levels of education multiplied by the number of students in school, then multiplied by the per capita GDP, and then adding up all levels of demanded education funding. In 2010, the total demand of regular schools for education funding were RMB994.7 billion (calculated at constant prices in 2000).

Dividing the "total demand for education funding of regular schools" by the "proportion of regular school expenditure in total education expenditure", we can get the total demand for education funding. In 1999, the proportion of regular school expenditure in total education expenditure was 80.2%, and in 2003 it rose to 84.4%. China will progressively develop vocational education, especially technical vocational education during the 11th Five-year Plan period. Therefore, we believe that the proportion of regular schools' expenditure in total education expenditure will show a downward trend, assuming a decline to 75%. In this case, in 2010, China's total demand for education funding were RMB1.3263 trillion (calculated at constant prices in 2000).

Fourth, calculate the total demand for government education funding.

In this step, we multiply the total expenditures on education at all levels by the proportion of fiscal education expenditure in the total education expenditure, and

Table 5.9 Parameters for estimating education funding demand in 2010

Item	Primary school	Middle school	High school	Higher education
Per-student expenditure index (%)	15	20	40	120
Gross enrollment rate (%)	100	98	80	25
Number of students in regular schools (10,000 people)	9797	5284	2410	2130
Proportion of fiscal education expenditure in total education expenditure (%)	95	95	50	40
Proportion of regular school fiscal expenditure in total fiscal education expenditure (%)	33		31	21

Table 5.10 Estimation results of demand for education funding in 2010

Item	2010
GDP (RMB billion)	21,467.7
Total expenditure on education (RMB billion)	1326.3
Proportion of total expenditure on education in GDP (%)	6.18
Total government expenditure on education (RMB billion)	856.4
Proportion of total government expenditure on education to GDP (%)	3.99

Note The absolute value of all types of funds are calculated at constant prices in 2000

then add up the fiscal education expenditure at all levels to obtain the total demand for government funding in regular schools. In 2010, the total demand for government funding in regular schools in China were RMB642.3 billion (calculated at constant prices in 2000).

Further, the total demand for education funding can be calculated by dividing the "total demand for fiscal education funding of regular schools" by "the proportion of regular schools in the fiscal education expenditure". In 1999, the proportion of regular school expenditure in the total government education expenditure was 82.2%, and in 2003 it rose to 85.7%. Given the Chinese government's strong willingness to develop vocational education during the 11th Five-year Plan period, we assume that the proportion of regular school expenditure in the total government education expenditure will also show a downward trend. We assume that it will fall to 75%. Under this assumption, in 2010, the total demand for government education funding would be 856.4 billion yuan (calculated at constant prices in 2000).

Fifth, calculate the ratio of total demand for government education funding to GDP.

According to the data released by the World Bank, based on the constant price of US dollar in 2000, China's per capita GDP in 2005 was US$1436, and the population was 1.3045 billion. China's GDP in 2005 was US$1.8728 trillion by multiplying these two. Calculated at an exchange rate of US$1 to RMB8.1046, China's GDP in 2005 was RMB15.1781 trillion. Further assuming an average annual growth rate of being 7.18% of China's GDP during the 11th Five-year Plan period, we obtained that China's GDP will reach RMB21.467 trillion by 2010.

Finally, by dividing the total demand for education funding and the total demand for government education funding by GDP in 2010, the ratio of total demand for education funding to GDP and the ratio of total demand for government education funding to GDP were obtained, 6.18% and 3.99%, respectively (See Table 5.10).

5.2.2 Estimation with Econometric Regression

According to the education development goals in the 11th Five-year Plan, the gross enrollment rate of higher education will be 25% and that of high schools will be

80% by 2010. Regardless of dropouts it can be assumed that by 2010 the structure of the school-age population by education level will be as follows. Primary school graduates account for 0%, middle school graduates 20%, high school graduates 55%, junior college graduates 10%, undergraduates 10% and postgraduate 5%. Years of education at all levels of education were calculated according to the standards in the last row of Table 5.11. The average number of expected years of education of the school-age population in China in 2010 will be 12.4 years.

Substituting the above values into the estimation results of the regression Model (5.3), the international average of the public expenditure ratio can be obtained, which is 4.49%. It is not difficult to find that this result is greater than the prediction result (4.37%) based on Model (5.1), and also greater than the prediction result (4.11%) based on Model (5.2). This shows that if we estimate the demand for education funding with the international average, the demand would exceed the supply.

It should be noted that dropouts are not considered here. During the 11th Five-year Plan period, China's high school gross enrollment rate was set at 80%. With such a high target, the dropout rate will be inevitably higher, the reasons for which can be various. First, dropouts from middle schools in rural China are still very common. During the 11th Five-year Plan period, it will be difficult to ensure that middle school students do not drop out, and it is even more difficult to assume that high school students do not drop out. Second, high school education is non-compulsory education in China, so students have to pay tuition and fees, which will be a heavy burden for families with financial difficulties. Therefore, even if the government will provide admission to high school to 80% of middle school graduates, the actual rate of students that would actually complete high school education can be expected to be significantly lower than 80%. Under such circumstances, the expected average years of education of the school-age population in China in 2010 will be less than 12.4 years, and the corresponding international average of the public expenditure ratio will thus be lower than 4.49%.

Table 5.11 Proportion of school-age population at all levels and corresponding years of education in 2010

Education level	Primary school	Middle school	High school	Junior college	Undergraduate	Postgraduate	Total
Percentage (%)	0	20	55	10	10	5	100
Years of education	6	9	12	14.5	16	19	12.4

5.2.3 *Conclusions and Policy Recommendations*

This chapter uses statistical data and econometric regression to study China's public spending on education during the 11th Five-year Plan period, from both the supply and demand side.

On the supply side, if the economic development level is the only factor considered, the international average of the public expenditure ratio corresponding to China's economic development level in 2010 should be 4.37%. If fiscal revenue capacity and fiscal allocation structure are also considered, the corresponding international average of the public expenditure ratio should 4.11%.

On the demand side, if we only consider the current status and development goals of China's education, the total fiscal education expenditure in 2010 should account for 3.99% of GDP. If we also use international comparison and econometric regression to estimate the ratio corresponding to China's educational development goals, the international average of the total demand for government education funding as a proportion of GDP should be 4.49%.

To sum up, the appropriate proportion of China's fiscal education expenditure to GDP should be around 4% by 2010. This ratio is in line with the fiscal education funding demand ratio of 3.99%, and does not exceed the fiscal supply capacity of 4.11% estimated above. Finally, the premise of ensuring this ratio is that during the 11th Five-year Plan period, China's GDP maintains an average annual growth rate of about 7.18%, the proportion of fiscal revenue to GDP and the proportion of fiscal education expenditure to total fiscal expenditure not lower than the 2004 level.

References

Carnoy, M. (2000). *International Encyclopedia of Economics of Education* (Ed., Trans. Min, W., et al.). Higher Education Press.

Chen, L., et al. (1988). International Comparison of the Proportion of Educational Expenditure in the Gross National Product. *Research on Educational Economics*. Shanghai People's Publishing House.

Chen, L., et al. (1992). International Comparison of Public Education Investment. *Research on Education Investment Decision-making*. Peking University Press.

Liu, Z., & Yuan, L. (2006). Study on the Ratio of Public Education Investment in China. *Journal of Higher Education, 2*, 62–66.

Wang, R., et al. (2003). China's Public Education Finance System: Challenges and Reforms. *Stepping from a Large Country in Population to a Powerful Country in Human Resources*. Edited by the Task Force for Report on China's Education and Human Resources. Higher Education Press.

World Bank. (2006). *World Development Indicators 2006*. https://openknowledge.worldbank.org/handle/10986/8151

Yue, C. (2003). Proportions of Educational Investment: An International Comparison. *Stepping from a Large Country in Population to a Powerful Country in Human Resources*. Edited by the Task Force for Report on China's Education and Human Resources. Higher Education Press.

Part II
Educational Opportunities and Resources Allocation

Part II consists of three chapters and conducts an empirical analysis on the equilibrium of China's educational development at all levels and the fairness of educational opportunities. Chapter 6, "Inequality in Resources Allocation for Compulsory Education", studies the unbalanced allocation of compulsory education resources in China from 1997 to 2000 using data from the Ministry of Education's county-level education finance statistics. From a sociology perspective, Chapter 7, "Adjustment in Geographic Distribution of Rural Primary and Secondary Schools", puts forward a preliminary analysis framework to understand the distribution adjustment of rural primary and secondary schools in China. Chapter 8, "Research on Equal Access to Higher Education", analyzes the distribution of higher education enrollment opportunities among different social classes from the two dimensions of quantity and quality.

Chapter 6
Inequality in Resources Allocation for Compulsory Education

China has made impressive achievements in the education sector since the founding of the People's Republic of China in 1949, and the accessibility of the nine-year compulsory education has been a focus of China's education policies in the past two decades. However, the efforts of making such education universally available, especially among rural populations, were met with challenges.[1] The two major obstacles, the unbalanced allocation of resources and financial strains in underdeveloped rural regions are closely linked to the funding system of compulsory education.

Changes began to take place in educational financing in the early 1980s. The funding system for education, once centralized and propelled by homogeneous income sources, transformed to one that is more loosely structured and with more diversified incomes (Tsang 1996). School finance reforms took place in the context of nationwide public fiscal reforms, which resulted in counties and lower administrative divisions taking on the financial obligations of compulsory education. Funding comes from both government budgets and other channels, which inevitably gave rise to two issues: uneven resource distribution across different regions and disparities in per-pupil expenditure. Analyses of the current allocation of funding show that such issues are hardly unique in the education sector, other public departments are faced with similar challenges (Park et al. 1996; Wang and Hu 1998). Resolving them will undoubtedly improve social equality, educational resource efficiency, and social stability (Tsang 2003).

As pointed out by World Bank research in 1999, a significant obstacle faced by China's education sector in the new century is the financial strains and disparities. The research suggests that streamlining the funding system and putting counties instead of townships in charge of securing educational investment would take the burden off townships, and resource gaps within counties can thus be bridged. As the rural tax

[1] By the end of 2001, the gross enrollment ratio (GER) in middle schools stands at 88.3%. Those who are unenrolled are mostly from western and rural China. Source: 2001 National Statistical Communique on the Development of Education, June 13, 2002.

W. Min, *Educational Input, Resource Allocation and Returns to Human Capital*,
https://doi.org/10.1007/978-981-96-4687-6_6

reform started to roll out nationwide in 2001, the management of compulsory education also became responsibility of county-level governments, and there has been an increasing demand for a standardized and robust system for more resource allocations to local governments to help them address funding for compulsory education (Tsang 2003). In order to develop proper fiscal policies for this purpose, empirical research on the finances of compulsory education is crucial.

By delving into county-level data, this research provides descriptive statistical analyses on educational resource distribution and its imbalance, observes the trend in which such an issue developed from 1997 to 2000, and discusses policy implications that this study has discovered.

6.1 Analysis of School Expenditures: Methodology, Existing Research, and Data

A prevalent way to analyze educational resource allocation is to examine school expenditure. For budgeting and planning purposes, school spending is usually divided into operating expenditure and capital expenditure. Operating expenditure is defined as the input of resources consumed by the school in a year and can usually be broken down into personnel and non-personnel expenditure. Capital expenditure, on the other hand, is referred to as the input of resources that have longer lasting effects, usually more than one year (such as buildings and large equipment). It is worth pointing out that school expenditure is just one part of the total spending on compulsory education, but usually the most significant one. Therefore, it is oftentimes the center-of-attention for policy analyses. Education cost outside schools (such as hiring private tutors, spending on learning materials, and loss of personal income due to the pursuit of education etc.) might also be substantial and can be a major source of education inequality and uneven distribution of academic resources. However, comprehensive data on private education expenditure is difficult to obtain.

China is a large and culturally diverse country with varying degrees of socioeconomic development across different regions. Hence, any analyses on the imbalance of educational and social development must factor in the disparities between different geographic locales, urban and rural areas, and different ethnic minority groups and regions. According to the fifth national census, in 2000, rural residents comprised 64% of the total Chinese population. In order for the Ministry of Education to universalize the "nine-year compulsory education" stage by stage, 31 provinces, autonomous regions and municipalities directly under the central government were commonly categorized into "three tiers". The most economically and educationally advanced "Tier 1" consists of the nine coastal provinces and municipalities in East China. The least developed "Tier 3" includes the five ethnic autonomous regions and the four least advanced western provinces (Qinghai, Gansu, Yunnan, and Guizhou). "Tier 2" consists of the thirteen provinces in central China. In 2000, ethnic groups made up 8.41% of the total population, and most of them reside in 635 county-level ethnic autonomous areas (including the counties and banners in autonomous regions and prefectures), which takes up 64% of the total land area. In these regions, 46% of the population are ethnic groups.[2]

In the studies of educational finance, common indicators of education inequality include adjusted statistical range (the difference between the 95th percentile value and the 5th percentile value), adjusted range ratio (the ratio of the 95th percentile value to the 5th percentile value), the coefficient of variation (standard deviation divided by mean), the Gini index, and the Theil index etc. The Theil index can be more easily decomposed (the Gini index is also decomposable but is inevitably with redundancy). The equation for the overall Theil index (T) is:

$$T = \frac{1}{n}\sum \frac{x_i}{u}\log\left(\frac{x_i}{u}\right) \tag{6.1}$$

In this chapter, x_i represents the per pupil expenditure of the i_{th} for county and equivalent administrative unit. The value range of the Thiel index is 0 to log (n). The overall Theil index can be decomposed into two components: intra- and inter-group inequality. Assuming that there are multiple groups within the smallest unit in the sample, the intra-group inequality coefficient (T_w) is:

$$T_w = \sum \left(\frac{n_k u_k}{nu}\right) T_k \tag{6.2}$$

Here, T_k is the overall Theil index of the k_{th} group. n_k and u_k represent the number of samples and the per pupil expenditure in the k_{th} group. As displayed in the equation, the intra-group inequality coefficient is the weighted average of inequality coefficients of all groups. Inter-group inequality coefficient (T_b) equals the overall Theil index minus the intra-group inequality coefficient: $T_b = T - T_w$.

By the early 1990s, a decentralized funding system had taken shape in order to pull together more resources for compulsory education. Since then, the academic community has been studying the impact of this system on education equality. Some studies took place on a provincial level, such as Mun Chiu Tsang's research in 1994 on 29 provinces, autonomous regions, and municipalities (Tsang 1994). According to Tsang, in 1989, the province with the highest per student expenditure for primary education spent 5.2 times more than the province with the lowest expenditure did, and for secondary education (middle schools and high schools), this number is 4.5 times. Another research by Du Yuhong and Wang Shanmai (2000) discovered that the gap in total expenditure for primary education widened between 1978 and 1996, yet for secondary education, the extent of inequality remained mostly unchanged. Other researches studied the data by dividing the provinces into groups. One example is a research by Jiang Minghe in 1995. It found out that in terms of budgetary expenditure per pupil, the ratio of developed regions (provinces such as Jiangsu,

[2] National Bureau of Statistics: *China Statistical Yearbook 2000*, Beijing: China Statistics Press, 2000, p. 37.

Zhejiang, and Guangdong) to underdeveloped regions (provinces such as Anhui, Henan, and Guizhou) increased to 2.14 from 1.61 (Jiang 1995).

Analyzing provincial-level data has its own significance, for the province is an essential administrative level, and the data is easily accessible. However, such analyses did not touch upon the intraprovincial inequality, which could also be jarring and is usually the focus of education policies. The earliest research which analyzed the expenditure per pupil in compulsory education using county-level data is done by Jiang Minghe in 1992. Jiang's research included data samples from 374 counties and illustrated the correlation between a region's per pupil expenditure and its local average income. Since the 1990s, there have been more researches gauging the intraprovincial inequality by examining county-level data,[3] and they mostly came to the conclusion that the per pupil expenditure correlates with the local average income (which means it does not reach "fiscal neutrality"). Some studies also explored the trend of educational inequality over time. Method wise, adjustd statistical range, adjusted range ratio, the coefficient of variation, the Gini index, and the Theil index are the preponderant indicators for measuring such inequality. As for the pieces on whether the expenditure per pupil reaches "fiscal neutrality", some researches, such as Pan's, used a simple unary linear regression while others, like Wang Rong's research in 2003, adopted the multiple linear regression. Wang used the hierarchical linear model, for the independent variants in the model have hierarchical differences. In comparison, this research highlights the imbalance of resource allocation in China's compulsory education mainly by conducting descriptive statistical analyses on the regional differences in per pupil revenue and expenditure.

In the next sections, the three following topics will be discussed in depth: (1) Schools' overall revenue and expenditure for compulsory education and the disparities between regions; (2) The extent of inequality in revenue and expenditure; (3) The trend in which the disparity in educational resource allocation evolves between the years 1997 and 2000.

Compared to previous studies, this chapter made the following improvements: First, areas with large ethnic minority populations are analyzed in addition to the traditional "three tiers" and the urban versus rural comparisons. Second, the extent of inequality in per pupil revenue and expenditure is carefully measured with multiple methods. Third, the imbalance in resource allocation and how it had evolved over time are well articulated. The time range of the study is three years (while Pan's research only covers one year). The data comes from the Ministry of Education, which compiled the education financial reports from primary administrative subdivisions and built a comprehensive county-level subdivisions database. The "county-level subdivisions" here include county units and equivalent administrative units, and affiliated counties of municipalities (prefecture-level). As the quality of the data of county-level financial reports continued to improve from 1997 to 2000, the data collected in 2000 already covers the majority of the county-level subdivisions in the country. Therefore, compared to those which used data prior to 2000, the study of

[3] Zhang Li, *Facing Poverty* Nanning: Guangxi Education Publishing House Co., Ltd., 1998.

this chapter offers a more comprehensive picutre of the educational inequality in China.

Available data sources show that approximately 3100 county-level subdivisions that have institutions of primary education (primary and middle schools) are included, and almost all county-level subdivisions in the 31 provincial-level divisions are in the year of 2000 database. The aggregated number of enrollment for primary schools in the database roughly equals 97% of the actual number, and the number of enrollment for middle schools is slightly higher than the actual number.[4] The overall school expenditure consists of operating and infrastructural expenditures (including spending on large equipment). Operating expenditure can be broken down to personnel and public expenditure. Personnel expenditure is mainly composed of salaries and benefits for faculty and staff, hardly any spent on students. Public expenditure includes spendings on day-to-day management, supplies and student services, equipment, facility maintenance, inbound and outbound travel, and other administrative affairs etc. According to the schools' revenue reports, the total revenue comes from government budgetary used for management and infrastructure, urban and rural educational surcharges, income from miscellaneous fees, school-run enterprises, work-study programs, fundraising, and donations etc. In the expenditure statement, each expenditure item also seperately records expenditures that are both budgetary and extrabudgetary. Meanwhile, in county-level statistics, educational funding in the form of government programs is also included.

The indicators used for measuring ineuqliaty in this chapter include adjusted statistical range, the adjusted range ratio, the coefficient of variation, the Gini Index, and the Theil Index etc. In order to better compare the study of this chapter to the other ones, the calculation of the Gini index was conducted in two ways. One is a method of exhaustion, meaning that every county is included, and the equation is:

$$G = \frac{2}{n}(1y_1 + 2y_2 + \cdots + ny_n) - \frac{n+1}{n} \tag{6.3}$$

G is the Gini index; n represents the total number of county-level subdivisions, and y_i is the share of the i_{th} subdivision's expenditure in the total expenditure, with $y_1 < y_2 < \cdots < y_n$.

Another method is to generate a Lorenz curve using regression and calculate the area under the curve (equation omitted). The results produced by both methods of calculation are almost identical.

[4] Enrollment data for primary and middle schools in 2000 comes from the *Statistical Bulletin on* China's *National Educational Development*, Ministry of Education, 2002. The number of middle school enrollment in the database is larger than that in the Bulletin, for the database includes institutions that offer both middle school and high school education, and their expenditure on the middle-school level were not separately recorded. For the purpose of calculating per pupil expenditure of middle schools, this chapter counts every high schooler as 1.5 middle schoolers. Therefore, the enrollment number shown in the database is higher than the number in the *Bulletin*.

6.2 School Revenues and Expenditures for Compulsory Education in 2000

Table 6.1 provides a detailed picture of the per pupil expenditure broken down by region in the year 2000. All the average revenue and expenditure in this chapter are weighted by the number of students in the respective county-level subdivisions.

In 2000, the national average of per pupil expenditure for primary schools stands at RMB789.68, 95.38% of which is operating expenditure (which means only less than 5% of the total spending went to education infrastructure). As for middle schools, the national average is RMB1303.32, 91.72% of it is operating expenditure. In developing countries, such high percentages are not unusual.[5] The per pupil expenditure for middle schools is about 66% higher than that of primary schools,[6] and the gaps between urban and rural areas are substantial for both educational stages with urban areas spending 85% more money on each student. In non-ethnic minority regions, per pupil expenditure is higher than that in ethnic minority regions, but the difference is not drastic (although the gap is wider at the middle-school level). "Tier 1" regions have much higher per pupil expenditure than "Tier 2" and "Tier 3" regions do. "Tier 1" regions spend almost twice as much on each student as "Tier 2" regions, and the difference between the two is bigger than the difference between urban and rural areas. As shown by Table 6.1, the per pupil infrastructure spending also varies by region, and the variation is particularly pronounced in lower secondary education. A region with sound educational infrastructure would have 10% of the total expenditure spent on infrastructure etc., while that ratio in less developed "Tier 2" and "Tier 3" regions is only 7.12% and 6.6%. If looking at absolute amount, the gap in expenditure in terms of infrastructure is even more glaring than the one in total expenditure.

Table 6.1 also displays the share of personnel spending in operating expenditure (which consists of personnel and public expenditure). For middle schools, personnel spending takes up 3/4 of the operating expenditure, and the proportion for primary education is close to 2/3. It is safe to say that regions with high per pupil expenditure (urban, non-ethnic minority, and "Tier 1" regions) have a lower percentage of personnel spending than regions with relatively paltry per pupil expenditure (rural, ethnic minority, and "Tier 2" & "Tier 3" regions). Namely, public expenditure takes up a smaller share for higher-spending regions than it does for lower-spending regions. If looking at absolute amount, the gap in public expenditure per pupil is even wider than that in total expenditure.

This chapter calculates various types of public expenditure in different regions as well as their respective shares in the total public spending. The results show

[5] Usually, over 90% of the expenditure for primary education in developing countries is operating expenditure. The rate for lower secondary education is about 80%–85%. M. Tsang, Cost analysis and educational policymaking: A review of cost studies in education in developing countries, *Review of Educational Research*, Vol. 58, No. 2 (1988), pp. 181–230.

[6] This difference is resulted from a higher student/teacher ratio of middle schools. The sample shows the student/teacher ratio of middle schools is 17.1 and that of primary schools 22.3.

Table 6.1. Per pupil expenditure in 2000

Item	Total expenditure (RMB)	Operating expenditure (RMB)	Personnel expenditure (RMB)	Operating/ total (%)	Personnel/ operating (%)
Primary schools					
National average	789.68	753.24	557.08	95.38	73.96
Urban average	1195.21	1128.94	796.75	95.25	70.58
Rural average	644.98	619.09	471.75	95.52	76.20
Urban/rural	1.85	1.82	1.69		
Non-ethnic minority Regions average	796.83	759.90	558.84	94.46	73.54
Ethnic minority Regions average	746.59	713.10	546.46	95.99	76.63
Non-ethnic/ ethnic	1.07	1.07	1.02		
Tier 1 average	1201.34	1139.52	815.54	94.85	71.57
Tier 2 Average	611.30	588.13	442.5	96.21	75.24
Tier 3 average	682.75	646.71	496.98	94.72	76.85
Tier 1/Tier 2	1.97	1.94	1.84		
Tier 1/Tier 3	1.76	1.76	1.64		
Middle schools					
National average	1303.32	1195.41	778.00	91.72	65.08
Urban average	1626.03	1485.65	968.69	91.37	65.20
Rural average	880.93	833.52	581.89	94.62	69.81
Urban/rural	1.85	1.78	1.66		
Non-ethnic minority Regions average	1330.73	1216.77	788.99	91.44	64.84
Ethnic minority Regions average	1098.74	1035.98	696.01	94.29	67.18
Non-ethnic/ ethnic average	1.21	1.17	1.13		

(continued)

Table 6.1. (continued)

Item	Total expenditure (RMB)	Operating expenditure (RMB)	Personnel expenditure (RMB)	Operating/ total (%)	Personnel/ operating (%)
Tier 1 average	1930.42	1741.75	1109.52	90.23	63.70
Tier 2 average	1001.35	930.10	613.28	92.88	65.94
Tier 3 average	1075.51	1004.51	674.80	93.40	67.18
Tier 1/Tier 2	1.93	1.87	1.81		
Tier 2/Tier 3	1.79	1.73	1.64		

that different regions demonstrate similar spending patterns. For instance, the most sizable item in all the regions' public expenditure is facility maintenance fee (national average is 33.26% for primary schools and 34.54% for middle schools), and the smallest is inbound and outbound travel (national average is 1.41% for primary schools and 1.26% for middle schools). However, facility maintenance fees take up smaller shares in higher-spending regions than they do in lower-spending regions, and for those items that are directly related to teaching activities, the opposite situation is true. For example, in primary education, facility maintenance fee in "Tier 1" counts for 30.18% of the total public expenditure, while this number for "Tier 3"is 44.80%. Teaching-related items like expenditure on supplies and student services take up 29.11% for "Tier 1", while "Tier 3" only spends 20.73% on the same items. Since the difference in per pupil public expenditure is already substantial (more significant than the difference in overall per pupil expenditure), a much higher percentage of instruction-related spending in "Tier 1" than in "Tier 3" implies an even more drastic gap in absolute numbers.

Expenditure and revenue are two sides of the same coin. Therefore, the total amount of revenue per pupil, which consists of budgetary and extrabudgetary revenue, is investigated in this chapter as well. The amount of budgetary and extrabudgetary revenue in different regions, along with the percentages of different sources of extra-budgetary revenue, are also calculated (chart omitted). The results show that in 2000, the amount of total per pupil expenditure is roughly the same as the total per pupil revenue across the country (per pupil revenue is approximately RMB11 more than per pupil expenditure in primary education, and the surplus for middle schools is around RMB26). The per pupil budgetary revenue in 2000 marks RMB541.7, taking up 68.24% of the total revenue (which means less than 1/3 of the total revenue is extra-budgetary); For middle schools, budgetary revenue stands at RMB827.97, taking up 62.29% of the total revenue (which means a little over 1/3 of the total revenue is extrabudgetary). A general pattern here is that a region with higher revenue per pupil would also have a higher percentage of extrabudgetary revenue (this phenomenon is less pronounced at the middle school level). Meanwhile, the research found that ethnic minority regions generally have a higher percentage of budgetary revenue, even though their overall revenue per pupil is lower than that of non-ethnic minority regions. For primary schools, the percentage of budgetary revenue in total revenue for ethnic and non-ethnic minority regions are 79.84% and 66.43%, which shows that ethnic minority regions in fact have higher per pupil revenue than non-ethnic minority regions (RMB606.61 versus RMB537.31). As for middle schools, per pupil budgetary revenue respectively takes up 70.93% and 61.33% of the total revenue for ethnic and non-ethnic minority regions, yet the amount of budgetary revenue for ethnic minority regions is lower than that of non-ethnic minority regions (RMB797.73 versus RMB832.03). The results indicate that government budget plays a more significant role in ensuring the universalization of compulsory education in areas with large ethnic minority populations, or that compulsory education in areas with large ethnic minority populations relies more heavily on budgetary grants from the government.

In 2000, miscellaneous fees became the largest source of extrabudgetary revenue. For primary schools, it counts for 30.82% of the total extrabudgetary revenue. The second largest source is educational surcharges (rural, urban, and regional educational surcharges) collected by all levels of governments, which takes up 29.58%. For middle schools, 34.21% of the extrabudgetary revenue comes from miscellaneous fees, while only 19.22% of it is from educational surcharges. If looking at extrabudgetary revenue by region, schools located in urban areas have a significantly bigger share of self-generated incomes in their extrabudgetary revenue portfolios than rural schools do (28.30% versus 14.17% for primary education, almost twice as high and three times higher if looking at absolute amount).

By comparing budgetary revenue per pupil and personnel expenditure (99.9% of which is spent on faculty salaries), one will discover that the national average budgetary revenue per pupil for primary education cannot cover an average salary for a faculty (RMB547.17 versus RMB557.08). For lower secondary education, the budgetary funding per pupil is 6.5% higher than the personnel expenditure per pupil (RMB827.97 versus RMB778.00). If breaking it down by region, in rural and non-ethnic areas, the budgetary revenue at primary school level cannot fully cover the faculty salary, and the same is true for "Tier 1" and "Tier 2" regions. However, as mentioned above, schools in "Tier 1" regions are more capable of generating extrabudgetary revenue. Therefore, paying for faculty salaries and benefits and securing the public budget should not be as difficult for "Tier 1" as it is for "Tier 2".

The analyses above indicate that for less developed regions and rural areas, financial strains in education are a common issue. Many schools are barely staying afloat, and some are even on the edge of closing down. Meanwhile, the abiding low quality of facilities and equipment (low spending on infrastructure) and inadequate public grants will not only affect enrollment rates but also the quality of education (Tsang 2001).

6.3 Disparities in Per Pupil Expenditures among Schools

Table 6.2 shows the extent of inequality in per pupil expenditure for compulsory education in 2000 measured by different indicators.

Table 6.2. The extent of inequality in per pupil expenditure for compulsory education in 2000 measured by different indicators

Item	Adjusted range	Adjusted range ratio	Coefficient of variation	Gini Index	Theil Index	Intra-provincial inequality	Percentage in total intra-provincial inequality (%)
Primary schools	1486.68	5.64	0.76	0.348	0.242	0.172	71.10
Middle schools	3065.08	7.51	0.85	0.319	0.262	0.183	69.80

The indices above reflect the disparities in per pupil expenditure for compulsory education. One thing to note is that the highest and the lowest 5% of the extrema were already eliminated when calculating the adjusted statistical range and the adjusted range ratio. Yet even so the differences between the highest and the lowest per pupil expenditure for primary schools and middle schools still respectively stand at RMB1486.68 and RMB3065.08. The adjusted range ratio for middle schools and for primary schools are 5.64 and 7.51, which means that for primary education, the county-level subdivisions on the highest end (but not the highest ones since the top 5% was already eliminated) spend 5.5 times more money than the ones on the lowest end (but not the lowest ones since the bottom 5% was already eliminated). The coefficients of variation at both levels exceed 0.75 and 0.85 (generally, a coefficient of variation of over 0.5 signifies a high variation in a set of values). According to all the five indices in the table above, lower secondary education suffers from far worse inequality in per pupil expenditure than primary education does. A decomposition of the Theil index also shows that most of the expenditure inequality in compulsory education takes place within provinces. At least 2/3 of the inequality is intra-provincial.

Currently, county-level subdivisions shoulder the majority of responsibilities of carrying out compulsory education in China while all other levels of governments play supportive roles at their own paces. Since the 21st century, the central government has been funding compulsory education in underdeveloped regions at an unparalleled scale, and provincial-level governments also launched special campaigns to back such efforts. From the perspective of public finance, the spillover effect of public goods such as compulsory education could reach far more than just local communities (For example, with the process of urbanization and industrialization, the laborforce in rural areas that receive compulsory education would migrate to metropolises and industrial hubs). Moreover, compulsory education is important, even crucial, in building a civil, modern society, promoting social stability and boosting national cohesion, which is why the central government and provincial-level governments are undoubtedly obliged to successfully universalize compulsory education. Analyzing indices of inequality could inform different levels of governments in their efforts of eliminating inequality in per pupil expenditure, but the root causes for educational inequality might be extremely complicated. Whether there is excessive educational inequality in any administrative divisions may depend on the efforts made by the local government, or the difficulty of ensuring equity in education in a region.

Table 6.1 reflects the disparities in per pupil expenditure between urban and rural areas, and this research is able to investigate how much such disparities contribute to the overall expenditure inequality because the general database contains the aggregated data of both "urban schools" and "rural schools" in most county-level subdivisions. To calculate the overall Theil index, every provincial-level division is viewed as a whole.[7] To calculate the intra-group Theil, every county-level subdivision is viewed as a group with two units in each group: urban schools aggregated and rural schools aggregated). With these two indices, we can calculate the proportion of every provincial-level division's urban-rural disparity in the overall inequality. Here, the national average of such proportion is simply deduced by calculating the mean (without weighting each province by the number of enrollment) of the proportions of urban-rural disparity in all provinces.

The results show that the urban-rural disparity takes up a little less than 1/3 of the total expenditure inequality for primary education (32.7%) while the number for lower secondary education is a little more than 1/3 (34.7%, a breakdown of results by province is omitted). If looking at each provincial-level division, for primary schools, urban-rural inequality counts for 20%-45% of the total expenditure inequality with the highest being Chongqing (45.9%) and the lowest being Zhejiang (merely 5.8%). For middle schools, urban-rural inequality takes up the biggest proportion in Guizhou (56.6%) and the lowest in Ningxia (17.5%). If compiling the data from both educational stages (by calculating the mean), urban-rural inequality takes up the largest proportion in Guizhou (close to 50%), Anhui (48%), and Chongqing (47%), all of which are provincial-level divisions with less developed economy. In relatively developed regions with a strong presence of township and village enterprises, urban-rural inequality is shown to have a less prominent effect, the lowest being Guangdong (16%), Zhejiang (17%), and Jiangsu (21%). For the three more developed municipalities, Beijing, Shanghai, and Tianjin, their weights of urban-rural inequality in overall expenditure inequality roughly equal the national average with Tianjin being slightly lower and Shanghai slightly higher. However, whether urban-rural inequality takes up a large proportion in overall inequality is not necessarily relevant to the actual extent of inequality in a province. For example, the urban-rural disparity is not significant in Jiangsu's overall expenditure inequality, but Jiangsu is the province with the widest expenditure gap (Theil index marks 0.191 for primary schools and 0.197 for middle schools). Shandong is the second worst in terms of its disparity in expenditure, but its urban-rural inequality also takes up a smaller share than the national average. Both Jiangsu and Shandong see a tremendously uneven economic growth within provinces, which dwarfs the impact of urban-rural inequality. Such a pattern closely mirrors the overall situation in China: the gap in expenditure between urban and rural schools are eclipsed due to the more severe socioeconomic disparities

[7] The smallest unit of study here is not county-level subdivisions, but a compilation of data of township or village schools.

among different regions within provinces (individual results of all the provinces are omitted).

Since the sources of funding for schools' expenditure are clearly marked in the database, this research respectively calculates the extent of inequality of the following nine categories: total per pupil expenditure, per pupil operating expenditure, per pupil public expenditure, total budgetary expenditure per pupil, budgetary operating expenditure per pupil, budgetary public expenditure per pupil, total per pupil extrabudgetary expenditure, extrabudgetary operating expenditure per pupil, and extrabudgetary public expenditure per pupil (results omitted). All the five inequality indicators show that the most severe inequality is seen in per pupil budgetary public expenditure. Calculating the adjusted range ratio would be infeasible, for the lowest 5% of the values in the category is 0. Namely, over 5% of the county-level subdivisions' budgetary public expenditure is zero. Needless to say, the budgetary expenditure in these regions all went to the salaries of faculty and staff. Studies show that adequate funding for public expenditure is crucial to delivering quality education (Lockheed and Verspoor 1992), and a lack of such funding will surely affect the quality of compulsory education in some regions.

Public expenditure is indispensable for school's daily operation. Due to inadequate government input, public expenditure in many regions must rely on extrabudgetary income, which is unstable and oftentimes subject to policy changes. For a long time, the saying "the government funding keeps schools open, but education surcharges support school operations" reflects the harsh reality of compulsory education in many places. In early 2000s, tax reforms in rural areas resulted in a shift away from educational surcharges, fundraising, and volunteer service, which means miscellaneous fees have become the major source of funding for school's public expenditure. In addition, the wide implementation of the "single fee system" regulated the tuitions and fees in compulsory education. Starting in 2004, the central government launched the policy of "exemption of miscellaneous fees, exemption of book fees, subsidy for living expenses" in west and central China. Though the timeline of policy implementation is not set in stone, the introduction of the policy indicates that given time, a free compulsory education in underdeveloped, rural areas is an inevitable trend. This means that miscellaneous fees, the major source of funding for public expenditure will almost definitely be scrapped. Previous analyses have also suggested that schools in underdeveloped, rural areas are less capable of generating income for themselves (these types of incomes are also unstable and can hardly be considered as a steady source) than urban schools are. Therefore, if the government funding fails to cover schools' public expenditure, some regions in the country would have difficulties keeping the schools open, and leading to dire consequences.

6.4 Changes in School Revenue Expenditures and Disparities in Per Pupil Expenditures (1997–2000)

This chapter also utilizes the data from the grassroots level reports on education finance in 1997 to conduct statistical analyses on the fiscal imbalance and per pupil revenue and expenditure for compulsory education. The results are juxtaposed with the ones in 2000. Between 1997 and 2000, the per pupil expenditure for primary education grew by 26.24% (gauged with the constant-price of 2000), registering a much faster growth than lower secondary education's 14.79%. For primary schools, the per pupil expenditure in ethnic minority regions enjoyed a more significant growth than that of non-ethnic minority regions (37.46% versus 24.88%), while the growth rates of urban and rural schools remained roughly the same (with the per pupil expenditure grows a little faster for rural schools). If breaking down the results by region, for primary education, the per pupil expenditure of "Tier 1" and "Tier 3" provinces grew much faster than that of "Tier 2" provinces (Tier 1, 2, 3 respectively 30.22%, 16.84%, and 40.57%). For lower secondary education, the situation is similar, but there is a discernible gap in growth rate between urban and rural schools (15.96% and 10.2%). Table 6.3 shows how the ratios of per pupil expenditure among different regions evolve during the three years.

It is worth pointing out that the results in 1997 and 2000 are not inferred from the same group of county-level samples. There are many county-level subdivisions missing 1997 data, and the inconsistency of the samples affected the accuracy of the calculation. If the samples from both years were considered as merely surveys on all county-level subdivisions, the data in 2000 offers a more comprehensive view of the situation. In the 1997 database, Tibet Autonomous Region only has compiled provincial-level data, and provinces like Jiangxi, Yunnan, and Jilin are missing data from a large number of county-level subdivisions. According to Table 6.3, the urban-rural gap in expenditure for primary schools narrows between 1997 and 2000. Since the expenditure of "Tier 3" has a higher growth rate than that of "Tier 1", and the growth rate of "Tier 1" higher than that of "Tier 2", the gap between "Tier 1" and "Tier 3" had become narrower, and the gap between "Tier 1" and "Tier 2" wider. For middle schools, three out of the four sets of ratios in Table 6.3 saw an increase in the three years. As for the non-ethnic minority region to ethnic minority region ratio of per pupil expenditure, the gaps at both educational stages were closing up.

Table 6.3. Ratios of per pupil expenditure among different regions in 1997 and in 2000

Item	Primary schools		Middle schools	
	1997	2000	1997	2000
Urban schools/rural schools	1.99	1.85	1.65	1.85
Non-ethnic minority regions/ethnic minority regions	1.17	1.07	1.29	1.21
Tier 1/Tier 2	1.76	1.97	1.61	1.93
Tier 1/Tier 3	1.90	1.76	1.82	1.79

As for per pupil revenue, the conclusions closely resemble the ones on per pupil expenditure. However, a lot has changed in the three years in terms of schools' revenue structure. In 1997, the budgetary revenue of primary schools took up just over half of the total per pupil revenue (55.46%). In 2000, over 2/3 of the revenue was budgetary (68.24%). For middle schools, the budgetary revenue took up 53.68% of the total per pupil revenue in 1997, and by 2000, this number was also close to 2/3 (62.29%). If breaking down the results by region, the percentage of the budgetary revenue in total revenue per pupil in areas with large ethnic minority populations (and "Tier 3" provinces where ethnic groups constitute the majority of the population) experienced the most substantial growth. For example, in 1997, the budgetary revenue took up roughly 2/3 of the total revenue per pupil for primary schools in ethnic regions (65.14%), while this proportion in 2000 grew to almost 80% (79.84%). During this time, governments scaled up their input in compulsory education significantly (in fact, the increase in public funding came almost exclusively from government input, and the extrabudgetary revenue decreased for both primary and lower secondary education). The structure of extrabudgetary revenue also underwent significant changes. In 1997, educational surcharges were the biggest source of extrabudgetary revenue, yet in 2000, it has fallen behind miscellaneous fees and became the second largest. For middle schools, educational surcharges were only the third largest source, following miscellaneous fees and self-generated revenue. Previous analyses have pointed out that extrabudgetary revenue are hardly stable. Thus, an increase in government input should be able to provide a stronger safety net for compulsory education.

Table 6.4 reflects the extent of inequality of per pupil expenditure and their evolvement over the three years manifested in the five indicators.

According to Table 6.4, the inequality in per pupil expenditure at both educational stages deepened over the years and was more substantial for lower secondary education. However, different indicators captured the different aspects of expenditure inequality. Adjusted statistical ranges saw dramatic changes for both primary and middle schools. Both the Gini Index for primary education and the Theil index for lower secondary education saw a surge in 2000. It can be inferred from the equation that the Theil index is sensitive to the changes in extrema (which is why Theil index is also referred to as "entropy index" as extrema are more heavily weighed during

Table 6.4. Evolvement of per pupil expenditure inequality over the years

Item	Primary schools		Middle schools	
	1997	2000	1997	2000
Adjusted statistical range	967.40	1486.68	1825.40	3065.08
Adjusted range ratio	5.03	5.64	4.91	7.51
Coefficient of variation	0.72	0.76	0.70	0.85
Gini Index	0.330	0.348	0.315	0.319
Theil Index	0.234	0.239	0.240	0.255
Intra-provincial inequality/overall inequality (%)	75.20	71.10	79.90	69.80

calculation). Comparatively, the Gini index responds more to the changes happening to the middle part of the distribution. A substantial change in the Theil index for middle schools means that compared to the middle part, the extrema on both ends of the sample set underwent bigger changes. To prove these conclusions, researchers calculated the McLoone index and the Verstegen Index for middle schools. The former is calculated by dividing the summation of the bottom 50% of the values in the set by the median then multiplied by n/2: An increased McLoone index suggests less inequality in the per pupil expenditure. The Verstegen index, on the other hand, is calculated by dividing the summation of the top 50% of the values by the median then multiplied by n/2. A decreased Verstegen index indicates less inequality in the per pupil expenditure. When being analyzed in addition to the other indicators, the McLoone Index and the Verstegen Index can be used to identify the specific part of the distribution that gives rise to the changes in the extent of the expenditure inequality. For instance, an increased coefficient of variation signifies deeper inequality. If the McLoone index goes down while the Verstegen Index hardly changes, it means that the worsening of inequality is caused by the withering expenditure of the schools at the bottom of the distribution (compared to the median of that year). According to the calculation, from 1997 to 2000, the McLoone index for middle schools decreased to 0.709 from 0.739, and the Verstegen index went up to 1.988 from 1.789, meaning that all county-level subdivisions across the country saw increasing inequality in educational expenditure. To be more specific, subdivisions with already lower per pupil expenditure had growth rates slower than those at the higher end of the distribution. For primary education, the McLoone index decreased to 0.685 from 0.708 while the Verstegen index increased to 1.858 from 1.816. The smaller change in the latter means that the main reason for worsening inequality is the slower growth rate of the administrative divisions with lower expenditures.

According to the Theil indices and their decompositions in both years, the overall inequality in education expenditure worsened between 1997 and 2000. The proportion of intra-provincial inequality shrank while that of inter-provincial inequality swelled. If looking at absolute numbers, intra-provincial inequality experienced little changes and even dwindled. This shows that the main culprit for the worsening inequality in per pupil expenditure is the widening gap in expenditure among different provinces.

6.5 Conclusion and Reflections

In the year 2000, the operating expenditure per pupil for primary and middle schools took up 94% and 92% of the total expenditure of their respective educational stages. Spending on personnel accounted for about 3/4 of the total for primary schools and 2/3 of the total for middle schools. Although the spending pattern is similar across different regions, the per pupil expenditure in terms of absolute numbers wildly varied. The gaps between urban and rural and between "Tier 1", "Tier 2" and "Tier 3" were simply jarring. While schools in areas with large ethnic minority populations spent less on their students, they are not far behind their counterparts in non-ethnic minority regions.

Certainly, the difference in expenditure in compulsory education can be traced back to the funding system. Schools in economically advanced regions enjoy more adequate budgetary funding, and their abilities to mobilize extra-budgetary resources are also stronger than those in less developed regions. As for underdeveloped areas and ethnic regions, their schools rely much more heavily on budgetary funding, and since most of it is spent on personnel, the schools' public expenditure is largely inadequate. The nine-year compulsory education in more advanced regions is readily available to all students, and the goal for these regions is to improve educational quality. Underdeveloped regions are striving to make compulsory education accessible to all, and some regions are still struggling to complete the task. Meager government funding makes it difficult to provide quality education, which will not only widen the gap between different regions but will also pose obstacles for the overall universalization of compulsory education.

All five indicators included in this chapter show that disparities in per pupil expenditure is substantial for primary and lower secondary education. Among all the expenditure items, public expenditure suffers from the worst inequality, and within public expenditure it is the budgetary public expenditure that sees the most inequality. A decomposition of the Theil index suggests that about 2/3 to 3/4 of the overall inequality comes from within provinces, while urban-rural inequality only takes up roughly 1/3. The wide expenditure gap between urban and rural schools pales in comparison with the disparities among different regions.

By juxtaposing the results of 1997 and 2000, one can discover that the degree of inequality in the overall per pupil expenditure worsened over time, and this trend seemed to continue on: county-level subdivisions that are on the top of the distribution enjoy growth rate much higher than those at the bottom, and the gaps between urban and rural and between "Tier 1" provinces (mostly coastal provinces) and inland regions had a tendency to widen.

The fiscal imbalance in compulsory education mirrors the uneven economic development of China (Wang and Hu 1998). Although the extent of overall inequality in per pupil expenditure did not change dramatically between 1997 and 2000 (reflected in the calculation of the two more complex inequality indicators), evidence shows that the gaps among different regions continue to grow (as reflected by some of the simpler inequality indices, increased proportions of intra-provincial inequality and deepening urban-rural disparities).

Remedying the crippled funding system of compulsory education requires efforts from both inside and outside the education sector (Tsang 1996). External efforts include pushing for socioeconomic development and alleviating poverty in underdeveloped and rural areas. Since late 1990s, the central government has been focusing on west China by putting in place enabling policies for peasants which would advance rural economy. The effects of such policies are yet to be examined by future research.

Fixing the issues in a decentralized system of funding oftentimes requires intergovernmental transfers (Tsang and Levin 1983). Building a robust, standardized system for mobilizing government funding involves many different aspects, some of which are relevant to this chapter.

First, the respective scopes of responsibilities of the central and provincial governments. Till now, most government programs are still initiated by the central government to which the provincial and lower-level governments are required to provide supplemental funds. This mechanism has three problems: (1) it is yet to be institutionalized; (2) the scale of such funding is too small to bridge the gap; (3) provincial governments do not take a proactive approach nor play a significant role in allocating the funding.

By decomposing the Theil index, one can find that (1) Inequality in per pupil expenditure mostly happens intra-provincially; (2) inter-county inequality is the main composition of intra-provincial inequality, and the urban-rural difference within counties plays relatively minor roles; (3) although inter-provincial inequality only counts for a small proportion in the overall inequality, it seems to have worsened in these three years. (1) and (2) indicate that provincial governments should play a bigger part in ameliorating the inequality within provinces. Of course, (1) does not necessarily mean that provincial governments need to provide 60%-70% of the funding. The causes for expenditure inequality among county-level subdivisions, oftentimes related to both provincial-level and state-level policies, are complicated. The findings in this chapter are not indications that provinces are historically culpable in causing the inequality. In addition, adjusting the intergovernmental transfer mechanism brings about another issue, which is whether underdeveloped provinces in west China are capable of fixing the fiscal imbalance in the education sector by themselves. Raising this question itself implies that central government is imperative in the problem-solving process. Meanwhile, (3) suggests that the central government needs to do the heavy lifting despite the relatively limited presence of provincial-level governments. The respective roles they play in government programs depend on their financial capacities. Findings from this chapter are intended for informing future policies: provincial governments need to strive to make a bigger impact in government programs, but the importance of the central government should not be overlooked. More details on this matter would require in-depth analyses in the future.

Second, the use of government funding. The fiscal issue with China's compulsory education is seen as two main problems in this chapter: financial strains in underdeveloped, rural regions and the jarring inequality. Since it is unnecessary and infeasible to curtail the spending on education in economically advanced regions, the only viable method is to allocate all the government funding to underdeveloped regions. By doing this, not only financial difficulties in underdeveloped regions will be alleviated, the extent of inequality will also be reduced.

Third, the roles and effects of governmental and non-governmental educational resource. The government is obliged to ensure that every child receives (quality) compulsory education, and it is a widely acknowledged fact that education is a fruitful investment itself for both individuals and the society (World Bank 1995). The responsibility of delivering education lies with governments at all levels. Although school selection fees and privatization of education have become the hot topics in recent years (Tsang 2003; Kwong 1997), the government should remain at the center of universalizing compulsory education to ensure its fairness and efficiency as well as social mobility. Privatization and school selection during compulsory education should be approached and handled with caution.

Fourth, the disparity between ethnic and non-ethnic minority regions. In the past, there were no studies on per pupil expenditure of ethnic and non-ethnic minority regions utilizing surveys of county-level data. This chapter, through data analyses, discovers that the expenditure per pupil in ethnic minority regions is lower than that of non-ethnic minority regions, but the difference is hardly as substantial as the urban-rural disparity. Due to data limitations, the comparison did not take place between schools and between individuals. Even within ethnic autonomous regions, ethnic minority groups and the Han ethnic group may demonstrate different expenditure patterns. Moreover, situations may vary for different ethnic autonomous regions (Postiglione 1999), which itself is a matter worthy of in-depth investigation.

Fifth, the imbalance of education finance. As demonstrated in this chapter, employing a single indicator for everything or simply comparing the means of different sets of values might be misleading for developing a clear understanding of the imbalance in education finance. The results above show that some indicators such as the statistical range in expenditure per pupil may have increased drastically within the three years, but some other intricate indicators for measuring the overall inequality did not experience significant changes. Studying the imbalance in education finance and its consequences requires further exploration of theories and methodology.

References

Du, Y., & Wang, S. (2000). Imbalance in Educational Development. *Economic Analysis of Educational Policy*. People's Education Press, 76–109.

Jiang, M. (1995). Market Economy and Reform of Educational Finance. *Educational Research, 2*, 15–19.

Kwong, J. (1997). The Remergence of Private Schools in Socialist China. *Comparative Education Review, 41*(3), 244–259.

Lockheed, M., & Verspoor, A. (1992). *Improving Primary Education in Developing Countries: A Review of Policy Options*. Published for The World Bank. Oxford University Press.

Park, A., Rozelle, S., Wong, C., & Ren, C. (1996). Distributional Consequences of Reforming Local Public Finance in China. *The China Quarterly, 147*, 751–778.

Postiglione, G. (1999). *China's National Minority Education: Culture, Schooling, and Development*. Routledge Press.

Tsang, M. (1994). Costs of Education in China: Issues of Resource Mobilization, Equality, Equity and Efficiency. *Education Economics, 2*(3), 287–312.

Tsang, M. (1996). Financial Reform of Basic Education in China. *Economics of Education Review, 15*(4), 423–444.

Tsang, M. (2001). Intergovernmental Grants and the Financing of Compulsory Education in China. *Harvard China Review, 3*.

Tsang, M. (2003). School Choice in the People's Republic of China. *Choosing Choice: School Choice in International Perspective*. Teachers College Press.

Tsang, M., & Levin, H. (1983). The Impact of Intergovernmental Grants on Educational Expenditure. *Review of Educational Research, 53*(3), 329–367.

Wang, S., & Hu, A. (1998). *The Political Economy of Uneven Development: The Case of China.* Routledge.

World Bank. (1995). *Priorities and Strategies for Education: A World Bank Review.*

Chapter 7
Adjustment in Geographic Distribution of Rural Primary and Secondary Schools

Since late 1990s, the adjustment in geographic distribution of rural primary and secondary schools[1] has become a common phenomenon in China. In general, there are many practical studies and news reports on the adjustment in geographic distribution of rural primary and secondary schools in various regions, but there are relatively few analyses of academic significance. Most studies focus on the reasons and benefits of the adjustment in geographic distribution, but few studies examine the adjustment process itself. From the perspective of sociology, this chapter proposes a preliminary analysis framework for the components and contents involved in the adjustment in order to understand the process of adjustment in geographic distribution of rural primary and secondary schools in China, and then uses this framework to analyze the distribution adjustment of rural primary and secondary schools in Yunnan Province.

7.1 Issues and Inadequacies in Relevant Studies

School distribution refers to the geographic distribution of schools in a country or region. Geographic distribution of schools is directly related to the fairness and efficiency of educational resource allocation. The geographic adjustment of schools is mostly due to changes in school-age population or adjustments in regional planning. Since the reform and opening up, the nationwide adjustment in geographical distribution of rural primary and secondary schools in China mainly occurred in two historical periods. The first is the "decentralized school-running" period, which is featured by nationwide universal compulsory education movement in the mid-to-late

[1] In China, primary and secondary education takes 12 years to complete, divided into primary, junior secondary (middle school) and senior secondary (high school) stages. Primary education has 6 years schooling, while junior secondary stage has 3 years schooling. The 9-year schooling in primary and junior secondary schools pertains to compulsory education. General senior secondary education lasts 3 years.

W. Min, *Educational Input, Resource Allocation and Returns to Human Capital*,
https://doi.org/10.1007/978-981-96-4687-6_7

1990s. With the popularization of compulsory education, "village-run schools" were introduced in order to increase the enrollment rate of primary and secondary schools, especially to follow "the principle of proximity" so that students enter the nearby schools. In this period, rural primary and secondary schools rapidly expanded in number and geographic space. The second is "centralized school-running" period that is still in progress since 2000. With the progress of rural tax and fee reform, the rural compulsory education management system has also changed. Rural compulsory education has been transformed from schools administered by local rural residents to by governments, and county-level governments start taking the main responsibility for school funding. In order to reduce expenditure and improve efficiency, large-scale geographic adjustments have been initiated across the country. In general, the school-running models dominated by the above two periods are different, and the process of school geographic adjustment is also quite different.

The adjustment in geographic distribution directly involves the reallocation of educational resources, as well as fairness and efficiency of rural compulsory education. After 2000, regions that have popularized nine-year compulsory education in rural areas were facing great pressure to improve the quality of education. If the adjustment in geographic distribution fails to achieve more balanced distribution of educational resources, efficiency loss and serious inequality will become inevitable. The speed of geographic adjustment is another issue in improving the fairness and efficiency of rural education. If the adjustment is aggressive and fast, more students can enjoy high-quality educational resources in a relatively short period of time, which is conducive to promoting educational equality. However, if the adjustment is too fast without necessary supporting measures keeping up, related burden generated from the adjustment will exceed the financial capability of some families, which may cause students from these families to drop out of school and trigger more severe inequality. Therefore, there is a dilemma between equality and efficiency in the process of adjustment in geographic distribution of rural primary and secondary schools.

Consequently, the following issues require further research. Which factors affect the decision-making in geographic adjustment of rural primary and secondary schools? How is the adjustment policy implemented and how is the implementation method determined? What factors would affect the speed of geographic adjustment? How to balance the fairness and efficiency issues caused by the adjustment? In the process of geographic adjustment, which groups are vulnerable, and how can their interests be protected? Judging from the existing domestic and foreign literatures, there are few studies on the adjustment process, and there are not many focusing on the above issues.

Some Chinese scholars have reviewed foreign literatures on the adjustment in geographic distribution of schools.[2] Foreign researches have mainly focused on the following four aspects: the reasons for the geographic distribution adjustment, the goals of the adjustment, the consequences of the adjustment, and measures to avoid

---

[2] Shi Renbing, Foreign Studies and Enlightenment on School Layout Adjustment, International and *Comparative Education*, Issue 12, 2004.

the adverse effects of the adjustment. Regarding the reasons for the geographic distribution adjustment, it is generally believed that changes in the school-age population are the main cause. There are generally two goals of school geographic adjustment. One is to facilitate enrollment, and the other is to improve the efficiency of educational investment. In the case of conflict between the two goals, the goal is generally to increase benefit of educational investment as much as possible while ensuring convenient enrollment. According to foreign researches, school close down could have impact in the following aspects: (a) acceptance by students and parents; (b) teaching organization of the school before close down; (c) interests of different local social groups; (d) preservation of local culture. Some studies have put forward a number of measures to reduce the adverse effects of geographic distribution adjustment, such as (a) improving education planning; (b) retaining necessary small-scale schools in places with low population density; (c) innovating the educational organizing methods and making good use of school buildings for small-scale schools; (d) strengthening job-transfer training of the remaining teachers and helping them achieve a smooth career transition.

The relevant research in China on the geographic distribution adjustment of rural primary and secondary schools can be roughly divided into two categories. The first category is academic research, which have had few findings, not to mention outstanding work. Among them, the Yunnan Academy of Educational Sciences' work on the benefit comparison between the decentralized model and the centralized model in the distribution of primary schools is representative. The second category is experience reports in newspapers and periodicals by local government officials (such as the director of the Education Commission or the director of the Bureau of Education) in charge of the adjustment, mainly including the background, conditions, ideas and strategies of the adjustment, etc.

7.1.1 Efficiency Comparison Between Decentralized and Centralized School-Running Models

With funding from the Department of International Development of the United Kingdom, the Yunnan Academy of Educational Sciences organized a research project named A Comparative Study on the Costs and Benefits of Teaching Posts and Comprehensive Primary School Education. The study took "teaching posts"[3] as a typical model of decentralized primary schools and took "comprehensive primary schools"[4] as a typical model of centralized primary schools. The study found that there are currently two typical models of primary schools in Yunnan Province. In the decentralized model, teaching posts and village primary schools are established based on the principle of "students entering nearby schools", with enrolling distance

[3] The "teaching post" has less than six grades.

[4] The "comprehensive primary school", typically known as "*wanxiao*", refers to a school that has complete primary education from Grade one to Grade six.

no more than 3 km. In the centralized model, teaching posts are gradually removed, so students go to comprehensive primary schools, and schools provide boarding service to students who live more than 3 km away from the school. By comparing the efficiency of the two models, the study found that the centralized model shows greater overall efficiency than the decentralized model in terms of human resource, material resource, financial resource and educational resource. Further analysis found that the quality of pupils at comprehensive primary schools is significantly better than that of the teaching posts. Pupils at comprehensive primary schools have broader knowledge, more comprehensive skills, and can achieve better comprehensive development. In addition, the average annual education cost of comprehensive primary schools is lower than that of teaching posts. The study also found that the social benefits of comprehensive schools are greater than teaching posts. For example, comprehensive schools are more organized, more active, and more advantageous than teaching posts in promoting the physical and mental development of students.[5]

7.1.2 Practitioners' Experience and Discussion of Practical Issues

7.1.2.1 Reasons for Adjusting the Distribution of Primary and Secondary Schools

Most local officials and school principals believe that the change in the school-age population is the main factor leading to the adjustment in geographic distribution. However, there are many factors that may cause changes in the school-age population. For example, both decline in birth rate and migration flows caused by urbanization and market economy may lead to a decrease in the local school-age population. Ni Liren, principal of a middle school, believes that market economy may have an impact on the geographic distribution of middle schools. In his opinion, the original distribution of middle schools was based on administrative regions, and was influenced by the concepts of "school at the doorstep" and "middle school run by every village". Under the market economy, the value of education is more affirmed, and parents with financial capability will send their children to the county or township middle schools. Coupled with the impact of domestic migration, the number of students in township middle schools will greatly increase.[6] Yang Xiangsen, the former Director of the Education Commission of Jingmen City in Hubei Province, points out that the change in the peak number of students in school is also an important reason for the geographic distribution adjustment. Taking Jingmen as an example, the city has entered the peak of middle school enrollment since 2000. From 1998 to 2002,

---

[5] Yunnan Academy of Educational Sciences, A Comparative Study on the Costs and Benefits of Teaching Posts and Complete Primary School Education, 2003.

[6] Ni Liren, Market Economy and the Layout of Middle Schools, *Journal of Lishui Teachers College* (Social Science Edition), Issue 1, 1995.

the city had a net increase of more than 20,000 first-year middle school students. The number will gradually fall after the peak, leading to the necessity of relocating educational resources.[7]

7.1.2.2 Methods and Investment of the School Distribution Adjustment

Most rural areas with inconvenient transportation have to establish boarding system to adapt with the school distribution adjustment. However, building boarding schools is largely restricted by financial capability. Gao Shengfeng,[8] the former Director of the Yidu Bureau of Education, believes that lack of a clear running body is a big issue in developing rural boarding primary schools, "In recent years, declined enrollment in some villages has caused comprehensive primary schools to be degraded to teaching posts, or even revoked. The students from some villages were rearranged to a boarding school jointly run by several villages. In practice, inadequate cooperation and coordination among villages is a common problem, due to lack of clear management body and responsibilities, as well as inadequate leadership. The villages who originally had their own schools believed that their school-running obligations disappeared after their village schools were closed. Meanwhile, boarding schools lack the enthusiasm to provide boarding service, as they believe that running a boarding system would not benefit the children of their own village." Gao argues that government funding could not fully cover the construction, maintenance and equipment purchase of rural primary schools due to limited financial resources. Therefore, giving full play to the enthusiasm of villages in running schools is the cornerstone of the rural education development. In terms of management structure, it is feasible to adopt a model of operated by villages and supervised by township, and villages take responsibility in improving the conditions for boarding primary schools. To be specific, township leaders took the lead in coordinating relevant school-running units and village leaders to establish a school management committee, clarifying the responsibility of each unit. For example, Panjiawan, a village of the Yidu city, issued the Regulations of Panjiawan Unified School Council, and funded a unified school through the approval of the school council and villagers' committees.

Yang Xiangsen introduced that Jingmen has implemented a "Two Systems and One Concentration" approach to promote the distribution adjustment of primary and secondary schools since 1999. The "Two Systems" are the "boarding system for primary schools in mountainous areas" and the "nine-year consistent system for small towns". "One Concentration" refers to the "centralization of rural primary and secondary schools". That is, to locate schools in accordance with population density, and gradually "primary schools will be located in relatively bigger villages where the

---

7 Yang Xiangsen, Dynamic Control of the Distribution of Primary and Secondary Schools, *Hubei Education*, Issue 12, 2001.

8 Gao Shengfeng, Discussion on the Development and Regulation of Rural Boarding Primary Schools, *Hubei Education*, Issue 10, 2002.

local farm markets are located, middle schools will be located in township administrative centers, and high schools will be located in where the county government is located." In practice, measures such as "reorganization", "transfer" and "expansion and merger" have been adopted.[9] "Reorganization" means transforming redundant rural high schools into middle schools, and transforming redundant primary schools into kindergartens, teaching posts, rural adult schools or work-study bases. In addition, small-class teaching is implemented in comprehensive primary schools with relatively few students. "Transfer" means that to ensure that educational resources are not left idle or lost, transferring the remaining school buildings to the township or village committee, so that they can function as local villagers' night schools, nursing homes, medical rooms, or cultural centers. The redundant teaching equipment is deployed to central schools to reserve necessary educational resources for a future enrollment peak. "Expansion and merger" are to expand the enrollment scale of existing middle schools on the one hand, and to merge or transform primary schools with better conditions into middle schools on the other hand. In this way, a smooth transition to cope with the enrollment peak of middle schools can be realized without building new schools or heavily investing in school expansion.

7.1.2.3 Resistance from Localities

Some education administrators and principals engaged in the front line reported that the geographic distribution adjustment of rural primary and secondary schools faced not only financing difficulties, but also resistance from local and indigenous ideas. In the Chinese society, running school has always been highly valued and honored by local communities. Therefore, school closures involve the interests and honor of the local government and villagers, and thus may be resisted. Some villages of Anhua County still tried to run their own schools.[10] A middle school principal strongly felt locality's influence on the geographic distribution adjustment, and called on "the government should dare to undertake responsibilities and actively coordinate the relationship among townships" and "all townships should focus on the big picture, overcome localism, and break administrative regionalism".[11] Yuan Xianrong, then deputy magistrate of Tianzhu County, believed that there are multiple reasons why villagers were unwilling to see their local school closed or merged. Village schools were usually built with funds raised from local villagers, so they have emotional bond with local schools. Meanwhile, the relationship between villages will also

---

[9] Yang Xiangsen, Dynamic Control of the Distribution of Primary and Secondary Schools, *Hubei Education*, Issue 12, 2001.

[10] Li Maolin, et al., A Solid and Efficient Leap: The Secrets of the Layout Adjustment of Primary and Secondary Schools in Anhua County, *Hunan Education*, Issue 19, 2003.

[11] Ni Liren, Market Economy and the Layout of Middle Schools, *Journal of Lishui Teachers College* (Social Science Edition), Issue 1, 1995.

affect running of unified schools, as villagers may "be afraid that their children will be bullied if they have to go to school in other villages".[12]

7.1.3 *Limitations of Existing Research*

The research by the Yunnan Academy of Educational Sciences demonstrates that comprehensive primary schools can bring more economic and social benefits than teaching posts, and thus established a theoretical basis for the geographic distribution adjustment policies of Yunnan Province. The method used in the research provided a reference, but there are some limitations regarding the comprehensive study on the geographic distribution adjustment of primary and secondary schools. For example, the research only involved a comparison between comprehensive primary schools and teaching posts, failing to consider the distribution adjustment of middle schools. In addition, the study did not involve the distribution adjustment process, not to mention diverse factors involved in the process. If these issues are not treated seriously, the goal of the distribution adjustment may not be achieved. Therefore, further research is needed on the geographic distribution adjustment process. The reports from practitioners are mostly empirical, summarizing some experiences and lessons, as well as analyzing several issues, all of which are mostly limited to their local areas, failing to analyze the overall situation across the country, or to provide academic analysis on the geographic distribution adjustment of rural primary and secondary schools.

Therefore, it is necessary to put forward an overall framework to analyze the geographic distribution adjustment of rural primary and secondary schools across China.

7.2 Analytical Framework for Adjustment in Geographical Distribution of Rural Primary and Secondary Schools

Drawing on relevant research at home and abroad and practices in geographic distribution adjustment, the following issues need to be considered when analyzing the adjustment process of rural primary and secondary schools in China.

- Why is it necessary to conduct geographic distribution adjustment? (for any region, what are the major motivations and resistance to the adjustment? Does the decision to adjust the geographic distribution of rural primary and secondary schools come from instructions of the central government or the local government? Or is it just the wishes of the grassroots education administrative officials, or the needs of local people?)

[12] Yuan Xianrong, Difficulties and Countermeasures in the Layout Adjustment of Schools in Poor Mountainous Areas, *Guizhou Education*, Issues 1 and 2, 2001.

- What are the basic conditions for the geographic distribution adjustment? Such conditions will directly affect the handling of possible issues in the adjustment, such as the acceptance of the local residents, the arrangement of redundant school staff, full-time teachers and substitute teachers after the merger, as well as fundraising for renovating or expanding school buildings, etc.
- In what way is the geographic distribution adjustment carried out? Is it radical, led by administrative power, requiring completion in a short period of time? Or is it gradual, under the guidance of the government, with parents spontaneously sending their children to schools in towns or counties?
- The geographic distribution of schools reflects the interest pattern of governments at all levels and stakeholders. How to deal with issues such as fund allocation, public goods sharing and personnel arrangement in the adjustment process?
- In the process of geographic distribution adjustment, will the status of disadvantaged groups deteriorate and will their interests be harmed? How to solve the additional burden on families and children with financial difficulties caused by the adjustment?
- What are the related consequences of the adjustment?

To answer the questions above, we try to design a framework to analyze the distribution adjustment of rural primary and secondary schools.

7.2.1 *The Background and Rationale of Geographic Distribution Adjustment*

As early as the 1980s, some areas in China had adjusted the geographic distribution of rural primary and secondary schools because of changes in the school-age population. However, according to related reports, the geographic distribution adjustment across the country was mainly performed in the middle and late 1990s and after 2000, indeed a lot happened after 2002. In some areas, adjusting the geographic distribution of rural primary and secondary schools was not initiated until 2003 and 2004. Therefore, in the past 10 years, the adjustment in various regions was not at the same stage, and the problems faced may be very different. Since the early 1990s, there have been major measures on universalizing rural compulsory education by various levels of government, such as the Campaign for Compulsory Education, the first to fourth Basic Education in Poor and Minority Areas Project by the World Bank, the National Compulsory Education Project, and the National Dilapidated Building Renovation Project, as well as rural tax and fee reform that have been gradually rolled out nationwide since 2000, etc. Most of these major projects or policies required corresponding geographic distribution adjustment of primary and secondary schools in various regions. The impact of these major projects or major policies varies from place to place. In addition, financial conditions of places are different, so challenges faced in the adjustment process also different.

In a nutshell, the background of the geographic distribution adjustment of rural primary and secondary schools, or the source of the legitimacy of the adjustment policy, is mainly concentrated in two aspects: pursuit of efficiency in the economy and improvement of education equality in the society.

7.2.1.1 The Scale and Benefits of School Running

Most provinces in China have achieved universal nine-year compulsory education around the mid-1990s. In the process of popularizing compulsory education, the model of establishing schools in every village was promoted to achieve enrollment at the closest location. Under this school-running model, schools are scattered and small in scale. At that time, multi-channel financing for rural compulsory education made this model feasible, because rural schools mainly relied on local residents to raise funds. Establishing a local school was directly related to the vital interests of the local people, therefore it was relatively easy to mobilize the people to donate to the local school.

Around 2000, the basic conditions that supported the scattered school distribution structure changed radically. In some areas, primary and secondary schools were eventually unable to keep running due to the decrease in number of students. This situation occurred earlier in more advanced areas, and later in less developed ones. The following reasons may have caused the situation.

- China implemented a family planning policy in rural areas in the 1980s, which led to a sharp decline in the number of births and a consequent decrease in the school-age population.
- With deepening of modernization, people's willingness to have more children is decreasing. In addition, China implemented a strict family planning policy at that time, which gradually changed the structure of school-age population. In many places, the peak of enrollment has shifted from primary school to middle school, and then to high school.
- The impact of urbanization. The distribution of educational resources in China is unbalanced, and the quality of education in cities or towns is better. With accelerated urbanization, rural students' desire to study in cities or towns increased, and urbanization provided them with ways to do so. In particular, migrant workers may send their children to schools in towns or where they work, resulting in a decrease in the number of students in rural schools.
- Competition among schools. In recent years, competition among rural schools has intensified. Parents are more willing to send their children to schools with better quality and higher reputation, which has led to a sharp decline in the number of students in schools with worse conditions. Emergence of private schools in some places has also intensified the competition.
- Fast and convenient transportation in the process of urbanization has changed people's "sense of distance" and made it much more convenient for local people to travel between urban and rural areas. Consequently, there have been competitions

among cities, counties, towns, and rural areas for excellent teachers and students. Private primary and middle schools in large or medium-sized cities attracted a large number of excellent teachers from counties or districts within a certain radius. After losing excellent teachers, county schools will take advantage of their location and attract better teachers from towns or villages within the county. In this way, after level-by-level pumping, quality of education in rural primary and secondary schools could become worse as it goes to lower-level schools, and there is even a phenomenon of "hollowing out". Under such circumstances, students are more likely to leave rural schools and transfer to other schools for better education, and it will be more difficult for weak rural schools to recruit enough students.

When investigating in Xinjiang Uygur Autonomous Regions, the author found that the above-mentioned reasons have also appeared in Barkol Kazak Autonomous (hereinafter referred to as Barkol) County, which can be used as a case to vividly illustrate the school distribution situation caused by the above factors.[13] Barkol is a designated poverty-stricken county in Hami Prefecture of Xinjiang, also a border county and minority autonomous county. According to statistics at the beginning of September 2006, there were 6313 primary school-age children in the county. Among them, 1307 students had registered permanent residence in the jurisdiction but were studying outside the county (i.e., transient students[14]), accounting for 20.7% of the total number of school-age children. In the rural areas of Barkol with 3432 primary school-age children and 986 transient students, this proportion was close to 30% (28.7%). At the middle level, the county had a total of 3308 middle school-age students, of which 840 went to school elsewhere, accounting for 25.4% of all middle school-age teenagers. Among them, the total number of school-age teenagers in urban middle schools was 474, and only 60 studied outside the jurisdiction, accounting for 12.7%. The total number of middle school-age teenagers in agricultural areas was 1823, and there were 590 students studying outside the jurisdiction, accounting for 32.4%. The total number of middle school-age teenagers in pastoral areas was 1011, and the number of students with registered permanent residence studying outside the jurisdiction was 190, accounting for 18.8%. Obviously, the proportion of students in Barkol's agricultural areas studying outside the jurisdiction was much higher than that of urban and pastoral areas. To further analyze the situation of transient students in 7 villages and towns in the agricultural areas of Barkol, the number of students studying abroad was divided into primary and middle schools as shown in Table 7.1.

As shown in Table 7.1, the proportion of school-age students going to school outside the jurisdiction of the agricultural townships of Barkol was higher at both levels. Among them, Shannan Development Zone is close to Hami City and had the

[13] Information about Barkol Kazak Autonomous County comes from Guo Jianru, A Study on Investment and Benefits of Rural Compulsory Education in Areas with large ethnic minority populations of Western China, Graduate School of Education of Peking University, 2007.

[14] The "transient students" refer to students whose household registration (*hukou*) or school registration is inconsistent with the school they are attending. For example, a student whose registration is at school A but actually is studying at school B.

Table 7.1 Transient students in rural primary and secondary schools in Barkol

Name of township	Primary school level			Middle school level		
	School-age population (people)	Number of transient students (people)	Percentage of transient students (%)	School-age population (people)	Number of transient students (people)	Percentage of transient students (%)
Dahe	1434	489	34	781	316	40
Kuisu	770	175	23	378	108	29
Huayuan	345	41	12	183	26	14
Shirenzi	617	189	31	331	85	26
Shannan development zone	121	70	58	67	42	63
Santanghu	100	13	13	58	4	7
Liangzhongchang	45	9	20	25	9	36
The county total	6313	1307	20.7	3308	840	25.4

highest proportion of transient students at both levels, 58% at the primary level and 63% at the middle school level. In towns with larger school-age population, such as Dahe, Shirenzi, and Kuisu, the proportion of students enrolled in schools outside the town was also pretty high. The proportion of students attending outside primary schools of Dahe reached 34%, and that of middle schools reached 40%.

The situation of studying outside of Barkol's agricultural areas is further divided into two categories, namely, out-of-town and out-of-county, as shown in Table 7.2.

It can be seen from Table 7.2 that among the county's primary-level transient students, 68% were studying in other counties. In Shannan Development Zone, Kuisu and Dahe Town, the proportion of students studying in other counties was higher, 97%, 85%, and 82% respectively. The proportion of middle school level transient students in the three townships was also very high, 100%, 90% and 73%, respectively. Shannan Development Zone had more students attracted to Hami City due to geographical proximity. Kuisu and Dahe had a higher proportion of students studying in other counties, mainly in places where their parents work or schools with better education quality.

It can also be seen from Table 7.2 that in some townships, there were more students studying outside the jurisdiction of the town and within the county, such as Huayuan, Santanghu, and Liangzhongchang. 64% of the middle school students in Shirenzi studied in another town of the county. The investigation found that most of the students schooling outside their hometown but within the county attended schools in the county seat. This can be found from the survey of the student source of Barkol No. 1 Middle School, a middle school in Barkol, as shown in Table 7.3.

Among the 273 students in the first grade of Barkol No. 1 Middle School, 70.0% were from outside the school's jurisdiction. 63.3% of the 311 second-year and 68.7% of the 335 third-year students were from outside the jurisdiction. Contrary to Barkol

Table 7.2 Children schooling outside their hometowns in Barkol

Name of township	Primary school students					Middle school students				
	Total number (people)	Out-of-town		Out-of-county		Total number (people)	Out-of-town		Out-of-county	
		Total (people)	Percentage (%)	Total (people)	Percentage (%)		Total (people)	Percentage (%)	Total (people)	Percentage (%)
Dahe	598	109	18	489	82	435	119	27	316	73
Kuisu	206	31	15	175	85	120	12	10	108	90
Huayuan	166	125	75	41	25	123	97	79	26	21
Shirenzi	292	103	35	189	65	238	153	64	85	36
Shannan Development Zone	72	2	3	70	97	42			42	100
Santanghu	78	65	83	13	17	53	49	92	4	8
Liangzhongchang	45	36	80	9	20	20	11	55	9	45
The county total	1457	471	32	986	68	1,031	441	43	590	57

Table 7.3 Number of students of Barkol No. 1 middle school

First grade			Second grade			Third grade		
Total (people)	Within the jurisdiction (people)	Outside the jurisdiction (people)	Total (people)	Within the jurisdiction (people)	Outside the jurisdiction (people)	Total (people)	Within the jurisdiction (people)	Outside the jurisdiction (people)
273	82	191	311	114	197	335	105	230
Percentage (%)	30.0	70.0	Percentage (%)	36.7	63.3	Percentage (%)	31.3	68.7

No. 1 Middle School which had attracted more high-quality students from villages in the county, in some towns of Barkol, the number of students for primary and secondary schools had greatly declined. Among them, two schools were the most typical. Zhanjiang Minhan School in the Shannan Development Zone had 8 teachers but only 13 students, the Shirenzi School had 11 teachers but only 30 students. The school principals from Dahe Town reported that their local excellent students were massively transferring to Barkol No. 1 Middle School, making it difficult for local rural schools to survive.

From the case of Barkol, we can see the impact of better educational resources, urbanization, labor mobility, and competition from high-quality schools within the county on the distribution of students. For the disadvantaged schools in the competition, it means fewer students with more teachers and worse inefficiency. Since it is impossible to invest additional resources in the losing rural schools, keeping operating such schools will also have an impact on their students' equitable access to high-quality educational resources.

7.2.1.2 The Pursuit of Fairer Educational Resource Allocation

China's rural policies have undergone major changes since late 1990s. The Chinese government strives to build a harmonious society. Governments at all levels are required to establish a public finance system and compensate rural areas and villagers. During the 10th Five-year Plan period, the central government invested all the incremental education funds in rural education. Under the leadership of the central government, local governments at all levels began to prioritize more balanced allocation of educational resources and tilt educational resources towards rural areas.

The popularization of modern basic education generally follows an inter-regional hierarchy system, and the allocation of modern educational resources is correspondingly distributed along the hierarchical system. Within a province, from the provincial capital city to prefecture-level city, then to county units—townships—and rural areas, quantity of educational resources decreases level by level. The lower the school level, the lower the quality of education. Although modern compulsory education has a history of nearly a hundred years since it was introduced in China, there are still teaching posts and one-teacher schools in many rural areas. In these teaching posts, the curriculum is incomplete, with no music, physical or art education. Some village-based primary schools in the western region are still seriously short of basic hardware and teaching staff. Therefore, it is difficult for them to implement curriculum reform and provide quality education to rural students.

During the annual National People's Congress (NPC) and the Chinese People's Political Consultative Conference (CPPCC) sessions (the "Two Sessions") in recent years, education, especially rural education, has become a hot topic. Proposals from the Two Sessions and media opinions have put pressure on the government. Many local governments have begun to pay attention to the education gap in rural areas and education resource balancing strategies have been implemented. The traditional small and scattered distribution of rural primary and secondary schools has obviously become a major obstacle to quickly shortening the gap between rural and urban education, as the cost would be too high for the government to make all the scattered rural schools reach the average level of urban schools.

7.2.1.3 The Rural Basic Education Management System Reform and the Government's Finance Pressure

The overall time schedule for the geographical distribution adjustment of rural primary and secondary schools in China is relatively tight, and in a certain area, the adjustment time arrangement is relatively concentrated. This has a lot to do with the government's leading role in the adjustment process and carrying out the adjustment in an administrative manner. The direct driving force for the government to dominate the adjustment process includes financial pressure on local governments and political pressure from higher-level governments. These two kinds of pressures are rooted in the major changes in China's compulsory education management system, particularly the education financing system after 2000.

Around the mid-1990s, when nine-year compulsory education in rural areas was popularized in eastern and central China, the financial responsibility for compulsory education in rural areas was mainly borne by local rural residents. After 2000, when the eastern and central regions were consolidating and improving nine-year compulsory education in rural areas, and the western regions were accelerating universal rural compulsory education in rural areas, the management system and finance system of rural basic education changed. Rural basic education changed from township management to county-based management. The rural tax and fee reform abolished the "three deductions" (for public reserve funds, public welfare funds and management fees) and the "five charges" (rural education surcharges, family planning, militia training, rural road construction and subsidies to entitled groups) collected from villagers, and education surcharges and reserve funds were also cancelled. Then agricultural taxes were gradually abolished across the country. In January 2006, the Regulation of the People's Republic of China on Agriculture Tax was abolished. Since then, funds to support rural education from villagers were greatly reduced and could only rely on the county government.

In many rural areas in central and western China, county and township finances are basically still supported by government funding. Teachers, accounting for a large proportion, more than half in many places of local personnel, were financially supported by local finances. As a political task, teachers' salaries should be guaranteed first under public finance. This may lead to dissatisfaction toward the education sector from other departments of the local government, and put the education sector under great pressure. After the implementation of county-based management, county-level finance has to bear more education investment. Therefore, county-level governments have greater motivation to pursue economies of scale in school running. In some counties, local finances are not self-sufficient, and most of the fiscal expenditure including education expenditures depend on transfer payments from higher-level governments. Transfer payments often pose requirements for higher efficiency, which will also prompt local governments to adjust the distribution of rural schools.

When local governments are under pressure from higher-level governments to adjust the rural school distribution, the strong administrative mobilizing capabilities of the government management system during the planned economy period can easily be used, forming a top-down movement. For example, if a provincial or municipal government decides to vigorously implement the school distribution adjustment, it will make the adjustment an important part of the county and township governments' performance evaluation, and thus accelerate the adjustment.

Among the above-mentioned factors, reduction of rural school-age population is fundamental, which exposed the flaws of scale inefficiency and poor quality of the "village-run school" that was originally carried out for universal compulsory education. Obviously, the "village-run schools" structure will not be able to support better or fairer education. It gives legitimacy to local governments for the school distribution adjustment, but it does not necessarily mean that government's behavior has been recognized by the society. Local governments have to strive for the support of the local community to resolve resistance from locals.

7.2.2 The Geographic Distribution and Interest Pattern of China's Rural Education

7.2.2.1 School Distribution Reflects the Pattern of Interest While the Distribution Adjustment Changed the Controlling Structure of Rural Schools

The geographic distribution of education is a spatial reflection of the interest pattern. The spatial pattern reflects the interest arrangements of various stakeholders, such as villages, township-level governments, county governments, and the interest relationships among students, parents, and different types of teachers.

The geographic distribution of rural primary and secondary schools is basically a vertical top-down structure, with high schools located in county towns at the top, township middle schools in the middle, village-level schools with a large number of primary schools and teaching posts at the bottom. Teaching posts and comprehensive primary schools have a very close relationship with the local community, because their school assets are closely related to the local community's input. For example, the schools' land and buildings may be provided by villages, and most of the students come from the local villages. Some full-time and substitute teachers are also from the local villages. These rural schools' operation is affected by local villages in many aspects.

The rural tax and fee reform have effectively changed the way external forces affect rural schools by establishing a county-based rural compulsory education management system. Teachers' salaries are uniformly paid by the county government. Education funding is also directly appropriated by the county government. The power and ability of villages in rural school running are greatly weakened, the impact of local forces greatly reduced. Especially after the dismissal of substitute teachers from local villages, rural schools are staffed with only full-time teachers and school funding mainly rely on the government. Financially, rural schools then become public schools and an extension of the public education system in the countryside instead of being a simple graft with rural organizational structures. The rural tax and fee reform have reduced the legitimacy of rural community's influence on education, while most rural areas have not generated new forms of organization to participate in local school management.

The school distribution adjustment during or after the tax and administrative charge reform can cause more complicated issues. The adjustment spatially "pulled" schools out of the countryside, making schools gradually concentrated in towns, counties and cities. Education is a public good, and a local school can bring honor as well as direct and indirect benefits to the local community. For example, it is more convenient for local children to go to a local school, and for parents to communicate with teachers in time. If the local school is merged, these benefits will disappear. Moreover, if the school is mainly funded by the local community, the dissolution of the school will directly involve the disposal of related assets. The merger of primary schools will involve the relationship between the school and the local villages, and the distribution adjustment at the middle school level will involve more villages, even townships.

7.2.2.2 Spatial Distribution Patterns of Rural Schools

The geographic distribution adjustment of rural primary and secondary schools has many forms, which can be summarized as follows: (a) schools jointly run by several adjacent villages, such as selecting a site in the center of several villages and building a new school; (b) building a nine-year consistent school in the center of several adjacent villages, and merging all the surrounding primary and middle schools; (c) schools run by local community and enterprises jointly; (d) two village schools complementing each other by running different grades, with one principal appointed to be responsible for school administration; (e) schools co-sponsored by cross-township; (f) setting up a central branch: all middle and upper grade students will go to the central branch school and lower grade students will stay in the village schools with classes of mixed grades (not an independent school), the central branch will implement all-around management; (g) entrusted schools: a school is unable to complete the teaching work of every grade, and entrusts students of some grades to another school; (h) boarding schools; (i) setting up teaching posts: combine the upper grades of several schools into one school, and change the lower grades into teaching posts; (j) interspersed merger: school A's several grades are merged into school B, and school B's several grades are merged into school A; (k) schools run by groups: in some places in Zhejiang Province, a teaching group is established with a high-quality and well-known local school as the leader, the teaching group manages local public primary and secondary schools across villages and towns, implements overall supervision of education quality, and uniformly allocates educational resources, etc.[15]

In several provinces such as Heilongjiang, Hubei, Hunan, and Zhejiang, the above-mentioned practices were mostly adopted. Particularly, several neighboring villages or administrative villages, and several neighboring towns jointly running schools under the leadership of the higher-level government is a common practice.

7.2.2.3 Stakeholders Involved in Joint School-Running

In the process of distribution adjustment of rural primary and secondary schools, village-village joint school-running and town-town joint school-running are common forms. Joint school-running is actually an organizational form of contract, the core of which is coordination of interests. Therefore, it is necessary to conduct a detailed analysis of the interests and stakeholders involved in this organizational form.

1. *Schools Jointly Run by Villages*

This arrangement involves issues such as which school should be appointed as the dominant school, how the assets of the merged schools should be disposed of, how the assets of the new schools will be composed of, how to share rights and interests among villages (such as sharing of land purchase and campus construction costs, etc. It may also involve the naming rights of the new school, whether the new school name should be based on where it is located or just use a new name, etc.), potential conflicts and disputes in new school distribution planning and implementation, and how to resolve such conflicts and disputes, etc.

As mentioned earlier, schools are regarded as a kind of public welfare and a symbol of social reputation in rural society, so investing in schools has become the focus of symbolic capital competition. Some villagers may take various measures to oppose closures or mergers of schools in their community. To this end, villagers can put pressure on the local government, or raise funds to build their own schools and hire teachers to run the schools. For this kind of problem, there are many solutions in reality, such as rebuilding a new school at the center of several villages, and merging the original schools in each village to balance related interests. Ning'an County in Heilongjiang Province adopted this method in its rural school distribution adjustment. There were four primary schools in the five villages, Linjiang, Lincheng, Jiaoyu, Xingsheng, and Xinsheng, all of which are in the eastern part of Ning'an Town. They chose a school site in the center village, and all the villages raised funds to build the first primary school of Ning'an Town. The new school's maximum service

[15] The Investigation Group on Optimizing Educational Resources Allocation in Primary and Secondary Schools, A Survey Report on Adjusting the Layout of Primary and Secondary Schools, *Education Exploration*, Issue 2, 2000.

radius is only 1.5 km. Similarly, seven villages of Lianhua Area, Bohai Town, jointly built a school with standard nine-year schooling in Tianxin Village in the central area. The new school absorbed all the original six primary schools and one middle school, and also dispatched school buses daily to pick up students on time for the three distant villages. In order to fund the new school, the Ning'an City Education Commission signed agreements with each participating village. The agreement states the terms of how much each village should pay each year to prevent villages that do not run school after joining the new school from doing nothing.[16] A field study in Suyu County of Jiangsu Province found, when several villages jointly build a school, some villages are willing to donate part of their land to the school for free in order to strive for the school to be located within the territory of the village. Guidong County of Hunan Province established a system of "cooperation in building school, operating school and managing school". Schools involved in multi-township and multi-village education set up a joint committee, and involving towns and villages jointly assume the responsibility of school running according to the statutes of the joint committee.[17]

2. *Joint School Running Across Townships*

This involves coordination among towns, but the coordination has a cost. According to the author's survey in Henan's rural areas, students of some villages have traditionally attended schools in other towns due to geographical proximity to other towns. However, in the geographic distribution adjustment, schools were established in their own villages.

3. *School Closure or Merger Related to Funding from Overseas Chinese*

The school geographic adjustment process will also involve the closure and merger of some schools built with donations from overseas Chinese. The overseas Chinese donating funding to set up schools is a manifestation of their love, and thus they have won high social honors in local areas, which is more common in Guangdong and Fujian provinces. Therefore, how to protect the enthusiasm of overseas Chinese in supporting China's education during the geographic adjustment process deserves serious consideration.

4. *Define the Rights and Interests of Residents and the Power of Educational Administration when Making School Distribution Adjustments*

During the process of adjustment, merger of schools in some urban communities has led to disputes over rights between the community and the Education Bureau.[18] This is the case in Qianxi Community of Haizhu District in Guangzhou City. The local

---

[16] Yang Ping, A Useful Exploration in Rural School Layout Adjustment, *School Administration*, Issue 12, 1998.

[17] Li Lun'e, et al., Improving Benefits by Adjusting School Layout: Understanding Educational Development in Poverty-stricken Areas from the Guidong Phenomenon, *Hunan Education*, Issue 2, 1999.

[18] http://gz.focus.cn/msgview/21484/2/17464053.html, To refute Haizhu Education Bureau's reply, September 10, 2004.

community questioned the arrangements and reasons for the closure and merger of their community supporting school, and resisted the Education Bureau's decision. Similar problems may also occur in rural areas, although strategies adopted may be somewhat different.

5. *Funding Structure Among Different Levels of Governments*

The allocation of funding between upper and lower level governments in geographic distribution adjustment includes how to allocate the proportion shared by the central and provincial governments; how much funding should be provided by the county and township governments. Although rural compulsory education implements a county-based management system, many local county-level governments usually try to encourage townships to carry out relevant distribution adjustments. Meanwhile, the funding and responsibility sharing ratio between the county and township-level governments should be determined according to the importance attached by the township government to the school adjustment and the local finance affordability.

6. *Disposal of Related Assets and the Interest Coordination among Related Investors*

Investors include not only individual families, villages and towns as a whole, but also county- and township-level governments. The school spatial location reflects an interest pattern, which is the result of all relevant parties' joint action. It is worth exploring proper methods in dealing with the issues above.

7.2.3 Decision-Making, Administrative Process and Methods in the School Geographic Adjustment

China has a vast territory with large regional disparities, and levels of social, economic and educational development vary from region to region. The time to popularize nine-year compulsory education in rural areas and the level of compulsory education development vary greatly. Therefore, the basis for the geographic distribution adjustment, the pressure and factors impacting the adjustment are also different, which may cause different regions to adopt very different methods in managing the adjustment.

7.2.3.1 Educational Policies and Administrative Methods of the Central and Provincial Governments

The central and provincial governments generally have two types of requirements for the geographic distribution adjustment of rural primary and secondary schools. The first type is mandatory constraints, such as rigid regulations on the staffing of primary and secondary schools, combining relevant standards with the performance assessment of local officials. The second type is principled regulations. Requirements for vulnerable group protection often fall into this category. Mandatory constraints are usually rigid and are the main content when higher-level governments evaluate lower-level governments. Principled regulations are often flexible. In the geographic distribution adjustment, it is naturally easy to highlight the former, while the latter usually becomes a negotiable and even insignificant. Therefore, some local governments often ignore public interests in order to ensure their performance evaluation. This reflects the double-edged sword characteristics of bureaucracy. While ensuring the superficial effect of policy implementation, bureaucracy may ignore or deviate from public interests, the original intention of the policy.

7.2.3.2 Two Main Administrative Methods of County Governments

The geographic distribution adjustment of rural primary and secondary schools is usually implemented by governments at all levels from top to bottom. The pressure exerted by the provincial or higher-level governments on lower-level governments will greatly affect the administrative method adopted by local governments. In general, China's local governments usually have adopted two ways in the distribution adjustment of rural primary and secondary schools. One way is to take use of administrative power to launch promoting campaigns, which are deployed within a certain time limit and completed at a relatively fast speed. The other way is to use guidance and/or inducement, which is slower and the adjustment process requires more use of market mechanisms, planned and step-by-step implementation in accordance with the population decline trend, and finally bringing students to the target schools. These two ways are similar to the "imposed change" and "induced change" proposed in the theory of institutional change. In imposed changes, administrative mobilization is the main force. In the mid-1990s, most provinces in China adopted this method to popularize the nine-year compulsory education in rural areas. The distribution adjustment of primary and middle schools in most areas was also implemented with this method after 2000. But there were some places adopting "induced change" approach in the distribution adjustment. Local education administrative authorities usually implement distribution adjustment in a relatively modest manner, concentrating high-quality resources in some center schools, and allowing these schools to naturally attract local population.

Under what conditions will the local government tend to adopt the method of imposed change and under what conditions will it tend to adopt the method of induced change? The following factors may have an important impact on the adjustment method chosen by the local government:

- Administrative pressure from superiors. In the central and western regions of China, and even some less developed areas in the east, some county governments are still accustomed to administrative and imposed manners in policy implementation, so they may naturally tend to adopt this method in the school geographic distribution adjustment. In order to speed up the adjustment, higher-level governments usually take three ways to motivate lower-level governments. The first is to adopt a "one size fits all" policy, which strictly controls the staffing of primary and secondary schools. The second is to provide rewards and incentives based on the speed of completing the adjustment. The third is to link government officials' work in school adjustment with their annual performance evaluation.

- The administrative tradition and culture of local governments. In areas where market economy is relatively developed, the government has a strong sense of the rule of law, and local people have a strong sense of individual rights protection, then the local government is less likely to adopt mandatory changes.
- Fiscal capability of the local government. In areas where the local government has relatively abundant financial resources, two methods can be adopted: the local government can make hard adjustments and then fiscally subsidize schools, or it can also continuously strengthen center schools to make them attractive to students and parents. In areas where local governments do not have sufficient financial resources to support concentrated school running, rural school dismantling and merging is always slower. For example, for many poor areas in Yunnan Province, all the local governments can do is to merge teaching posts with village-run comprehensive primary schools. However, as our field study shows, in Zitong County of Sichuan Province, there are very few comprehensive schools in villages, so rural primary school students have begun to transfer to schools located in township centers.
- Geography and transportation. In areas with better geographical conditions, it is easier to run schools in a centralized manner due to convenient transportation, and there is no need to set up a boarding system. Therefore, the local government can greatly reduce the number of schools. However, it is much more difficult to do so in areas with complex geographical environment and inconvenient transportation, such as mountainous areas.
- Local residents' affordability and desire to accept the school distribution adjustment. The adjustment brings not only direct or indirect economic burden to local people, but also psychological impacts. In particular, rural schools named after local villages, which are mainly built with local funding, have become an important part of the local cultural system. School closures and mergers may be unacceptable to many local people. This is especially the case if a village school is merged into other neighboring villages.
- The level of educational development. If compulsory education has been popularized, parents would have a strong desire for their children to receive high-quality education. The distribution adjustment will generally not cause more students to drop out of school. In some areas, the distribution adjustment was carried out in a planned and step-by-step manner, often combined with some other major projects. This may make it easier for local people to accept the adjustment. If local compulsory education is less popularized, or local education is less developed, the distribution adjustment would be more likely to be resisted by the local people.

- The speed and scale of decline in school-age population. If school-age population has decreased significantly, or has been slowly decreasing but has shown a significant decrease after a long period of time, local people will be more willing to accept large-scale and rapid adjustment.
- Resistance from local teachers. The dissolution of schools will inevitably involve rearrangement of teachers. Before the school geographic adjustment, some regions had more substitute teachers, while some had fewer substitute teachers and more full-time teachers. Generally, in areas where there were more substitute teachers, there was little resistance to the distribution adjustment, as substitute teachers were all temporary employees. In areas where there were fewer substitute teachers and more full-time teachers, school merger would encounter greater resistance from teachers. In Barkol County of Xinjiang, rural schools were mostly overstaffed. In some small primary and middle schools, number of teachers was even close to that of students. However, due to limited government financial resources and limited local employment opportunities, local government cannot provide re-employment opportunities for teachers who would suffer from job loss during the school distribution adjustment. The local education administration authority thus was worried that large-scale school distribution adjustment will cause dissatisfaction from local teachers, and thus cannot effectively carry out large-scale distribution adjustments.[19]

7.2.3.3 Case Study: Mandatory Administrative Methods of County Governments

In Zibo City of Shandong Province and Suqian City of Jiangsu Province, the basic adjustment approach was cadres at all levels contracting a certain area within the specified time, such as county cadres contracting townships, township cadres contracting villages, combined with guiding public opinion, mobilizing all the stakeholders by public conferences, and promoting best practices in the region.

Case 1. The Geographic Distribution Adjustment Practice in Zibo City of Shandong Province

Zibo's rural primary and secondary school distribution adjustment meeting was held in its Zhoucun District on September 22, 2004. The leaders of Education Bureau put forward seven major requirements for the work:

- Clarify priorities. The focus of the distribution adjustment for Zibo's rural primary and secondary schools is to do everything possible to complete the tasks in 2004. Those schools that should be closed and merged will be done. The construction of new schools must get started in 2004.

[19] Guo Jianru, Report on Investment and Benefits of Rural Compulsory Education in Ethnic Minority Regions in Western China, Graduate School of Education of Peking University, 2007.

- Supervision at all levels. The education administrative departments at all levels must do a good job in supervising the adjustment process. The city will organize relevant personnel to conduct supervision on a county-by-county, town-by-town, and school-by-school basis to guarantee the progress in a timely manner. Results of the all level supervision should be reported to the relevant departments of the municipal government as well as county governments and education administrative departments.
- Focus on publicity. To vigorously publicize the significance, goals, tasks, achievements and experience of distribution adjustment through various forms. The purpose is to seek the support of all administrators, win the understanding of parents and the general public, and create a good social atmosphere for promoting the adjustment of rural primary and secondary schools.
- Gain support from paired assistance providers. Further seek the support of all paired assistance providers and fully mobilize the forces of all sectors of society to support the school distribution adjustment. In particular, this is of greater significance to mountainous and reservoir areas.
- Guide scheduling. All administrative departments of education should make timely arrangements for the adjustment and give scientific guidance in a timely manner.
- Review and awards. Timely review the achievements made in the adjustment of the distribution of rural primary and secondary schools and honor those districts, counties and townships that have completed the annual adjustment tasks, and incorporate this review into the scope of supervision and evaluation of districts, counties and townships.
- Implement accountability. To decompose the goals and tasks of school distribution adjustment to each division of the education administration, and to each township and each individual. The members of the leadership team of the municipal education bureau should cover the districts and counties, and the members of the leadership team of the county education administrative department should cover the townships to supervise and guide in a timely manner to ensure the completion of the task of adjusting the distribution of rural primary and secondary schools.[20]

Case 2. The Geographic Distribution Adjustment Practice in Suqian City of Jiangsu Province

In 2001, the Suqian city government took the distribution adjustment of primary and secondary schools and the renovation of dilapidated school buildings as major projects. At the same time, it included the progress of the two projects in the performance evaluation of local government officials. Each county/district government signed a responsibility contract with the city government. The city government established a special leading group for the two projects, with an executive deputy mayor and executive deputy secretary as group leaders, and members of leaders from government agencies such as education, finance, planning, construction, agriculture, land, and taxation. The city decided to win a "tough battle" by pooling all the resources

[20] Zibo Bureau of Education News Relwase. The rural primary and secondary school distribution adjustment meeting was held. September 2004.

available, and required the county party committees and governments to mobilize extensively and work hard. In some counties, government secretaries and supervisors participated in person, and each cadre at or above the middle level in the education administration was in charge of a township or a school. Under such a mobilization and incentive system, the rural school distribution adjustment in Suqian City has indeed fulfilled the task very well. During the "Two Sessions" in 2003, a representative analyzed the problems posed by the approach the government mobilized and implemented the school redistribution policy.

In response to the adjustment of the distribution adjustment of primary and secondary schools, the municipal government and education authorities have successively issued a series of relevant documents and measures, which have achieved certain results. However, there are still some issues that need to be addressed in the entire implementation process.

- *Inadequate publicity. Education is the concern of thousands of families, and the distribution adjustment touches the vital interests of various stakeholders. During the operation process, the education administrative department did not hold parents' meetings and briefing meetings communicating with all parties in a timely manner, but implemented the administrative order as soon as it arrived. So parents, society and even schools lacked necessary information and understanding, and lacked awareness of the importance of distribution adjustment. Consequently, they behaved negatively, resulting in failure in completing the adjustment in some areas as scheduled.*
- *Emergence of new inferior schools due to action with undue haste. The Provincial Department of Education required all localities to complete the distribution adjustment, with related tasks of renovating dilapidated school buildings and improving inferior schools completed in three to five years based on actual conditions. The city*'s *goal was to complete it within three years and strive for two years. Considering issues easily arising in the adjustment, the City Education Bureau clearly required that in practice, construction should be prior to closures, renovation prior to closures. Disorderly and blind closure or merger is strictly prohibited. However, to complete the required tasks in time, schools were often closed before renovated or new ones were built in some areas, resulting in a sudden increase in the number of students in the new center schools. The original buildings and teaching equipment could no longer meet daily needs, and a lot of safety risks have emerged. Lack of supporting facilities has also led to declining teaching quality and new inferior schools emerging.*
- *Merging schools but not building new schools is inconsistent with the original intention of "adjustment" to facilitate students' nearby enrollment. Many areas adopted a simplistic approach to the distribution adjustment, just closed or merged most schools, without considering whether the center school*'s *location is convenient for students and parents. Many parents had to send children to and pick them up from school by riding forty to fifty miles every day, although there are buses available, many rural families may not be able to afford to take the buses*

every day. Such inconvenience indeed had affected the normal work and life of rural families.[21]

The bureaucratic administrative system has a strong ability to mobilize social resources. Under China's planned economic system, implementing various reforms administratively was taken as the most important approach. Some local governments were still accustomed to this approach. For example, in Suqian many other reforms were also promoted through mandatory manners. Therefore, local governments were accustomed to apply the same approach to the distribution adjustment of rural primary and secondary schools. However, the administrative bureaucracy places special emphasis on being accountable to the superiors rather than subordinates, so the general public are often in a disadvantaged position and their interests are often ignored. The result of administrative mobilization, mandates, excessive policy steps may lead to conflicts with the original intention of "adjustment" and harm the interests of the public.

7.2.3.4 Case Study: Induced Methods of Local Governments at County/City Level

There is no doubt that government plays a driving role in the process of school distribution adjustment, but more importantly, some local governments seized the trend and gave full play to designated schools. Guidong County and Anhua County in Hunan Province are relatively successful cases in this regard.

Case 1. The Geographic Distribution Adjustment Practice in Guidong County of Hunan Province

Guidong's approach was summarized as "everyone moving to a better chair" by Li Lun'e.[22] With one or two new "chairs" made, those who used to sit on the slightly old chairs move to the new "chairs", and then those who used to sit on the half-old "chairs" move to the slightly old ones. By changing chairs one by one, everyone feels that they have moved to a better chair and thus are willing to accept the change. In Guidong county, the adjustment first relocated Chengguan Middle School and the County's No. 1 High School to newly built campuses, leaving their old campuses to the two secondary schools. The former secondary vocational school's buildings were handed over to the county's No. 2 High School, and the adult secondary school's buildings were handed over to the Zhaiqian middle school. If township middle schools were closed or merged, school buildings of the merged school were handed over to the township central primary school, and the township central primary school's old buildings may be grouped together and handed over to agricultural schools or to be used to build teachers' housing. In this way, school mergers did not require new

---

[21] Wang Dongping, Some Suggestions on the Layout Adjustment of Primary and Secondary Schools, Suqian City Forum. http://www.suqian.gov.cn/sqlh/011/rdvzx2003_011_015.htm.

[22] Li Lun'e et al., Improve Benefits by Adjusting School Layout Understanding Educational Development in Poverty-stricken Areas from the Guidong Phenomenon, *Hunan Education*, Issue 2, 1999.

funding to build new schools, but only moving schools to other "chairs", and each "chair" is better and more comfortable than the older one.

Case 2. The Geographic Distribution Adjustment Practice in Anhua County of Hunan Province

Anhua County is a county in Hunan Province. It integrates mountainous areas, reservoir areas and old revolutionary base areas. After a detailed field study, Li Maolin described Anhua's case in a research paper.[23]

In 1999, with the approval of the party committee and government of Anhua County, adjustment of school distribution was carried out in accordance with some clear principles, which included scientific planning, targeted guidance, easier issues first, urgent issues first, making full use of local conditions, and adjusting step by step. The county government clarified that the most critical task was to build center schools' reputation and thus students and parents will aspire to them. The key points in developing center schools included:

- Equipped with state-of-the-art hardware. After middle schools were all merged to the township central schools, central schools' teaching quality has been significantly improved with advanced hardware facilities. Some students from other towns have also sought to go to the township middle school.
- Hire excellent teachers. The county education bureau required that teachers in center schools must meet multiple criteria, including well-trained and devoting, having qualified education and excellent basic skills. The principals and backbones teachers of center schools were sent to Hunan Normal University and county training schools for further training. Dafu Town focused on improving school conditions, selecting the best teachers to teach in the center school, and thus the center school became the best school of the town. A total of 28 schools were removed and merged smoothly.
- Provide outstanding management services, in particular for boarding schools. In the process of adjusting the distribution of rural primary and secondary schools in Anhua County, the local government played a very important role, such as formulating plans, dismantling and merging inferior schools, actively communicating with relevant stakeholders, etc. Anhua County established a double linkage mechanism between the education sector and townships. The county government as well as each township set up a leading group for the distribution adjustment, responsible for planning, guidance, coordination, inspection, supervision, assessment, reward and punishment. The people's congress at the county and township levels were also functioning in approving the adjustment plans in their regions. The county party committee and the county government incorporated the adjustment into each township's dual-civilization progress assessment. It was stipulated that the newly-built schools in towns and villages must conform to the overall adjusting plan, capital investment to schools to be dismantled or merged must be ended, and funding allocation of future education projects would be linked to the progress of the distribution adjustment. Under the premise of not causing student

[23] Li Maolin et al., Efficiencyy and a Solid Leap Forward: Anhua County's Experience in Adjusting the Layout of Primary and Secondary Schools, *Hunan Education*, Issue 19, 2003.

dropout, RMB4000 was awarded for each school closed or merged. The county education bureau included the adjustment progress into the annual assessment of towns by rewarding ten townships every year. Overall, the measures taken by the government were mainly induced. In implementation, the principle of "no close down or merger until conditions are ripe, and no close down or merger until the masses accept" has avoided a lot of potential resistance.

7.2.4 *Fund Demand and Investment Mechanism of the School Distribution Adjustment*

7.2.4.1 Fund Demand

Generally, expenditures required for the school distribution adjustment mainly include the following.

1. *Infrastructure costs*

Infrastructure costs are affected by the level of economic development, the goals of educational development, and the existing school distribution of an area. Within the same area, the infrastructure costs are mainly related to the existing school distribution. If the center school does not have enough buildings after merger, new buildings will need to be built or old ones renovated. Or if there is no proper school to function as the center school, it may be necessary to construct a new campus at a new site. If one of the schools is used as the center school, its campus can be expanded on the original basis. If the upper grades are concentrated into the center school, and the other schools become teaching posts with only lower grades, there may be no need for much infrastructure investment. In some mountainous areas with inconvenient transportation and less developed economy, large-scale distribution adjustment will require a lot of investment in infrastructure, especially if a boarding system is necessary.

2. *Personnel expenditures*

Personnel expenditures include two parts. One is the compensation for substitute teachers to be dismissed. In the distribution adjustment, most substitute teachers need to be removed when schools and teaching posts get closed or merged. The compensation system for substitute teachers is different among regions. Generally, compensation is determined by years of service. In some places, a one-time compensation of RMB3000 will be given to substitute teachers whose years of service are within a certain number. The other part of personnel expenses is fund to hiring new public teachers, due to the removal of substitute teachers. Newly hired public teachers are mostly college graduates, and their monthly income may be several times that of substitute teachers. If there are students in the lower grades of primary school that have to live in accommodation, childcare staff costs will further add to personnel expenses.

3. *Schooling expenses*

The distribution adjustment will directly bring about an increase in the schooling cost for students, especially accommodation and living expenses in the boarding system. Transportation expenses will occur for students whose families live far from school. Schooling expenses may be borne by families, or they may be subsidized by the government or borne by local communities.

4. *Other expenses*

The distribution adjustment will also produce some hidden costs. For example, some parents may choose to pick up and drop off their children at school every day due to safety concerns. In some areas, grandparents even rent an apartment close to the school to accompany their grandchildren.

Which institution or individuals should bear the above-mentioned expenses in the process of distribution adjustment depends on the local institutional arrangements as well as funding sources.

7.2.4.2 Possible Funding Sources for School Distribution Adjustment

1. *The Central Government Funding*

Since late 1990s, China's central government has increased its fiscal investment in basic education. The central government has promised that all the newly increased education funding during the 10th Five-year Plan period will be used for rural basic education. The state's direct investment in school distribution adjustment is relatively small, but many funds allocated in conjunction with the distribution adjustment are also available in the adjustment. For example, infrastructure and dilapidated building renovation funds in compulsory education projects are all related to basic construction.

The central budget has also supported distribution adjustment of some provinces. For example, in Henan Province, the distribution adjustment of primary schools, especially primary schools in mountainous areas, was the key. The central government gave Henan Province RMB200 million in special funds for universalizing nine-year compulsory education and basically eliminating illiteracy among young and middle-aged adults. The special funds were mainly used for the construction of boarding schools in rural areas, especially mountainous areas.[24] In principle, eastern provinces are more developed, and thus were able to fund the distribution adjustment by themselves. The central government had certain support for the central region, and more support for the western region.

2. *Provincial Government Funding*

[24] Distribution Layout Adjustment of Rural Primary and Secondary Schools in Henan Province. *Henan Daily*. August 20, 2004.

With changes in the rural compulsory education management system, the provincial government's responsibility in compulsory education has been continuously strengthened. Provincial governments have increased their support for less developed areas since 1990s. In implementing the rural tax and fee reform and the new rural compulsory education system, the provincial government has been actively promoting the distribution adjustment of rural primary and secondary schools, and imposed pressure on the city and county governments in implementing the distribution adjustment. For example, the distribution adjustment method in Suqian area in northern Jiangsu had a lot to do with the local administrative tradition, but it was also directly related to the mandatory requirements, even with a deadline for completion, by the provincial government. The director of the education department of Jiangsu Province has set a clear quantitative target for the distribution adjustment. The provincial government granted RMB100 million funds to advance the distribution adjustment, and subsidized the merged schools.

Since 2003, the distribution of Jiangsu's primary and secondary schools will be changed. Within two years, the number of primary schools in the province will be reduced to 9000, and the number of middle schools will be reduced to about 2200. The focus of 2003 is rural primary schools. Wang Bintai, Director of the Provincial Department of Education, said at the work conference on the distribution adjustment of primary and secondary schools and the "Three-New and One-Bright"[25] *project that was held. By the end of 2002, the province had 13,372 primary schools. In 2003, more than 4300 schools will have to be closed. In addition to facilitating joint action of middle schools and primary schools, actively promoting the boarding system, strengthening the construction of center schools, and temporarily retaining a few teaching posts in remote areas, the Provincial Department of Education will allocate RMB100 million to advance the distribution adjustment. For a few difficult counties in the northern and middle area, calculated based on the number of schools at the end of 2000, a local government will receive from the provincial government a subsidy of RMB30,000, RMB60,000, and RMB100,000 for each primary school, middle school, and senior high school removed. For places with more advanced economy, the local government should provide funds for the distribution adjustment by themselves.*

In some rural schools in northern Jiangsu, several students have to share one broken desk, with only one incandescent lamp in the classroom, and it is common that the school does not even have one intact podium. To this end, the Provincial Department of Education plans to implement the "Three-New and One-Bright" project for rural primary and secondary schools in two years to improve their basic conditions. In 2003, the project will be implemented in some counties and cities in northern Jiangsu.[26]

Prior to the large-scale distribution adjustment of rural primary and secondary schools, Jiangsu Province had provided fiscal support to several counties and cities

---

[25] "The new desks, new benches, new podium, bright lights" —Tr.

[26] Jiangsu Province adjusting the distribution of rural primary and secondary schools, more than 4300 primary schools will be closed, *Yangtse Evening Post*, July 3, 2003.

in northern Jiangsu for early distribution adjustment. For example, in 2001, Jiangsu formulated a plan for the distribution adjustment of primary and secondary schools, and allocated RMB250 million in special funds for the distribution adjustment and the renovation of dilapidated buildings. Most of the funds were allocated to rural areas in northern Jiangsu, where establishment and adjustment of rural primary and secondary schools were mainly planned by the county government. A total of 3476 primary and secondary schools were merged throughout the year, and another 1524 were converted into teaching posts.[27]

Guangdong is a more developed province in China. In adjusting rural primary and secondary schools, the provincial government invested considerable funds. According to the Guangdong Provincial Department of Education, by 2007, the Guangdong Provincial Department of Finance has planned to allocate more than RMB2.8 billion to support five cities outside the Pearl River Delta to carry out the distribution adjustment. The Provincial Department of Finance will also allocate RMB355.2 million for the third-batch school building renovation in old revolutionary base areas, including 1184 primary schools. In addition, living allowances for boarding students from families with a per capita income less than RMB1500 will be approved and delivered.[28] In 2003, the Provincial Government proposed that they would basically complete the distribution adjustment of rural schools in three years. In 2003 alone, the provincial government allocated RMB500 million of special funds to support the distribution adjustment of primary and secondary schools in eastern, western and northern Guangdong.[29]

3. *County Government Funding*

County governments are the main decision-making and implementing agencies for the distribution adjustment of rural primary and secondary schools. The fiscal resources available to county governments have a large impact on whether and what kind of distribution adjustment can be achieved, because not all counties and cities can get sufficient fiscal support from the central and provincial government. Funds for the distribution adjustment in many places mainly rely on local governments. Local governments usually adopt multiple methods to raise funds and treat different schools differently, such as Lingshi County, Shanxi.

Lingshi County of Shanxi Province raised funding through multiple channels such as the state, society, and individuals, to promote the distribution adjustment of primary and secondary schools. Constructing schools in the county seat and county affiliated schools will be incorporated into the overall urban planning. The distribution adjustment will be implemented with the county government's overall planning

[27] The "county-based" system of Jiangsu's rural basic education shows its effectiveness, Ministry of Education of China, January 17, 2002.

[28] Boarding primary and middle school students will receive living allowances, Jinyang Net-*New Express* September 23, 2004.

[29] Liu Kun, Guangdong's Taxes and Fees Reform will Definitely Get Rid of Huang Zongxi's Law, *Southern Metropolis Daily*, July 11, 2003.

and townships as the mainstay. From 2003 to 2004, the county government will allocate RMB4 million of special funding for the distribution adjustment. The implementation will be adopted in strict accordance with each township's fiscal capability and actual costs. In addition, funding obtained from the provincial and city government this year and next will be used as rewards and funding supplements for the distribution adjustment. The townships should take measures to increase investment in education, and secure the funding for the distribution adjustment.

4. *Township Government Funding*

Before the reform of rural tax and fee, township governments were responsible for rural compulsory education and township finance had to provide teachers' salaries and other operating funding for local schools. After the reform, the county-based management system was established, so fiscal responsibilities of townships were alleviated. In most rural areas, teachers' salaries are uniformly allocated by the county government in the form of special settlements. However, rural townships and villages still have certain responsibilities in local school running. The responsibilities of townships with insufficient fiscal resources are mainly to assure public security and strive for public support for local school running, such as mobilizing school-age children to go to school. Some rich townships still have the desire and ability to invest in schools and improve school-running conditions, where county governments usually also require them to assume certain financial responsibilities in the distribution adjustment. For example, Jiande city in Hangzhou has such a provision that required townships to provide 70% of the funding for the distribution adjustment.

5. *Funding from the Village*

After the reform of rural tax and fee, rural school management and related financial responsibilities have been transferred to the county level, but some wealthy villages still provide subsidies for the increase in schooling costs caused by the merger of the village school. For example, Leping town in Sanfeng district of Foshan City in Guangdong Province has provided two-level subsidies for students' transportation expenses. "As some students go to school far away, each township arranged a shuttle bus to pick up students to and from school. Leping Town arranges 25 buses per day. The expense is subsidized by the township government and village committees. Students and their families only pay RMB80 per semester."

6. *Funding from Rural Residents*

Before the reform of rural tax and fee, rural compulsory education funding was mainly from fundraising or education surcharges collected from local villagers, and paid in the form of the village or township government appropriation. The distribution adjustment has caused schooling costs to increase for many rural families, such as housing and related transportation expenses. Some parents from mountainous areas even had to rent an apartment close to the center school to accompany their children, further adding to schooling costs. The schooling costs were mostly borne by local families, and only a few poor families could receive government subsidies, but the the amount and scope of subsidies were restricted by the government's fiscal resources.

7. *Self-Raised Funds by Schools and Education Agencies*

The main channels of schools' self-raised funds are bank loans, loans from other organizations or individuals, and the surplus of miscellaneous fees from students. In addition, school-run enterprises and related work-study programs, temporary schooling fees, etc. may also become sources of funding. In the distribution adjustment, the proceeds from the sale and lease of school buildings of merged schools will also be used as part of the school's self-raised funds.

8. *Other Funding Sources*

Other funding sources may include funding support from paired assistance programs, pre-payments of the construction contractors, social donations, etc.

The amount and proportion of funds that different counties could obtain from the above-mentioned channels are quite different. Some sources of funds are only a possibility, and in fact they are basically useless or do not need to be used.

7.2.4.3 Funding Solutions of Rural School Distribution Adjustment

1. *Raising Funds Through Multiple Channels*

Multi-channel funding includes funds from governments at all levels, such as the central, provincial, prefecture, and city government, as well as the county and township government. Many places tried to fund the distribution adjustment by various channels. Here we provide two case analyses to illustrate the funding structure of the distribution adjustment. One is about Zibo city of Shandong Province, and the other is about Suqian city of Jiangsu Province.

Case 1: Funding Sources for the Distribution Adjustment in Zibo City of Shandong Province

According to the preliminary estimate, Zibo city needed about RMB400 million to complete the distribution adjustment of rural primary and secondary schools. In order to raise sufficient funds, Zibo city adopted the following approaches. The first is to strive for support from higher-level government. The second is to allocate special funds from the city budget. Each district, county and township gave special funds for the school distribution adjustment and exempt related administrative charges associated with school construction. The city government also used special funds to subsidize and reward some rural primary and secondary schools in the distribution adjustment. The third is to make sure that education surcharges of all counties and townships mainly used for the distribution adjustment. The fourth is bank loans. The fifth is to start to collect four types of education administrative fees and use them in education. The four types of administrative fees include compulsory education fees of urban employees, vocational education fees of enterprises and public institutions, compulsory education fees of hotels and aquatic products. The sixth is to carry out city's Notice on Educational Support for Mountainous Areas and townships along the Yellow River, and to support paired assistant programs. The seventh is to dispose the assets of merged schools and use all the income from asset disposal for the distribution adjustment. The eighth is to mobilize social donations, encouraging schools and enterprises to coordinate in school operations. The ninth is to check and ratify the amount of investment, make overall planning of fund use, ensure full appropriation and efficiency.

Case 2: Funding sources for the distribution adjustment in Suqian city of Jiangsu Province

Suqian is a newly-built prefecture-level city and a typical agricultural city. Its economic and social development was lagging behind in the province. According to statistics at the end of 2000, the city's total fiscal revenue was only RMB1.127 billion, 1/20 that of Suzhou. The per capita net income of villagers was less than RMB3000. Suqian city needed about RMB840 million to complete the distribution adjustment and dilapidated building renovation project, then about RMB300 million input required every year. In 2001, the provincial government allocated only RMB38 million as special funds to the city. Due to the lack of financial resources, most of the funding needed for the distribution adjustment and dilapidated building renovation had to be raised by counties, townships, and schools.[30]

Shuyang county raised RMB57 million through multiple channels. In addition to the RMB10 million budget reform fund at the beginning of the year, the county government strived for support from the Edward Education Fund, the Shaw Education Fund and local Shuyang people who registered in Shuyong but work in other areas, mobilized public donations, and encouraged enterprises and individuals to participate in school running. By using social capital, the county raised adequate funds for the distribution adjustment. The main leaders of Gaoxu township, Shuyang county and the principals of primary and secondary schools had travelled to Nanjing twice to communicate with higher-level leaders, and finally won the support of officials at the provincial government.

Facing the dilemma of limited financial resources and a huge funding gap, Suyu county worked hard to raise funds from bank loans, social donations, disposing assets of closed/merged schools, and revitalizing existing assets. As a result, the county government managed to invest RMB40.605 million to ensure a smooth start of the distribution adjustment and dilapidated building renovations.

Sucheng district secured funding in accordance with the "five some" approach, namely, the higher- level government providing some, the district government and townships allocating some, local education authorities raising some, primary and middle schools contributing some, and cadres and the masses donating some. The whole district has successively raised more than RMB20 million.[31]

---

[30] Wang Min, et al., Doing great things with great effort: A Documentary of Suqian City's primary and secondary school distribution adjustment, *Jiangsu Education*, No. 3, 2002.

[31] Wang Min, et al., Doing great things with great effort: A Documentary of Suqian City's primary and secondary school distribution adjustment, *Jiangsu Education*, No. 3, 2002.

Although all the regions tried to raise funds for the distribution adjustment through multiple channels, there were big differences in the funding structure of different regions. The funding structure is related to the financial situation and fundraising ability of local government. In all the funding sources, social capital played an important role.

2. *Using Social Capital in the Distribution Adjustment*

Social capital refers to social resources in a relatively stable social network that can help achieve certain goals, formed by individuals or groups of people in the course of long-term interaction. Social capital plays an important role in resource distribution, and has been a hot topic in sociology since late 1990s. Coleman believed that social capital has many forms, such as obligations and expectations, authority relationships, norms and effective punishments, and multifunctional organizations.[32] Judging from the cases of Zibo and Suqian, social capital played a very important role in providing funding to the distribution adjustment.

Using social capital in the distribution adjustment of rural primary and secondary schools is based on a strong authority system and organizational system in the local area. First, this refers to a strong government mobilization system, which can effectively combine forces and resources of various departments to achieve certain social goals. Second, a pairing assistance system formed by administrative arrangements was also very important. Third, the local community's support was another key. If there is a tradition of raising funds and donating to local education, funds will be relatively easy to obtain. The local government attached great importance to organizing such social capital, so that wealthy local people can better support local education.

3. Gaming in Forming the Input Structure

The distribution adjustment of rural primary and secondary schools involves multiple parties, in which the motivations, interests and responsibilities of related parties are very different. Therefore, there is mutual restraint and even a game among the main parties. If the provincial government plans to complete the distribution adjustment in a short period of time, as in the more developed provinces such as Jiangsu and Guangdong, or hopes to complete the task ahead of schedule, the provincial government will appropriate more funding accordingly.

There is also such a game between counties and towns. Despite the county-based management system in rural education, the county government may divide fiscal responsibility to towns under it as much as possible. For example, in Deyang city in Hangzhou, townships had to provide 70% of the funding. Generally, higher-level institutions have more advantages in the game over lower-level ones. This is very obvious in disputes over fiscal responsibility sharing among townships, village committees, and villagers in local school removal or merge. Many places did not provide corresponding compensation for the increase in schooling costs due to school closures, and these costs were finally borne by local villagers. In some

[32] James Coleman, *Foundations of Social Theory* (Chinese Edition), translated by Deng Fang, Beijing: Social Sciences Academic Press (China), 1999.

places, there have been elderly people renting houses around schools to accompany their school-age grandchildren.

7.2.5 Flow of People and Things in the Distribution Adjustment

The school distribution adjustment involves the flow of teachers and students, as well as the flow of funds and things, such as school equipment, books, tables, chairs, benches, etc. This part analyzes how resources flow, and how the flow of these resources will affect the interests of relevant stakeholders.

7.2.5.1 Flow of Teachers

Flow of teachers can be divided into three categories: (1) Flow of substitute teachers, *gongban* teachers[33] and school leadership. Generally speaking, substitute teachers are most likely to be removed in the adjustment. (2) Flow of *gongban* teachers has two forms. One is free flow throughout the county or even the city based on complete market competition. The other is restricted flow subject to the education department's approval. In the restricted flow mode, teachers tend to move from remote areas to towns close to the county seat, and finally to the county seat. The basic education is seriously uneven across different regions in China. In some areas, primary, middle and high schools are not completely separated at all stages. There are still middle school classes in some primary schools, or high school classes in middle schools. With the distribution adjustment, the phenomenon of mixed classes will gradually disappear. Accordingly, some teachers will be transferred to middle schools, or other teachers may be merged into a new middle school or primary school. (3) Flow of leadership of merged schools varies greatly from place to place. Mostly, they are either reappointed to the leadership team of a center school or compete for positions in other schools.

7.2.5.2 Flow of Students

The local government has the responsibility to ensure that students do not drop out of school under China's nine-year compulsory education system. Therefore, flow of students has become a more critical issue in the distribution adjustment. The flow of students has the following types. First, all students flow to the newly established school. Second, most students flow to the new school, and a small number go to other schools closer to their families. Third, a small number or individual students transfer to a better local school. Fourth, a small number or individual students drop out of

[33] "Gongban teacher" refer to teachers in China's public school system.

school because of the distance between the school and their family or the increased financial burden on their family after the adjustment.

In order to enable as many students as possible to attend the new school, the new school will adopt various measures to reform its organizational structure and improve its service system. For example, the new school may provide or expand the boarding system, hire nurses to take care of the lower-grade primary students, provide facilitating services such as school buses, teacher escort or older students taking younger home and so on. Some schools have added special protective measures, such as marking a special road for students around the school.

The flow of students to the new school embodies the collective effort of school, family, students, government, and local community. Schools have to make all kinds of preparations. Parents are faced with various choices. The local community must cooperate with schools. For example, the school may coordinate with relevant village committees and ask them to take care of the students passing by.

7.2.5.3 Asset Disposal

Ownership of school assets is the most controversial issue in the asset disposal of the merged/closed schools. According to related laws and regulations, school assets are educational assets, owned by the school during the school's duration, and should be owned by the related administrative department after the school is merged. In reality, diversified sources of school assets have led to disputes in disposing of them. Under the system of multi-channel financing for compulsory education, most rural primary and secondary schools were funded and built by local villagers. The local villagers did not understand why the school assets did not belong to them after the school was withdrawn, and could not accept it emotionally.

In this case, asset disposal may depend on the ability of relevant parties to claim their ownership, and it may eventually lead to the following results. The first is to transfer the school assets to the local village committee free of charge or lease them with little charge. The second is to auction the assets. The third is to keep and provide these assets to a local kindergarten. The fourth is to have the new center school manage the assets. However, it is difficult for the new school to effectively manage the assets. In some places, the new center school has to send a teacher and a class to stay in the village, in order to maintain the old school buildings, which will delay the adjustment.

7.2.5.4 Vulnerable Groups

How to protect the interests of vulnerable groups must be highly valued in the adjustment, especially whether the adjustment will make it more difficult for children from poor families to go to school. This will be discussed further below.

7.2.6 *Effects of the School Distribution Adjustment*

7.2.6.1 Types of Effects

The school distribution adjustment can have economic and social effects. Economic effects are mainly reflected in whether the government's investment achieves economic benefits, which can be divided into short-term effects and long-term effects. Short-term effects are to compare the direct changes before and after the distribution adjustment, and long-term effects need to calculate the investment and the changes in several years after the distribution adjustment. Commonly used indicators to measure economic effects include hardware indicators and software indicators. Hardware indicators include those such as the school's average campus area per student and modern experimental instruments or facilities. Software indicators include quality of teachers, students' academic performance, and improvement of students' overall quality, etc. For example, government of Deqing county calculated the economic benefits of their distribution adjustment as such. "It can reduce the investment in equipment and facilities of primary and secondary schools by RMB39.65 million at a time, reduce the following costs or expenses by a considerable amount each year, including school building maintenance costs RMB2 million, equipment and facilities maintenance costs RMB860 thousand, and operational expenses RMB1.05 million. In addition, it will save the county government RMB900 thousand in personnel expenses, equivalent to 150 substitute teachers' salary each year. It will reduce fiscal burden of the county and township government as well as villages."[34]

Social effects of the school distribution adjustment are mainly reflected in three aspects. First, whether students can adapt to the new environment, and whether the new environment after school merger is conducive to improving students' overall growth and their academic performance. Second, whether the school distribution adjustment has a positive impact on the local culture. Third, whether the situation of the disadvantaged groups is improved after the adjustment.

7.2.6.2 Student's Adaptability

The key criterion to measure the success of school distribution adjustment is to look at its impact on students' learning and growth, which is reflected in two aspects. One is students' enthusiasm for school, and the other is students' learning quality. The following indicators can be used to measure these two aspects: (a) schools' dropout rate, enrollment rate, and retainment rate; (b) students' academic performance, for example, the pass rate and excellence rate of the county's unified examination; (c) proportion of students getting further education.

The impact of the distribution adjustment on students' academic performance is more complicated, which may bring about favorable results, such as expansion of

[34] The burden of school running reduced, the benefits of the layout adjustment of Deqing's primary and middle schools are significant, *Xijiang Daily*, 2003-10-15.

campus area per student, schools' ability to offer all the courses required, completeness of teaching equipment, improvement in teachers' qualifications, and so on. The distribution adjustment may also bring some negative impacts, such as oversized classes with each student receiving less attention from teachers, etc. The key is to thoroughly study the impact of distribution adjustment on students and possible mechanisms that produce these effects.

7.2.6.3 Impacts on Disadvantaged Groups

Students and their families are in a weaker position in the distribution adjustment, relative to the government and schools. If students' families are further classified, there are two types of groups more likely to be at a disadvantage.

First are families with financial difficulties. Although the distribution adjustment has improved the quality of local education, and provided better conditions for students' comprehensive development, it may cause problems, for example, the direct increase of financial burden on families, especially poor families. Therefore, it is necessary to examine the following issues. (a) Which schooling costs have been added for local families after the distribution adjustment? How are the additional food and accommodation costs covered if there is a boarding system? (b) In addition to the direct costs, indirect costs such as time cost increased from escorting children to and from school also need to be considered. (c) How many students drop out of school due to the increased schooling costs caused by the distribution adjustment?

Another vulnerable group is ethnic minority groups, especially ethnic minority families in mountainous areas. Not only the parents need to bear direct or indirect increase in costs, their children also have to face challenges such as adapting a new schooling environment with a different language and strange cultural customs and habits.

7.2.6.4 Other Issues

Since 2000, the distribution adjustment of rural primary and secondary schools in most regions of China was related to a series of changes that have been taking place in China's urban and rural society, especially urbanization and industrialization. In this process, people flow upward along the hierarchical chain of regions. The distribution adjustment of rural primary and secondary schools has followed the same path, gradually shifting the distribution of schools from scattered teaching posts to comprehensive village primary schools, then to a central primary school of the township, or from multiple middle schools to one middle school in each township, then to one middle school of several neighboring townships, and finally most students concentrated in the county seat.

The distribution adjustment of rural primary and secondary schools corresponds to more convenient and faster transportation brought by modernization and globalization. The primary and middle school stage is a key phase for an individual's socialization. Social groups formed during this period are of great significance to the development of students throughout their lives. After the distribution adjustment, the geographical scope of students' interaction circle will become larger, which will form a common feeling and identity on a larger scale of population, and lay the foundation for forming a new social community on a larger scale.

7.3 Application of the Analytical Framework: A Case Study of Rural Primary and Secondary Schools in Yunnan Province

The conditions and methods used by Yunnan Province in the distribution adjustment of primary and secondary schools in rural areas may be different from those in other parts of the country, but the basic analytical framework developed above can still be used for its analysis. At the end of 2004, the Institute of Educational Economics of Peking University and the Academy of Educational Sciences of Yunnan Normal University co-organized a research team to conduct a field investigation on Yunnan Province's rural education. The distribution adjustment of rural primary and secondary schools is one of the important contents of this investigation. This part is based on the investigation.

7.3.1 Factors Affecting the Distribution Adjustment in Yunnan Province

Yunnan Province, as a border province with a concentration of ethnic groups, faced very different conditions and foundations for the distribution adjustment of rural primary and secondary schools than the eastern coastal areas and many inland provinces in China.

- Less developed economy with more financial difficulties. Due to the low level of social and economic development, especially in mountainous areas and areas with large ethnic minority populations, many counties could not be financially self-sufficient. Under such economic and financial conditions, it was difficult to implement large-scale and intensive school distribution adjustment.
- Change in school-age population. The national birth rate has significantly declined in China, However, in the mountainous areas and areas with large ethnic minority populations of Yunnan, the family planning policy was much looser. And some ethnic groups could have as many children as they wish. Therefore, although the school-age population was also decreasing in Yunnan like other provinces, the magnitude of the decrease was smaller, or much smaller.
- Complicated geographical conditions. Yunnan is located in a mountainous area in southwestern China. The distribution of local population is much scattered, which

has brought great difficulties to the distribution adjustment. In contrast, Inner Mongolia and other areas with large ethnic minority populations have much better geographical conditions, with flatter terrain and more convenient transportation, which is conducive to adjust the distribution of local schools on a large scale and concentrating students to center schools.

- Greater linguistic and cultural challenges. With many ethnic groups, Yunnan's modern basic education in areas with large ethnic minority populations must consider cultural and language differences in each area. This adds to the geographical challenges in the distribution adjustment.
- Less pressure from the higher-level government. Basic education in Yunnan has been lagging behind most other provinces. Some counties and cities have just completed universal nine-year compulsory education and some have not yet. In these places, the main task of rural primary and secondary schools was not improving efficiency, but ensuring access to basic education and enrollment rate. Therefore, these places generally faced less pressure from the higher-level government in the distribution adjustment.
- Latecomer advantages induced from slower popularization of rural compulsory education, which can be reflected in three aspects. (a) It was possible for Yunnan to learn relevant experience and lessons from the inland provinces, and to systematically consider the changes in school-age population and the school distribution adjustment in popularizing compulsory education. (b) With a stronger economy and society, the central government is more likely to increase the transfer payments to backward regions. Yunnan Province thus can get more funding support in the distribution adjustment of rural primary and secondary schools. (c) Economic and social development has made local villagers richer, and they will thus attach more importance to their children receiving better education, leading to less resistance to the distribution adjustment from local communities.
- Greater support in cultivating excellent management talent. Yunnan Province have successively gained funding support from many educational projects offered by the World Bank and various state ministries and commissions. These projects mostly required integrating the school distribution adjustment into local education planning. As a result, it was possible to cultivate local talents in education management in implementing these projects, which played a key role in the distribution adjustment. Due to serious shortage of local fiscal resources, Yunnan's rural education was more affected by external resources and factors, and relevant experience thus could be better absorbed. For example, some areas have put forward the idea of "projects following planning, funds following projects, audits following funds".
- Better opportunities. With support from the central government and international organizations, Yunnan Province has continued to launch large educational programs and projects, and county governments will have more opportunities to adjust the school distribution with various support from these programs and projects.

To summarize the above factors, the distribution adjustment of primary and secondary schools in Yunnan Province may not have as large policy fluctuations as the eastern and central provinces in China, and may be carried out in a more planned and smooth manner. At the same time, the distribution adjustment in Yunnan may have stronger and longer effects on its basic education.

7.3.2 Funding Sources and Methods of Yunnan's School Distribution Adjustment

The investment method is one of the key issues in the school distribution adjustment of rural primary and secondary schools in Yunnan Province. The source and structure of funding are subject to various factors.

7.3.2.1 Adjustment Methods and Funding Demand

Funding demand is closely related to the method and implementation of the distribution adjustment. At the same time, the choice of adjustment method and implementation are mainly determined based on the corresponding sources and quantity of funding. According to the field study, the overall distribution adjustment of rural primary and secondary schools in Yunnan Province can be divided into three types according to geographic and economic conditions. The first type is those areas with more advanced economies and favorable geographic conditions. These areas had begun to close and merge village primary schools into township central primary schools, and would retain only a few teaching posts in individual villages in the next few years. In such areas, middle schools had transformed from being run by each township to jointly run by several towns. Anning, a county-level city under the jurisdiction of the provincial capital Kunming, was an example of this type. The second type is the areas with the least developed economies, poor geographic conditions and complex ethnic minority groups. In such areas, the school distribution adjustment so far had mostly been developed to gradually merge teaching posts in every village into its comprehensive primary schools, and middle schools have not yet run across towns. Such areas were represented by Wenshan Prefecture. The third type is the areas between the first and second types.

The relevant documents of Yunnan Province indicate that the focus of Yunnan's rural education was still popularizing compulsory education in areas with large ethnic minority populations, that is to say, the focus was on the second type of areas mentioned above. From a national perspective, difficulties in popularizing compulsory education were mainly concentrated in mountainous areas and areas with large ethnic minority populations. In almost all provinces, developing boarding and semi-boarding schools was the key solution. Establishing boarding schools required larger campus, more dormitories and corresponding management personnel, all of which meant more funding. In addition, boarding schools would induce higher schooling costs for families. Financial capability of local families and ways to provide subsidies to poor families had to be taken into consideration in the adjustment.

7.3.2.2 Fiscal Support from the County or Prefecture Government

1. *Differences in Fiscal Capability Among Local Governments*

The fiscal strength gap among regions in Yunnan Province is relatively large. According to the proportion of external financial resources in the available fiscal revenue, the Yunnan Provincial Department of Finance divides the province's regions into three categories:

- Prefectures and counties with external financial resources account for more than 60%, and these counties lack the ability to provide internal revenue to meet their expenditure needs, so have to rely heavily on fiscal subsidies from higher-level governments. These areas include mainly three autonomous prefectures, Wenshan (60%), Nujiang (68%), Diqing (81%), and 30 counties including Ludian;
- The proportion of external financial resources is between 20 and 60%. These prefectures and counties have a certain ability to provide their own revenue, but they still cannot get rid of the fiscal subsidies from the higher level government;
- The proportion of external financial resources is less than 20%. There are mainly four prefectures (Kunming, Yuxi, Chuxiong, Dali) and 19 districts and counties including Chenggong.[35]

Differences in fiscal strength were also manifested at the county-level, and the degree of differences among counties was getting larger and larger. In 1994, county-level governments' financial disparity within Yunnan reached 2.97, and remained at 2.20 in 1999.[36] As shown in Table 7.4, the proportion of external financial resources of all the prefectural and county governments had increased year by year since the tax distribution system reform in 1994, implying the increasing dependence of county-level finances on higher-level, especially city-level and provincial-level governments.

To take Wenshan Prefecture as an example, the basic fiscal conditions of the prefecture and counties under it is shown in Table 7.5.

It can be seen that neither Wenshan Prefecture itself nor any of its counties was financially independent. In 2003, the prefecture government's fiscal revenue was

[35] Yunnan Provincial Department of Finance, The Operation of the Financial Management System of the Tax Distribution System in Yunnan Province, Budget Department of the Ministry of Finance (ed), *China's Intergovernmental Fiscal Relations*, Beijing: China Financial & Economic Publishing House, 2003: 754–757.

[36] Yunnan Provincial Department of Finance, The Operation of the Financial Management System of the Tax Distribution System in Yunnan Province, Budget Department of the Ministry of Finance (ed), *China's Intergovernmental Fiscal Relations*, Beijing: China Financial & Economic Publishing House, 2003: 754–757.

Table 7.4 External financial resources in total financial resources of prefecture, county-level governments in Yunnan province (Unit: %)

Item	(1994–1999)					
	1994	1995	1996	1997	1998	1999
All levels average	13.2	20.1	11.7	27.3	19.0	22.2
Prefecture and city level average	−0.7	3.8	−4.4	14.1	−1.0	−0.2
County level average	23.1	29.5	21.0	33.9	29.4	33.7

Source Yunnan Provincial Department of Finance, The Operation of the Financial Management System of the Tax Distribution System in Yunnan Province, Budget Department of the Ministry of Finance (ed), *China's Intergovernmental Fiscal Relations*, Beijing: China Financial & Economic Publishing House, 2003: 754–757

Table 7.5 Fiscal revenue and expenditure of counties in Wenshan prefecture in 2003

Region	Fiscal revenue (RMB million)	Fiscal expenditure (RMB million)	Revenue/Expenditure
The prefecture total	478.95	2172.81	0.22
Wenshan county	171.09	342.30	0.50
Yanshan county	65.48	211.93	0.31
Xichou county	21.89	167.46	0.13
Malipo county	28.08	199.90	0.14
Maguan county	43.66	223.62	0.20
Qiubei county	36.88	207.22	0.18
Guangnan county	43.99	269.99	0.16
Funing county	33.93	215.44	0.16

Source General Office of the Yunnan Provincial Government and the Yunnan Provincial Statistics Bureau, *The Economic Work Manual for Yunnan's Leading Officials, Year 2004*, Kunming: The Ethnic Publishing House of Yunnan, 2004

only 22% of its expenditure. The county with the best fiscal situation was Wenshan County, the capital of the prefecture, whose fiscal revenue accounted for only half of its expenditure. Under such a fiscal system, the city's major investment could only rely on transfer payments from the provincial and the central government, and education was no exception. The Wenshan Prefecture Education Bureau analyzed the educational investment of the Prefecture and Yunnan Province from 1998 to 2002, as shown in Table 7.6. Wenshan Prefecture's educational investment accounted for more than 100% of its local fiscal revenue in each year, and in 2002 it even reached 146%.

From Table 7.6 we can see that Wenshan prefecture's local fiscal revenue was far from enough to cover its educational investment, and the same was true for the counties under Wenshan prefecture. Take Malipo county as an example as shown in Table 7.7. The county's fiscal revenue was RMB28.08 million in 2003, while its

Table 7.6 Educational investment: Wenshan prefecture vs Yunnan province (1998–2002)

Scope	Year	Educational investment (RMB million)				Local fiscal revenue (RMB million)	Local fiscal expenditure (RMB million)	Educational investment accounting for local fiscal revenue (%)	Educational investment sccounting for local fiscal expenditure (%)
		Special funding from higher levels	Budget allocation by the local level	Extra-budgetary funding allocation	Total				
Wenshan prefecture	1998	35.38	250.96	50.05	336.39	326.69	1213.31	102.97	27.22
	1999	41.73	269.68	61.66	373.07	349.39	1295.22	106.78	28.80
	2000	39.70	317.99	55.30	412.99	366.66	1426.01	112.64	28.96
	2001	39.01	423.97	57.15	520.13	449.66	1939.94	115.67	26.81
	2002	43.46	469.60	91.16	604.39	413.96	1903.17	146.00	31.76
	Total	199.45	1732.20	315.32	2246.97	1906.36	7777.65	117.87	28.89
Yunnan province	1998	138.60	315.30		17,267.00	37,805.00			18.22
	1999	135.16	599.26		17,810.00	41,390.00			18.48
	2000	193.00	389.10		19,110.00	49,640.00			18.48
	2001	214.10	379.50		20,500.00	53,000.00			19.26
	2002	223.56	497.81		22,890.00	58,800.00			19.05
	Total	904.42	2180.97		97,577.00	240,635.00			

Source Wenshan Prefecture Education Bureau, November 2004

educational investment alone was RMB76.09 million. That year's fiscal revenue only accounted for 36.9% of the same year's total educational investment.

2. *Possibility of Funding from Township Governments and Local Residents*

Before the rural tax and fee reform, the multi-channel funding system for rural compulsory education played a key role in Yunnan's rural education. After the rural tax and fee reform and the rural basic education management system reform, townships' income from villagers dropped significantly, and township governments immediately fell into financial distress, unable to provide enough funding to rural education. In addition, funding from local villagers for local education became very little after education surcharges and public reserve funds were cancelled, and more constraints have been imposed on the procedures and amount of public fundraising in rural areas. In 2003, education surcharge from rural areas was RMB535,000, plus some tuition and fees. In the following years, the rural education surcharge was abolished, and tuition and fees were exempted.

In the case of prefectures, counties and townships with serious fiscal difficulties and no more mass funding channels, the funding needed for the distribution adjustment of rural education could only rely on the support from the central and provincial governments, which will result in a deeply dependent local government fiscal system. Special funds provided by the central and provincial government accounted for almost 100% of all the special funds received by Malipo County in 2003.

7.3.2.3 Fiscal Support from the Central and Provincial Government

To support education in poverty-stricken areas, the central government and Yunnan Province have implemented a number of basic education development projects, which mainly include the followings.

1. *The National Compulsory Education Project in Poor Areas (NCEPPA)*

From 1998 to 2000, the State Council implemented the first phase of the National Compulsory Education Project in Poor Areas, with a total investment of RMB812.5 million, including RMB325 million from the central government, RMB325 million from the provincial government, and RMB162.5 million from prefecture and county governments. The funds were allocated to 69 key counties for poverty alleviation and development. A total of 267 primary schools were newly built, 1121 renovated or expanded, school buildings with an area of 965,700 square meters newly built, renovated or expanded. 27 new middle schools were newly built, 192 renovated or expanded, school buildings with an area of 322,800 square meters newly built, renovated or expanded. From 2001 to 2005, the state implemented the second phase of the National Compulsory Education Project in Poor Areas, with a total investment of RMB555 million, of which RMB370 million was invested by the central government and RMB185 million by the provincial governments. The funds were allocated to 40 key counties for poverty alleviation and development. The plan was to renovate or expand 383 primary schools, construct new school buildings with an area of 87,000

Table 7.7 Malipo county's education funding structure in 2003 (Unit: RMB10 thousand)

Total	Special funds					Social donations		Education surcharges		Others	Other operating funds (schools and administrative departments at all levels)
	Subtotal	The central and provincial government	Prefecture government	County government	Townships	Subtotal	Rural area	Urban area	Rural area		
7609.9	2390.5	2384.5	6	0	0	14.7	0	47.9	53.5	90.4	5012.9

Note Relief funds of RMB1.347 million for poverty-stricken students in the year of 2003 were not included in this Table 7.7. The data was provided by Malipo County, November 2004

square meters, renovate or expand 286 middle schools, and construct new school buildings with an area of 41,000 square meters.

2. *The Border School Project*

In September 2002, the Yunnan Provincial Party Committee and the Provincial Government formulated the Action Plan for the Revitalization of Basic Education in Yunnan Province, and implemented the Five Major Projects. One of the Five Major Projects was to improve school conditions in border areas and develop primary and secondary schools at border ports and important passages. With special funding from the central government, the provincial government decided to build about 100 border schools and improve the conditions of compulsory education in 25 counties or cities, and enhance the quality of education in the border areas from 2002 to 2005. In 2002 and 2003, a total of RMB104.141 million was invested in the construction of border schools, including RMB83 million from the central government, RMB5 million from the provincial government, and RMB16.141 million from prefectures and schools. The project covered 8 prefectures and 25 counties or cities, 61 border schools, 88 construction projects with a total building area of 146,801 square meters.

3. *The "Three Exemptions" Project*

Since 2000, the provincial government has arranged a special fund of RMB18 million to implement the "three exemptions" project in border villages of 25 counties. The "three exemptions" refers to textbook fees, miscellaneous fees, and stationery fees all exempted, and the project benefited 140,000 primary school students. In 2002, the special fund was increased to RMB44 million, and the scope of subsidies was expanded to primary and middle school students in border poverty alleviation towns. In 2003, the provincial government made the expansion of "three exemptions" project one of the government's projects for public support. The provincial fiscal funding was increased to RMB52 million, and the scope of "three exemptions" was expanded to 7 areas with large ethnic minority populations of less than 100,000, providing RMB150 per student per year for primary schools and RMB250 for middle schools. The number of beneficiaries rose to 320,000.

4. *Living Allowance for Boarding and Semi-boarding Students*

In 2002, the provincial government invested RMB45 million as special education funding for the living allowance of 3,750 semi-boarding students, with an annual subsidy of RMB120 per student. The subsidy covered 375,000 students. During the 10th Five-year Plan, another RMB7.2 million was added each year, and a total investment of RMB36 million has been added by 2005.

5. *The Rural Boarding School Construction Project*

From 2004 to 2007, the State invested RMB1 billion to build 567 rural boarding schools, including RMB900 million from the central government and RMB100 million from the provincial finance. This project is implemented in 35 key counties of national poverty alleviation and development work, focusing on the reconstruction and expansion of rural boarding middle schools and primary schools. The 567 rural boarding schools include the renovation and expansion of 471 schools and the construction of 96 new schools, with a planned investment of RMB986.8 million (including RMB900 million of central government funds and RMB86.8 million of provincial supporting funds). There was also RMB918.504 million of civil construction funds, accounting for 3.57% of the total funds. The project plans 334 middle schools, accounting for 58.91% of the total number of schools under the project, with planned investment of RMB734.008 million (including central government funds of RMB669.437 million, and provincial supporting funds of RMB64.571 million), accounting for 74.38% of the total investment. The project plans 183 primary schools, accounting for 32.3% of the project schools, with planned investment of RMB139.795 million (including central government funding RMB127.351 million and provincial supporting funds of RMB12.444 million), accounting for 14.17% of the total investment. Among the project schools, there are 19 schools with first to nineth grade education, accounting for 3.35% of all schools, and the planned investment capital of RMB33.533 million (including RMB30.581 million of central government funding, and RMB2.952 million of provincial supporting funds), accounting for 3.4% of the total investment. There are 31 other types of schools planned by the project, accounting for 5.47% of the project schools, and the planned investment capital of RMB79.464 million (including RMB72.631 million from the central government fund and RMB6.833 million from the provincial supporting funds), accounting for 8.05% of the total investment.

All the relevant data of the project items are summarized in Table 7.8.

The following conclusions can be drawn from Table 7.8.

- Since 1998, the central government and Yunnan Province have invested a lot of money in border counties, and counties with large ethnic minority populations. Therefore, universal compulsory education in these counties was the focus of the central and provincial governments.
- The special transfer payments from the central government were far greater than those from the provincial government. With regard to the above-mentioned five major projects, the central government alone has allocated nearly RMB1.7 billion for educational development in Yunnan Province, while the provincial government has provided about RMB700 million.
- In Yunnan, border counties and counties with large ethnic minority populations were highly overlapped with each other. Therefore, the central and provincial governments were likely to have invested in the same area multiple times through various projects, although the key target areas of each project were different. This is of great significance in helping the counties in popularizing compulsory education. These counties' education has undergone great changes with the intensive capital investment from the central and provincial governments, and Malipo is a representative area in this respect.

Table 7.8 Yunnan's major education projects supported by the Central and Provincial Government (1998–2004)

Project name	Project period	Structure of funding sources (RMB million)				Funding used in compulsory education		Key areas invested
		Central government	Provincial government	Prefecture or county matching	Total	Primary schools	Middle schools	
NCEPPA (Phase I)	1998–2000	325	325	162.5	812.5	267 newly build, 1,121 renovated/ expanded	27 newly build, 192 renovated/ expanded	69 key counties for poverty alleviation and development
NCEPPA (Phase II)	2001–2005	370	185		555	383 renovated/ expanded	286 renovated/ expanded	40 key counties for poverty alleviation and development
The border school project	2002–2005	83	5	16.141	104.141	100 border schools newly built, including 61 border school between 2002–2003		25 border counties
The "Three exemptions" project	2000		18			140,000 pupils		25 border counties
	2002		44			Primary and middle school students in border poverty alleviation towns		

(continued)

Table 7.8 (continued)

Project name	Project period	Structure of funding sources (RMB million)				Funding used in compulsory education		Key areas invested
		Central government	Provincial government	Prefecture or county matching	Total	Primary schools	Middle schools	
	2003		52			RMB150 per student per year	RMB250 per student per year	7 areas with large ethnic minority populations of less than 100,000, 320,000 students covered
Living allowance for boarding and semi-boarding students	2002			RMB45 million, an additional RMB7.2 million every year during the 10th five-year plan	A total of RMB36 million added by 2005			3,750 schools/ 375,000 students covered, RMB120 per student per year
The rural boarding school construction project	2004–2007	900	100		1000	To renovate or expand rural boarding primary and middle schools		35 Key counties for poverty alleviation and development

Source Institute of Educational Economics of Peaking University, the Academy of Educational Sciences of Yunnan Normal University, Research on the Development of Yunnan's Rural Education, 2004

7.3.2.4 Take Malipo County as an Example

Malipo is a border county. Thanks to the support of related special funding, such as the border school project, the local rural schools close to the border have been greatly improved, and local students have enjoyed free education and boarding subsidies. Malipo is well-known throughout the Counterattack in Self-Defense on the Sino-Vietnamese Border, and its high reputation helped the county to obtain special funding from the central and provincial governments and social donations, which made possible the rapid development of the county's education. Through the coordination of the Ministry of Foreign Affairs in the pairing assistance program, the county has received foreign donations of more than RMB20 million in a few years, equivalent to the county's annual fiscal revenue. Among the county's special income in 2003, special funding from the central and provincial levels reached RMB23.845 million, which was 84.9% of the county's fiscal revenue in that year.

Therefore, Malipo County's educational investment has been highly dependent on external financial resources. It is only possible for a financially difficult area to achieve leap-forward educational development by obtaining large amounts of external funding. However, if external funding cannot be sustained or stabilized, it will have a devastating impact on local education.

7.3.2.5 Characteristics and Challenges of Yunnan's Education Funding

The education funding structure of Yunnan Province had its own distinctive features, which were mainly manifested in four aspects. First, local fiscal revenue was severely inadequate, leading to a highly dependent and unitary fiscal system, which made transfer payments from governments above the county level play an important role in the distribution adjustment of rural education. Second, international donations and special projects had an active role in promoting the development of Yunnan's education. Third, pairing assistance and social donations were also effective ways to add to Yunnan's education funding. Fourth, in managing and using external financial resources, the administrative leadership of the local education department was very important.

Deep dependence on external financial resources may cause the following problems. First, expectations from higher-level governments may be too high, beyond the reality of the local area, which may lead to insufficient follow-up improvement. Second, local governments may be overly concerned with the numerical objectives, ignoring the quality aspect, resulting in superficial rather than substantial development. A survey in Yunnan found that although many full-time teachers in primary and secondary schools met the academic qualification required by the education authority, these qualifications were mainly obtained through correspondence, and there might be no connection between their academic qualifications and the courses they teach. In addition, in some areas that have popularized nine-year compulsory education, school dropout rate was still high and students' academic performance still poor. Third, with extensive external investment in a certain period, the progress of education may surpass the local socio-economic development and take the lead in a short period of time, but in the long run, local education is still subject to the overall level of economic and social development, especially local culture and economic strength.

Finally, the current transfer payment system is not yet perfect, and there may be a game between governments at different levels due to unclear responsibilities. With the central government's strong willingness and fiscal support in boosting local education, even counties and townships with certain local fiscal resources would choose to rely on transfer payments from higher-level governments. The central and provincial transfer payments may crowd out the local funding that should have been used for education in more developed counties and townships. Therefore, the educational transfer payment system needs to be normalized.

7.3.3 *Administrative Methods of the Distribution Adjustment in Yunnan Province*

The special factors facing the distribution adjustment of rural education made it impossible for Yunnan Province to fast complete the distribution adjustment, therefore, the provincial and city governments didn't require quick implementation in the first place. Given large gaps in socio-economic development and cultural and racial diversity within Yunnan Province, administrative methods adopted by different local governments were also very different. The counties surrounding large and medium-sized cities, such as Anning, a county-level city under the jurisdiction of Kunming, were in sharp contrast with Wenshan Prefecture. In Anning, school merging across different towns had emerged prior to the distribution adjustment, while Wenshan Prefecture was still in the stage of merging teaching posts to comprehensive primary schools in villages.

7.3.3.1 Outline of Yunnan's Rural Education Distribution Adjustment

Yunnan Province is one of the provinces with the largest number of native people and the highest proportion of ethnic group populations in China. Due to historical, geographical, ethnic, cultural and economic factors, Yunnan's rural education has presented a pattern of "many schools, many one-teacher and one-student schools, many teaching posts, and many small-scale schools", which was necessary to enable all the school-age children to receive compulsory education. Since the 9th Five-year Plan, governments at all levels and relevant departments across the province had started to adjust the distribution of rural primary and secondary schools and the adjustment of rural primary schools had achieved significant progress. From 1998 to 2003, a total of 7439 rural primary schools and 911 village comprehensive primary schools were closed. By 2003, the province had 2275 regular middle schools, including 421 high schools and 1854 middle schools, with 40,822 classes, 2,284,619 students in school, and an average class size of 56 students. The minimum service radius of the schools was 3 km and the maximum more than 150 km. The average population covered by the schools was about 20,000. At the primary level, there were 20,296 regular primary schools and 19,154 teaching posts, with 153,371 classes, 4,418,821 students in school, an average class size of 29 students, the largest 65 students and the smallest only 2. The minimum service radius of the primary schools was 3 km and the maximum 85 km. The average population covered was about 2000 people.[37]

Dan Zeng, the former deputy secretary of the provincial committee of the CPC, who was in charge of education in Yunnan Province, believed that Yunnan's school running had to endure a low starting point and high cost. 93% of its primary schools, 83% of its primary school students, 70% of middle schools and 57% of middle school students lived in rural areas. Moreover, "the province's mountains and rivers are crisscrossed with long borders, and the population of some prefectures is quite scattered, resulting in scattered distribution of schools, high cost and low efficiency in school running.[38]

7.3.3.2 The Provincial Government's Guidelines on Rural Education Distribution Adjustment: Adjusting Step by Step and Developing Boarding Schools

Yunnan Province did not mobilize a strong administrative force like the eastern and central provinces in the distribution adjustment, but emphasized that it should be carried out gradually according to the actual situation. Dan Zeng, mentioned some guidelines in his speech at the symposium for the leaders of prefecture/cities and higher education institutions on educational reform and development of Yunnan Province in 2004. He said, we must "proactively and steadily advance the educational reform, and make sure that reform measures are adapted to the level of economic and social development of our province". "We must respect the law of educational development, promote gradual and steady development, and proceed from the reality of our province, from the needs of the masses and society. We must be positive but not aggressive, prudent but not conservative. All the plans and measures must be adapted to the economic and social reality of our province and must be in line with the people's bearing capacity. A best plan cannot be implemented if it is unacceptable or unbearable to the majority of the people." "Old revolutionary base areas, areas with large ethnic minority populations and border areas must seek truth from facts and avoid blindly benchmarking developed areas." Regarding the distribution adjustment, Dan Zeng believed that county-level governments should be given the

---

[37] The data comes from Research on Rural Education Development in Yunnan Province, the Institute of Educational Economic of Peking University, 2004.

[38] Dan Zeng, Speech at the research briefing on the high school education, November 2003, meeting materials for the research briefing on the education reform and development of Yunnan Province.

power to coordinate the adjustment of compulsory education schools in its jurisdiction, in accordance with the principle of "improving the overall efficiency of school running, concentrating schools, merging or adding schools based on the specific situation". In conjunction with the construction of rural boarding schools, county-level governments should expand the scale of boarding and semi-boarding schools, balance convenience of attending school and expansion of schools, and ensure enrollment of all the school-age children.[39]

The adjustment of education distribution is mainly driven by the government, but the extent of the government's promotion is often determined by the local finance strength and acceptance of local people. The previous analysis shows that the focus of Yunnan Province's education was still popularizing and consolidating compulsory education, and thus the distribution adjustment only required removing or merging teaching posts into comprehensive primary schools. During the 10th Five-year Plan period, the intensity of the distribution adjustment has been strengthened, but the focus was still to remove and merge some village primary schools in mountainous areas and teaching posts in a planned and step-by-step manner. The main method was to develop boarding and semi-boarding schools for the upper grades of primary schools. Through the rural boarding school project, 35 poverty-stricken counties planned to remove 842 schools, and build, renovate or expand 600 boarding schools from 2004 to 2007.

7.3.3.3 Two Typical Modes: Anning Mode vs. Wenshan Mode

In October 2004, the Institute of Educational Economics of Peking University and the Academy of Educational Sciences of Yunnan Normal University jointly conducted a survey of rural education in Yunnan Province. The survey was conducted in Anning, a county-level city under the jurisdiction of Kunming, economically more developed, and Wenshan Zhuang and Miao Autonomous Prefecture, an economically underdeveloped ethnic minority autonomous prefecture. The distribution adjustment in Anning and Wenshan can reflect the big picture of Yunnan's educational development.

1. *Anning Mode: Running Schools Across Townships and "Upgrading One by One"*

In Anning City, there was a phenomenon similar to "everyone moving into a better chair" in Guidong County, Hunan Province. Using the opportunity of Kunming's reservoir resettlement project, Anning got special funding for school construction from the resettlement funds, and also applied for other funds from the Kunming municipal government. All the money was used to supplement funds for the school

[39] Dan Zeng, Grasp the key points, break through the bottleneck, and comprehensively promote the education reform and development of Yunnan Province, *Yunnan Bulletin*, Issue 14, 2004.

distribution adjustment. Anning's main approach was to jointly run high schools across several townships, of which two newly-built middle schools were each shared by three townships. The original township middle school campus was then handed over to the center comprehensive primary school of the township. After the township center primary school was relocated, its remaining campus was transferred to village primary schools, and the village schools' buildings were reserved for village kindergartens. In this way, all the schools' hardware was upgraded, and the township and village comprehensive primary schools became more attractive to students from smaller village schools or scattered teaching posts. Some townships even gave their government compound to secondary schools.

Some towns in Anning City had started to consider concentrated school running very early, and had gradually absorbed students at village primary schools and teaching posts into townships. With the gradual expansion of the center school campus, the township center school's ability to attract students in a larger radius has been increasing, and its advantages in improving teaching quality have become more and more obvious. Recognition and acceptance of local people have led to little resistance in accelerating the distribution adjustment. However, there were still various obstacles. To give an example, a village school, which had been built with a donation of more than RMB3 million from an entrepreneur, was planned to be removed and merged to the township center school in the adjustment. The plan was strongly resisted by the village and the donor. The county education bureau had to cancel the plan to maintain social enthusiasm in school running.

2. *Wenshan Mode: Gradually Merging Teaching Posts into Comprehensive Primary Schools*

The overall distribution adjustment of rural education in Wenshan Prefecture was still at the early stage, gradually merging teaching posts to village comprehensive primary schools. At this stage, local resistance is relatively easy to deal with because the scale of adjustment is fairly small. In field interviews, some township leaders believed that the principals of school districts were more active than the township government in the adjustment, as the township center school was also responsible for school district supervision. The principals believed that after the merger, schools could be better managed in a more concentrated manner and teaching quality would be improved. The gentle and gradual adjustment method of Wenshan Prefecture can be seen from the relevant progress year by year, as shown in Table 7.9.

7.3.4 Resource Flow in the Distribution Adjustment of Rural Primary and Secondary Schools

Education resources mainly include human, financial, and material resources. Some counties and cities in Yunnan Province had different ways to deal with the remaining school assets after the distribution adjustment. Some sold these assets, some rented out school buildings, and others transferred the assets to local village committees.

Table 7.9 The distribution adjustment progress of Wenshan's primary schools (1997–2003)

County	Students in school (2003)	Number of schools and teaching posts each year (schools in the first column and teaching posts the second)														Number of erductions		Estimated reduction in 2004	
		1997		1998		1999		2000		2001		2002		2003		Schools	Teaching posts	Schools	Teaching posts
		(1)	(2)	(1)	(2)	(1)	(2)	(1)	(2)	(1)	(2)	(1)	(2)	(1)	(2)				
Wenshan	47,135	223	259	221	250	176	280	261	186	253	177	161	265	157	163	66	96		33
Yanshan	59,511	441	262	434	268	447	237	420	242	425	210	418	208	420	174	21	88	11	50
Xichou	21,086	236	149	230	133	228	129	226	128	218	131	212	122	208	98	28	51	1	7
Malipo	26,258	181	259	149	280	147	261	150	252	170	203	162	199	154	197	27	62	2	4
Maguan	29,931	329	214	313	169	287	123	269	95	252	88	242	83	235	73	94	141	1	2
Qiubei	60,897	241	647	248	638	263	603	271	592	282	538	253	563	259	522	−18	125	0	61
Guangnan	91,670	610	650	543	678	572	620	588	564	569	548	550	547	529	540	81	110	0	0
Funing	37,413	335	374	321	354	320	320	308	300	284	300	287	273	274	277	61	97	−3	6
Total	373,901	2596	2814	2459	2770	2440	253	2493	2359	2453	2195	2285	2260	2236	2044	360	770	12	163

Source Institute of Educational Economics, Peaking University, Research on Rural Education Development in Yunnan Province, 2004

It depends on perceptions of local villagers and principals about these assets. Some insisted that school assets are educational assets and should not be transferred to the local village committee. In order to protect these assets, some school district principals had to leave a class and a teacher of the merged school at the original campus. In some school districts, buildings of merged schools were transferred to the local village committee free of charge. The principal in charge of this matter believed that these buildings were constructed by the local villagers and should be left to them.

The distribution adjustment of rural primary and secondary schools inevitably involves the placement of the public and substitute teachers of merged/closed schools, especially the placement of substitute teachers.

7.3.4.1 Reasons for Existence of Substitute Teachers

In the last century, rural primary and secondary schools in China had to hire a large number of middle or high school graduates as teaching staff. They were part of the *minban* teachers[40] that had become an important measure to rapidly strengthen basic education in rural areas with very limited human and financial resources. As the economy and society became more developed, *minban* teachers were listed as a historical problem that should be resolved. By the end of the 1990s, many localities adopted various methods such as recruiting more qualified teachers, transforming *minban* teachers to regular teachers, dismissing unqualified *minban* teachers, and elder teachers retiring, in order to basically solve the problem of *minban* teachers. However, a number of *minban* teachers failed to transform to regular teachers for various reasons, such as failing required exams. Later, some of the *minban* teachers who had failed to transform to regular teachers became substitute teachers in the twenty-first century. However, many substitute teachers are newly hired, and most of them are also middle or high school graduates with rural *hukou*, just like the *minban* teachers in the twentieth century. The main reasons why there are so many newly hired substitute teachers in recent years may include the following.

The first is shortage of teachers. Dismissing most *minban* teachers caused schools to have to supplement public teachers from college graduates. However, there might be too few college graduates assigned or willing to fill in positions of retired teachers, leading to persistent shortage of public teachers. Some other reasons may lead to temporary lack of public teachers. For example, some primary and middle school teachers may be transferred to government agencies for some time, or some public teachers may be absent for pregnancy or illness. All the factors above will lead to demand for substitute teachers.

The second is unbalanced distribution of regular teachers, the so-called *gongban* teachers. Rich counties may have sufficient or even too many *gongban* teachers, but

[40] "*Minban*" teachers refer to "teaching staff in rural schools in China who are not included in the official staff of the state. They are the main form of supplementing the shortage of teachers in rural compulsory education.

few of these teachers are willing to teach in impoverished or mountainous areas. Under a system allowing free flow of teachers, this phenomenon may be more common, which is the case for Anning City and Wenshan Prefecture. In Wenshan and other prefectures and counties, there were many scattered teaching posts due to geographical conditions. In the absence of special subsidies for teaching in remote mountainous areas, some teaching posts were unable to retain regular teachers, leading to necessity for substitute teachers.

The third is financial constraints. By taking advantage of a segmented teacher market, some local governments were willing to retain some substitute teachers, rather than replacing all of them with regular teaching staff for financial reasons. The counties under the jurisdiction of Wenshan Prefecture where teachers were an enviable high-income group. However, within the group of teachers, there was a serious problem of unequal pay for equal work between substitute teachers and regular teachers. The income of regular teachers consisted of at least the following: (1) the "state standard salary" consisting of basic salary, position ranking salary, and allowances based on years of teaching; (2) the "three subsidies" provided by the provincial government, namely, border subsidies, plateau subsidies and price subsidies, with an amount of RMB180-RMB240/month; (3) the "other subsidies" of RMB105/month, also provided by the provincial government; (4) the provincial "intellectual allowance", RMB60/month for undergraduates, RMB50/month for junior college graduates, RMB30/month for graduates from technical secondary schools and others; (5) the provincial government introduced an increase of RMB400 subsidy in 2003, of which RMB200 provided by the provincial government and RMB200 by the local government. Wenshan failed to provide the prefecture subsidy due to fiscal difficulties. To add the above five items together, if the minimum state standard salary was RMB800/month, the monthly income of a regular teacher would be at least RMB1,315. This was 3.45 times the maximum monthly salary of substitute teachers in the prefecture, 12.1 times the minimum monthly salary, and 7.1 times the average monthly salary of substitute teachers. In this way, the local government could keep more funds by hiring fewer regular teachers and retaining more substitute teachers.[41] For example, as of October 2004, there were still 325 substitute teachers in Malipo county. Regarding why it was not possible to replace substitute teachers with regular teachers within one or two years, the County Education Bureau explained that the county-wide teacher establishment approved by the county government was sufficient, but each year the personnel establishment of the educational system approved by the county government was limited. For example, in 2004, only 100 positions were approved at first, and 150 were reached with extra effort. The county government's strict control over the number of positions in the education system was mainly due to fiscal difficulties.[42]

[41] Institute of Educational Economics Peking University, "Research on Rural Education Development in Yunnan Province", 2004.

[42] Institute of Educational Economics Peking University, "Research on Rural Education Development in Yunnan Province", 2004.

7.3.4.2 The Composition of Substitute Teachers: Taking Malipo as an Example

Substitute teachers in Yunnan Province are still a relatively large group. In Wenshan Prefecture, the basic situation of substitute teachers is shown in Table 7.10.

Substitute teachers in Malipo county accounted for 10% of all the substitute teachers in Wenshan Prefecture. As of October 2004, there were 325 substitute teachers in Malipo county. The composition was as follows.[43]

- 316 people among the 325 indicated the time they started working as a substitute teacher, accounting for 97.2%. Among them, 137 people were hired after 2000, accounting for 43.4% of the 316 substitute teachers. The number of substitute teachers employed in 2000, 2001, 2002, 2003, 2004 was 22, 7, 20, 29, 59, respectively, accounting for 6.9%, 2.2%, 6.2%, 9%, and 18.4% of the total. 141 people were employed in the 1990s, accounting for 44.6%. From 1980 to 1989, 37 people were hired, accounting for 11.7%. Only one person was hired in March 1976. This shows that the county was still hiring new substitute teachers in early 2000s.
- Among the 325 people, 27 did not indicate their Hukou category. Among the 298 people giving their Hukou information, 38 were from non-agricultural and urban households, 18 from agricultural and grain households, and 242 from agricultural households, accounting for 12.8%, 6% and 81.2%, respectively.
- Among the 321 people included in the statistics, 9 graduated from junior colleges, 72 from technical secondary schools. 99, 133 and 8 substitute teachers were senior high school, middle school and primary school graduates, accounting for 30.8%, 40.5%, and 2.5%, respectively. The academic qualifications of most substitute teachers did not meet the requirements for public teachers.

Wenshan Prefecture has actively dismissed substitute teachers. As of March 2004, among the eight counties in Wenshan Prefecture, Wenshan and Maguan had no substitute teachers. There were 3,865 substitute teachers in the other six counties, and the six counties were also taking measures based on their own conditions to replace substitute teachers.

7.3.4.3 Hiring and Dismissing Substitute Teachers in the Distribution Adjustment

Hiring and managing substitute teachers in Wenshan Prefecture was mainly conducted by the county or township government. Therefore, there were two types of substitute teachers: county-hired and township-hired. In Malipo County, all substitute teachers were hired by the county education bureau, and the costs were borne by the county government. The procedure was generally that the county education bureau and the county personnel bureau discussed and determined the number of substitute

[43] Institute of Educational Economics of Peking University, "Research on Rural Education Development in Yunnan Province", 2004.

Table 7.10 Overview of substitute teachers in Wenshan prefecture as of October 2004

County	Number of substitute teachers	Hiring agency		Academic qualifications				Income (RMB/month)		
		County government	Township government	Junior college	Technical secondary school	Senior high school	Middle school or below	Highest	Lowest	Average
Yanshan	1193	41	1152	116	853	119	105	385.75	108.5	171.99
Xichou	157	157	0	8	74	32	43	170	170	170
Malipo	333	333	0	8	57	116	152	184	139	170
Qiubei	1,014	972	42	27	448	281	258	310	280	292
Guangnan	998	135	863	52	575	327	44	360	110	149
Funing	170	170	0	0	92	44	34	160	160	160
The Prefecture overall	3865	1808	2057	211	2099	919	636	385.75	108.5	185.5

Note The substitute teachers in Wenshan County and Maguan County have all been dismissed. This table is compiled based on the "Table of Substitute Teachers in Wenshan Prefecture" provided by Wenshan Prefecture Education Bureau on October 30, 2004

teachers to be hired, and then the county finance bureau would allocate the funding for substitute teachers' salary according to the number and standards approved by the county personnel bureau. The decision-making of substitute teachers employed by the township was generally in the township, and most of the funding was provided by the township.

In many areas, substitute teachers were dismissed with a subsidy, which was determined by the teacher's length of service. Teachers with more years of teaching received a subsidy of RMB3000, and those with a shorter period of time were simply dismissed without any subsidy. As substitute teachers were temporarily hired, most of them could not focus on teaching due to the following factors. First, substitute teachers teach the same courses and have the same workload as the regular *gongban* teachers, but they have far less income, much lower social status, and thus strong sense of deprivation. Second, substitute teachers could be dismissed any time, with little chance of transforming to a regular *gongban* teacher, no sense of career security. Third, substitute teachers may quit whenever there is another job that offers more money than teaching. This state of mind of substitute teachers might affect the educational quality of the schools they serve.

In March 2004, Wenshan Prefecture conducted a survey of the six counties where there were still substitute teachers, and analyzed the main puzzles as well as problems as shown in Table 7.11.

As shown in Table 7.11, the main reasons leading to unsettled mind of substitute teachers are related to the policy of the distribution adjustment. To alleviate substitute teachers' unstable mind or solve the relevant problems as soon as possible is of great significance to ensuring educational quality.

7.3.4.4 The Distribution Adjustment and Flow of Teachers Have Caused the "Hollowing Out" of Rural Educational Resources

The distribution adjustment generally causes the flow of teachers to increase. The combination of teacher flow and the distribution adjustment will then lead to increasing educational resource concentration in designated schools such as comprehensive primary schools and center schools in some rural areas. Village primary schools and teaching posts, especially those in remote mountainous areas, will be faced with even fewer educational resources, i.e., "hollowing out" of educational resources is getting worse.

In some counties and cities in Yunnan, there are four methods in assigning public teachers to the remaining teaching posts after the distribution adjustment. The first is punitive administrative assignment, in which teachers who have offended their leaders or colleagues or made mistakes are assigned by the county education bureau to a certain rural school. The second is teachers who fail to win a better position in competition go to teach at the remaining teaching posts. The third is sending volunteers, such as college students voluntarily teaching to remote areas. Fourth is a mixed form of the above three. For example, the local government can stipulate that a teacher must work for one to two years in teaching posts or village primary schools

Table 7.11 Survey of main problems faced by substitute teachers in Wenshan prefecture

County and number of substitute teachers	Main puzzles and problems
Yanshan (1193 people)	• Low income • No hope of transforming to regular teachers • No dismissal subsidy when replaced by new teachers
Xichou (157 people)	• Those having got required academic qualifications were still unable to transfer to regular teachers • Most of substitute teachers would be dismissed with some allowance unpaid • Some substitute teachers have served many years, and would have no or few financial resources and no livelihood guarantee. Some previously dismissed teachers still had not received the dismissal subsidy
Malipo (333 people)	• Low income and family financial difficulties • No opportunity to take the recruitment examination. Even the opportunity comes, they still cannot compete on an equal footing with the fresh graduates of colleges and secondary schools, and thus no hope for transfer to regular teacher • Substitute teacher may be dismissed any time
Qiubei (1014 people)	• Whether those who have obtained a technical secondary school education or above would be included in the national recruitment examination. If they were hired as full-time personnel, how to verify their length of service (teaching years) and professional title • The same comprehensive scores were required for the substitute teachers as the fresh graduates of universities in the national recruitment examination, while some substitute teachers had to work long hours or work in remote mountainous areas, leading to unfair competition
Guangnan (998 people)	• Low income • Those who have obtained a technical secondary school education or above before 2001 hoped to be allowed to take the recruitment examination of public institutions • It was better to quit sooner under the policy of "dismiss one (substitute teacher) for hiring a new (regular teacher)"
Funing (170 people)	• Substitute teachers have heavy work load and long working hours, with much less income than public teachers • Whether substitute teachers with many years of teaching can tranfer to regular teachers • Whether compensation or subsidy are provided to dismissed substitute teachers
The prefecture total (3865 people)	

Source Wenshan Prefecture Education Bureau, Substitute Teachers in Wenshan Prefecture, March 2004

before reassigned to schools in the county seat. In the distribution adjustment, how to maintain the teaching quality of grassroots schools is an important issue. Judging from the practice of some counties and cities in Yunnan Province, this problem has not been well resolved. On the contrary, with the liberalization of the teacher market, the problem is getting worse.

7.3.5 Effects of the Distribution Adjustment for Rural Primary and Secondary Schools

Research on the effects of rural primary and secondary school distribution adjustment can distinguish short-term effects and long-term effects. The short-term effects include positive effects and negative effects.

7.3.5.1 Positive Effects of the School Distribution Adjustment

The positive effects of school distribution adjustment can be roughly divided into economic and social effects. Economic effects include improving the efficiency of school running and saving educational resources. Social effects are mainly reflected in creating better conditions for students' all-round development. From the field survey and related information, most of the economic and social goals set for the distribution adjustment of some counties in Anning city and Wenshan prefecture have been achieved.

7.3.5.2 Negative Effects of the School Distribution Adjustment

The distribution adjustment of rural primary and secondary schools in Yunnan may have brought about the following negative effects.

- The distribution adjustment caused negative emotions among the substitute teachers of the merged and closed schools.
- The flow of teachers caused by distribution adjustment has caused "hollowing out" of educational resources of the lower level rural schools. When good teaches leave, excellent students will also leave. As a result, the lower the level of education, the worse the quality of education, which will inevitably have an adverse impact on educational equity.
- The impact on disadvantaged groups is obvious. The impact on poor families and families in ethnic minority areas is an important dimension to measure the fairness of education distribution policies. In the distribution adjustment in some places in Yunnan, government and schools adopted various methods to reduce the distribution adjustment's impact on disadvantaged groups, such as increasing subsidies for students from poor families and redistributing subsidies for boarding

students. Schools revised the standard of food subsidy for boarding students from the provincial government, by splitting one student's subsidy into two shares or two shares into three, thus benefiting more students with the same amount of funding. In 2005, the state implemented the "two exemptions and one subsidy" policy, under which the central government will pay all the textbook expenses for children from poor families in rural areas during the compulsory education stage, and provide living subsidies to poor students in boarding schools. In 2006, the western region took the lead in implementing a new mechanism of supporting rural compulsory education, in which tuition and miscellaneous fees for rural students will be all exempted. These measures will undoubtedly play an important role in alleviating the burden on poor families caused by the distribution adjustment.

7.3.5.3 Long-Term Impacts

With continuous modernization and globalization, the originally isolated mountainous areas and ethnic minority areas have become more and more connected with the economic and social system in a larger geographic scope. The original boundaries have been merged or disappeared, and people's sense of space and distance has been changing. The continuous upward clustering of school distribution along the geographical hierarchical system is the result of this background, and it is also a manifestation of modernization and globalization. The adjustment of school distribution will play an extremely important role in breaking the traditional isolated regional concept and forming a new and broader one.

It is an inevitable trend in the modern era to reduce campuses and teaching posts, to promote centralization schooling and to develop boarding schools. Large schools can attract more qualified teachers and experts in relevant fields, and will be more qualified to deal with all kinds of issues in school running, as well as cultivate students' adaptability. For example, larger schools may provide students with better health care facilities, such as an in-school infirmary or health department, and modern transportation, etc. to deal with students' health issues, which is nearly impossible for a remote teaching site. In addition, students at center schools have access to more qualified sports equipment and physical education courses, lowering the overall health risks of students.

School life provides important conditions for the socialization of each individual and the formation of modern personality. The larger the school, the more separated it is from the traditional local concept, and the closer it is to the modern society. The organizational form of a large school itself is a feature of the modern society. In such an organizational environment, it is necessary for students to live with fellows from other places, which is conducive to forming students' social skills, making them happier and better at interacting with others. Even conflicts with classmates are helpful in forging students' sense of cooperation and ability to cooperate and compete with others.

7.3.6 Suggestions on the Distribution Adjustment of Rural Primary and Secondary Schools in Yunnan Province

On the whole, the distribution adjustment of rural primary and secondary schools in Yunnan Province has shown a trend of steady implementation, which is closely related to the current status of Yunnan's rural compulsory education and its financial capability. The basic conditions will continue for quite a long time in most parts of Yunnan. Therefore, it is necessary to put forward some suggestions for the distribution adjustment to be further implemented in the future.

- Emphasizing on the importance of the actual needs of local education. The distribution adjustment funding in Yunnan Province is highly dependent on transfer payments from higher-level governments. Therefore, the adjustments may be greatly affected by the intentions of superiors, so there may be problems of sacrificing local autonomy and ignoring the opinions of local people, and putting forward what do not comfort to the actual development conditions of local education. Local policymakers need to be vigilant about these possible drawbacks.
- Mobilizing social capital. Yunnan's educational development has received lots of donations from the international and domestic organizations and social groups. Meanwhile, many places in Yunnan have established paired assistance relationships with other provinces or national ministries and commissions. These relationships are essential for Yunnan to obtain more financial support and comprehensive assistance in the future.
- Adhering to the gradual approach in the distribution adjustment. The gradual approach is adapted to the current conditions of local education, the financial capability of local governments and the bearing capacity of local people, and thus is effective.
- Paying attention to cultural diversity. Yunnan is a province with many ethnic minority groups. In the distribution adjustment, the integration of ethnic education and modern education should be highly emphasized. The distribution should not only be based on the geographical distance, but also the cultural circle of each ethnic group.
- Highlighting the key points and difficulties, and combining the adjustment with popularizing compulsory education. The focus of Yunnan province should be overcoming difficulties in popularizing rural compulsory education in border counties, and ethnic minority counties. In these areas, developing boarding systems and running boarding schools with the help from the central and provincial government is a better solution.
- Improving the transfer payment system. Transfer payments from the central and provincial government should be intensified. In addition, the responsibilities of the central, provincial and local governments in developing rural compulsory education should be clarify and formulated in relevant regulations, so that local governments and education authorities can form stable expectations for the development of local education and make long-term arrangements.

- Policy implementation needs to be tailored to local conditions. Regional differences within Yunnan Province are quite prominent, and different policies should be adopted to distinguish the conditions of different places. The areas currently still universalizing the nine-year compulsory education still face many tasks in infrastructure construction. These areas should first estimate future demand for local education and make planning in accordance with the changes in local population. For areas that have completed the nine-year compulsory education popularization earlier, local school-age population having shown a significant decline, and improving educational quality having become the key issue, accelerating the distribution adjustment may be considered. For areas that are between the above two types and have just universalized the nine-year compulsory education, consolidating the local compulsory education system may be the key, and a large-scale distribution adjustment may not be proper. The distribution adjustment of rural primary and secondary schools is a long-term and evolving task, as the school-age population is constantly changing, and it is impossible to accomplish the whole task at one stroke. In addition to adjusting the distribution according to the endurance and acceptance of the local government and people, it is also necessary to make full use of all the resources available.

The allocation of rural compulsory education resources, including human, financial and material resources, etc. is geographically reflected in the distribution structure of primary and secondary schools, and the fairness and efficiency of allocation will also be directly reflected in the school distribution structure. Therefore, the distribution adjustment will directly affect the fairness and efficiency of the distribution of educational resources. The spatial distribution of schools is also an interest structure, directly related to the rights and interests of government at all levels and related stakeholders, such as students, parents, teachers, etc. The distribution adjustment involves interactions for interest coordination and competition among different stakeholders. The interactions will directly affect the distribution adjustment, as well as the interests of related vulnerable groups.

Regarding the spatial distribution of schools as a social structure, this chapter proposes a framework to analyze the mechanisms of various social groups shaping the spatial distribution of schools, and uses this framework to study the distribution adjustment of primary and secondary schools in Yunnan Province. The framework developed here may have a certain significance for understanding the nation-wide rural school distribution adjustment. However, research on the rural school distribution adjustment in Yunnan Province is still very preliminary and tentative, without enough attention to some important aspects, such as changes in students' academic performance as well as the overall effectiveness and efficiency of the adjustment. Such issues require more specialized and in-depth research in the future.

Chapter 8
Research on Equal Access to Higher Education

8.1 Two Hypotheses on the Size of College Enrollment and Equal Access

There has been a worldwide expansion in education since the twentieth century. In the process of educational expansion, has the impact of student socioeconomic background on equality of educational opportunities changed? What has been changed? In other words, can the degree of educational equality be improved by expanding the scale of education? In the study of these issues, two theoretical hypotheses have emerged: the maximally maintained inequality (MMI) hypothesis proposed by Raftery in 1993 (Raftery and Hout 1993) and the effectively maintained inequality (EMI) hypothesis proposed by Lucas in 2001 (Lucas 2001).

Raftery et al. studied the relationship between the expansion of secondary education and equal access in Ireland in 1993. Ireland's secondary education has been expanding steadily in the twentieth century, especially in the latter half of the 1960s. The research of Raftery et al. found that with the changes in scale and the implementation of a series of fiscal policies on equalizing educational opportunity, the impact of family background on educational opportunity was weakening. However, the barriers between strata have not disappeared. As a result, Raftery et al. proposed the MMI theory. The core arguments can be distilled into two key points. First, the continuous expansion of education does not necessarily lead to changing impacts of family social status on people's educational opportunities. Second, educational inequality does not decrease when the rapid increase in educational opportunities exceeds the aggregate demand of society. Only if the educational needs of the most advantaged socioeconomic group have reached a certain saturation point, or have reached the "maximization" of a certain level of education, the difference in educational opportunities at that level between the advantaged and disadvantaged may be reduced. Otherwise, parents with high socioeconomic status will always look for various ways to maximize their children's educational opportunities.

W. Min, *Educational Input, Resource Allocation and Returns to Human Capital*,
https://doi.org/10.1007/978-981-96-4687-6_8

The MMI theory has exerted significant influence since its inception. However, the proposition advanced by MMI—namely, "when a certain level of education becomes widespread, the impact of a family's socioeconomic background on educational opportunities at that level will diminish and may even vanish"—has been questioned and criticized by Lucas et al. Lucas pointed out that MMI does not take into account the differences in the quality and type of education, thus failed to reveal the profound relationship between family socioeconomic background and educational opportunities. Lucas then put forward the EMI theory. He believed that when the equality in terms of quantity is achieved at a certain educational level, the inequality in educational quality should be considered. The advantaged social group will ensure the advantages of their own and their children's educational opportunities whenever and wherever possible. If there is significant and universal imbalance in the quantity of educational opportunities for different social groups, the group will gain a quantitative advantage. But if the imbalance in the quality of educational opportunities is universal, the most advantaged socioeconomic group will gain a qualitative advantage. As long as a certain level of education has not been popularized, the group with superior socioeconomic status will use various resources to ensure their access to that level of education. Once this level of education is popularized, they will use their abilities to ensure their education of the same quantity but better quality.

Both EMI and MMI emphasize the social strata competition among families, and both believe that the impact of a family's social background is significant when a certain education level is not universalized. Nevertheless, there is disagreement between EMI and MMI. MMI believes that the impact of family background for universalized education levels could be zero, while EMI believes that for any universalized education level, the competition will revolve with the type and quality of education, and not only inequality exists, but the impact should not be insignificant.

The concept of educational opportunity involves different perspectives. We can group different research perspectives into three categories. (1) Research on the status of educational participation at a certain level. The analysis from this perspective focuses on the equalization of educational development at the quantitative level, for example, examining the equality of educational opportunities through the distribution of schooling years or the enrollment rate of a certain level of education. (2) Research on the participation of different quality or type of education. This perspective focuses on qualitative differences rather than quantitative differences. For example, divide higher education into general higher education and higher vocational education to study the participation of different types of higher education; examine the equalization of educational opportunities according to different quality levels such as human resources and material resources or social reputation. (3) Research on the equalization of educational benefits. For example, study the distribution of educational benefits, including employment opportunities, occupations, income, etc. MMI focuses on the first perspective, while EMI focuses on the second perspective. Both MMI and EMI provide valuable findings that respectively shed light on aspects not revealed by the other, so the combination of the two theories will contribute to a deeper understanding of the expansion of higher education in China and changes in the distribution of opportunities at different levels.

8.2 Empirical Study Findings of Equal Access to Higher Education in China

Since the 1990s, the enrollment of China's higher education has been increasing. The increase in enrollment has undoubtedly provided more higher educational opportunities. As the scale increases, how does the distribution of higher education opportunities in different social groups change? Does the expansion of scale weaken the influence of family economic background on enrollment opportunities?

This chapter will provide empirical analysis for the above issues from two aspects. One is to look at changes in the level of equalization through the study of urban residents' access to higher education regardless of the type of higher education institutions. The other is to look at changes in the distribution of higher education opportunities among students with different socioeconomic backgrounds in different types of universities and colleges.

8.2.1 The Distribution of Higher Education Enrollment Opportunities for Urban Residents without Quality Considerations

This section analyzes the composition of family socioeconomic background for family members under the age of 23 with a college degree or above (including those who have received or are receiving higher education) (hereinafter referred to as "college students") by using the data from the urban household survey conducted by the National Bureau of Statistics of the People's Republic of China in 1991 and 2000. From Figs. 8.1 and 8.2, it is easy to see the changes in the distribution of different income groups of college students.

In Fig. 8.2, the horizontal axis represents the family economic background of "college students" in ascending order, and the vertical axis indicates the cumulative percentage of "college students". If members of different economic backgrounds have equal access to higher education, the Lorenz Curve[1] is the 45° straight line, known as the line of equality. It has a slope of 1 which illustrates perfect equality in income or wealth. The Lorenz Curve lies beneath the 45° line of equality. The further away the curve is from the 45° line, the greater the income or wealth inequality in an economy.

Figure 8.2 shows that the Lorenz Curve was closer to a 45° curve in 2000 than in 1991. At the same time, we follow the approach of the Gini coefficient and define the "Gini Coefficient of Higher Educational Opportunity." The coefficient is between 0 and 1. A zero coefficient implies that higher educational opportunities are absolutely equal in each income group. An increase in the coefficient implies deeper inequality.

[1] Developed by economist Max O. Lorenz in 1905, the Lorenz Curve graphically shows the degree of income or wealth inequality in an economy.

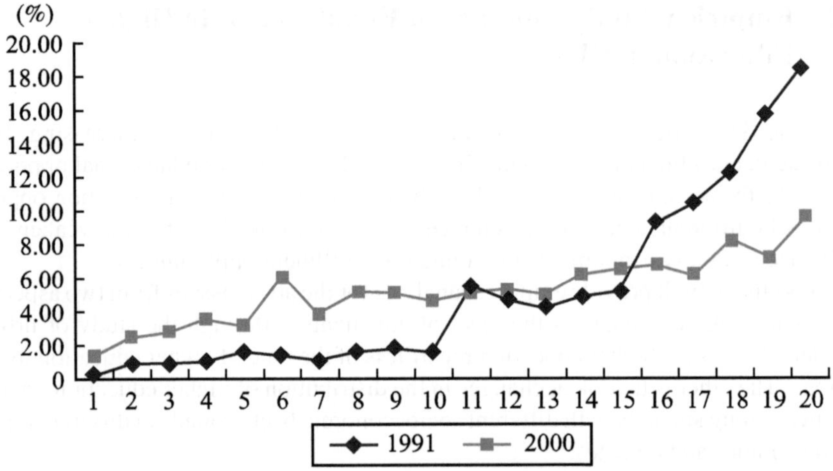

Fig. 8.1 Distribution of college students in different socioeconomic groups

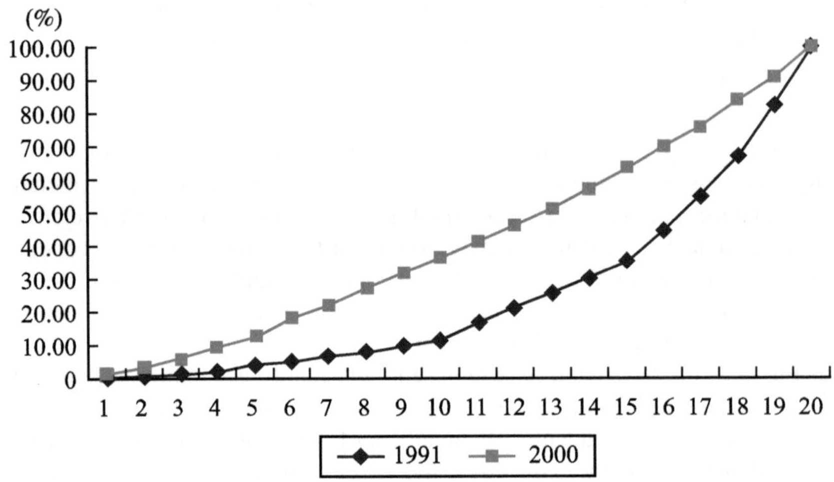

Fig. 8.2 Cumulative distribution of college students in different socioeconomic groups

The calculated values of the "Gini Coefficient of Higher Educational Opportunity" in 1991 and 2000 are 0.4746 and 0.1520, respectively, which indicate that the distribution of "college students" among people with different socioeconomic conditions has been significantly more equalized.

In addition to the analysis of the family's economic status, we also analyzes the educational level of the parents (head of the household) of "cóllege students". Table 8.1 shows that compared with 1991, the proportion of "college students" from households whose heads are at a relatively low educational level in 2000 has increased

Table 8.1 Distribution of college students by household head's education level (unit: %)

Education level (head of household)	1991	2000
College degree and above	44.8	30.8
Technical secondary school	15.0	13.8
High school	14.8	18.4
Middle school and below	25.4	37.0

significantly. In other words, the equal distribution of "college students" among people with different educational backgrounds has changed significantly.

In summary, the analysis shows that families with lower socioeconomic and educational backgrounds have significantly improved their participation in higher education. Compared with 1991, the equalization of higher educational opportunities in 2000 has improved significantly.

In fact, with the reform of the higher education funding system during the 1990s, the proportion of tuition and fees in the entire source of higher education funding has changed significantly. Non-budgetary funds, especially tuition and fees, have been playing an increasingly important role in higher education funding. In 1995, public expenditure on higher education accounted for 73.29% of the total funding, but declined to 55.23% in 2000, instead, the tuition and fees increased from 11.89% to 21.09%, respectively. The proportion of tuition and fees in per student expenditure increases year by year, rising from 6% in 1990 to 16% in 1995 and then to 31% in 2000. Tuition and fees accounted for 28% and 12.62% respectively in per capita net income for rural and urban residents in 1990, rising to 67% and 25% in 1995, 160% and 61% in 1999. Although the cost recovery policy has played a vital and active role in supporting the expansion of the higher education system, the rapid increase in tuition has led to common concerns about the detriment to equal access to higher education.

The following aspects may explain the improved equalization in access to higher education in urban China shown by the statistical results above:

First, the expansion of higher education has brought about a general increase in higher education participation for all social strata, especially middle and lower classes. In 1991, the number of students enrolled in regular colleges and universities was 2.04 million, but increased to 5.56 million in 2000. The expansion of enrollment may largely offset the negative impact of rising private costs of higher education on enrollment opportunities. This fact supports the MMI theory to some extent.

Second, the private return on China's college graduates has significantly increased in the 1990s. Studies have shown that the private Mincer rate of return on higher education in China was 3.78% in 1991 and 13.1% in 2000, showing a significant rise (Chen et al. 2003). Compared with the internal rate of return that considers both private costs and private benefits, the Mincer rate of return, which only reflects private benefits, may play a more critical role in determining people's willingness to pay for higher education. In other words, when people decide whether to get higher education, they consider more the future benefits of higher education graduates.

Third, the data used above includes only urban households. It is unclear whether the results will still hold if rural data is also considered.

Fourth, the higher education system itself has a pyramid structure with noticeable differences in quality and types of education within the system. However, due to data limitations, this research cannot distinguish the enrollment of different types of higher education. In order to further deepen the research, the following empirical analysis will use other data to explore the changes in higher education enrollment from a quality perspective.

8.2.2 *Changes in Distribution of College Students from Different Socioeconomic Backgrounds with the Type and Quality of Higher Education Institutions Considered*

Some scholars have provided insights on changes in access to different types of higher education institutions (HEIs) in China. Most believe that family background is an essential factor affecting enrollment opportunities. However, due to different research designs and data sources, there is no consistent conclusion on changes in enrollment opportunities, especially changes and trends for different types of HEIs (such as Xie and Li 2000; Ding 2000). This section uses data from the survey of different types of HEIs across the country in June 2004 and analyzes the family socioeconomic background of undergraduates matriculated in various years.

The quality of HEIs can be graded according to different criteria. For this chapter, we divide the 15 sample colleges into two types by their name recognition and attractiveness to students. Tier 1 colleges refer to colleges and universities under the direct jurisdiction of the Ministry of Education and other ministries or under the "985 Project". Tier 2 colleges include those not in Tier 1. Considering the attractiveness to students, this section will classify all the agricultural, forestry, and geological colleges and universities in Tier 2.

8.2.2.1 Family Occupational Background of Students

The family occupational background of a student is an important indicator reflecting the socioeconomic background of the student. This part of the research will use the father's occupation to represent the occupational background of a family.

First, based on the occupational structure data of the fifth national census in 2000, we divided the proportion of students with various family occupational backgrounds by the proportion of the corresponding occupational population in the total population. If the result of the ratio is 1, it indicates that the proportion of students in this type of occupation and those who are engaged in this type of occupation in the entire labor market is roughly the same; if the ratio is less than 1, it means that

Table 8.2 Ratio of father's occupational background to corresponding occupations

Item	Tier 1	Tier 2	Tier 1/Tier 2
Farming, forestry, animal husbandry, side-line production and fishery	0.27	0.49	0.54
Blue collar workers in cities	0.73	0.76	0.95
General management staff	3.61	3.20	1.13
Senior professionals	2.82	1.92	1.46
Heads of units or departments	10.62	6.58	1.62

Table 8.3 Changes in fathers' Occupational Index

Item	Student enrollment year			
	2000	2001	2002	2003
Tier 1 colleges	56.8	55.4	57.8	58.4
Tier 2 colleges	51.8	50.9	48.2	51.1
Tier 1/Tier 2	1.10	1.09	1.20	1.14

the proportion of students in this type of occupation is lower than the proportion of people engaged in such occupations in the labor market, and vice versa. Table 8.2 reflects the fathers' occupational background of college students.

Table 8.2 shows that the higher educational opportunities obtained by people from families of farming, forestry, animal husbandry, side-line production, fishery and blue collar workers are significantly less than the proportion of the population engaged in the occupation in the social population (the ratio is smaller than 1), while students from families of these two categories of occupational background get fewer chances of admission to Tier 1 colleges than Tier 2 colleges (the value of Tier 1 is less than that of Tier 2). Students from families of the other three sectors have a significantly higher ratio of receiving higher education than the general public (all ratios greater than 1). In particular, those who came from professional backgrounds as unit leaders have 10 times and 6 times more chances of getting admission to Tier 1 and Tier 2 colleges respectively than the expected proportion of the general social population. The differences in access to higher education are significant.

Second, in order to comprehensively evaluate the occupation of a group, we build an Occupational Index[2] by assigning values to different occupations and using the proportion of different occupations as the weights for weighted summation. It is not difficult to see that the higher the Occupational Index value of a certain group, the higher the social status of the group, and vice versa. Table 8.3 shows the changes in fathers' Occupational Index by college levels.

[2] The calculation of "Occupational Index": First assign values to different occupations, then use the proportion of different occupations in the total personnel as the weight to perform a weighted sum. The absolute value of the occupational index has no special meaning and is mainly used to examine the trend of dynamic changes.

Table 8.4 Changes of student enrollment with fathers' occupation in farming, forestry, animal husbandry, side-line production and fishery

Item	Student enrollment year			
	2000	2001	2002	2003
Tier 1 colleges	0.187	0.175	0.141	0.177
Tier 2 colleges	0.296	0.297	0.340	0.312
Tier 1/Tier 2	0.632	0.589	0.415	0.567

Table 8.5 Changes in the proportion of students with fathers' occupational background as heads of units or senior professionals

Item	Student enrollment year			
	2000	2001	2002	2003
Tier 1 colleges	0.324	0.306	0.364	0.359
Tier 2 colleges	0.258	0.221	0.202	0.227
Tier 1/Tier 2	1.256	1.385	1.802	1.581

Table 8.3 shows that for students matriculated in the same year, the Occupational Index of their fathers in Tier 1 colleges is higher than that of the students' fathers in Tier 2 colleges. Over time, the Occupational Index of Tier 1 has an upward trend compared with that of the Tier 2 colleges.

Third, among all the occupations, people often focus on the weakest and the strongest occupational stratification. The most disadvantaged occupations are those engaged in farming, forestry, animal husbandry, side-line production, and fishery. The most powerful occupations include the heads of government agencies, business executives, as well as senior professionals. Table 8.4 shows the change in the proportion of students whose fathers' occupation is farming, forestry, animal husbandry, side-line production and fishery. Table 8.5 shows the changes in the proportion of students whose fathers' occupation are heads of enterprises or senior professionals.

Table 8.4 shows that for the same enrollment year, the proportion of students with fathers' occupational background in farming, forestry, animal husbandry, side-line production, and fishery in Tier 1 colleges is lower than that of Tier 2 colleges. Over time, the proportion of Tier 2 colleges seems to have a downward trend.

Table 8.5 shows that for the same enrollment year, the proportion of students with fathers' occupational backgrounds as unit leaders or senior professionals in Tier 1 colleges is higher than that in Tier 2 colleges. Over time, the proportion of Tier 1 colleges shows a rising trend compared with Tier 2 colleges.

8.2.2.2 Changes in the Students' Family Educational Background

Family educational background is an important factor reflecting the socioeconomic background of students. This section uses the father's education level to represent

Table 8.6 Changes in fathers' Educational Index

Item	Student enrollment year			
	2000	2001	2002	2003
Tier 1 colleges	47.8	47.9	50.6	52.3
Tier 2 colleges	46.8	45.3	43.1	45.8
Tier 1/Tier 2	1.02	1.06	1.18	1.14

the family's educational background. In order to make a comprehensive evaluation of the education level of a certain group, this research builds an "Educational Index". Similar to the Occupational Index above, we first assign values to different education levels, and then use the proportion of different education levels as weights for weighted summation. The absolute value of the Educational Index has no special meaning and is mainly used to examine the trend of changes. According to the weight assignment of education at all levels in the Educational Index calculation, it is not difficult to see that the higher the Educational Index of a certain group, the higher the social status of the group, and vice versa. Table 8.6 is the Educational Index of fathers of students matriculated in different years by college types.

Table 8.6 shows that for the same year of enrollment, the educational index of fathers of students in Tier 1 colleges is higher than that of fathers of students in Tier 2 colleges. Over time, the ratio of the Educational Index of Tier 1 colleges to that of Tier 2 colleges shows a rising trend.

8.2.2.3 Influencing Factors for Entering Different Types of Colleges

Based on the above analysis, this part further uses logistic regression to explore the impact of family socioeconomic background on whether a student can be admitted to Tier 1 colleges.

The dependent variable is a dummy variable (Y_1) for entering Tier 1 colleges. The independent variables include (1) family economic status (Eco); (2) whether the father is the "head of unit or department" or "senior professional" (Ocu-1–2); (3) whether the father is in agriculture, forestry, animal husbandry, side-line production, and fishing or a worker (Ocu-7–8); (4) whether the student comes from an urban area (Residency); (5) the enrollment year (Time). The results of logistic regression analysis are shown in Table 8.7.

As shown in Table 8.7, the opportunity to obtain high-quality higher education (Tier 1 colleges) is significantly correlated with a student's birthplace, family economic background, and father's occupation. For example, among all college students, the opportunities for urban students to get admitted to Tier 1 colleges are 1.48 times that for rural students (see the Exp(B) value of the Residency variable). Among all college students, if the father's occupation is farming, forestry, animal husbandry, side-line production, and fishery, or blue-collar workers, the student's chance of getting admitted to Tier 1 colleges is minimal (only 0.768 times).

Table 8.7 Logistic regression results

Vatiable	Coefficient B	Standard error	Significance level	Exp(B)
Residency	0.392	0.049	0.000	1.480
Eco	0.047	0.005	0.000	1.048
Ocu-1–2	0.123	0.060	0.042	1.130
Ocu-7–8	−0.265	0.054	0.000	0.768
Constant	833.549	42.072	0.000	

However, if the father is a unit leader or a senior professional, the student's chance of entering Tier 1 colleges gets significantly higher than others. Family income also has a significant positive impact on admission to Tier 1 colleges.

Based on the above empirical analysis results of the quality stratification of higher education institutions, we have reached the following conclusions:

- Students from families of farming, forestry, animal husbandry, side-line production, and fishery or blue collar workers have significantly lower access to higher education. Such students have even fewer chances to attend Tier 1 colleges. Opportunities are significantly higher for the students with family background of management personnel in enterprises and public institutions, senior professionals, and heads of units or departments. In particular, those with such occupational backgrounds as heads of units get 10 times and 6 times that of the expected proportion of the general public in Tier 1 or Tier 2 colleges. The difference in access to higher education is noticeable.
- Father's Occupational Index for students in Tier 1 colleges is significantly higher than that of the students in Tier 2 colleges. The index for students in Tier 1 colleges showed a trend of gradual increase over time, while that in Tier 2 colleges showed a trend of decline from 2000 to 2002.
- The proportion of students in Tier 1 colleges with occupational background in farming, forestry, animal husbandry, side-line production, and fishery is significantly lower than that in Tier 2 colleges. The proportion of students in Tier 1 colleges with occupations in agriculture sectors showed a decreasing trend over time, while that in Tier 2 colleges showed an increasing trend from 2000 to 2002.
- The proportion of students in Tier 1 colleges with an occupational background of heads of units or departments or senior professionals is significantly higher than that in Tier 2 colleges. Moreover, this proportion has shown an increasing trend over time, while that in Tier 2 colleges has shown a decreasing trend from 2000 to 2002.
- The Educational Index of fathers of students in the Tier 1 colleges is significantly higher than that in Tier 2 colleges. The index for Tier 1 colleges has increased significantly, however, the index did not show the same trend of change for Tier 2 colleges although there was a significant decline from 2000 to 2002.
- Factors such as family economic status, father's occupation, birthplace, and others have a significant impact on students' access to Tier 1 colleges.

The above empirical studies on the distribution of higher educational opportunities in China provide a basis for the interpretation of MMI and EMI theory at different levels. On the first level, with higher educational expansion, the degree of equal access to higher education reflected by quantitative indicators increases significantly. This result is consistent with the MMI hypothesis. On the second level, when quality factors are considered, the distribution of higher educational opportunities does not show a more equalized trend. On the contrary, high-quality higher education has shown a tendency to be more inclined to advantaged social groups, and non-elite colleges do play an essential role in expanding access to higher education for the disadvantaged groups. From the second level, EMI can better explain the actual situation in China.

8.3 Identifying the Causes

China's college admissions are based on the score of the national college entrance examination as the only criterion. Whether it is the national college entrance examination or the unified college entrance examination of various provinces and cities, the system guarantees the correspondence between college access opportunity and examination score. Although there are issues of fairness in the allocation of enrollment quotas in college admissions, and economically disadvantaged groups need to consider affordability when making higher education choices, from the perspective of the enrollment mechanism, the college entrance examination scores still play a decisive role, and do not discriminate against those from rural areas and disadvantaged family economic backgrounds. So, what are the reasons for the disproportionate preference for high-quality university education opportunities to socially advantaged groups? Here are two possible reasons.

- Due to the enormous demand of urban residents for high-quality primary and secondary education, private investment, including school selection fees, has become an essential source of income for elite primary and secondary schools. In early 2000s, national fiscal policy for compulsory education has aimed at improving equalization of public sector investment in primary and secondary schools, but the effect of implementation is not satisfactory. The increased public education investment in backward schools is far behind the sum of public and private resources obtained by high-quality schools. This has created a huge gap in terms of the quality of public education between urban and rural areas, and the gap among different regions is likely to further widen. The widening gap in the ability to obtain resources has enlarged the difference in teaching quality, especially in the English and computer courses, as such subjects or related abilities play an important role in the national college entrance examination.
- After-school tutoring has become an essential part of urban residents' investment in their children's education. The author's research on urban families' education expenditure shows that more than 70% of urban families spend on after-school

tutoring or hobby classes. Expenditure on off-campus education accounts for about 30%–40% of the total educational investment for urban residents. Meanwhile, there is a significantly positive correlation between expenditure on tutoring and family economic status. These analyses indicate that competition for better access to higher education has shifted from basic education within the formal school system to off-campus tutoring and enhancement. Students from families with socioeconomic advantages improve their academic performance and enhance high-status extracurricular activities such as music or sports through higher quality tutoring, which could help them gain bonus points in the college entrance, and then increase their chances of entering high-quality colleges and universities. In other words, the advantaged social stratum always maximizes the educational resources of their children in various ways.

8.4 Discussion and Policy Implications

Equalization of educational access in relation to quantity is important because it is, after all, a dimension of equal access to higher education. The history of some countries shows that the continuous expansion of higher education does not necessarily bring about increasingly equal access associated with quantity when higher education is far from universal. Therefore, the improvement of China's higher education access for urban residents in the 1990s has a positive significance for improving the fairness of the entire society.

Nevertheless, it is not enough to focus solely on the participation rate in higher education (that is, the expansion scale or quantity). In addition to the quantitative perspective, equal access to higher education at different quality levels is also a critical aspect. In fact, the degree of equal access after stratification within the education system is closely related to the education system of a country. Raftery et al. have explained the reasons why MMI ignored the quality of education. They believe that because Ireland's secondary education implements a unified national curriculum and students across the country receive the same content of education at the same time, the quality factors within the education do not seem to be necessary. Obviously, this condition does not hold for China. There are significant differences within China's higher education system, and the degree of differentiation among different universities in terms of resources and reputation is very significant. Therefore, in addition to quantitative differences, our research also considered qualitative differences. The quality difference is a more profound indicator to measure the equality of access in China's education system. When the scale of education expands rapidly, the importance of quality differences will inevitably replace the importance of quantitative differences, and it will increasingly become the basis for people to choose higher education. The empirical analysis in this chapter shows that while the participation rate, which reflects the quantity of higher education, shows an unequal reduction, the degree of inequality in quality has continued and even increased. Therefore, to understand the changes in the distribution of opportunities in China's higher education, it is necessary to analyze both the changes in opportunities related to quantity and the changes in opportunities related to quality. The combination of the two can make the analysis more comprehensive.

The findings of this chapter has the following policy implications.

For a period of time, a dilemma of student loans in China's higher education is that commercial banks are willing to provide loans for elite colleges and universities, but lack the enthusiasm for granting loans to non-elite colleges and universities. Our research results show that it is the non-elite local colleges and universities that recruit a large number of children from socially and economically disadvantaged families. Proper policies to increase loans to students at non-elite higher education institutions are necessary to improve equal access in higher education.

Concerns about access to higher education usually focus people's attention on the fiscal policy of higher education, including tuition, student financial aid policy and so on. However, in addition to economic factors, family's educational resources, social capital, etc. also play a role that cannot be ignored and may be decisive. As the scale of China's higher education expands, financial aid policies are also being built, which allow students with a relatively disadvantaged social and economic background to get more opportunities for higher education, but it still has not changed the situation that the advantaged groups have more opportunities for high-quality higher education, and the inequality even tends to worsen. The authors argue that the reason for this might stem more from institutional deficiencies outside the higher education financial system. Therefore, in addition to improving the financial aid policy for higher education, a series of related social and educational policies should also be improved. It is necessary to reflect on the admission selection mechanism of China's higher education, and we can learn from the relevant mechanisms and policies of other countries to ensure the admission of disadvantaged groups. For example, elite colleges and universities can allocate a certain number of admissions each year to rural students and those with disadvantaged social and economic backgrounds, not only providing them with financial support, but also taking appropriate care in admissions.

It is a general phenomenon that family background affects children's educational opportunities to varying degrees in any society. In fact, the education of children from disadvantaged groups will be restricted and affected by various conditions such as family income, parental education level and so on. The resistance to entry into higher education already exists in the primary and secondary education stages. The social and economic disadvantaged classes all over the world are disadvantaged to varying degrees in terms of educational opportunities. To achieve complete equal access in the strict sense is a near-utopian ideal in both developed and developing countries. However, the unremitting pursuit of equality of educational opportunity should never be underestimated by policymakers of all countries. If the idea of equal opportunity is unduly trampled, and the family socioeconomic background becomes the decisive factor in a person's access to higher education, that will have profound and long-term adverse social impacts. In order to build a harmonious society, improve educational opportunities for disadvantaged groups, and minimize the differences in educational opportunities between disadvantaged and dominant groups, it is necessary to conduct an in-depth analysis of the mechanisms causing the differences and explore possible solutions. The goal of public policy should be to manage and mitigate the extent of intergenerational influence in educational or economic status. With the expansion of enrollment scale, the government can improve the equal access to higher education through a more reasonable and balanced allocation of educational resources as well as continuous reform of fiscal policy. With the scale expansion, the reform of the education system and the education financing system will not only affect whether people have access to higher education, but also become an essential factor in determining the type and quality of higher education they will receive.

References

Chen, X., Chen, L., & Xia, C. (2003). Rates of Return to Schooling in Urban China: Changes in the 1990s. *Peking University Education Review, 2*, 65–72.

Ding, X. (2000). A Survey Report on Students with Different Family Incomes in China's Colleges and Universities. *Research on Education Tsinghua University, 2*, 102–108.

Lucas, S. (2001). Effectively Maintained Inequality: Education Transitions, Track Mobility, and Social Background Effects. *American Journal of Sociology, 106*(6), 1642–1690.

Raftery, A., & Hout, M. (1993). Maximally Maintained Inequality: Expansion, Reform, and Opportunity in Irish Education, 1921–75. *Sociology of Education, 66*(1), 41–62.

Xie, W., & Li, X. (2000). Investigation and Research Report on Higher Education Equity. *Economic Analysis of Education Policy*. People's Education Publishing House.

Part III
Education and Human Resource Allocation

Part III consists of three chapters, which comprehensively examine the impact of education on employment, job satisfaction, job mobility, industry choice, job promotion, and income levels. Chapter 9, "Survival Analysis Based on Unemployment Duration after Graduation and Education Level", studies the overall level of unemployment duration of urban youth groups above middle school and above, and uses the life table method to give the unemployment rate of groups with different education levels at different points in time. Chapter 10, "Education and Job Autonomy," explores how different levels of education affect job satisfaction through matching with a certain amount of work autonomy. Chapter 11, "Education, Job Mobility and Income", focuses on the relationship between individual education level and job mobility, and analyzes the impact of education on job mobility rates and types of mobility, as well as changes in income.

Chapter 9
Survival Analysis Based on Unemployment Duration After Graduation and Education Level

Unemployment has become a great challenge plaguing China's social and economic development since the late 1990s. According to the *Blue Book of the Chinese employment (2005)*, youth unemployment has become prominent while the problem of reemployment of laid-off workers has not been fundamentally solved. Young people are a disadvantaged group in the labor market, as they are vulnerable to unemployment due to lack of experience and on-the-job training opportunities. The large proportion of youth in the unemployed population is a notable issue in various countries. Studies have shown that young people falling into unemployment at the beginning of their working lives can lead to serious consequences, including significantly greater possibility of future unemployment (Lynch 1989) and much lower future income (Corcoran 1982; Ellwood 1979). In addition, unemployment in early adulthood may bring about a series of social issues, including anti-social behavior such as crime (Farrington et al. 1986), drug and alcohol abuse (Levin 1983). Furthermore, the unemployed population is not randomly distributed, young people with poor education, low parental income and low parental professional reputation are more likely to experience unemployment than those with good education, high parental income and high parental professional reputation (Rees and Gray 1982). Faced with severe unemployment in China, we need to pay attention to youth unemployment, understand their transition from school to work, so as to establish an effective linking mechanism between the education system and the labor market.

There are many studies regarding youth unemployment in the international arena. Some explored the causes and relevant factors of youth unemployment. For example, some scholars pointed out that the education system's failure to train qualified graduates for the labor market causes youth unemployment (Fraser 1980). Some scholars analyzed the factors affecting youth unemployment from three aspects: human capital, social capital, and personal capital. Poor human capital includes lack of high-school qualifications, poor reading skills, low IQ scores, and limited parental resources. Poor social capital includes growing up in a single-parent family, family conflicts, etc. Poor personal capital refers to youth involved in anti-social behaviors

W. Min, *Educational Input, Resource Allocation and Returns to Human Capital*,
https://doi.org/10.1007/978-981-96-4687-6_9

faced with greater risk of unemployment (Caspi et al. 1998). There is also a lot of literature that focuses on the consequences of youth unemployment. For example, some scholars found that unemployed young adults may experience more family conflicts (Conger et al. 1994). Human capital theory points out that unemployment reduces the opportunities for young adults to learn skills and makes them less competitive in the labor market (Becker 1975). Labor market segmentation theory believes that employers tend to use previous unemployment experience as a signal to distinguish employees with lower productivity.

In China, there are many studies on youth employment and unemployment, but the focus is on college graduates. Some scholars summarized the current status of college graduates' employment from three aspects and proposed future research directions. The aspects include investigating the employment situation of college graduates, reasons for difficulties of college graduates getting employed, and policies to promote employment (Yue 2004). Some scholars studied the employment of college graduates from the perspective of education equality, examined the impact of family background on college students' employment, and concluded that graduates from families with different backgrounds have different employment results (Wen 2005).

To summarize literatures on youth unemployment, we found that foreign studies managed to reveal the inner mechanism of youth unemployment from multiple aspects and levels with the help of ingenious model building and variable selection. Chinese scholars made considerable progress in studying the employment of college graduates and promoted timely policy adjustments. However, only studying employment of college graduates is far from enough, as a lot more young adults in China have only received primary and secondary education. The unemployment for them has never been paid enough attention in policy making. It is necessary to extend the research to the unemployment of less educated youth. In addition, existing studies on youth unemployment issues mostly focus on static analysis at a certain point of investigation, unable to understand the long-term dynamic characteristics of the transition from unemployment to employment. For example, the existing literature lacks estimates of the unemployment rate of youth at different time points after graduation. Few studied the time length of youth unemployment or relevant factors that may affect it, not to mention incorporating the time characteristics in policy recommendations. Limitations of conventional research methods are a main reason for this situation.

Education level is considered as a key factor in studies on youth employment/unemployment. A large number of empirical studies support a significant positive correlation between an individual's education level and his/her lifetime income. Both human capital theories and screening theories have strong explanatory power in explaining the relationship between one's education level and income. However, neither of them can deduce that the higher one's education level, the shorter one's transition period from school to getting hired. One possible reason is that a person with a higher education level tends to have higher expectations for his/her future job. When looking for a job, a person wants to find a position that he/she thinks valuable and is willing to take. Similarly, when hiring employees, an employer needs to balance the productivity required by a position and the wages having to be paid. Much empirical evidence show that the unemployment issue of a society is not due to shortage of total jobs, but the fact that many applicants with limited skills have unrealistic expectations of getting high-income and high-level jobs. The structural conflict between the jobs provided by the labor market and the graduates provided by the education system will make the relationship between unemployment duration and education level more complicated.

What is the relationship between the level of education and unemployment duration for young adults in urban China? Can higher level of education shorten graduates' job search time in the labor market? To answer these questions, this chapter expands the object of youth unemployment research from college graduates to other education level groups, such as young adults with middle school and high school education. By using survival analysis methods, we try to study the relationship between the time length of youth unemployment and their level of education, as well as the dynamic characteristics of the transition from searching for a job to getting hired for young people with different levels of education.

9.1 Methodology and Data

The existing research on unemployment issues mostly used ordinary statistical analysis methods, such as least square regression or logistic regression, to explore factors affecting unemployment. These traditional methods all used cross-section data for analysis. However, in real life, people's employment status changes with time, which can be described with a set of longitudinal data composed of a series of continuous interrelated cross-section data. At the same time, the values of explanatory variables on different cross-sections also change during the observation period. Traditional methods cannot correctly describe and explain the complicated process from one's initial status in job seeking to the end status of being employed or not. What's more, they cannot distinguish the status change from unemployment to employment, and it is difficult for them to accurately reflect the actual dynamics between the beginning and end of the observation period, causing loss of information and systematic deviations in estimation. Survival analysis solves the limitations of traditional methods by establishing "censorship", which can reveal dynamic characteristics. It is suitable for studying laws in a dynamic process of event occurrence and exploring how various explanatory factors affect probabilities of different durations. Survival analysis is a statistical analysis method commonly used by biomedical researchers and epidemiologists. At present, it has been applied in actuarial science, reliability engineering, economics, demography and criminology, but it is not well applied in research of unemployment issues.

This chapter attempts to use survival analysis to explore the relationship between the unemployment duration of China's urban youth groups and their education level. The data comes from the China's Urban Household Education and Employment Survey-2005 by the Institute of Economics of Education, Peking University. We choose urban youth aged 15–29 years old with middle school education or above from the total sample of the survey and conduct survival analysis with SPSS for data processing.

In this chapter, the survival time is defined as the length of time an observed individual spends from graduating (from school) until he/she gets the first job, which is also called the unemployment duration. By the end of the survey, those who are willing to work but are not yet employed are defined as censored data. We define whether the observed individual starts to work as the survival state variable, which has two values: 1 = start to work, 0 = censored. This chapter also uses the life table to calculate the unemployment rate of young adults with different education levels at a certain time point after graduation from school. In addition, we use the Kaplan–Meier method to compare the difference in the unemployment duration of youth groups with different education levels, and use the COX model to analyze the impact of education level on unemployment duration.

9.2 Statistical Description of Sample Data

9.2.1 *Statistical Description of Employment Status of Urban Youth*

Table 9.1 shows the employment distribution of the urban youth aged 15–29. If those currently at work, laid-off, unemployed, and waiting for job assignment are collectively referred to as the population willing to enter the labor market, among all the 2465 people willing to enter the labor market, 1951 can get a job, 79.1% of all the people willing to get a job ending up having one. In other words, a considerable proportion of young people are unemployed despite their willingness to work.

9.2.2 *Employment Status by Education Level*

Table 9.2 shows the employment situation of young people aged 15–29 who are willing to enter the labor market by education level. With the increase in education level, the unemployment rate decreases. Here, unemployed rate is defined as the ratio of the number of people who are willing to enter the labor market but have not obtained a job to the total number of people who are willing to enter the labor market.

Table 9.1 Employment distribution of urban population aged 15–29

Item	Employment status		Frequency	Percentage (%)
	Missing samples		383	6.5
Willing to enter the labor market	At work		1951	33.3
	Unemployed	Laid off	36	0.6
		Unemployed	396	6.8
		To be assigned	82	1.4
Unwilling to enter the labor market	Incapable to work		16	0.3
	Housework		44	0.8
	To go to school		17	0.3
	At school		2,848	48.7
	Deceased		47	0.8
	Other non-employed		31	0.5
Total			5851	100.0

Table 9.2 Employment status by education level

Education level	Employment status				Total (5)	Unemployment rate (6) (6) = ((2) + (3) + (4))/(5) (%)
	Work (1)	Laid-off (2)	Unemployed (3)	To be assigned (4)		
Primary school	11	1	8		20	45.0
Middle school	225	8	138	11	382	41.1
High school	603	18	155	26	802	24.8
College	633	7	71	26	737	14.1
Undergraduate and above	470	2	22	19	513	8.4
Total					2454	

9.3 Findings from the Survival Analysis

9.3.1 Unemployment Rate of Young Adults with Different Levels of Education

In the statistical description of the sample data, the unemployment rate obtained is the unemployment rate at the end of the survey, which cannot reflect the dynamic characteristics of the rate during the observation period. The life table method of survival analysis can help solve this problem by estimating the unemployment rate at different points in time, so as to dynamically describe the characteristics of the unemployment rate of groups with different education levels. This chapter divides education level into middle school, high school, college, and undergraduate and above. The unemployment duration is divided into groups with each interval being 0.5 years long. The results after sorting are shown in Table 9.3, which shows that among the population aged 15–29 willing to enter the labor market, there are 347 individuals with middle school education, 608 with high school education, 376 with college education, and 221 with undergraduate and above.

Table 9.3 reflects the distribution of unemployment rates among people of different education levels. For example, 93.82% of the middle school graduates (calculated according to the data in this chapter, the lower limit of 0.5 years of an unemployed period is considered that a person getting employed in the year of graduation) are unemployed in the year of graduation, and 83.77% of them stay unemployed one year after graduation, etc. Table 9.3 also reflects that for the unemployment rate at the same time point (such as a year after graduation), the unemployment rate decreases with the increase of education level. The unemployment rate is in descending order of education level, from middle school, high school, to college and undergraduate and above. In other words, young people with a higher level of education are more likely to get jobs faster in the labor market.

9.3.2 *Kaplan–Meier Analysis of Graduates of Different Education Levels*

We use the Kaplan–Meier method to compare the unemployment duration for young people with different education levels.

Table 9.4 shows that the median duration of unemployment for middle school graduates is 5.5 years, and that for high school graduates and people with college, undergraduate education and above is 2.5 years and 1.5 years, respectively. As mentioned above, the length of unemployment of less than 0.5 years implies that an individual gets a job in the year of graduation. After adjusting the above median time accordingly, the actual median duration of unemployment for youth groups with education at middle school, high school, college and undergraduate level is 5 years, 2 years and 1 year, respectively. With the improvement of education level, the median duration of unemployment shortens sharply. Table 9.4 also shows the 95% confidence interval of the median duration of unemployment for graduates of different education levels.

Table 9.5 is a summary of observations analyzed by the Kaplan–Meier method for graduates of different education levels. It shows that among the 1,552 valid observations, 43.23% of those with middle school education, 28.62% of those with senior high school, 23.40% of college graduates, and 15.38% of those with undergraduate education and above, failed to get their first job despite their willingness to work. All of these observations constitute the censored data.

Table 9.6 is an overall comparison of the unemployment duration for graduates of different education levels. It shows that there are significant differences in the

Table 9.3 Distribution of unemployment rates with different education levels

Lower limit of the unemployment duration of the segment	Middle school		High school		College		Undergraduate and above	
	Number of observations in segment	Cumulative unemployment rate up to the upper limit of the segment	Number of observations in the segment	Cumulative unemployment rate up to the upper limit of the segment	Number of observations in segment	Cumulative unemployment rate up to the upper limit of the segment	Number of observations in segment	Cumulative unemployment rate up to the upper limit of the segment
0	347	1.0000	608	1.0000	376	1.0000	221	1.0000
0.5	347	0.9382	608	0.7997	376	0.6839	221	0.5174
10.5	312	0.8377	470	0.5922	242	0.4424	106	0.2794
20.5	271	0.7183	335	0.4274	145	0.3109	48	0.1490
30.5	224	0.6525	222	0.3495	90	0.2127	21	0.0671
40.5	193	0.5476	157	0.2771	54	0.1520	8	0.0581
50.5	150	0.4789	111	0.2282	30	0.1460	6	0.0387
60.5	119	0.4363	75	0.2019	20	0.1369	4	0.0387
70.5	96	0.3971	56	0.1804	11	0.1369	3	0.0258
80.5	74	0.3568	33	0.1739	6	0.0913	2	0.0258
90.5	57	0.3228	21	0.1633	4	0.0913	2	0.0129
100.5	43	0.2977	11	0.1633	4	0.0913	1	0.0129
110.5	31	0.2748	4	0.1633	4	0.0913	–	–
120.5	19	0.2325	3	0.1633	4	0.0913	–	–
130.5	5	0.2325	3	0.0327	4	0.0684	–	–
140.5	–	–	–	–	3	0.0684	–	–
150.5	–	–	–	–	3	0.0684	–	–
160.5	–	–	–	–	3	0.0137	–	–

Table 9.4 Median duration of unemployment for young adults with different education levels

Education level	Median duration of unemployment (years)			
	Unemployment duration	Standard error	95% confidence interval	
			Lower bound	Upper bound
Middle school	5.50	0.53	4.45	6.55
High school	2.50	0.13	2.25	2.75
College	1.50	0.14	1.22	1.78
Undergraduate and above	1.50			

Table 9.5 Unemployment status of groups with different education levels

Education level	Subtotal (1) (1) = (2) + (3)	Number of people working (2)	Number of people unemployed (3)	Censored ratio (4) (4) = (3)/(1) (%)
Middle school	347	197	150	43.23
High school	608	434	174	28.62
College	376	288	88	23.40
Undergraduate and above	221	187	34	15.38
Total	1552	1106	446	28.74

unemployment duration for graduates of different education levels, and the P values of the three test statistics are all less than 0.05.

Figure 9.1 is the survival curves, which show that the higher the level of education, the lower the unemployment survival curve, indicating that the unemployment duration decreases as the education level rises. The results of Kaplan–Meier analysis also support the conclusion: youths with higher levels of education are more likely to get a job in the labor market, which is reflected in a shorter unemployment duration.

It can also be seen from Fig. 9.1 that there is a difference in time when the unemployment curve stabilizes. The curve for undergraduate and above stabilizes first, and that for middle school last. This suggests differences in time when the unemployment rate tends to stabilize for groups with different levels of education. Combining the life table, we can conclude that the unemployment rate of graduates of middle school, high school, college, and undergraduate and above starts to stabilize about 12 years, 9 years, 6 years and 5 years after graduation, respectively.

Table 9.6 Overall comparison of unemployment duration for graduates of different education levels

Item	Statistic	Degree of freedom	*P* value
Log rank	244.03	3	0.0000
Breslow	255.37	3	0.0000
Tarone-Ware	260.68	3	0.0000

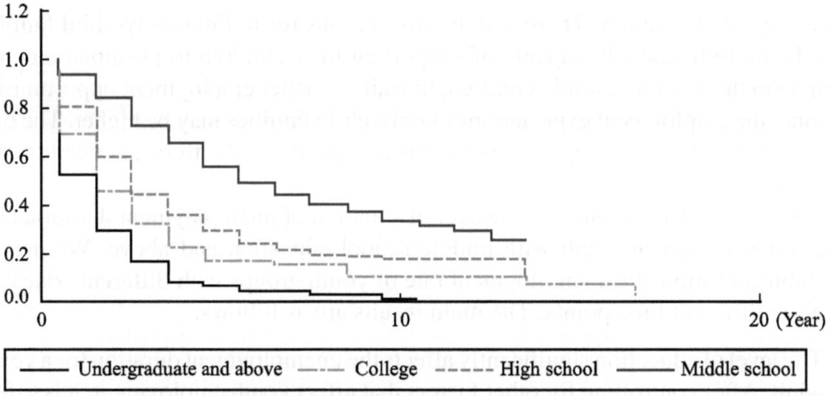

Fig. 9.1 Survival curve of unemployment duration by education level

9.3.3 Cox Regression

In survival analysis, Cox regression is usually used to study the impact of some variables on survival time. The Cox regression model is also called the proportional hazard model. It assumes that the hazard function at time t can be expressed as:

$$h(t) = [h_0(t)]e^{BX}, \quad \text{where, } BX = B_1X_1 + B_2X_2 + \ldots$$

B is a set of unknown regression parameters, and *X* represents a group of factors that affect the unemployment duration.

The model in this part attempts to explore whether an individual's education level affects his/her unemployment duration, with other variables controlled, including the person's gender, age, and family background. A person's family background includes whether he or she is the only child, parents' years of schooling, father's occupation, family income level, etc.

Cox regression results are shown in Table 9.7, which shows that the overall model is significant ($P = 0.000$). In the univariate test, the variables of only child, high school, college, and undergraduate education are all significant ($P < 0.05$). The coefficients of the three dummy variables, high school, college, and undergraduate and above are all positive, and the coefficient becomes larger with the improvement of education level. It implies that when the other factors remain unchanged, the higher the education level, the shorter the unemployment duration for a graduate. That is, the level of education is an important factor that affects the unemployment duration. It is worth noting that the coefficient of the only child variable is negative, which means that when other conditions remain unchanged, the unemployment duration for an only child may be longer than that for a non-only child, which is an interesting result. Experience and research have shown that it is possible for only-child families to invest more in education, which will benefit their children's employment. However, our findings suggest that young people from only-child families face relatively longer unemployment duration. There may be two reasons for it. First, only-child families may be more financially capable of supporting their children to postpone employment than those with multiple children, to wait for better employment opportunities. Second, the employment expectations of only-child families may be higher. The only child and their families may be unwilling to accept some job offers and would rather keep looking for better ones.

This chapter tries to analyze the overall situation of unemployment duration after graduation for urban youth with middle school education and above. We use the life table and show the unemployment rate of youth groups with different education levels at different time points. The main results are as follows:

- The level of education significantly affects the unemployment duration for a young adult. After controlling for other factors that affect youth employment, it is safe to say that investing in one's human capital such as education can significantly help shorten one's job search time after graduation. The results also find that only-child families may delay their children's employment due to higher expectations and stronger financial capabilities to support their children to postpone employment.
- From the perspective of time, the results show that there are differences in the average unemployment duration, the unemployment rate at a certain point, and the time when the unemployment rate tends to stabilize for youth with different education levels. This implies that the focus of employment policies should be different for youth with different levels of education. For example, in view of the different time points of the unemployed rate tending to stabilize, it may be a relatively long-term task to promote the employment of middle school and high school graduates, while the unemployment issue of college graduates is mainly concentrated in the first few years after graduation. For another example, the median duration of unemployment for middle school graduates is 5 years, which is a long period far beyond the time needed in general job hunting. Passionate and impulsive youths can have many achievements in 5 years. The employment policy can be designed and adjusted according to the characteristics of this group of youth.

This chapter defines the survival time interval in years, due to the limitation of data. If the data is specific to monthly intervals, unemployment duration can be studied specifically to the monthly level, and the results will be more accurate and the estimation error of unemployment duration can be reduced.

This chapter expands the research object of youth unemployment in China from college graduates to middle school and high school graduates, and highlights the time characteristics of youth unemployment. Future research on youth employment/unemployment may have more perspectives, including the relationship between one's personal characteristics during adolescence and performance in the labor market later on, comparative study of looking for a new job when having one or quitting a job to find another one, and the substitution effect of youth employment to adult employment, and so on.

The analysis of the causes of youth unemployment is always involved with relevant policies and mechanisms, including improving the existing education and training

Table 9.7 Cox regression results

Independent variable	Coefficient of independent variable	Standard error	Wald test value	Degree of freedom	Significance level	Hazard ratio
Age	−0.016	0.015	1.146	1	0.284	0.984
Father's years of schooling	0.008	0.014	0.368	1	0.544	1.009
Mother's years of schooling	0.009	0.012	0.488	1	0.485	1.009
Only child						
No (benchmark)						
Yes	−0.204	0.074	7.512	1	0.006*	0.815
Gender						
Female (benchmark)						
Male	−0.049	0.070	0.492	1	0.483	0.952
Father's occupation						
Industrial worker (benchmark)						
Professional technician	−0.060	0.097	0.383	1	0.536	0.942
Head of state agencies, party organizations, or enterprises and institutions	0.284	0.180	2.499	1	0.114	1.329
Office staff and management staff	0.050	0.098	0.258	1	0.611	1.051
Commercial worker	0.119	0.167	0.510	1	0.475	1.127
Service worker	0.013	0.154	0.007	1	0.932	1.013
Agriculture, forestry, animal husbandry and fishery worker	0.445	0.363	1.504	1	0.220	1.561
Freelancer	−0.457	0.462	0.979	1	0.322	0.633
Unclassifiable	0.513	0.588	0.760	1	0.383	1.670
Education level						
Middle school (benchmark)						

(continued)

Table 9.7 (continued)

Independent variable	Coefficient of independent variable	Standard error	Wald test value	Degree of freedom	Significance level	Hazard ratio
High school	0.659	0.107	38.246	1	0.000*	1.933
College	0.996	0.119	69.846	1	0.000*	2.708
Undergraduate and above	1.348	0.134	100.549	1	0.000*	3.848
Household income						
Lowest income (benchmark)						
Low income	−0.193	0.128	2.298	1	0.130	0.824
Middle-lower income	−0.204	0.132	2.385	1	0.122	0.815
Middle income	−0.042	0.131	0.106	1	0.745	0.958
Upper-middle income	0.000	0.133	0.000	1	0.999	1.000
High income	0.152	0.136	1.252	1	0.263	1.164
Highest income	0.206	0.144	2.065	1	0.151	1.229
Valid sample size	1273					
-2 Log Likelihood	11,583.952*					
df	22					

Note (1) Method = Enter. (2)* means statistically significant at a = 0.05 level

system to make it more adaptable to the needs of the job market, as well as evaluating the effects of existing employment and employment promotion policies and reform, etc. For example, some studies have shown that if some personal characteristics such as anti-social attitudes to life, lack of skills, or uncooperative habits affect young people's access to jobs, the policy of simply increasing jobs will not be effective (Corcoran and Hill 1976). Henry Levin (1983) pointed out that providing more educational opportunities to those with lower levels of education cannot solve the problem of youth unemployment, and the likely result is over-education. To further understand the employment of young people in China and relevant factors, we need to conduct more in-depth analysis and research from the perspective of system and policy based on the above empirical results.

References

Becker, G. (1975). *Human Capital: A Theoretical and Empirical Analysis, with Special Reference to Education* (2nd ed.) NBER.

Caspi, A., Wright, E. et al. (1998). Early Failure in the Labor Market: Childhood and Adolescent Predictors of Unemployment in the Transition to Adulthood. *American Sociological Review, 63*(3), 424–451.

Conger, R., Elder, G., et al. (1994). *Families in Troubled Times: Adapting to Change in Rural America. Social Institutions and Social Change.* Aldine de Gruyter.

Corcoran, M. (1982). The Employment and Wage Consequences of Teenage Women's Nonemployment. In *The Youth Labor Market Problem: Its Nature, Causes and Consequences* (pp. 391–426). University of Chicago Press.

Corcoran, M., & Hill, M. (1976). Persistence in Unemployment Among Adult Men. *Five Thousand American Families* (vol. 7, pp. 39–71). University of Michigan Institute for Social Research.

Ellwood, D. (1979). *Teenage Unemployment: Permanent Scars or Temporary Blemishes?* NBER Working Paper No. w0399, Available at SSRN: https://ssrn.com/abstract=261247.

Farrington, D., & Gallagher, B. et al. (1986). Unemployment, School Leaving, and Crime. *British Journal of Criminology, 26*(4), 335–356.

Fraser. M. (1980). *Extract from Address to the National Convention of the Young Liberal Movement.* Bundoora, VicLa Trobe University.

Levin, H. (1983). Youth Unemployment and Its Educational Consequences. *Educational Evaluation and Policy Analysis, 5*(2), 231–247.

Lynch, L. (1989). The Youth Labor Market in the Eighties: Determinants of Re-employment Probabilities for Young Men and Women. *The Review of Economics and Statistics, 71*(1), 37–45.

Rees, A., & Gray, W. (1982). Family Effects in Youth Unemployment. *The Youth Labor Market Problem: Its Nature, Causes and Consequences.* University of Chicago Press.

Wen, D. (2005). The Impact of Family's Social Economic Status on Higher Education Opportunity and Graduate Employment in China. *Peking University Education Review, 3*(3), 6.

Yue, C. (2004). Literature Review on China's Higher Education and Labor Market. *Economics of Education Research (Beida), 4.*

Chapter 10
Education and Job Autonomy

Development economists believe that developing countries should rely on their late-development advantages to imitate and learn developed countries' knowledge and technology, achieve a faster technological innovation rate than developed countries, and change their own endowment structure to promote economic development and narrow the gap with developed countries. As China's economic factor endowment changes and the gap with developed countries narrows, its capacity in absorbing endogenous knowledge will become stronger. Simultaneously, as we get closer to the technological frontier, more innovations will be necessary to achieve further technological advancement. Therefore, the Outline of the National Medium and Long term Science and Technology Development Program (2006–2020) takes independent innovation capacity as the mainline and building an innovative nation as the goal, giving a comprehensive plan and deployment for China's scientific and technological development in the next 15 years, and proposes to make China an innovative nation by 2020. This national policy was also brought about to meet the requirements of the era of knowledge economy.

10.1 Education, Human Resource Development and Technological Progress

Knowledge economy has become an essential feature of modern economic development. The "research and development system" is the heart of the entire system. Based on the essential role of knowledge in the economy, it can be considered that knowledge economy contains two sectors, the production sector and the consumption sector of knowledge. The function of the knowledge production sector is to innovate and update knowledge and technology and advance the boundaries of technology. The function of the knowledge consumption sector is to learn and use advanced knowledge and technology to promote the balance of technology distribution. Whether it

W. Min, *Educational Input, Resource Allocation and Returns to Human Capital*,
https://doi.org/10.1007/978-981-96-4687-6_10

is the process of knowledge absorption or innovation, knowledge workers are the most vibrant and important production factors. Drucker defined knowledge workers as "those who master and use symbols and concepts, and work with knowledge or information" (Drucker 1998). Without a good human resource development system for knowledge-based employees, it is difficult to release the enormous knowledge potential in economic organizations.

Education and training are the foundation and fundamental guarantee for the development of knowledge-based human resources. From the perspective of human capital theories, education can accumulate human capital, and employees who receive more education have higher productivity and a stronger ability to deal with labor market imbalances. From the perspective of screening hypotheses, education can provide employers with certain signals, and employees who receive more education have greater training potential. In the labor market, knowledge workers with higher education levels are faced with different job opportunities, working environments, working organization ways, and on-the-job training opportunities. Therefore, employees with varying levels of education adapt to different human resource development and management systems. Higher education provides a rich reserve of resources for the development and management of knowledge-based human resources. Because college graduates usually have strong learning ability and can improve the possibility of organizational innovation, the innovation and development capability of an organization is positively related to the number of college graduates it hires.

At the same time, the development and management of knowledge workers also include the selection, allocation, motivation, and retraining of talents. This is a systematic project that requires the formal school education system to provide a training model suitable for economic and social development and the labor market to allocate and train talents properly. In addition, internal working methods of organizations have changed, and more emphasis is placed on high-performance work systems that are supported by flexible production. Therefore, a talent development strategy should provide employees with learning opportunities and incentives in their jobs, taking full account of their educational background and what the job can offer. Such a strategy is of vital importance to stimulate talent potential, and to advance the frontier of knowledge and technology. This research focuses on the requirements of working environment and working style for highly educated talents, so as to explore the long-term effects of higher education on promoting employees' autonomy and motive to learn, and the role of higher education on technological innovation of economic organizations.

10.2 Education and Job Satisfaction

Job satisfaction is a research area of organizational behavior. Studies have shown that higher job satisfaction may lead to lower turnover rates and higher job performance. Job satisfaction is often used as an indicator to predict employee behavior and job performance (Freeman 1978; Levy-Garboua et al. 2001). Job satisfaction is also an important indicator of the overall state of life and affects people's happiness (van Praag et al. 2003). Therefore, job satisfaction can be used as an indicator to evaluate the effects of human resource management and development.

The focus on job satisfaction comes from exploring methods of employee motivation by industrial psychologists. Hoppock (1935) first began to study job satisfaction which was since then, widely studied by psychology and sociology, was defined as "an orientation of emotions that employees posses towards the role they are performing at work place". Freeman (1978) introduced job satisfaction as an economic variable into the analysis of economic behavior and believed that job satisfaction was a reflection of individual job utility. Previous studies on employee job satisfaction have attempted to build a function by combining individual characteristics and job characteristics. Job satisfaction is explained by factors such as gender, age, marital status, income, working environment, and the relationship between education and job matching (Clark and Oswald 1996; Allen and van der Velden 2001), as is shown in the following equation, $S = F(P, W)$, where P represents personal characteristic variables, and W represents work-related characteristic variables.

Among personal characteristics, the most closely related to this research is education level. Education is an important way of human capital investment and accumulation, and the first step in human resource development. Education affects organizations and people themselves through their adaptability and performance in the labor market. Education economics focuses on the relationship between education and job satisfaction from the perspective of the relationship between education and the labor market. It not only observes the impact of education on individual monetary income, namely income, but also pays attention to the impact of education on achieving of individual career goals and non-monetary benefits such as job health.

The ways in which education affects work are complex. Education affects not only many factors of employees' characteristics, including knowledge, skills, occupational needs, and expectations, but also many factors of their job characteristics, that is, their position in the labor market and thus jobs they can find. Moreover, education will also affect the matching of these two factors, thereby affecting employees' job satisfaction and work effort, and then affecting their labor productivity. Mun Chiu Tsang (1987) used this theory to study the impact of education on labor productivity and regarded employees' job satisfaction and work effort as mediating variables between education and labor productivity. Min Weifang and Mun Chiu Tsang (1990) also examined the impact of vocational education on labor productivity through the impact of education and job matching on job satisfaction. Both studies focused on the relationship between education and job satisfaction from the perspective of education economics, and laid the foundation for theoretical discussion and empirical research for subsequent studies.

In general, the impact of education on job satisfaction has many research directions: to control other variables to see the impact of education on job satisfaction (Clark and Oswald 1996); to study the influence of education and job matching on job satisfaction, that is, the impact of over-education and insufficient education on job satisfaction (Tsang 1987; Min and Tsang 1990; Verhofstadt and Omey 2003; Allen and Van der Velden 2001); to analyze the impact of different majors and job matching on job satisfaction (Vila and García-Mora 2005); to study the different patterns of job satisfaction determinants among people with different levels of education. Most studies have linked higher education to lower job satisfaction (Clark and Oswald 1996), but some found that more educated employees are more satisfied with their jobs than those with less education (Yuan and Ma 2002). The conclusions of studies from the perspective of overeducation are also inconsistent. Most studies believed that overeducation negatively affects the evaluation of job satisfaction (Battu et al. 1999; Belfield and Harris 2002; Johnson and Johnson 2000). For graduates with advanced degrees, their professional background affects the evaluation of job satisfaction, and ability to use professional skills learned at work can improve their job satisfaction (Belfield and Harris 2002; Allen and Van der Velden 2001).

Other personal variables such as gender, age, and marital status also affect job satisfaction. Studies have found that when many related variables and sample selection bias are controlled, women's job satisfaction is higher than that of men (Clark and Oswald 1996). The explanation for this is that women's employment expectations are lower than men's, and their lower expectations stem from their disadvantaged position in the labor market. As women's level of education increases and the proportion of those with higher education levels rises, the difference between their job satisfaction and men's tends to disappear. The relationship between age and satisfaction presents a U-shape, and job satisfaction reaches the lowest in the mid-career period (Clark et al. 1999). For people with different marital status, married people are more satisfied with their jobs than unmarried people (Federico et al. 1976).

Work-related variables include income, working hours, work unit size, occupational status, job autonomy, access to training opportunities, etc. (Freeman 1978; Clark and Oswald 1996; Belfield and Harris 2002). Theoretically, personal income has a positive impact on job satisfaction. But empirical research shows that the impact of income is mixed. Clark (1997) found that the level of income has a significant impact on income satisfaction and overall job satisfaction. However, Clark and Oswald (1996) found that the level of well-being reported by respondents was not closely related to income. Belfield and Harris (2002) further found no evidence that income determines job satisfaction for people with higher education. Given that people may be more interested in their relative position, some studies suggested that absolute income doesn't matter, but relative income does (Clark and Oswald 1996). By examining the importance of relative income, many studies have shown that relative income has some effect on job satisfaction, but overall, the effect is small (Clark and Oswald 1996; Neumark and Postlewaite 1998). Other studies have shown that for groups with higher education, job satisfaction is more affected by relative wages (Sloane and Williams 2000). However, job satisfaction is a comprehensive concept. The utility of a person's job is not only the balance between his income and leisure, but also the comprehensive evaluation of his monetized income and non-monetized income (Hamermesh 2001; Borjas 1979). Therefore, people's evaluation of job satisfaction should also include the evaluation of working environment and working style together with other non-monetized income. Knowledge management expert Mahen Tampoe put forward a model to motivate knowledge workers through empirical research. He believed that the four aspects of career development that employees with higher education value most are personal growth, job autonomy, business achievement, and income, among which job autonomy is a very important aspect (Zhang and Peng 2001). It can be seen that employees with higher education levels have a higher pursuit of job autonomy than others, so there will be differences in evaluating overall job satisfaction after obtaining autonomy. This has become the basis for this research, and it should also become the focus that cannot be ignored in developing people-oriented human resources.

10.3 Job Autonomy and Job Satisfaction

Hackman and Oldham (1976) defined job autonomy as the degree to which a job gives individuals the freedom, independence, and discretion in arranging work and deciding how it is done. Most studies on the influence of job autonomy on job satisfaction are conducted in the field of psychology (Anderson et al. 1992; Lander-sweerd and Bousmans 1994; Weaver 1977), sociology (Schienman 2002) and business (Bhuian and Al-Shammari 1996; Birdseys and Hill 1995). Locke (1976), a scholar of organizational behavior, theoretically elaborated that job autonomy was one of the factors affecting job satisfaction. Through theoretical analysis, Hu Bei (2003) summarized the factors affecting job satisfaction into three categories: job itself, work relationship, and work environment, among which job itself includes work content and autonomy. Since the degree of employee autonomy partly reflects the characteristics and requirements of job, there are many studies on the effect of job autonomy on job satisfaction in the field of professional jobs, most of which are on nurses (Finn 2001), salespeople (DeCarlo and Agarwal 1999), journalists (Lu 2004), etc. Studies found that their job autonomy affects their job performance by affecting their job satisfaction. These people's job characteristics determine that they are faced with changing and complex situations at work, and they need to have some autonomy to deal with them. The more autonomy they feel in their work, the more freedom and authority employees will have to choose ways to make customers more satisfied. Therefore, scholars are keen to study the impact of job autonomy on job satisfaction from the perspective of human resource management.

In the wave of globalization and knowledge economy, most work organizations have changed, and corresponding human resource management and development systems will also change. Levin summarized some characteristics of organizations in the industrial age: First, work organizations are generally large, hierarchical, and dehumanized. Employees' rights and responsibilities are divided according to their levels and nature of work. Each employee is placed in a command structure, in which a few managers are responsible for the overall planning. Some middle—level workers have both labor and supervisory responsibilities. This has resulted in an organizational and output model that strengthens overall management. Second, production plants of modern enterprises have a meticulous division of responsibilities. Many workers do not need to participate in any complete production and service process, but only need to repeat a few minutes of procedural work to complete the task. Third, the work of most workers in modern factories is not intrinsically attractive, so organizations emphasize motivating workers through external rewards such as continued employment, increased wages, or promotion, rather than through the intrinsic satisfaction of gaining experience. Fourth, status of work and occupation is divided according to gender and other personal characteristics. In other words, modern enterprises have a strict pyramid structure. This is a standardized and large-scale production model that has continued from large-scale industrial production. Because of its effectiveness to a certain extent, it may continue to extend in the new era. But a different form of organization has emerged, the so-called "high-performance workplace" (Bailey 1993). High-performance workplaces require workers at all levels to actively and intelligently participate in production. In such a high-performance work system, the tasks that workers participate in are not specific or fixed. High-performance workplaces require employees to take the initiative to make suggestions and give full play to their creativity in accomplishing the tasks and objectives of the organization. Employees are expected to be able to solve problems, find ways to improve methods, and work with people on their own initiative.

The trend of diversification, flattening, and flexibility of organization has driven the transformation of human resource management from the control-oriented management to the participatory management method. Anh Ngoc Nguyen, Jim Taylor and Steve Bradley (2003) conducted a study on the effects of job autonomy on employees in non-specific industries. The study divided job satisfaction into multiple dimensions, such as income satisfaction, marginal income, promotion prospects, job safety and job importance, and used the samples with education from 8th grade to 12th grade in the NELS (National Educational Longitudinal Study) survey to investigate the influence of job autonomy on different aspects of job satisfaction. They found a significant correlation between the degree of autonomy gained at work and all the five aspects of job satisfaction. With the increase of personal control over work, job satisfaction has been improved, and the most obvious improvement is from "no autonomy" to "a small part of autonomy." The improvement of women's job autonomy has a greater impact on job satisfaction than men's, especially on the dimension of job importance.

10.4 Education and Job Autonomy

The reason why job autonomy can affect job satisfaction is that job autonomy reflects the trust relationship between an organization and an individual (Baker et al. 1994), which is a reflection of the work content and the individual's daily working status. Trust between the organization and the individual is the prerequisite for success of the individual's career and realization of organizational goals. Lack of trust may lead to problems of non-cooperation or higher monitoring cost. Sitkin and Roth (1993) believed that trust is a kind of belief, attitude, or expectation that a certain behavior, a certain individual, team, or organizational output can be accepted or meet the requirements of participants.

Neoclassical economics believes that wages of employees are determined by their labor productivity, but the incalculability of labor productivity leads to adverse incentives for employees. Employees may be more inclined to focus on measurable job performance than on what the job really requires (Baker 2000). In order to avoid excessive supervision costs, employers are willing to build trust with employees, and employers are willing to pay employees efficiency wages (Ewing and Payne 1999). Efficiency wages motivate employees to work harder (Akerlof 1982; Akerlof and Yellen 1986). Sometimes, there is no completely clear definition of what employees should do, so the labor contract is incomplete and unclear. Especially for highly educated employees, measurement of their labor productivity does not simply depend on specific and clear terms (Allen and Van der Velden 2001), but on how they create opportunities to better achieve the employer's goals. Therefore, employers value employees' creativity, adaptability, and ability to better grasp opportunities. To better grasp opportunities and make the best use of one's own resources to complete the work, one needs to have a certain degree of autonomy. Autonomy is believed to largely reflect the trusting relationship between employers and employees. This trust is particularly important in positions where labor productivity is hard to measure or where employees are required to do creative work. At the same time, for knowledge workers with good better self-control and stronger motivation for self-realization, as long as they are given necessary training, deployment and leadership as well as challenging work, they can maximize their creativity at work.

Giving knowledge workers more autonomy is not only external requirements of their working environment, but also requirements of the employees themselves. Civic education in modern society conveys the concepts of equality and democracy to the educated. The democratic political ideology promoted by market economy also promotes citizens' demand for democratic participation and autonomy in economic activities. For higher education graduates, freedom has both cultural and traditional significance as well as practical significance, which terms of cultural traditions, universities have a tradition of academic freedom. It first originated in medieval European universities and expanded in German universities in the nineteenth century. Academic freedom at the time was limited to the right of teachers to teach their subjects freely in the classroom. In the United States in the twentieth century, the concept of academic freedom further expanded and profoundly influenced and promoted academic prosperity. Graduates of higher education who have been exposed to academic freedom are likely to place more emphasis on their autonomy and discretion in their own jobs. This tradition is even internalized as the value standard of their work and life. A study on the professional values of graduate students shows that "autonomy" is second only to lifestyle and achievement, in professional expectations (Hou and Li 2005).

In terms of practical significance, an autonomous organizational culture and work style provides a place for educated people to learn actively so that they can innovate in a certain free space. After the emergence of the concept of knowledge economy, the concept of learning economy was put forward, and it was believed that learning is a response to the era when knowledge becomes outdated more rapidly. Lorenz and Valeyre (2005) divided four work organization systems based on employees' autonomy and learning opportunities in work, which are autonomous learning system, dependent learning system, Taylor style, and traditional style. Among them, 85% of employees under the autonomous learning system can control their work pace and working methods. This system also permeates the idea of lifelong learning. Ways of lifelong education include school education, formal training organized by enterprises, and informal learning. Highly educated people acquire the habit of continuous learning and the ability to continue learning through formal training. The more they are exposed to the frontiers of knowledge and technology, and the more they can feel the speed of knowledge development, the more they need to respond to rapid changes. Although they often have more access to formal training, informal learning is equally important. Autonomous workplaces will provide space for informal autonomous learning. On the one hand, employees can learn by doing, accumulate experience in solving problems, and develop new methods when confronted with new challenges. On the other hand, they can learn from it and deal with it as they encounter it over and over.

10.5 Data and Research Design

10.5.1 Research Design

Education is closely related to human resource development, and employee satisfaction is an intermediate performance index of human resource development. Education affects job satisfaction in many ways, including career expectations, income, position, career development opportunities, and job autonomy. Job autonomy is an important aspect of job satisfaction. Education also affects job satisfaction by affecting job autonomy. On the one hand, education affects job characteristics and positions, etc., which makes it easier for people with higher education to gain the trust of employers and obtain higher job autonomy. On the other hand, since self-realization, liberal traditions, and autonomous learning habits require autonomy and discretion at work, people with higher education tend to be more satisfied with gaining more autonomy at work than people with less education. Therefore, different levels of education bring diversity in career pursuit. More education brings more attention to the non-monetized benefits of a job. In the past, studies simply established the relationship between education and job satisfaction, job satisfaction and job autonomy, and education and job autonomy. In particular, the relationship between education and job satisfaction has always been vague. Researchers can only make guesses to explain the impact mechanism of education based on the results of coefficient estimation. On the basis of controlling personal characteristic variables and job characteristic variables, this research introduces the interaction between education and job autonomy, and tries to explore how education affect job satisfaction through degree of job autonomy.

Based on literature review and theoretical analysis, this chapter puts forward three hypotheses:

Hypothesis 1:
In general, greater job autonomy leads to greater job satisfaction.

The empirical research in this chapter builds the function of job satisfaction on personal characteristic variables and job characteristic variables. Three models are introduced. Model 1 uses all the employees surveyed as a sample, job satisfaction as the dependent variable, job autonomy as the independent variable, and personal characteristic variables such as education level and work-related variables like income and position as control variables in regression analysis to examine the overall impact of job autonomy on job satisfaction.

Hypothesis 2:
The effect of job autonomy on job satisfaction varies with people's education level.

Lack of job autonomy will reduce the job satisfaction of more educated people to a greater extent, while full job autonomy will increase the job satisfaction of more educated people to a greater extent.

As mentioned in the theoretical analysis, in order to better examine the impact of the interaction between education and job autonomy on job satisfaction, in Model 2, the level of education is divided into two categories according to whether the respondents received undergraduate education or above, which interact with four degrees of job autonomy in order to explore the interaction between job autonomy and job satisfaction for different education levels.

Hypothesis 3:
Among factors that affect job satisfaction, more educated employees value job autonomy more.

In order to compare differences in influencing factors of job satisfaction among people with different education levels, the dependent variables and independent variable of Model 3 are the same as those of Model 1, while the difference is that the samples were divided into several sub-samples based on education level, and regression was conducted respectively to analyze whether job autonomy has different effects on job satisfaction compared with other job characteristics for groups with different education levels.

The operational definition of each variable is explained in detail in Table 10.1.

10.5.2 Methodology and Data Description

Since employee job satisfaction is a 5-point ordinal variable, the regression should use an ordered Probit regression model (McKelvey and Zavoina 1975). In this chapter, the ordered Probit regression method of STATA software is used.

Table 10.1 Variables and explanation

Variable	Explanation
Dependent variables	
Job satisfaction	Question: What is your overall satisfaction with your current job? The answer is a 5-point variable. Very satisfied is 5, relatively satisfied is 4, basically satisfied is 3, relatively dissatisfied is 2, and very dissatisfied is 1
Independent variable	
Gender	Male is 1 and female is 0
Marital status	Dummy variable. Married is 1 and unmarried is 0
Age	Squared age
Education	Years of schooling
Unit size	Total number of people employed
Income	Total revenue in 2004
Operating hours	Working hours per week
Growth at work	Question: "Do you agree with 'I am constantly learning something new by doing my present job.'?" The answer is divided into 5 dimensions, 5 for strong agreement, 1 for strongly disagree
Job autonomy	Question: "How is your relationship with the direct leader at work?" The options are as follows. My manager decides what I do and how I do it (no autonomy at all), marked as 1. My manager decides what I do and I decide how to do it (with some autonomy), marked as 2. My manager gives me some freedom to decide what to do and how to do it (with more autonomy), marked as 3. At work I am my own boss (with a lot of autonomy), marked as 4. The four options represent a progressive increase in autonomy at work
Employment category	Including the Party and government institutions and the military, public institutions, state-owned and holding enterprises, foreign-funded enterprises, enterprises with funds from Hong Kong, Macao and Taiwan, collectively-owned enterprises, private enterprises, partnership enterprises, individual business owner, self-employed, and other 11 categories. 10 dummy variables are set up based on the self-employed

(continued)

Table 10.1 (continued)

Variable	Explanation
Occupation	Positions include professional and technical personnel; heads of state departments and public institutions; clerks and management personnel; commercial workers; service workers; agricultural, forestry, animal husbandry and fishery workers; production workers, transportation workers and related personnel; freelancers; nine categories of other workers that are inconvenient to classify, and eight dummy variables are set based on production workers, transportation workers and related personnel
The interaction between education and job autonomy	Based on one with higher education and no autonomy, dummy variables include having higher education and complete autonomy, having higher education and much autonomy, having higher education and some autonomy, and having no higher education and complete autonomy, having no higher education and much autonomy, having no higher education with some autonomy, having no higher education and no autonomy

Data from the 2005 Urban Household Survey, funded by the China Education and Human Resources Project (see Tables 10.2, 10.3 and 10.4). Since it is to investigate the contribution of job autonomy to job satisfaction among people with different education levels, a sample of employed family members (excluding those who continue to work after retirement) was selected. The effective sample size is 5476, among which 55.1% are males and 44.9% are females. The youngest is 22 years old and the oldest is 69 years old, with an average age of 41.4 years old. People aged 22–29 years old account for 5.3%, people aged 30–39 years old account for 36.0%, people aged 40–49 years old account for 47.7%, and people over 50 years old account for 10.7%. Because the relevant data covered employment status of only the head of household and his spouse in the survey, the sample subjects tend to be older than the general population, and their careers focus mainly on professional and technical personnel (31.6%), clerical and managerial personnel (23.4%), and production workers (23.3%). Heads of other units account for 2.9%, business staff 7.9%, service personnel 9.2%, agriculture, forestry, and fishing workers 0.2%, freelancers 0.6%, and other workers 0.6%.

Employees with a college degree or above account for 39.2%, followed by those with technical secondary school education, accounting for 35.3%. Most of their positions have no or little job autonomy. More than 50% of them need to follow the directions of their direct leaders about what to do and how to do their job, and less than 10% of people have the freedom to decide what to do and how they work. It can be seen that current organizations are mainly using a control-oriented management system, and most employees' evaluation on their job satisfaction is basically satisfied (46.3%) or relatively satisfied (40.7%).

Table 10.2 Overall satisfaction with current job

Item	Number	Percentage (%)	Cumulative Percentage (%)
Valid sample			
Very dissatisfied	103.0	1.9	1.9
Relatively dissatisfied	506.0	9.2	11.1
Basically satisfied	2535.0	46.3	57.4
Relatively satisfied	2227.0	40.7	98.1
Very satisfied	105.0	1.9	100.0
Total	5476.0	100.0	

Table 10.3 Job autonomy

Item	Number	Percentage (%)	Cumulative percentage (%)
Valid sample			
No autonomy	2805.0	51.2	51.2
Some autonomy	1410.0	25.7	77.0
Much autonomy	751.0	13.7	90.7
Complete autonomy	510.0	9.3	100.0
Total	5476.0	100.0	

Table 10.4 Education level

Item	Number	Percentage (%)	Cumulative percentage (%)
Valid sample			
Primary school and below	121.0	2.2	2.2
Middle school	1272.0	23.2	25.4
High school	1935.0	35.3	60.8
Junior college	1261.0	23.0	83.8
Undergraduate	806.0	14.7	98.5
Postgraduate	81.0	1.5	100.0
Total	5476.0	100.0	

10.6 Findings and Conclusions

The study found that after controlling the variables of personal and job characteristics, job autonomy has a significant positive impact on job satisfaction (see Table 10.5). That is, more job autonomy can easily increase job satisfaction, and vice versa. This shows that, on average, people prefer a freer work environment. Therefore, the data supports hypothesis 1.

Table 10.5 Model 1 and Model 2 regression coefficients

Variable	Model 1 Coefficient (Z value)	Model 2 Coefficient (Z value)
Personal characteristic variables		
Male	0.070** (2.10)	0.081** (2.52)
Married	−0.103 (−0.39)	−0.079 (−0.30)
Age squared	9.61E−05*** (3.58)	8.99E−05*** (3.47)
Years of schooling	0.012* (1.93)	0.039** (2.06)
Job characteristic variable		
Unit size	4.89E−06 (1.28)	5.26E−06 (1.40)
Income	4.73E−06*** (6.54)	4.01E−06*** (6.71)
Operating hours	−0.007*** (−4.85)	−0.007*** (−5.05)
Growth at work	0.047*** (3.29)	0.051*** (3.71)
Job autonomy	0.068*** (3.83)	
Employed by the party and government institutions and the military	0.511*** (5.29)	0.491*** (5.31)
Employed by public institutions	0.496*** (5.64)	0.451*** (5.36)
Employed by state-owned enterprises	0.355** (2.12)	0.239 (1.48)
Employed by foreign-funded enterprise	0.282*** (3.40)	0.225*** (2.85)
Employed by Hong Kong, Macao and Taiwan enterprises	0.248 (0.96)	0.200 (0.77)
Employed by a collectively owned enterprise	0.208** (2.13)	0.151 (1.62)
Employed by a private enterprise	0.267*** (2.85)	0.205** (2.29)
Employed by a partnership enterprise	0.194 (1.03)	0.057 (0.31)
Self-employed	0.230** (2.26)	0.148 (1.46)
Other employment types	0.248** (2.26)	0.198* (1.92)

(continued)

Table 10.5 (continued)

Variable	Model 1 Coefficient (Z value)	Model 2 Coefficient (Z value)
Professional and technical personnel	0.159*** (3.34)	0.183*** (3.97)
Heads of state departments and public institutions	0.528*** (5.18)	0.513*** (5.12)
Clerks and management personnel	0.175*** (3.45)	0.185*** (3.78)
Commercial workers	0.072 (1.05)	0.055 (0.83)
Service workers	0.053 (0.85)	0.069 (1.17)
Agriculture, forestry, animal husbandry and fishery workers	−0.469 (−1.42)	−0.365 (−1.20)
Freelancers	0.142 (0.70)	0.219 (1.26)
Inconvenient to classify	−0.409* (−1.92)	−0.44** (−2.38)
Interaction between education level and work autonomy		
Higher education-complete autonomy		0.416*** (3.98)
Higher education-much autonomy		0.248*** (3.84)
Highly education-some autonomy		0.182*** (3.40)
No higher education-complete autonomy		0.338*** (4.04)
No higher education-much autonomy		0.119** (2.12)
No higher education-some autonomy		0.012*** (3.24)
No higher education-no autonomy		0.156*** (3.40)
Log likelihood	−5669.1021	−6156.6609

Note * $p < 0.1$, ** $p < 0.05$, *** $p < 0.01$

However, in current organizations, not all employees can get job autonomy, which is directly related to their positions. More fundamentally, the education they have received has affected their relative position productivity and capabilities that they may show in the workplace from the very beginning. People with different education levels are faced with different job opportunities, enter different positions, and show different abilities, and so gain different degrees of job autonomy. Through research on the interaction between education level and job autonomy, we find that people with lower education levels (middle school or below education level) show two major trends in their work style. Most of them (53.7%) have no autonomy at all. Plus, more than a quarter of them (26.4%) are self-employed or freelancers, and therefore have complete job autonomy. As for employees with higher education levels, the proportion of those who have no job autonomy at all decreases with the rise of education level, and the proportion of those who have gained autonomy also increases gradually. But at the same level of education, the proportion of people with no autonomy at all is the largest. Only in the postgraduate group, the proportion of employees with some autonomy exceeds those with no autonomy at all. This shows that the atmosphere of autonomous learning has not been generally established in current workplaces, highly educated employees have a lot of opportunities to strive for greater job autonomy.

Does the tilt of job autonomy opportunities to highly educated employees bring higher organizational performance? This can be explored from the interaction between education and job autonomy on job satisfaction. Among people who have no job autonomy at all, job satisfaction of people without college education is significantly higher than that of those with college education. As for people with autonomy in work, those with higher education have significantly higher job satisfaction than those without.

For groups without higher education, with the improvement of work autonomy, satisfaction shows a concave trend. In other words, for them, complete lack of job autonomy does not bring the lowest job satisfaction. This is different from the highly educated group, whose job satisfaction increases as they gain more job autonomy. From no autonomy to a certain degree of autonomy is a qualitative change in the way of working. In this working environment, highly educated employees are able to face a given task, choose suitable working strategies, and have the opportunity to try different methods. This is conducive to their autonomous learning and research, better absorbing knowledge, and achieving technological innovation, which is actually the most basic informal training for various sectors and positions.

A closer look at the highly educated population shows that the utility of autonomy at work is higher than that of income, growth at work, and leisure at work, see Table 10.6. Income brings less satisfaction to them than to the uneducated group, indicating that income is not the biggest source of job satisfaction and life happiness for the highly educated group. Instead, they value their job more. Among the group with higher education, those with a bachelor's degree or above value work autonomy more than those with junior college education, and those with junior college value income more than those with a bachelor's degree. It can be seen that within the group that received higher education, people's desire for job autonomy increases as education level continues to increase. Vocational universities focus on cultivating high-level technical talents and value operational skills. Undergraduate education is relatively focused on cultivating advanced compound talents. Income, autonomy, and other aspects of work have different effects on overall job satisfaction.

Human resources are precious wealth of a nation, and the education system shoulders the historical mission of comprehensively promoting quality education and bringing up tens of millions of specialized talents and a large number of creative

Table 10.6 Model 3 regression results

Model 3	Junior college degree and above	High school and below	Bachelor degree and above	Vocational university education
Job autonomy	0.111*** (3.96)	0.0239 (0.250)	0.126*** (2.87)	0.085** (2.26)
Income	3.52E−06*** (3.66)	7.01E−06*** (6.31)	2.47E−06** (2.16)	8.35E−06*** (3.49)
Growth at work	0.042** (2.36)	0.055** (2.44)	0.057** (2.09)	0.033 (1.33)
Operating hours	−0.009*** (−2.7)	−0.006*** (−3.91)	−0.015*** (−3)	−0.004 (−0.88)

Note Because the main focus is on the difference in satisfaction sources, only the coefficients and Z values of the four aspects that affect job satisfaction that are most concerned about in this chapter are listed. * $p < 0.1$, ** $p < 0.05$, *** $p < 0.01$

talents. At the time of knowledge economy, the training objectives and models of higher education should be clearer. Higher education needs to adhere to and strengthen the mode of cultivating learning habits and cultivating autonomy and innovative spirit. The training methods that prepare for lifelong learning will play a long-term role in promoting and innovating social, technological frontiers. At the same time, the idea of human resource development should be broadened, not only paying attention to formal training, but also to informal autonomous learning, and creating a freer platform for employees through changes in workplaces and work styles. The strategy to expand the opportunities for autonomous learning for highly educated talents is in a context where more and more workplaces are shifting from traditional hierarchization to more diversified and flatter structures in a transitional economy that requires innovative thinking, and in a society where the level of education and democratization of citizens is increasing. It will undoubtedly be an active promotion strategy, which will enable the country and individuals to obtain greater benefits through human capital investment in higher education.

References

Akerlof, G. (1982). Labor Contracts as Partial Gift Exchange. *The Quarterly Journal of Economics, 97*(4), 543–569.

Akerlof, G., & Yellen, J. (1986). *Efficiency Wage Models of the Labor Market*. Cambridge University Press.

Allen, J., van der Velden, R. (2001). Educational Mismatches Versus Skill Mismatches: Effects on Wages, Job Satisfaction and On-the-Job Search. *Special Issue on Skills Measurement and Economic Analysis, Oxford Economic Papers, 53*(3), 434–452.

Anderson. L., Tolson, J., et al. (1992). Job Autonomy as a Moderator of the Pelz Effect. *Journal of Social Psychology, 130*(5), 707–708.

Bailey, T. (1993). *Discretionary Effort and the Organization of Work: Employee Participation and Work Reform since Hawthorne*. Institute on Education and the Economy, Teachers College, Columbia University.

Baker, G., Gibbons, R., et al. (1994). Subjective Performance Measures in Optimal Incentive Contracts. *The Quarterly Journal of Economics, 109*(4), 1125–1156.

Baker. G. (2000). The Use of Performance Measures in Incentive Contracting. *The American Economic Review, 90*(2), 415–420.

Battu, H., Belfield, C., & Sloane, P. (1999). Overeducation Among Graduates: A Cohort View. *Education Economics, 7*(1), 21–37.

Belfield, C., & Harris, R. (2002). How Well Do Theories of Job Matching Explain Variations in Job Satisfaction Across Educational Level? Evidence for UK Graduates. *Applied Economics, 34*(5), 535–548.

Bhuian, S., & Al-Shammari. E. S. J. (1996). Organizational Commitment, Job Satisfaction and Job Characteristics: An Empirical Study of Expatriates in Saudi Arabia. *International Journal of Commerce and Management, 6*(3/4), 57–80.

Birdseys, M., & Hill, J. (1995). Individual, Organizational/Work and Environmental Influences on Expatriate Turnover Tendencies: An Empirical Study. *Journal of International Business Studies, 26*(4), 787–813.

Borjas, G. (1979). Job Satisfaction, Wages and Unions. *The Journal of Human Resource, 14*(1), 21–40.

Clark, A., & Oswald, A. (1996). Satisfaction and Comparison Income. *Journal of Public Economics, 61*(3), 359–381.

Clark, A., Geogellis, Y., & Sanfey, P. (1999). *Job Satisfaction, Wage Changes and Quits: Evidence from Germany*. Available at SSRN: https://ssrn.com/abstract=132109.

DeCarlo, T., & Agarwal, S. (1999). Influence of Managerial Behaviors and Job Autonomy on Job Satisfaction of Industrial Salespersons: A Cross-Cultural Study. *Industrial Marketing Management, 28*(1), 51–62.

Drucker, P. (1998). *Post-Capitalist Society* (Trans. Zhang, X.). Shanghai Translation Publishing House.

Ewing, B., & Payne, J. (1999). The Trade-Off between Supervision and Wages: Evidence of Efficiency Wages from the NLSY. *Southern Economic Journal, 66*(2), 424–432.

Federico, J.M., Federico, P., & Lundquist, G. W. (1976) Predicting Women's Turnover as A Function of 'Extend of Met Salary Expectations' and Bio-Demographic Data. *Personnel Psychology, 29*(winter), 559–566.

Finn, C. (2001). Autonomy: An Important Component for Nurses' Job Satisfaction. *International Journal of Nursing Studies, 38*(3), 349–357.

Freeman, R. (1978). Job Satisfaction as an Economic Variable. *The American Economic Review, 68*(2), 135–141.

Hackman, J. R., Oldham, G. (1976). Motivation Through the Design of Work: Test of a Theory. *Organizational Behavior and Human Performance, 16*, 250–279.

Hamermesh, D. (2001). The Changing Distribution of Job Satisfaction. *The Journal of Human Resources, 36*(1), 1–30.

Hoppock, R. (1935). *Job Satisfaction* (pp. 131–136). Harper and Brother.

Hou, Y., & Li, Y. (2005). A Quantitative Study on Professional Values of Postgraduates. *Science of Social Psychology, 5–6*.

Hu, B. (2003). An Empirical Study on Job Satisfaction of Mental Workers. *Science Research Management, 7*.

Johnson, G., & Johnson, W. (2000). Perceived Overqualification and Dimensions of Job Satisfaction: A Longitudinal Analysis. *The Journal of Psychology, 134*(5): 537–555.

Landerweerd, J., & Bousmans, N. (1994). The Effect of Work Dimensions and Need for Autonomy on Nurses' Work Satisfaction and Health. *Journal of Occupational and Organizational Psychology, 67*(3), 207–217.

Levy-Garboua, L., Montmarquette, C., & Simonnet, V. (2001). *Job Satisfaction and Quits: Theory and Evidence from the German Socioeconomic Panel*. CIRANO Working Papers 2001s-41, CIRANO.

Locke E. A. (1976). *The Nature and Causes of Job Satisfaction*. Rand McNally College Publishing Company.

Lorenz, E., & Valeyre, A. (2005). Organisational Innovation, HRM and Labour Market Structure. https://www.researchgate.net/publication/281948251_Organisational_Innovation_HRM_and_Labour_Market_Structure.

Lu, Y. (2004). Social Control and Independence: An Analysis of Job Satisfaction and Role Conflict of Journalists. *Modern Communication, 6*.

McKelvey, R. D., & Zavoina, W. (1975). A Statistical Model for the Analysis of Ordinal Level Dependent Variables. *The Journal of Mathematical Sociology, 4*(1), 103–120.

Min, W. F., & Tsang, M. C. (1990). Vocational Education and Productivity: A Case Study of the Beijing General Auto Industry Company. *Economics of Education Review, 9*, 351–364.

Neumark, D., & Postlewaite, A. (1998). Relative Income Concerns and the Rise in Married. *Journal of Public Economics, 70*(1), 157–183.

Nguyen, A., Taylor, J., & Bradley, S. (2003). *Job Autonomy and Job Satisfaction: New Evidence*. Lancaster University Management School Working Paper. https://www.research.lancs.ac.uk/portal/en/publications/job-autonomy-and-job-satisfaction-new-evidence(c62c01f2-bac6-4f84-b740-9a0ecdd92e4a)/export.html.

Schienman, S. (2002). Socio-Economic Status, Job Conditions, and Well-Being: Self-Concept Explanations for Gender-Contingent Effects. *Sociological Quarterly, 43*(4), 627–646.

Sitkin, S., & Roth, N. (1993). Explaining the Limited Effectiveness of Legalistic 'Remedies' for Trust/Distrust. *Organization Science, 4*(3), 367–392.

Sloane, P., & Williams, H. (2000). Job Satisfaction, Comparison Income and Gender. *Labour, 14*(3), 473–502.

Tsang, M. C. (1987). The Impact of Underutilization of Education on Productivity: A Case Study of the U.S. Bell Companies. *Economics of Education Review, 6*(3), 239–254.

Van Praag, B., Frijter, P., & Ferrer-Carbonell, A. (2003). The Anatomy of Subjective Wellbeing. *Journal of Economic Behavior & Organization, 51*(1), 29–49.

Verhofstadt, E., & Omey. E. (2003). *The Impact of Education on Job Satisfaction in the First Job*. Working Papers of Faculty of Economics and Business Administration, Ghent University, Belgium 03/169, Ghent University.

Vila, L. E., & García-Mora, B. (2005). Education and the Determinants of Job Satisfaction. *Education Economics, 13*(4), 409–425.

Weave, C. (1977). Relationship Among Pay, Race, Sex, Occupational Prestige, Supervision, Work Autonomy and Job Satisfaction in a National Sample. *Personnel Psychology, 30*(3), 437–445.

Yuan, S., & Ma, S. (2002). Empirical Research on Employee Satisfaction. *Journal of Technical Economics & Management, 3*.

Zhang, W., & Peng, J. (2001). Motivation System in Chinese Knowledge-Based Enterprises. *Science Research Management, 6*.

Chapter 11
Education, Job Mobility and Income

Global migration has been greatly promoted by a new round of global technological revolution and the development of financial markets in the late twentieth century. As a result, job mobility plays an increasingly important role in human resource allocation and economic development, and is also of greater significance to personal career growth and wealth accumulation. With the advance of market-oriented reform of China's economic system, human capital allocation in China has broken through various institutional obstacles set by the traditional administrative planning system and gradually transformed to a market-oriented labor flow system. A free labor market is of great significance to optimizing the efficiency of human resources and giving play to the special role of human capital in economic growth.

It is safe to conclude that on the one hand, individuals obtain fairer opportunities through a free labor market; on the other hand, free flow of labor improves the efficiency of resource allocation and facilitates economic development. At the same time, education becomes increasingly important in a free labor market, as people with different levels of education face different job opportunities and tend to make different decisions, thereby affecting their social status. Therefore, the relationship between education and job mobility under a certain social structure has become a perspective for investigation. A number of issues are worth exploring, such as what roles the government, individuals, and the labor market should play, and what experiences of other countries can be learned.

11.1 Literature Review

Job mobility, or labor mobility in a broader sense, is one of the central topics of labor economics and a long-standing subject of empirical studies. Foreign studies before the 1970s mainly focused on the allocative efficiency of the labor market. Researchers mostly studied employees' attitudes, job switch decisions, and the direction of labor

W. Min, *Educational Input, Resource Allocation and Returns to Human Capital*,
https://doi.org/10.1007/978-981-96-4687-6_11

flow in order to ascertain whether information, motivation, and workers' behavior were consistent with the assumptions of classical economic theories. Later, methods advocated by human capital theories, job search theories and some new econometric models injected vitality into the stagnant field of labor mobility. In these theories and related empirical studies, education, as an investment in human capital or an individual characteristic, is regarded as one of many independent variables to examine labor mobility in a labor market. In China, studies on the relationship between education and job mobility mainly touched on vocational education and adult education. Most studies focused on migration across regions, especially between urban and rural areas and from the west to the east. There are also some studies on laid-off workers in which job mobility is considered as an option for them after being dismissed, as well as some on promotion within the same organization.

11.1.1 Economic Theories on the Relationship Between Education, Job Mobility and Income

Human capital theories hold that one's social status and job change decisions depend on individual characteristics. One of their basic assertions is that with the improvement of education level, people's employability, adaptability, and flexibility will be improved, thus causing the number of unemployed and the unemployment rate to reduce. Based on the basic assumptions of a perfectly competitive labor market in neoclassical economics, Becker (1994) suggested that the Market Clearing Model believes that the better educated people are, the more they tend to invest in on-the-job training after being employed, which is why their occupations are more stable and earnings (wages) grow faster than others'.

The Experience Good Model believes that the sense of job suitability is a process of self-perception and cannot be known in advance. Employees gradually realize the nature of a job in the process of work. Therefore, job mobility is driven by growing work awareness of workers who have changed jobs (Nelson 1970). The Search Good Model argues that job mobility reflects workers' intention to move to more productive jobs, where productivity comes from the conscious compensation paid by employers (Lucas and Prescott 1974).

The interaction between human capital investment and job search behavior can be seen from the following argument (Jovanovic 1979). Better-educated workers tend to invest more in training, and they will continue to do so when they switch to another employer. Therefore, they expect to stay in an organization longer than other workers. According to this model, better-educated workers will search more thoroughly (not necessarily longer) in order to achieve greater wage earnings.

Screening Theory argues that the chance of promotion is greater when education level and job requirements match well. Formal education plays a greater role in employees' mobility among different career ladders than in promotion within the same career ladder. In addition, employees of higher ranks are more likely to switch between career ladders, while more senior workers are less likely to do so.

The labor market segmentation model focuses on the barriers of market segmentation to labor mobility and believes that inequality stems from the structure of the labor market. According to McNabb (1987) and Rosenfeld (1992), the Institutional Model emphasizes that the labor market is segmented, and social and institutional barriers prevent certain workers, especially those with poor education, from obtaining better jobs, thus limiting their access to upward social mobility through job changes.

In short, early studies on job mobility mostly focused on employees' individual characteristics such as education and experience. Since the mid-1980s, researchers have tried to explain job mobility more in terms of structural factors. Apparently, theories on individual characteristics have limitations in explaining the generation and reproduction of social class and inequality. Job mobility affects a person's social identity and career growth, which is not only determined by the resources individuals have, but also by institutional factors such as social organization and structure.

11.1.2 Empirical Studies on the Impact of Education on Job Mobility and Income

Existing empirical studies mainly examined the impact of education on job mobility from two aspects. The first was to analyze the impact of education on the rate of job mobility, and the second was to study income differences caused by job change for people with different education levels.

In terms of the effect of educational background on job turnover, Wang et al. (2001) studied labor mobility in three cities of China: Beijing, Wuxi of Jiangsu Province, and Zhuhai of Guangdong Province. He used "individual mobility rate"[1] to measure the mobility rate of employees. It is believed that there are different forces in labor supply and demand influencing the mobility of employees with different education levels. Therefore, there are indeed significantly different mobility rates for different education levels. In Beijing, the higher the level of education, the higher the mobility rate, but the labor force with secondary vocational education shows the highest mobility rate. In Wuxi, the population with higher education is less mobile, and workers with high school and middle education change jobs most frequently. In Zhuhai, the labor force with middle school and higher education shows a higher mobility rate. Research suggests that such regional differences can be explained by differences in employment structure of the three cities.

In terms of income difference among people with different education levels after job changes, Mincer (1986) divided wage changes caused by job switch into short-term and long-term changes, and the reasons for an employee to leave a job into

[1] Divide the number of job changes by the total job tenure of an individual to approximate the number of job change per unit of time. The higher the value, the higher the mobility rate.

two types: resignation and dismissal.[2] He found that, with the exception of older workers being laid-off, income of the workers changing jobs rise in both the short and long term. In 1996, Wang Rong used the data of the National Longitudinal Survey of Youth (NLSY) of America for an empirical study on the relationship between education, job mobility and wages, and drew three conclusions. First, for college-educated workers, the benefits of voluntary job changes caused by wage differences are positive. Second, for college-educated workers, their previous wages have a positive effect on their possibility of voluntary job change. Third, the educational return rate of workers with job changes is higher than that of those without any changes. By using the data from NLSY, Shin's study in 2003 found that, with or without controlling for structural variables, better educated workers have a higher rate of upward job mobility, and there is also a positive relationship between higher education level and reduced frequency of job change. Munasinghe and Sigman's study (2004), using the 1979–1994 panel data from NLSY, showed that workers who change jobs less often earn more than those who change jobs more frequently, and their jobs will change less frequently in the future, especially among experienced workers.

By reviewing the above empirical studies, we can find that: (1) Foreign research more reflects the negative relationship between education level and the frequency of job changes. Chinese scholars' research reflects both positive and negative relationships, dependent on the employment structure and institutional factors in different regions. It is related to the transition of China's labor market from less to more mobility, as well as the differences in economic development, the degree of openness of the labor market, and the structure of employment opportunities among regions. (2) Chinese scholars' research mainly focuses on the impact of education either on wages or job mobility, but systematic analysis of the interrelationship among education, job mobility and wage is neglected.

Based on the existing literature, we attempt to synthesize relevant theories, focus on the relationship between education level, job mobility and wages, and analyze the influence of education on the frequency and type of job mobility, as well as the wage changes associated with job changes with other factors controlled.

11.2 Theoretical Framework and Analysis Models

11.2.1 Theoretical Framework and Related Variables

In accordance with the above research objectives and the results of related literature, this chapter outlines a theoretical framework shown in Fig. 11.1 as the basis for hypotheses. This chapter believes that education has an impact on job mobility. The

[2] Short-term wage changes refer to the difference between the starting salary of a new job and the salary before the end of the previous job, while long-term wage changes refer to the wage gap between two jobs with similar employment years after deducting the impact of work experience.

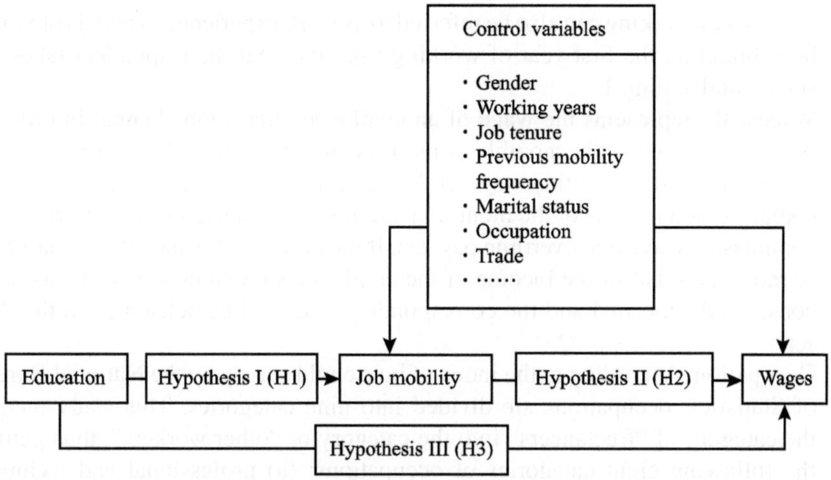

Fig. 11.1 A theoretical framework for the relationship between education, job mobility and wages

higher the level of education, the stronger the initiative of job mobility. One of the reasons why better educated people seek job change is for higher wages, thus in the labor market, the higher the education level, the higher the frequency of job change and the higher the earning (wages) from work. In addition, excessively rapid and frequent job change may be caused by other factors and thus will be considered as a distinguished value and eliminated in the sample.

The main variables are briefly described as follows.

1. Education. According to years of education, education is divided into five levels, including primary school or below, middle school (including ordinary middle school, secondary vocational middle school and intermediate mechanic junior high school), high school (including ordinary high school, secondary vocational high school, intermediate mechanic high school and secondary technical school), vocational college and bachelor's degree or above (undergraduate, master's degree and doctoral degree).
2. Job mobility. Job mobility in this chapter is defined as change of employer, regardless of whether it involves unemployment.

   Types of job mobility. Geographic, industrial, and occupational mobility are all components of job mobility.[3] According to the cause of job mobility, it can be divided into two types of job mobility: one is brought by the employer's dismissal, the other is caused by the employee's resignation or quitting.

   Frequency of job mobility. This is defined as the number of job changes since one started working divided by his/her years of working.

[3] This chapter examines job mobility across industries and occupations and does not conduct a separate study on geographic mobility.

Years of working can also be referred to as work experience, which is obtained by subtracting the first year of working from the year the respondent takes the survey and adding 1.

3. Wages. W_i represents the wage of an employee after a job change. In order to be consistent with the monthly wage used in calculating the return on a job change, the initial monthly wage of the current job is used to represent the total compensation income of the month, including basic salary, allowances, bonuses, commissions, average overtime pay, etc. If the current job's income is four times or more than that of the income of the employee's previous job, such cases are considered abnormal and the corresponding data will be deleted from the data set.
4. Occupation. According to the index of household survey by the National Bureau of Statistics, occupations are divided into nine categories. This study merges the category of "freelancers" into the category of "other workers", thus getting the following eight categories of occupations: (a) professional and technical personnel, (b) heads of government agencies, enterprises and institutions, (c) clerks and related personnel,[4] (d) business personnel, (e) service personnel, (f) agricultural, forestry, animal husbandry and fishery workers, (g) production workers, transportation workers and relevant personnel (hereinafter referred to as "production workers"), (h) other workers that are inconvenient to classify (including freelancers). In the econometric regression, "production workers" is taken as the benchmark, and the others are converted into seven dummy variables.

   To further facilitate the analysis, we further divide the above eight categories of occupations into two markets: the primary labor market, which includes (a) professional and technical personnel, (b) heads of government agencies, enterprises and institutions, and (c) clerks and related personnel; the secondary labor market, which covers all other occupations.
5. Industry. Based on the classification by the National Bureau of Statistics of the People's Republic of China,[5] we divide the 21 industries into 6 groups for empirical study: (a) "primary industry" (agriculture, forestry, animal husbandry, fishery); (b) "secondary industry" (including 4 industries such as mining, manufacturing, production and supply of electricity, heat, gas and water, and construction); (c) "circulation sector" (including four industries such as transport, storage and post, information transmission, software and information technology, wholesale and retail trades, and hotels and catering services); (d) "social production service and living service" (including financial intermediation, real estate, leasing and business services, scientific research, technical services and geological survey, water conservancy, environment and public facilities management,

[4] Clerks and related personnel include administrative clerks, political clerks, security clerks, post and telecommunications clerks, other clerical clerks and related personnel. Economic management professionals who have no professional titles and no college or technical secondary school education are excluded and incorporated into the secondary labor market.

[5] According to the industry classification standard formulated in 1985, the tertiary industry was further divided into four levels; this standard was abolished in 2003. Because the classification of the three strata of industries is too rough, we adopt the classification standard of 1985 in this chapter.

services to households and other services); (e) "quality service" (including 3 industries such as education, health, social security and social service, culture, sports and entertainment); (f) "public service" (including public management and social organization, international organization, military). In the econometric regression, "public services" is taken as the benchmark category, and the rest are converted into 5 dummy variables.

6. Type of ownership. According to the classification by the National Bureau of Statistics, 11 kinds of ownership are grouped into 3 categories: (a) state-owned units (including three types of units such as government agencies and the military, public institutions, state-owned and holding enterprises); (b) urban collectively-owned units (collective enterprises); (c) other forms of ownership (including seven types such as foreign-funded enterprises, enterprises with funds from China's Hong Kong, Macao and Taiwan regions, private enterprises, partnership enterprises, self-employed individuals and others). In the econometric regression, "urban collectively-owned units" is taken as the benchmark category, and the rest are converted into two dummy variables.
7. Organization size. To facilitate research and according to the index interpretation of household surveys, organization size is divided into four types according to the number of employees. (a) small organizations (1–40 employees), (b) medium organizations (41–150 employees), (c) relatively large organizations (151–650 employees), and (d) large organizations (650 employees or more). In econometric regression, "large organizations" is used as the benchmark category, and the rest are converted into three dummy variables.

11.2.2 Hypotheses and Models

Hypothesis I (H1):
The higher the education level, the higher the frequency of job change.

Hypothesis II (H2):
The frequency of job change and wages are positively correlated.

Hypothesis III (H3):
The higher the education level, the greater the possibility of earning higher wages by job change.

This chapter also examines the differences in income changes for job mobility between inter-industry and intra-industry mobility, and compares income differences of job mobility in primary and secondary labor markets.

Descriptive statistics and regression models are used in the chapter as shown in Eq. (11.1):

$$W_i = a + c_1T + c_2T^2 + \sum e_jDUM_j + \mu \tag{11.1}$$

Here W_{i} represents an employee's wages after a job change, T is years of working. c_1 and c_2 respectively represents the impact of previous job tenure and the square of that on wages; DUM_j is the set of dummy variables representing gender, marital status, organization size, ownership, occupation and industry.

We then introduce education level to Eq. (11.1) to test the impact of education on wages brought by job mobility, and obtain Eq. (11.2):

$$W_i = a + \sum f_i EDU_i + c_1 T + c_2 T^2 + \sum e_j DUM_j + \mu \tag{11.2}$$

where EDU_i is a binary dummy variable representing education level, f_i represents the impact of the corresponding education level on wages. If a certain education level is used as the benchmark, f_i represents the additional amount of wages brought by the difference between education level i and the benchmark.

Finally, we introduce *RPM*, a variable representing the frequency of job mobility, into Eq. (11.2) to test the impact of job change frequency on wages and obtain Eq. (11.3):

$$W_i = a + \sum f_i EDU_i + c_1 T + c_2 T^2 + dRPM + \sum e_j DUM_j + \mu \tag{11.3}$$

where d represents the wage change caused by the frequency of job change.

In addition, we separately run Eq. (11.3) for intra-industry and inter- industry mobility, labor mobility in the primary and secondary markets, as well as mobility caused by dismissal and resignation, so as to investigate the influence of education level on wage changes for different types of mobility.

11.3 Data Description

The data is adopted from the China's Urban Household Education and Employment Survey-2005 by the Institute of Economics of Education, Peking University. There are a total of 14,338 respondents, including employed and laid-off workers, among whom 9369 answered questions about job changes. 3345 respondents had never changed jobs, while 6024 have changed jobs. By excluding invalid samples, we obtain a total of 5560 valid samples that cover various regions and industries in China. Tables 11.1, 11.2 and 11.3 show the statistical description of the sample data.

11.3.1 Gender

There were 2976 males, accounting for 53.5%; 2584 females, accounting for 46.5%. The number of females is slightly lower than that of males, but overall, the difference is acceptable.

Table 11.1 Individual characteristics and job statistics of sample data

Individual characteristics and job statistics	Number of samples	Percentage (%)
Gender		
Male	2976	53.5
Female	2584	46.5
Marital status		
Married	5355	96.3
Others (unmarried, divorced, widowed, etc.)	205	3.7
Education level when entering the previous job		
Primary school or below	107	1.9
Middle school	1510	27.2
High school	2923	49.5
Higher Vocational College	674	12.1
Bachelor degree or above	346	6.2
Previous job tenure		
1–10 years	2902	52.2
11–19 years	1786	32.1
20 years or more	872	15.8
Years of working		
1–9 years	268	4.8
10–19 years	1662	29.9
20–29 years	2426	43.6
30 years or more	1204	21.8
Monthly wages		
RMB1-RMB100	1069	19.23
RMB101-RMB1,000	3549	63.83
RMB1,001-RMB10,000	934	16.80
RMB10,001 or more	8	0.14
Occupation		
Primary labor market	2817	51.1
Secondary labor market	2697	48.9
Industry		
Primary industry	166	3.0
Secondary industry	2266	41.0
Circulation sector	1194	21.6
Social production service and life service	609	11.0
Quality service	618	11.2
Public service	680	12.3
Type of ownership		

(continued)

Table 11.1 (continued)

Individual characteristics and job statistics	Number of samples	Percentage (%)
State-owned	3806	69.3
Urban collective-owned	721	13.1
Other types of ownership	962	17.5
Organization size		
Small	1428	25.7
Medium	1300	23.4
Relatively large	1367	24.6
Large	1361	24.5

Table 11.2 Number of job changes

Number of job changes	Number of samples	Percentage (%)
1	2001	36.00
2	2114	38.02
3	948	17.05
4	289	5.20
5	127	2.28
6+	81	1.46
Total	5560	100

Table 11.3 Frequency of job change and average wages by education level

Item	Frequency of job change (times/year)	Average monthly wages (RMB)	Average job tenure (years)
Middle school	0.0913	524.28	10.95
High school	0.1048	644.89	9.54
Higher vocational college	0.1482	986.49	6.75
Bachelor degree or above	0.1498	1251.33	6.68

11.3.2 Marital Status

There were 5355 married, accounting for 96.3%, and 205 unmarried, divorced, widowed or others, accounting for 3.7%. The proportion of married people is much larger than that of the other cases, so marital status is excluded in the regression.

11.3.3 Education Level When Entering the Prior Job

The numbers of samples with middle school education and high school education accounted for 27.2% and 49.5%, respectively, those with vocational college education taking 12.1%, bachelor's degree or above 6.2%, primary school education or below 1.9%, and the samples missing education information accounted for 3.1%. The structure indicates that the education level of most urban workers is high school, followed by middle school.

11.3.4 Years of Service in the Prior Job

Taking 10 years as an interval, the number of samples who have 1–10 years' service in their prior jobs accounted for 52.2%, those with 11–19 years accounting for 32.1%, and those with more than 20 years accounted for 15.7%. Overall, the sample size decreases with the increase of tenure.

11.3.5 Number of years Since the First Job

This refers to years a worker has from the first job to the current job. Valid samples with a range of 1 to 59 years were divided into four groups. Those who have worked for 20–29 years is the largest group, accounting for 43.6%. People who have worked for 10–19 years accounted for 29.9%, representing the second largest group. 21.7% of the sample have worked for more than 30 years, and 4.8% 1–9 years. The sample is overall roughly normally distributed.

11.3.6 Monthly Wage

The income level of valid samples were divided into four groups (measured by monthly wage), RMB1–100, RMB101–1000, RMB1001–10,000, and RMB10,001 and above. The number of samples with a monthly wage of RMB101–1000 was the largest, accounting for 63.83%. It was followed by the group with a monthly wage between RMB1–100 (19.23%) and RMB1001–10,000 (16.80%). The number of samples with a monthly income above RMB10,001 was 8, accounting for only 0.14% of the total.

11.3.7 Occupation

Occupations were divided by primary and secondary labor markets, with 51.1% of the samples employed in the primary labor market, and 48.9% in the secondary labor market.

11.3.8 Industry

The largest number of people were employed in the secondary sector (including mining, manufacturing, production and supply of electricity, gas and water, and construction), accounting for 40.8%. As for the tertiary sector, 21.5% of all the samples worked in commercial industries12.2% in public service, 11.1% in quality service, 11.0% worked in the production and living services. Only 3.0% were employed in the primary sector. There were 0.5% of the samples missing industry information.

11.3.9 Ownership of Employers

Party and government offices, military, public institutions, state-owned or state-holding enterprises accounted for 68.5% of the total sample. Urban collectively owned units accounted for 13.0%, while the other ownership types (including foreign enterprises, private enterprises and individually owned businesses, etc.) accounted for no more than 4% of each, and the total of them accounted for 17.3%. There were 1.2% of the samples missing information. The high percentage of government and state related ownership reflected the economic system dominated by state-owned economy in China at that time.

Table 11.2 describes the distribution of the number of job changes. The number of samples having changed jobs from 1 to 10 times accounts for 99.8% of the total. Among them, the number of samples with one and two job changes is the largest. After that, the job mobility frequency decreases sequentially.

In the job market, people with different education levels have different mobility mechanisms and different levels of income. At the same time, job mobility and income differences are also different due to factors such as gender, age, occupation, industry, and types of ownership. We find that, with the exception of the insignificant difference in wages between male and female with a bachelor degree or higher degrees, male workers with all the other education levels change jobs less often than their female peers, and earn higher average wages. Both the frequency of job change and average earnings decline with age. Employees in the primary labor market change jobs less frequently than those in the secondary, and there is no significant difference in average wages. In terms of industry distribution, employees of the circulation sector and social production service and living service sectors show higher job mobility and earn more wages, compared with those in quality services, public service and the primary industry. People working in state-owned organizations show less mobility and lower wages than those of urban collective-owned ones, while those of other forms of ownership change jobs most frequently and achieve the highest wages. The larger the unit size, the lower the frequency of labor mobility. In general, the average wage of medium and relatively large units is higher than that of small and large ones.

Table 11.3 shows the average monthly wages and frequency of job change of workers with different education levels. The research result indicates that the average monthly wages and education level are positively correlated. The frequency of job change also increases with the improvement of education level. There is no significant difference in the frequency of job change between workers with higher vocational college education and those with a bachelor degree or above.

11.4 Factors Influencing Job Mobility

To test Hypothesis I, we first run regressions on Eqs. (11.1) and (11.2) with the frequency of job change as the dependent variable. Table 11.4 shows the regression results.

Regression results for Eq. (11.1) show that both gender and the previous job tenure have a significant impact on the frequency of job change. Specifically, male employees' frequency of job change is 0.009 lower than female workers'. The average frequency of job change decreases by 0.004 for each additional year of the previous job tenure.

In terms of occupation categories, professional and technical personnel, heads of government agencies, enterprises and institutions, clerks and related personnel all show higher mobility rates than production workers, the benchmark category. Among them, the mobility rate of heads of the government agencies, enterprises and institutions is the highest. Compared with production workers, those with no significant difference in job mobility include business personnel, service workers laborers agricultural, forestry, animal husbandry and fishery, and other workers.

In terms of industry, the regression coefficients of the primary industry and quality service sector are not significant, and those of the secondary industry, tertiary industry, social production service and life service sectors are all significant and positive, indicating that there is no significant difference in the frequency of labor mobility in the primary industry and quality service sectors compared with the benchmark, public service sector. The labor mobility rate of the other three industries is higher, and that of the circulation sector is the highest.

In terms of ownership, there is no significant difference in labor mobility between state-owned units and urban collective-owned units, the benchmark category. Labor mobility of other forms of ownership units is much more than that of state-owned and urban collective-owned units, and the regression coefficient is 0.064. In terms of unit size, compared with large-sized units, workers in small-sized units change

Table 11.4 Results of multi-step regression with job change frequency as the dependent variable

Variable	Equation (11.1)			Equation (11.2)		
	Coefficient	Standard regression coefficient	T value	Coefficient	Standard regression coefficient	T value
Constant	0.121		14.786**	0.102		8.302**
1. Gender	−0.009	−0.042	−3.318**	−0.011	−0.052	−4.164**
2. Previous job tenure	−0.004	−0.272	−21.210**	−0.003	−0.249	−19.279**
3. Occupation						
Professional and technical personnel	0.016	0.068	4.083**	0.004	0.017	1.001
Heads of government agencies, enterprises and institutions	0.029	0.039	3.008**	0.013	0.017	1.298
Clerks and related personnel	0.013	0.044	2.718**	0.004	0.013	0.804
Business personnel	−0.002	−0.005	−0.282	−0.005	−0.013	−0.822
Service personnel	0.007	0.015	1.038	0.005	0.012	0.814
Agriculture, forestry, animal husbandry and fishery workers	−0.028	−0.022	−1.592	−0.025	−0.02	−1.454
Other workers	0.018	0.013	1.015	0.017	0.011	0.918
4. Industry						
Primary industry	−0.01	−0.016	−1.033	−0.007	−0.011	−0.715
Secondary industry	0.009	0.042	1.706*	0.011	0.049	2.008*
Circulation sector	0.023	0.088	4.016**	0.025	0.096	4.379**
Social production service and life service	0.017	0.048	2.697**	0.016	0.047	2.678**
Quality Service	0.004	0.012	0.646	0	0	−0.008
5. Types of ownership						
State-owned units	−0.002	−0.008	−0.459	−0.004	−0.018	−1.005

(continued)

Table 11.4 (continued)

Variable	Equation (11.1)			Equation (11.2)		
	Coefficient	Standard regression coefficient	T value	Coefficient	Standard regression coefficient	T value
Other ownership	0.064	0.223	12.517**	0.062	0.217	12.299**
6. Organization size prior to job change						
Small-sized	0.014	0.058	3.271**	0.016	0.064	3.648**
Medium-sized	0.007	0.026	1.594	0.006	0.023	1.437
Relatively large-sized	0.005	0.018	1.182	0.005	0.018	1.212
7. Education level						
Middle school or equivalent				0.012	0.051	1.261
High school or equivalent				0.018	0.084	1.876*
Higher vocational college				0.050	0.152	4.775**
Bachelor degree or above				0.065	0.145	5.779**
R2	0.191			0.207		
R2 after adjustment	0.188			0.204		
F value	66.652**			61.174**		
D-W value	1.785			1.79		
Sample size	5399					

Note ** means the significance level is 0.05, * means the significance level 0.1, and the unmarked means insignificance. The benchmark categories of each dummy variable are female workers, production workers, public service, urban collectively-owned units, large-sized units, primary school or below

jobs more frequently. There is no significant difference in labor mobility of medium-sized, relatively large-sized and large-sized units. This result implies that the larger the unit size, the larger the number of employees, the less the labor mobility.

With the dummy variable of education level incorporated, we run a regression for Eq. (11.2), the results of which are also shown in Table 11.4. The overall explanatory power of the model rises from 19.1% to 20.7%. The significance of the regression results of control variables such as gender, last job tenure, industry, ownership, and unit size did not change, and the magnitude of the effect on the frequency of job turnover changed slightly. Neither the significance of nor the ranking among control variables such as gender, tenure of previous job, industry, ownership and unit size changes, although the magnitude of impact slightly changes. Occupation is the most affected control variable, with all the T values becoming insignificant. This indicates that the impact of education level greatly dilutes that of occupation on the frequency of job change.

Among different levels of education, high school, higher vocational college and bachelor degree or above level education have a significant impact on the frequency of job change, and the coefficient increases with the level of education. There is no significant difference between impact of middle school and that of primary school or below on job mobility. This finding validates the proposed Hypothesis I (H1): the frequency of job change increases with the improvement of education level.

The positive relationship between education level and the frequency of job change conflicts with the findings of most empirical studies abroad, such as those using American youth as the research sample, but is consistent with the research by Wang Fenyu et al. on labor mobility in Beijing. The contradiction between domestic and foreign research results can be explained by the different mechanisms of labor market at home and abroad. In a relatively mature labor market with standardized mechanisms job seekers can quickly get a matching job with steady and satisfying paychecks, especially those well-educated. As a result, a negative relationship between education and job mobility is formed, which is in line with the interpretation of human capital theories. China's labor market, in contrast, is at an early stage of transition to a market-oriented mechanism after a long period of stagnation, just beginning to stimulate free mobility of labor on the supply side. Employees with higher education levels face more job opportunities particularly. On the demand side, employers prefer to hire better educated people, believing that they will show higher productivity and save job training cost. Therefore employers tend to offer more employee benefits and incentives to attract well-educated people. In this case, workers with higher education levels are very likely to change jobs more frequently than those with less education.

11.5 Factors Influencing Wages

11.5.1 Impact of Education and Job Change Frequency on Wages

This section is to test Hypotheses II and III, in other words, to examine the impact of job mobility on wages and that of education on wages in different types of mobility. Individual and job characteristics are first taken as control variables, and then dummy variables of education level and job change frequency are successively introduced for a multi-step regression. The results are shown in Table 11.5.

The results of regression Eq. (11.1) show that some of the control variables have a significant impact on work income. Previous job tenure has a significant impact on wages of the current job, and the relationship is quadratic. The longer the previous job tenure, the higher the wage of the current job. Among workers with job mobility, men earn more on average than women. For employees in various occupations,

Table 11.5 Regression results with wages as the dependent variable

Variable	Equation (11.1)		Equation (11.2)		Equation (11.3)	
	Coefficient	T value	Coefficient	T value	Coefficient	T value
Constant	289.351	3.328**	379.149	3.019**	263.911	2.092**
1. Gender	212.248	7.695**	188.397	6.881**	200.006	7.323**
2. Previous job tenure	8.601	1.662*	14.336	2.796**	21.234	4.083**
Square of previous job tenure	−0.111	−0.691	−0.174	−1.095	−0.296	−1.862*
3. Occupation						
Professional and technical personnel	278.838	7.152**	133.009	3.304**	129.117	3.221**
Heads of government agencies, enterprises and institutions	542.613	5.560**	350.416	3.596**	340.182	3.506**
Clerks and related personnel	163.004	3.462**	56.076	1.182	53.314	1.129
Business personnel	3.556	0.059	−34.43	−0.576	−31.475	−0.528
Service personnel	89.028	1.393	64.39	1.023	60.127	0.959
Agriculture, forestry, animal husbandry and fishery Workers	447.59	2.547*	461.769	2.663**	485.106	2.809**
Other workers	231.802	1.268	216.521	1.202	200.845	1.12
4. Industry						
Primary industry	−226.924	−2.308**	−184.62	−1.905*	−178.362	−1.849*
Secondary industry	49.884	0.915	68.663	1.278	59.004	1.103
Circulation sector	115.46	1.973**	146.112	2.533**	124.853	2.171**
Social production service and life service	216.275	3.507**	215.286	3.544**	201.217	3.325**
Quality service	34.794	0.561	−10.186	−0.167	−8.807	−0.145
5. Ownership						

(continued)

Table 11.5 (continued)

Variable	Equation (11.1)		Equation (11.2)		Equation (11.3)	
	Coefficient	T value	Coefficient	T value	Coefficient	T value
State-owned	−48.095	−1.121	−74.18	−1.751*	−69.411	−1.645
Other ownership	259.489	5.059**	243.144	4.812**	187.813	3.687**
6. Unit size						
Small-sized	−53.166	−1.206	−36.997	−0.851	−51.252	−1.182
Medium-sized	31.361	0.751	19.231	0.467	13.74	0.335
Relatively large-sized	0.497	0.013	−0.225	−0.006	−4.386	−0.115
7. Education level						
Middle school or equivalent			−238.221	−2.419**	−252.561	−2.575**
High school or equivalent			−81.157	−0.829	−102.784	−1.054
Higher vocational college			233.59	2.221**	184.131	1.754*
Bachelor degree or above			488.018	4.338**	423.969	3.772**
8. Frequency of job change					946.758	6.929**
R^2	0.044		0.074		0.082	
R^2 after adjustment	0.041		0.07		0.078	
F value	12.416**		17.878**		19.233**	
D-W value	1.793		1.802		1.81	
Sample size	5399					

Note ** means the significance level is 0.05, * means the significance level 0.1, and the unmarked means insignificance

compared with production workers, heads of government agencies, enterprises and public institutions enjoy the biggest wage increase by switching to a new job, followed by agricultural, forestry, animal husbandry and fishery workers, clerks and related personnel and professional and technical personnel. There is no significant difference between the changes in average monthly wages of business personnel, service personnel and other workers compared with production workers. Among workers who have changed jobs in different industries, the average income of workers in the production and living service sector and circulation sector is the highest, RMB216 and RMB115 higher than that in the public service sector, respectively. The average income of workers in the primary industry is about RMB227 lower than that of those in the public service sector. The average income of employees in the secondary industry and quality service sectors after job mobility are not significantly different from those in the public service sector. From the perspective of ownership, the change in average income caused by job change for employees of state-owned units and of urban collective-owned show no significant difference, and the average income of employees of other ownership units after job change rises by about RMB259 higher than that of employees of urban collective-owned units. Unit size has no significant impact on the change in average income in labor mobility.

Results of regression Eq. (11.2) in Table 11.5 show the impact of education level on income change caused by job change. After excluding the impact of control variables, except for high school education, all the other three education levels have a significant impact on income after job change, and the overall explanatory power increases from 4.4% to 7.4%. Due to job mobility, average income for workers with bachelor's degree and higher vocational college education increases by about RMB488 and RMB234 more than that of employees with primary school education or below, the benchmark. However, average income for workers with middle school education rise by about RMB238 lower than the benchmark in mobility. Although there is a slight deviation, on the whole, the results support a positive correlation between the level of education and income in terms of job mobility, which accords with the conclusion on the relationship between education and income in human capital theories, and is consistent with the findings of most empirical studies at home and abroad. It implies that people with higher education levels possess more human capital, and are more capable of dealing with unemployment or mismatch in the labor market, thus more likely to earn higher income by changing jobs.

Results of regression Eq. (11.3) in Table 11.5 show the impact of the frequency of job switch on income and the overall explanatory power also rises from 7.4% to 8.2%. It is verified that the frequency of job change and income are significantly positively correlated, which is consistent with common sense.

11.5.2 Impact of Education on Wages in Inter-Industry and Intra-Industry Mobility

We further compare the impact of education on income between inter-industry and intra-industry mobility, as shown in Table 11.6.

Table 11.6 Comparison of impact of education on income between inter-industry and intra-industry mobility

Variable	Total	Inter-industry mobility	Intra-industry mobility
Education level	191.836** (17.874)	163.752** (23.301)	229.764** (28.730)

Note ** means the significance level is 0.05, and the T value is in parentheses

Table 11.7 Comparison of impact of education on income between autonomous and forced mobility

Variable	Total	Autonomous mobility	Forced mobility
Education level	177.558** (21.456)	185.441** (32.732)	147.392** (25.241)

Note ** means the significance level is 0.05, and the T value is in parentheses

Table 11.6 shows that education level has a significantly positive impact on income in both inter-industry mobility and intra-industry mobility. The impact in inter-industry mobility is smaller than that of intra-industry mobility. For each level of education increased, the average income increases by RMB164 and RMB230 after inter-industry and intra-industry mobility, respectively.

11.5.3 Impact of Education on Wages in Autonomous and Forced Mobility

We previously defined autonomous and forced mobility as job change caused by quitting and layoff, respectively (see Table 11.7).

According to the results in Table 11.7, education level has a significantly positive impact on income in both types of mobility, the impact larger in autonomous mobility than forced mobility, which is consistent with general understanding. For each level of education increased, the average income after autonomous mobility increases by about RMB185, and in forced mobility the amount of increase is about RMB147.

11.5.4 Impact of Education on Income for Labor Mobility in Primary and Secondary Labor Market

Finally, we investigate whether there are differences in the change of income for employees in the primary and secondary labor market after job change. The results are shown in Table 11.8.

Table 11.8 Comparison of impact of education on wages between mobility in primary and secondary labor market

Variable	Total	Primary labor market	Secondary labor market
Education level	191.836** (17.874)	230.733** (27.221)	122.440** (22.308)

Note ** means the significance level is 0.05, and the T value is in parentheses

Again, there is a significantly positive correlation between education level and income in labor mobility for both primary and secondary labor markets. On the whole, the higher the education level, the greater the impact of education on average income. In addition, the positive impact of education is greater in the primary labor market than the secondary. For each level of education increased, the average income rise brought by mobility is approximately RMB231 and RMB122, respectively.

11.6 Conclusions

11.6.1 Relationship Between Education and Job Mobility

The hypothesis that education has a significant positive impact on the frequency of job mobility is verified. That is, the higher the education level of workers, the more likely they are to change their jobs. This is mainly related to the transitional features of China's economic system and labor market. Under the planned economy, jobs were allocated according to the official plan, so there was no free-flowing labor market, except an individual transferred work due to job position change or family reasons. With the economy transforming to a market-oriented system, the labor market arises, and people are allowed to change jobs for higher income and better career opportunities. In the transition of labor market, workers with better education are more willing and able to pursue better jobs, and thus show a higher mobility rate than those with lower education levels.

Contrary to general perception, male workers have a lower rate of job mobility than female workers, which remains to be studied. The negative correlation between the previous job tenure and the frequency of job mobility is confirmed, which is consistent with the widespread notion. In terms of occupational categories, government agencies, enterprises and institutions have the highest frequency of job change, followed by professional and technical personnel, clerks and related personnel. There is no significant difference among people in other occupations. In terms of industry categories, the circulation department of the tertiary industry has the highest frequency of job mobility, followed by social production service and life service sector and the secondary industry. There is no significant difference between the mobility of other industries and those in the public service sector. In terms of ownership, other ownership units (including foreign-funded enterprises, private enterprises, self-employed individuals) show the highest labor mobility rates, and there is no significant difference between state-owned and urban collectively-owned units. In addition, job mobility decreases as the unit size increases.

11.6.2 Relationship Between Education, Job Mobility and Income

By comparing job mobility frequency and income of different educational groups, as well as the regression results with job wages as the dependent variable, we draw the following conclusion: the higher the education level, the higher the job mobility frequency and the higher the income.

In terms of individual characteristics, female workers generally have higher mobility frequency, but a smaller income increase after job changes than male workers. Among those with a bachelor's degree or above, female workers' income after mobility is slightly higher than that of male workers. At all levels of education, the mobility of 30-year-old and younger workers is the strongest, followed by those aged 31 to 45. Employees aged 45 and over have the lowest mobility. Among various occupations, workers in the primary labor market are generally less mobile than those in the secondary labor market, and earn slightly more income after job changes. On the whole, employees in the circulation sector of the tertiary industry and the production and life service sector show higher mobility and earn higher income after changing jobs. Workers in the primary industry, quality service and public service sector have lower job mobility and lower income increase after job changes. Labor mobility in the secondary industry is different at each education level, and there is no obvious pattern in general. Among diverse types of ownership, with the exception of primary school education or below, the mobility of workers with various education levels increases in turn for state-owned, collective-owned and other ownership units, their income rise also increasing accordingly. In terms of unit size, job mobility decreases with the increase of unit size, and income change is not significant. However, the negative correlation between mobility and unit size is not stable among people with higher vocational college and higher education levels.

By comparing different types of mobility, we reach the following conclusions. For well-educated workers, income increase due to intra-industry mobility is greater than that of inter-industry mobility. Generally, the higher the education level, the more professional and specific the knowledge and skills are, and the better employees can retain their professional advantages by working within the same industry. Switching jobs across industries will weaken one's advantages in professional skills in the previous industry. Workers with higher levels of education enjoy a rise in income both in autonomous and forced mobility, the rise larger in autonomous mobility. Finally, positive impact of education on income is greater in the primary than in secondary labor market in job mobility. A possible reason might be that the primary labor market generally requires more professional skills from employees.

In summary, by examining the relationship between education, job mobility and income, this chapter further validates the human capital theory that the better educated a person is, the more human capital he/she has, and the stronger his/her ability to deal with temporary imbalances in the labor market.

References

Becker, G. (1994). *Human Capital: A Theoretical and Empirical Analysis, with Special Reference to Education*, 3rd edn. University of Chicago Press.
Jovanovic, B. (1979). Firm-Specific Capital and Turnover. *Journal of Political Economy, 87*(6), 1246–1260.
Lucas, R., & Prescott, E. (1974). Equilibrium Search and Unemployment. *Journal of Economic Theory, 7*(2), 188–209.
McNabb, R. (1987). Labor Market Theories and Education. *Economics of Education: Research and Studies*, 157–163.
Mincer, J. (1986). Wage Changes in Job Changes. *Research in Labor Economics, 8A*, 171–197.
Munasinghe, L. & Sigman, K. (2004). A Hobo Syndrome? Mobility, Wages, and Job Turnover. *Labour Economics, 11*(2), 191–218.
Nelson, P. (1970). Information and Consumer Behavior. *Journal of Political Economy, 78*(2), 311–329.
Rosenfeld, R. (1992). Job Mobility and Career Processes. *Annual Review of Sociology, 18*, 39–61.
Wang, F., Li, L., et al. (2001). *Labor Mobility in Urban China*. Beijing Publishing House.

Part IV
Education and Return on Human Capital

Part IV consists of four chapters that provide empirical research on the personal and social benefits of education and training. Chapter 12, "Return on Education for Urban Residents," uses quantitative analysis to estimate the return on education at all levels in China and analyzes dynamic trends. Chapter 13, "The Role of Education in Promoting Labor Productivity", finds that in China's labor market, the positive correlation between education and income reflects not only the signaling role of education, but also the effect of education on improving labor productivity in economic units. Chapter 14, "The Impact of Education on Income of Different Groups", uses Gini coefficient statistical indicators and quantile regression methods to empirically study the income differences, education differences and the relationship between income and education among different urban groups. Chapter 15, "Urban Residents' Education and Intergenerational Income Mobility", analyzes the characteristics of China's urban residents' income intergenerational mobility through indicators such as the income intergenerational inheritance and mobility index, and the income intergenerational elasticity coefficient, and then uses the general path analysis techniques and binary logistic regression models to explore the function of education in promoting intergenerational income mobility.

Chapter 12
Return on Education for Urban Residents

After decades of economic reform, income distribution in China has undergone profound changes, and the income gap among different population groups has widened. The once highly equalized income distribution pattern has gradually shifted to a diversified pattern of income distribution based on various factors such as labor input, capital investment, and labor value. The impact of education on personal income has thus received increasing attention, as employees with more education earn higher wages. This income advantage, at least a large part of it, is considered to be brought by education, and naturally becomes a major factor explaining mass demand for education.

Calculated based on the average income of workers with different education levels, return on educational investment and rates of return on education reflect the relative performance of employees with corresponding levels of education in the labor market. Return on education and return rates on education can be used to measure the externality of education, as well as to analyze dynamics of supply and demand of the corresponding labor market for each education level, which can provide reference to schools and government sectors in planning and decision-making. For individuals and households, return on educational investment and rates of return to different levels of education represent expected benefits (and costs) of the corresponding level, which are essential factors in making educational decisions. In the academic discussions at the beginning of the implementation of China's higher education cost-sharing policy, personal benefits of education were one of the rationales justifying charging tuition and fees. With the tuition and fees system of non-compulsory education having been implemented for years and having attracting the attention of the entire society, return on investment in education and rates of return on education should also be able to provide reference in evaluating and improving the tuition system.

Technically, calculating rates of return on education requires income and education data for employees groups with different educational levels. In some cases, data on individual costs or social costs for various levels of education is also required.

W. Min, *Educational Input, Resource Allocation and Returns to Human Capital*,
https://doi.org/10.1007/978-981-96-4687-6_12

The data extracted from the China's Urban Household Education and Employment Survey-2004 and the supplementary questionnaire survey contained relevant information, enabling us to calculate the return on education for urban residents in China.

12.1 Salary of Workers with Different Levels of Education

In the data extracted from the China's Urban Household Education and Employment Survey-2004, there were a total of 38,568 employee samples between the age of 16 and 70, with their employment status being employed or unemployed (including idle youth not seeking employment, unemployed people, and other unemployed people such as college graduates looking for a job). Table 12.1 shows the average annual salary for samples with different education levels.

As shown in Table 12.1, the average annual salary of China's urban labor force (including unemployed persons) was RMB12,482 in 2004. It is also clear that the average annual salary rises with the improvement of education level. Except for the few samples that have never attended schools or only attended literacy classes, all the rest samples with a higher education level earn more annual average salary than those with a lower education level. Among them, samples with only primary school education have the least average annual salary of only RMB6248, while those with postgraduate education have the highest salary, RMB36,893.

We further divide samples of each education level into subgroups by age to analyze how the average annual salary changes for different age groups with different education levels. Table 12.2 shows the data.

The statistical results in Table 12.2 show two significant trends. (1) Among workers of each age group, those with higher education levels have higher salaries, showing a positive correlation between education level and annual salary for all age

Table 12.1 Average annual salary of different education levels

Level of education	Average annual salary (RMB)	Number of samples
Illiteracy	8609.434	49
Literacy classes	10,472.64	40
Primary school	6248.077	1044
Middle school	8137.304	9962
High school	10,547.75	10,576
Secondary vocational school	12,608.42	5186
Junior college	16,529.02	8321
Undergraduate	22,326.66	3198
Postgraduate	36,893.28	192
Total	12,481.59	38,568

Table 12.2 Average annual salary of workers with different education levels by age (Unit: RMB)

Age	Primary school	Middle school	High school	Secondary vocational school	Junior college	Undergraduate	Postgraduate
15–19		1694.1	1830.2	2035.0			
20–24	1321.3	2527.8	5539.4	7017.8	9464.8	13,324.4	
25–29	2308.5	4902.8	8181.6	8859.0	11,650.8	18,760.2	23,424.8
30–34	4150.3	5830.2	9251.1	11,147.0	15,014.2	20,932.3	36,520.4
35–39	5155.5	6713.4	10,021.2	12,494.2	16,683.5	23,067.3	36,167.0
40–44	5264.7	7909.2	10,843.6	13,899.0	17,687.4	23,365.3	37,149.3
45–49	5784.3	8909.5	11,511.5	15,498.1	19,739.2	24,699.2	44,943.1
50–54	7687.4	10,531.3	12,418.8	15,921.6	19,366.5	26,591.6	48,843.6
55–59	7131.9	10,839.5	14,614.5	16,529.5	20,023.6	27,029.2	29,207.8
60–64	6168.2	8016.9	11,519.2	15,436.9	20,009.2	26,813.7	
65–69	5751.9	6178.3	9564.5	8896.4	15,225.7	16,943.4	
Total	6248.1	8137.3	10,547.8	12,608.4	16,529.0	22,326.7	36,893.3

groups. (2) All education level groups show the same pattern, that is, salary increases first and then decreases with age. Except for those with graduate degrees, the average annual salary of all other groups increases monotonously with age before the age of 59, and declines after the age of 60. The age-income curves in Fig. 12.1 show this trend.

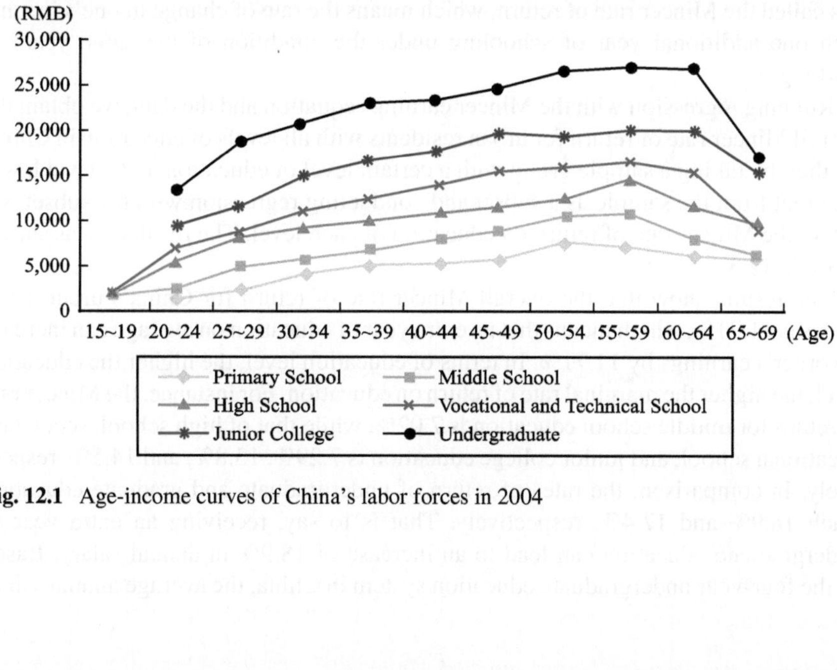

Fig. 12.1 Age-income curves of China's labor forces in 2004

12.2 Mincer Rate of Return on Different Levels of Education in China

In educational economics, there are two most commonly used indicators to reflect the level of educational returns: the internal rate of return, and the Mincer rates of return. The Mincer rate of return refers to the marginal rate of return to education calculated by using the Mincer earnings equation, providing estimates of the rate of change in income for one additional year of education. Calculation of the internal rate of return requires data on both the cost of education and the income of graduates after employment, while the estimation of the Mincer rates of return only requires data on the income of graduates. Here the Mincer rate of return is calculated.

The Mincer earnings equation is as follows:

$$\text{Ln}Y = \alpha + \beta * S + \gamma_1 * X + \gamma_2 * X^2 \tag{12.1}$$

Y is the employee's earnings, S is years of schooling, and X is years of working. According to labor employment theories and empirical evidence of labor markets of various countries, years of working have a quadratic impact on income. After an employee's earnings reach its peak at some point, it starts to decline as his/he years of working further increase. The coefficient β of the variable S can be defined by the following formula.

$$\beta = \frac{\partial \ln Y}{\partial S} = \frac{\partial Y/\partial S}{Y} \approx \frac{\Delta Y/Y}{\Delta S} \tag{12.2}$$

β is called the Mincer rate of return, which means the rate of change in one's income with one additional year of schooling under the condition of the same years of working.

Running regression with the Mincer earnings equation and the data, we obtain the overall Mincer rate of return for urban residents with all levels of education in China. Further, by taking a sample group with a certain level of education and a level lower than that from the sample as a subset and conducting regression with the subset, we obtain the Mincer rate of return on education of each level. The results are as shown in Table 12.3.

The results show that the overall Mincer rate of return for China's urban labor forces is 11.71%, which means that an extra year of education on average can increase a worker's earnings by 11.71%. In terms of education level, the higher the education level, the higher the marginal rate of return on education. For instance, the Mincer rate of return for middle school education is 7.02%, while that of high school, secondary vocational school, and junior college education is 7.29%, 13.8%, and 14.5%, respectively. In comparison, the rates of return of undergraduate and graduate education reach 18.9% and 17.4%, respectively. That is to say, receiving an extra year of undergraduate education can lead to an increase of 18.9% in annual salary. Based on the four-year undergraduate education system in China, the average annual salary

Table 12.3 Estimation results based on the Mincer earnings equation (urban data in 2004)

Item	Overall	Middle school	High school	Secondary vocational school	Junior college	Undergraduate	Postgraduate
Constant	7.5371	7.8273	7.8897	7.2280	7.1087	6.6352	6.9114
Years of working	0.0226	0.0318	0.0240	0.0369	0.0219	0.0195	0.0211
Square of years of working	−0.0002	−0.0003	−0.0002	−0.0005	−0.0002	−0.0001	−0.0003
Years of schooling	0.1171	0.0702	0.0729	0.1380	0.1451	0.1892	0.1740
R^2	0.153	0.050	0.051	0.092	0.105	0.166	0.062

Note The estimated coefficients of all variables are significant at the 0.01 level

Table 12.4 Overall Mincer rate of return for Chinese workers in multiple years

Item	1991	1995	2000	2004
Constant	6.785	7.649	7.469	7.5371
Years of schooling	0.02953	0.04655	0.08472	0.1171
Years of working	0.05648	0.03371	0.03114	0.0226
Square of years of working	−0.0008275	−0.0003594	−0.000213	−0.0002
R^2	0.273	0.150	0.154	0.153

Note The estimated coefficients of all variables are significant at the 0.01 level

of workers completing undergraduate education is 75.4% higher than that of high school graduates of the same age.

12.3 Changes Over Time in Mincer Rate of Return on Different Levels of Education

Rates of return on education for each year in China can be calculated based on the urban household survey data provided by the National Bureau of Statistics. Here we calculate the Mincer rate of return in Year 1991, 1995, 2000[1] and 2004 by using the household survey data of each corresponding year. The sampling range and sample size of each year are: the Year 2004 data includes 38,568 worker samples from 12 provinces, the 2000 data includes 25,323 samples from 30 provinces, the 1995 data includes 25,802 samples from 29 provinces, the 1991 data includes 26,158 samples from 30 provinces. The calculated results are shown in Table 12.4.

[1] Chen et al. (2003a).

Table 12.5 Mincer rates of return on education of all levels (Unit: %)

Year	Postgraduate	Undergraduate	Junior college	High school	Middle school
1991		3.78		2.72	1.60
1995	7.23		5.33	3.87	3.62
2000	13.1		9.97	6.53	4.86
2004	17.4	18.9	14.5	7.29	7.01

Note (1) In the Year 1991 survey, no distinction was made between undergraduate and junior college level; (2) Graduate level was not distinguished in the survey data in Year 2000 and before

The results show that China's Mincer rate of return in 1991 was 2.95%, 4.66% in 1995, 8.47% in 2000, and reached 11.71% in 2004. Throughout the 1990s, the rate of return rose year by year, from 2.95% in 1991 to 8.47% in 2000. The rates of return were still slightly lower than the international average but getting closer. According to the summary of Psacharopoulos and Patrinos, the international average rate of return to education in Year 2000 was 9.9% in non-OECD countries in Asia, 7.1% in Europe, the Middle East as well as non-OECD countries in North Africa, 12% in Latin America and the Caribbean, and 11.7% in sub-Saharan Africa, 7.5% in the OECD countries, and the global average was 9.7%.[2] At the beginning of the twenty-first century, the rate of return on education in China continued to rise, reaching 11.7% in 2004, slightly higher than the average of 9.9% in non-OECD countries in Asia and the global average of 9.7% the same year.

Similarly, by taking the labor group with a certain level of education and a level lower than that from a year's sample as a subset and conducting the Mincer earnings regression, we obtain the Mincer rate of return on education of each level in each year. The results are shown in Table 12.5.

As shown in Table 12.5, the major characteristics and changes over time in Mincer rates of return on education at different levels since the 1990s are as follows:

First, the rate of return on education at all levels has increased significantly over time, among which the rate of return on undergraduate education has increased from less than 4% in 1991 to 18.9% in 2004, that on middle school education from less than 2% to 7% in 2004.

Second, the higher the education level, the higher the rate of return on education. Cross-year survey data consistently show that workers with higher education levels not only have an absolute higher level of income, but also the higher the level of education, the greater the increase in their income brought by receiving an additional year of education.

Third, the estimated results in 2004 show that the rate of return on higher education in China reached 18.9%, which indicates that the current Chinese workers that have completed higher education enjoy considerably higher income. This result helps to explain the continued strong demand for higher education in China.

[2] Psacharopoulos and Patrinos (2002).

12.4 Characteristics of Changes in Mincer Rate of Return on Education

In China, the relationship between education and income is characterized by several stages. In the early stage of reform and opening up, the misplacement in income distribution with "the income of intellectual professional less than of that of manual workers" was one of the hot issues concerned by the entire society. Investigation and survey on labor remuneration found the unreasonable relationship between education and income, the more education a worker received, the less income he/she had.[3] In the early 1990s, with reforming of the economic system that aimed at the socialist market economy, the investment value of education started to emerge in China, and people with higher levels of education began to acquire higher income. Rates of return on education were positive according to surveys in that period, but well below the international average.[4] In the late 1990s, rates of return on education in China increased faster. As of 2000, the Mincer rate of return on education was only slightly lower than the international average.[5] Since 1998, China's higher education started to expand so rapidly due to enrollment expansion that people began to doubt whether the rate of return on education would decrease with so many more college graduates entering the labor market in years.[6] Nevertheless, studies have shown that rates of return on education continued to increase in China after entering the twenty-first century. Based on the data of 2004, China's Mincer rate of return on education slightly exceeded the international and regional average, reaching 11.7%. However, the Mincer rate of return to China's higher education further reached 18.9%, a relatively high level whether compared with historical data or international data.

The analysis also finds that the continuous increase in rates of return on education in China is because young workers with higher levels of education were remunerated with much higher income than their peers with lower levels when newly entering the labor market. A data analysis of the mid-1990s found that the return on education for newly employed young workers that completed higher education was higher than that of middle-aged workers employed before the reform and opening up.[7] Using data from Year 2004, we can further analyze this trend.

By taking the salary of workers with high school education as 1, we extend the Mincer earnings equation to include the interaction in terms of years of working and years of schooling.

$$\text{Ln}Y = \alpha + \beta * S + \gamma_1 * X + \gamma_2 * X^2 + \gamma_3 SX \tag{12.3}$$

---

[3] Li (1995, p. 7).

[4] Chen and Min (1998).

[5] Chen et al. (2003a)

[6] Chen et al. (2003b)

[7] Chen and Min (1999).

where the coefficient γ_3 of the interaction term between years of schooling and years of working indicates the direction in which the educational gap of income changes with years of working. γ_3 being positive indicates that the educational gap of income expands with the increase of years of working, and the age-income curves for various education levels diverge; γ_3 being negative indicates that the educational gap of income decreases with the increase in years of working, and the age-income curves for various education levels converge. This method is commonly used in education economics research to test human capital theories or screening hypotheses.[8]

The results show that the younger the age, the greater the income gap between different education levels. The most recent college graduates entering the labor market have the greatest income advantage. To explain in detail, this regression analysis found that the coefficient of the interaction term in the expanded Mincer earnings equation was significantly negative (−0.001,52, with a significance level 0.000,0), indicating that the fewer the years of working, the higher the rate of return on education. Not aimed for the dispute between human capital theories and the screening theory, the results here imply the reasons for the continuous increase in rates of return on education in China. That is, graduates who have newly entered the labor market enjoy much higher income, and the income advantage of the better-educated workforce expands over time, causing the overall average rate of return on education to increase. This result further implies that the Mincer rate of return on education in China will continue to rise if the current income distribution system does not undergo major adjustments.

12.5 Education Costs and Internal Rate of Return on Different Levels of Education

The Mincer rate of return reflects the marginal benefit of education and is widely used because its calculation only requires graduates' income data. Strictly speaking, the Mincer rate of return only implicitly represents the cost of education in terms of years of schooling. It cannot reflect the impact of changes in the direct cost and opportunity cost of education on the educated. A commonly used indicator that can reflect the cost–benefit efficiency of education is the internal rate of return, i.e. the discount rate that makes costs and net benefits of education equal. The equation for calculating the internal rate of return is as follows:

$$\sum_{t=1}^{n} \frac{B_t}{(1+r)^t} = \sum_{t=1}^{m} C_t \times (1+r)^{m-t} \tag{12.4}$$

[8] Li (2005).

where, B_t is the educational benefits in the tth year; C_t is the education costs in the tth year; m is the total schooling years for that level of education; n is the number of years in which the educatees have income after graduation; r is the internal rate of return of that level of education.

Based on the education cost data of the China's Urban Household Education and Employment Survey 2004, the average annual expenditures per student at all levels of schools are as shown in Table 12.6:

Using the education costs calculated above and the earnings simulated by the quadratic equation of job tenure as the benefits of education, as well as the average annual salary of graduates with one higher level of education and the same years of working as the opportunity cost of education, we calculate the internal rate of return on all levels of education in year 2004, under Alpha coefficient (the income differences attributable to level of education) being 1, 0.8 and 0.6, respectively (see Table 12.7).

Table 12.7 shows that the internal rate of return in China (when the Alpha coefficient is 1) is respectively 12.7% for middle school, 9.2% for high school, 8.2% for junior college, and 10.7% for undergraduate education. It has increased since the mid-1990s, but still much lower than the global average. The global average of the internal rate of return on primary, secondary and higher education is 26.6%, 17.0%,

Table 12.6 Average annual expenditures per student at all levels of education (Unit: RMB)

Item	Primary school	Middle school	High school	Junior college	Undergraduate
Total expenditures	**2286.2**	**3914.3**	**6101.1**	**10,568.9**	**13,898.4**
Tuition and miscellaneous fees	480.7	881.0	1763.0	5116.9	6101.8
Accommodation	20.1	77.0	163.4	807.6	1258.6
Study materials	269.8	420.9	624.2	700.5	885.9
Food	235.8	407.7	934.9	2844.8	4120.9
School uniforms	67.9	91.0	96.5	81.3	82.5
Transportation	57.9	117.7	203.5	315.8	433.9
Extra fees to attend a better school	250.2	847.0	1323.1	193.8	196.7
Extracurricular classes	676.4	566.5	466.3	152.7	269.4
Private tutoring	86.0	275.7	301.5	8.8	50.9
Other fees	141.5	229.7	224.8	346.7	497.8
Education costs	**1382.3**	**2842.4**	**5108.6**	**7351.1**	**10,370.7**

Note Education costs include tuition and miscellaneous fees, accommodation, study materials, food, school uniforms, transportation, extra fees to attend a better school, etc. For college and university students, RMB2709.6, the national average food expenditure per person in urban areas in 2004 is to be subtracted from the corresponding number in the Table 12.6

Table 12.7 Internal rate of return on various education levels (1996 vs 2004)

Year	Alpha coefficient	Middle school (%)	High school (%)	Junior college (%)	Undergraduate (%)
1996	1	N/A	5.47	6.86	6.78
	0.8	N/A	N/A	5.49	5.49
	0.6	N/A	N/A	3.93	4.00
2004	1	12.7	9.2	8.2	10.7
	0.8	10.8	7.2	6.8	9.0
	0.6	8.6	5.2	5.1	7.0

and 19.0%, respectively.[9] The internal rate of return on education in China is still relatively low, which should be attributed to China's higher level of private education costs.

In summary, using data extracted from the China's Urban Household Education and Employment Survey-2004, we calculated that the overall Mincer rate of return to education was 11.7% in 2004, among which the Mincer rates of return to middle school, high school, junior college, undergraduate and graduate education were 7.01%, 7.29%, 14.5%, 18.9%, and 17.4%, respectively. Historical comparison found that the Mincer rates of return on education in China have been continuously improving since the 1990s, and this trend continued until the beginning of the twenty-first century. As of 2004, the marginal benefits of education in China have reached or even exceeded the international average level, and China's education has entered a stage of high return on investment. The higher income of young employees with advanced degrees implies that the rate of return on education is likely to continue to increase in the future. Nevertheless, the private costs of education in China are also higher compared with the international average, leading to lower internal rates of return on all levels of education and a limited rise in the overall internal rate of return in the past ten years. With more attention from the government and society, the rapid increase in private education costs in China is expected to be curbed. In addition to the increase in private benefits of education, it is reasonable to expect that the private internal rate of return on education at all levels will continue to increase in the future.

References

Chen, X., & Min, W. (1998). Rate of Returns to Individuals in China's Higher Education. *Journal of Higher Education, 6*.

Chen, X., & Min, W. (1999). Expected Returns to China's Higher Education and Labor Marketization. *Educational Research, 1*.

[9] Psacharopoulos and Patrinos (2002).

Chen, X., Chen, L., & Xia, C. (2003a). Rates of Return to Schooling in Urban China: Changes in the 1990s. *Peking University Education Review*, *2*, 65–72.

Chen, X., Ran, C., & Chen, L. (2003b). Rates of Return to Private Schooling in Urban China: Changes in Recent Years. *Raising Adequate Resources for Education*. People's Education Press.

Li, F. (2005). *The Screening Function of Education: The Perspective of China's Labor Market*. Ph.D. Dissertation, School of Education, Peking University.

Li, Y. (1995). Introduction. In *Social and Economic Benefits of Education*. Guizhou People's Publishing House.

Psacharopoulos, G., & Patrinos, H. (2002). *Returns to Investment in Education: A Further Update*. World Bank Policy Research Working Paper, No. 2881, World Bank.

Chapter 13
The Role of Education in Promoting Productivity

Empirical studies conducted in different parts of the world mostly support the conclusion that there is a statistically positive relationship between the level of education and income. However, they differ significantly in how such a relation is explained. In the 1960s and 1970s, the human capital theory and the screening hypothesis, which had attracted the attention of scholars and politicians worldwide, provided explanations that seemed to conflict with each other. The human capital theory believes that a person can obtain more knowledge and skills through education, which will then help increase his or her productivity at work. Higher productivity in turn will bring him/her higher income. In other words, employers offer higher salaries to employees with higher productivity, and higher productivity comes from more education. Human capital theory regards education as an investment to improve personal skills and focuses on the productive role of education. The screening hypothesis, on the other hand, doubts the productive role of education in promoting productivity. It believes that a person's productivity or ability may be more of an innate talent, not the result of education, or that education does not significantly increase individual productivity. In other words, employers pay higher salaries to employees with higher education because employers believe that education is an effective signal of a person's productivity. Unlike the human capital theory, the screening hypothesis focuses on the informational role of education and believes that education is a screening tool that can distinguish between high and low productivity.

A large number of empirical studies have been carried out on the effectiveness of the relationship between education and income explained by these two theories from different angles and using data from different countries and regions. These studies attempted to identify and measure the productive and informative components of education. One of the widely used methods is to examine the basic Mincer earnings function and its various extended forms, which were then used to compare the contribution of education to income in competitive and non-competitive sectors, to find out if schooling has an effect on productivity, or if it is reflected in the reward of

W. Min, *Educational Input, Resource Allocation and Returns to Human Capital*,
https://doi.org/10.1007/978-981-96-4687-6_13

personal abilities as demonstrated by one's schooling or diplomas (Psacharopoulos 1979).

Psacharopoulos (1979) believed that the productive role of education is positively correlated with the degree of competitiveness, while the informative role of education has a negative correlation with the degree of competitiveness.[1] That is, in highly competitive sectors, income and productivity are more closely linked in a sense that education has a more prominent role in promoting productivity, and education has a weaker signaling role. On the contrary, in less competitive sectors, the link between income and productivity is weak. The wage system is more of an administrative decision based on seniority, in which the role of education in productivity is not reflected, and education is more like a signaling tool.

Different conclusions were drawn in empirical studies in different countries that compared the effects of education and work experience on income in competitive and non-competitive sectors. Some studies supported the human capital theory, i.e. the relationship between education and income reflects the role of education in productivity (Psacharopoulos 1979; Lee 1980; Cohn et al. 1987; Arabsheibani and Rees 1998; Clark 2000). Some studies have, however, obtained mixed results of the two, with evidence supporting the human capital theory and others backing the screening hypothesis (Lambropoulos 1992; Ziderman 1992; Brown and Sessions 1999; Lee and Miller 2004).

Mincer (1973) believed that individuals with different educational levels may have varying abilities, but that does not affect their earnings on a continuous basis. Psacharopoulos (1979) assumed that income differences caused by differences in ability are all covered by the constant term of the Mincer earnings function. Therefore, if the rate of return of education in the competitive sector is higher than that in the non-competitive sector, it means that education has an "intrinsic productive value." Based on the characteristics of the British labor market, Psacharopoulos assumed in his study that public administration is a "non-competitive" sector, and distributive trade is a competitive sector, because the former functions under a more hierarchical and bureaucratic structure. His research found that the rate of return to education in distributive trade is higher than that of public administration and believed that the results of his study support the assertion that education has an effect on productivity.

Lee (1980) extended the standard Mincer earnings function in his study by adding factors such as years of schooling and work experience. These product terms were added in order to find out whether education has a further effect on income after a person enters the labor market. The study found that the coefficient of the product term is positive in both public and private sectors, with a significance level of 5%. And the coefficient of the product term is higher and more significant in the private sector than in the public sector. Based on the above empirical results, Lee (1980) concluded that education has a universal productive function in both the competitive sector and the non-competitive sector, and the productive function of education is more obvious in the competitive sector.

[1] Some scholars disagree with this assertion, such as Ziderman (1992). It will be discussed further in this chapter.

Ziderman (1992) conducted relevant tests with two different sets of data from Israel and found in one test that educational returns were higher in government sector than in business, while the other test result was just the opposite. Based on the mixed results, Ziderman believes that the productive value of education may be more common in some regions or countries, while in other regions, education is more of a manifestation of informative value.

In discussions on the productive function vs the informative function of education, Mincer once summarized, "*In a world with incomplete information, as long as the ability is an input element in the education process, the production and screening effects of education in promoting productivity are not mutually exclusive. Controversies may focus on which of the production promotion and screening effects of education is more important for income.*" (Mincer 1980, p. 125) Some scholars have further pointed out that the composition of the productive and informative components of education is determined more by the local culture, social and economic systems of different countries (Brown and Sessions 1999).

Empirical studies on the relationship between education level and income of Chinese workers since the 1990s showed that there is a close link between education level and lifelong income, and investment in education will lead to a higher private rate of return (Chen et al. 2003). Is such a higher private rate of return on education in China a reflection of education's productive or screening function or a combination of the two? For hundreds of years China had an education system that played the role of screening, that was to select government officials through examinations, such as the imperial examinations in ancient times. Modern China has a strategy that puts more emphasis on human resource development, based on the productive function of education. Meanwhile, China's economy has been undergoing a huge transformation since the beginning of the reform and opening up. The proportion of the public sector in economy has been declining, and the private sector has gradually become the main driving force for China's economic development. Even within the public sector, economic transformation is in full swing, with the restructuring of state-owned enterprises, the reduction and downsizing of government departments and so on. All this shows that the current labor market of China is increasingly competitive both in private or public sector of the economy.

Hence the question is: what is the nature of the relationship between education and income in China, a country that has a long history of education and culture and where the social and economic systems are undergoing rapid transformation? Does the individual return of education come from the society's recognition of the role of education in screening talent, or does it represent the contribution that education makes to increasing labor productivity? To what extent do the productive and screening functions of education each play their roles? As the market economy continues to improve, and competition in the labor market becomes more intense, will there be changes in the productive and informative functions of education? What are the trends for these changes? These are the questions this chapter intends to answer. We hope to evaluate the productivity promotion and screening effect of education in China's labor market by comparing the educational return rates in different sectors and regions. At the same time, through a comparison of the educational returns of workers entering the labor market at different times, the trend of changes in the informative and productive function of education is verified, which will, to some extent, reflect the marketization process of China's labor market.

13.1 Hypotheses

During the planned economy era, China implemented a human resource and wage system that was designed as part of the planned economy, and as a result, the effect of education on labor productivity could not be fully reflected in salary. Education background was more of a basis for determining the salary level, so education mostly functioned as a signal device. With the reform of the salary system and greater autonomy that each organization now enjoys in staffing and pay scale setting, education has become more important in promoting productivity, in addition to its traditional role as a value signal of education, i.e. the productive function of education should be more and more fully reflected in income. This chapter attempts to prove that under China's specific labor and salary system, education not only has a signal effect in determining the level of income but also has the effect of increasing labor productivity. This productive function of education becomes more evident with the deepening of economic restructuring.

By referring to the discussion of Psacharopoulos (1979) on competitive and non-competitive sectors, and comparing the characteristics of China's labor market, we make the following observations on the degree of competitiveness in China in different economic units, regions, and time periods:

- Competitiveness of an economic unit gradually increases with the reduction of its state-owned components. To be specific, from state-owned enterprises, collective enterprises, to other ownership enterprises, labor competitiveness is getting higher and higher[2];
- Competitiveness increases with the level of regional economic development. Specifically, western regions are less competitive than other regions such as the more developed coastal areas;
- Competitiveness increases with the deepening of market economic reforms. Specifically, China's labor market has been more competitive since the 1990s than before the 1990s.

The research hypothesis is that the effect of education on productivity will be more fully reflected in income as the degree of labor market competitiveness increases. That is, the rate of return to education in a competitive labor market should be higher

[2] The composition of China's state-owned economy and collective economy is very complex, and many state-owned enterprises and collective enterprises are no less competitive than private enterprises and foreign-funded enterprises. However, due to the limitations of existing theories and current data, this study cannot provide a more accurate method to distinguish "competitive" and "noncompetitive" sectors. But according to the general social experience, in general, the competitiveness of the labor market will increase with the decrease of the state-owned component.

Table 13.1 Positive correlation between competitiveness in labor market and the rate of return to education

Item	Type of business ownership			Regional economic development		Work start year (before or after 1990)	
	State-owned	Collective ownership	Other ownerships	Western	Non-western	Before	After
Competitiveness	Weak	Second weak	Strong	Weak	Strong	Weak	Strong
Education rate of return	Low	Second lowest	High	Low	High	Low	High

than that in a weakly competitive labor market, and the difference can be attributed to employers' recognition of the role of education in promoting productivity. Based on the above discussion and observations on the competitiveness of China's different types of economic units, different regions, and different time periods, the following empirically testable hypotheses can be further deduced as shown in Table 13.1.

1. As the labor competitiveness of state-owned, collective, and non-state-owned economic types increases successively, their educational returns should also increase successively.[3]
2. Since the competitiveness of the non-western labor market is stronger than that of the western labor market, the educational return rate of the former is higher than that of the latter.
3. The labor market since the 1990s has become more competitive than the one before the 1990s, and China's labor and personnel management system basically follows the principle of "old measures applied to older generations and new measures for younger ones". Therefore, the educational return rate of the workers who joined the workforce after 1990 is higher than that of those who started working before 1990.

13.2 Empirical Results

The data set used in this chapter comes from a nationwide survey of urban households (excluding Tibet and Taiwan region) conducted by the Urban Research Team of China's National Bureau of Statistics in 2000. The data set includes 25,312 samples, of which 54% are males and 46% are females. The data set contains indicator variables

[3] The composition of China's state-owned economy and collective economy is very complex, and many state-owned enterprises and collective enterprises are no less competitive than private enterprises and foreign-funded enterprises. However, due to the limitations of existing theories and current data, this study cannot provide a more accurate method to distinguish "competitive" and "non-competitive" sectors. But according to the general social experience, in general, the competitiveness of the labor market will increase with the decrease of the state-owned component.

such as workers' annual income, education level, and years of work, as well as information about workers' employment status and home province or city.

By using Mincer's earnings equation, the regression results of different ownership types, different regions, and different time periods are shown in Table 13.2.

Table 13.2 indicates the following points:

- The educational returns of the state-owned enterprise group (column I), collectively-owned enterprise group (column II), and other ownership group (column III) are 7.79%, 7.94%, and 10.7%, increasing gradually. The results verify the first sub-hypothesis. Among them, the difference in the educational rate of return between the state-owned economy and the collectively-owned economy is not apparent and this difference is not significant even when dummy variables are added. In contrast, the educational rate of return of other ownership types is significantly higher than that of the state-owned and collectively-owned sectors, and the difference between them is significant with the dummy variables added. This shows that personal income in other ownership types is more closely linked to individual productivity, and the productive function of education to improve individual earning ability is better demonstrated than in the state-owned or collectively-owned enterprises.

Table 13.2 Regression results from using Mincer's earnings equation

Item	State-owned (I)	Collective ownership (II)	Other ownership (III)	The western region (IV)	The non-western regions (V)	Years of working before 1990 (VI)	Years of working in/after 1990 (VII)
Constant term	7.478 (262.34)[a]	7.336 (77.72)[a]	7.536 (66.22)[a]	7.292 (193.27)[a]	7.532 (232.52)[a]	7.522 (169.63)[a]	7.188 (117.63)[a]
Years of schooling	0.0779 (42.96)[a]	0.0794 (11.86)[a]	0.107 (13.10)[a]	0.0821 (31.53)[a]	0.0865 (40.59)[a]	0.0827 (46.42)[a]	0.0923 (21.39)[a]
Years of working	0.0396 (23.90)[a]	0.014 (2.15)[b]	0.034 (4.98)[a]	0.0420 (19.80)[a]	0.0260 (12.50)[a]	0.0263 (8.45)[a]	0.104 (7.15)[a]
Square of years of working	−0.0004 (−9.70)[a]	0.0002 (1.22)	−0.0005 (−2.38)[b]	−0.0004 (−8.43)[a]	−0.0001 (−2.05)[b]	−0.0001 (−1.83)[c]	−0.0057 (−4.43)[a]
Adjusted R-squared	0.155	0.082	0.136	0.200	0.137	0.125	0.104
Number of samples	19,991	2674	1318	8065	16,978	19,435	5607

Note The western region refers to 11 provinces and autonomous regions in the west except Tibet. The value in parentheses is the T value, "a" means the significance level is 1%, "b" means the significance level is 5%, and "c" means the significance level is 10%

- The educational returns of the western region group (column IV) and the non-western region group (column V) are 8.21% and 8.65% respectively, and the increase in non-western regions is slightly higher than that of the western region. Adding the dummy variable of the region brings the significance level of this difference to 5%. This also enables the second hypothesis to be verified, that is, in non-western regions, due to the higher level of economic development and higher competition in the labor market, the productive function of education can be better reflected.
- Through a comparison of years of working, we found that the educational return rate of the group that started working before 1990 (column VI) is 8.27%, while that of the group that started working after 1990 (column VII) is 9.23%, the former significantly lower than the latter. Using the same method of dummy variable, we further found that the difference in educational return rate in different time periods is significant, at a level of 5%. Therefore, the third hypothesis has been verified, i.e. the productive function of education is increasingly reflected in income due to the higher degree of competition in the labor market of China after the 1990s as compared with before the 1990s. Along with future economic reforms, it is predicted that the degree of competition in China's labor market will continue to increase, and the productive function of education will be more reflected.

13.3 Methodology

Some scholars do not think that the productive and screening functions of education can be evaluated by comparing the educational rate of return in labor markets with different degrees of competitiveness. For example, Ziderman (1992) believed that Psacharopoulos (1979) and many subsequent studies have all failed to prove that the productive and informational functions of education can be defined simply by comparing educational returns. Like Psacharopoulos (1979), Ziderman (1992) discussed the comparison of the rates of return on education between the competitive private sector and the non-competitive public sector, and argued that the return on education in the public sector may be higher or lower than in the private sector depending on public policy decisions. Therefore, trying to compare the rate of return to education in the public and private sectors is meaningless for testing the productive and screening functions of education. This is because, for the public sector which may correspond to the "non-competitive" sector, the screening hypothesis may not be an appropriate tool since just like the human capital theory, whose analysis is based on the labor market with "perfect competition", "benefit maximization", and "wage equals marginal labor productivity" rather than the "non-competitive" sectors. Scholars also pointed out that relative rate of return on all levels of education depends on the overall wage structure, which in turn is mainly affected by the political bargaining power of workers. Therefore, the education rate of return of a non-competitive labor market may be more affected by political and social factors, which will cause a big deviation to the result of researches that study only education's impact on labor income.

However, this chapter still holds that even though human capital theory and screening hypothesis are based on "fully competitive labor market", their principles can still be applied a "non-competitive" labor market. This is because a non-competitive labor market can be compared to a screening employment environment, while a competitive employment environment can be compared to a non-screening employment environment.[4] The real labor productivity of producers in the former is less easy to observe, so the signal effect of education is stronger. On the contrary, the real labor productivity in the latter is easier to be directly observed, so the productive effect of education is stronger. In this way, if the return rate of education is higher in a non-screening labor market, that is, in a more competitive employment environment, it indicates that the productive function of education has been reflected. Therefore, it makes sense to test the productive function and informative function of education by comparing the difference in educational returns between a competitive and a non-competitive labor market.

13.4 Conclusions

The composition of China's labor market is complicated, and there are multi- dimensional differences in regions and ownership types, which lead to differences in the degree of competitiveness in labor markets in different regions and ownership types. The difference in competitiveness is directly reflected in the difference in salary, which leads to the differences in the rate of return of education. The research of this chapter, as it is designed, indicates that in China's labor market, the positive correlation between education and income not only reflects the signaling role of education, but also reflects the increasing importance attached to the function of education to improve labor productivity in economic units and its effect on personal income.

The research in this chapter examines and compares the educational return of state-owned, collectively-owned, and other types of economic units, and concludes that the educational return rate is positively correlated with the degree of competitiveness of different ownership. This also shows, in a different way, that the wage system of state-owned economic units is more based on seniority, and education is to a large extent used as a basis to determine the salary level. In other economic units, however, the role of education in promoting productivity has been better reflected.

An analysis of different regions found that the western region, with a less competitive labor market, has a slightly lower rate of return to education than the more competitive non-western region. This shows that the more developed a region is, the more value of education can be reflected in labor income. This partly explains why college graduates are less inclined to work in the western region even though they

[4] Refer to Riley's research (1979) for the definition of the screening and non-screening employment environment.

often find it more difficult to find jobs in other regions. Even if they get a job in the west, they may find that the skills they acquired in college have little use in the workplace, or at least the value of higher education cannot be reflected in salary.

It has been found, however, that there is an obvious trend for improved educational return, with continuous deepening of market economy, as evidenced in the comparison of the two groups that started working in different periods. This shows that with increased competition in the labor market, education not only produces the signal effect for salary, but also helps promote productivity and personal earning ability. That is to say, there is now a growing trend for education to play a much bigger role in improving productivity as China's economic reforms expand to wider areas.

Based on the above study, we can argue that research on China's education and human resources should not just focus on the education system itself. It is also important to look at the labor market that is closely related to education. A reasonable level of competition in the labor market helps to reflect the productive function of education. Only when such a function plays a more important role, households and government will be motivated to invest more in education. Therefore, research on education and human resources in China should focus not only on enhancing the internal efficiency of the education system but also on strengthening the development of the labor market to better reflect the external efficiency of education. Only in this way can China's human resource development effectively promote the growth of social wealth while genuinely increasing individual income.

References

Arabsheibani G., & Rees, H. (1998). On the Weak Versus the Strong Version of the Screening Hypothesis. *Economics of Education Review*, *17*(2), 189–192.

Brown, S., & Sessions, J. (1999). Education and Employment Status: A Test of the Strong Screening Hypothesis in Italy. *Economics of Education Review*, *18*(4), 397–404.

Chen, X., Chen, L., & Xia, C. (2003). Rates of Return to Schooling in Urban China: Changes in the 1990s. *Peking University Education Review*, 2, 65–72.

Clark, A. (2000). *Signaling and Screening in a Transition Economy: Three Empirical Models Applied to Russia.* CERT Discussion Papers 0003, Centre for Economic Reform and Transformation, Heriot Watt University.

Cohn, E. et al. (1987). Further Evidence on the Screening Hypothesis. *Economics Letters*, *25*(3), 289–294.

Lambropoulos, H. (1992). Further Evidence on the Weak and Strong Versions of Screening Hypothesis in Greece. *Economics of Education Review*, *11*(1), 61–65.

Lee, K. (1980). Screening, Ability, and the Productivity of Education in Malaysia. *Economics Letters*, *5*(2), 189–193.

Lee, Y., & Miller, P. (2004). Screening and Human Capital in the Australian Labour Market of the 1990s. *Australian Economic Papers*, *43*(2), 117–135.

Mincer, J. (1973). *Schooling, Experience and Earnings.* National Bureau of Economic Research.

Mincer, J. (1980). Human Capital and Earnings. In *Wealth, Income and Inequality* (2nd ed., pp. 103–128). Oxford University Press.

Psacharopoulos, G. (1979). On the Weak versus the Strong Version of the Screening Hypothesis. *Economics Letters*, *4*(2), 181–185.
Riley, J. (1979). Testing the Educational Screening Hypothesis. *Journal of Political Economy*, *87*(5), S227–S252.
Ziderman, A. (1992). Evidence on Screening: P-tests for Israel. *Economics of Education Review*, *11*(1), 67–69.

Chapter 14
The Impact of Education on the Income of Different Social Groups

At the beginning of twenty-first century, the income gap in China continues to widen. Data published in 2005 by the United Nations Development Program indicates that China's Gini index in 2002 had reached 0.45 (UNDP 2005). As shown by the experience of many countries and regions, a society would be rife with conflicts when the GDP per capita is growing from US$1000 to US$3000, which is the phase China is currently in. In the process of building a harmonious society and achieving common prosperity, income gap, a phenomenon attracting extensive attention worldwide, has become an issue China must tackle head on.

Studies have proposed numerous explanations for the existence of income gap: rapid growth of the private sector, differences between industries and types of ownership, urban–rural economic dichotomy and labor market segmentation, and patterns of distribution molded by a combination of factors such as disparities in geography and resource endowment, social hierarchy and market economy, etc. (Chen et al. 2004; Cai 2003; Guo 2002; Lin 2004; Li 2003). Li Shi and Zhao Renwei (1999) summarized the explanations above into three main factors: sweeping changes in social system, growth and structural changes in the economy, and policies developed by government agencies. Building upon previous research, Dong Xian'an (2004) further summarized these elements into human capital, physical capital, and geographic advantages (i.e. enabling policies developed by the central government for coastal regions).

Theories on human capital consider education as an investment. According to early human capital theories, education is the most essential means to accumulate human capital, and it is a great equalizer in income distribution (Schultz 1960; Mincer 1974; Becker 1975). Some later scholars studied the impact of education on different income levels by starting with the mechanisms of the labor market: They analyzed the profile of the labor force by education attainment, the dynamic of the supply and demand of the labor force, and the impact of the expansion or decline of education. In their opinions, education helps narrow the wealth gap, and the degree to which it is able to bridge the gap depends on how the demand curve of the labor force

W. Min, *Educational Input, Resource Allocation and Returns to Human Capital*,
https://doi.org/10.1007/978-981-96-4687-6_14

responds to the expansion of education. (Ahluwalia 1976; Knight and Sabot 1983). Particularly, opportunities for education and human capital have a substantial impact on income, and the empirical research by Li Shi, Chen Yuyu, Bai Xuemei et al. echo this statement—the difference in human capital is the main reason for income disparities (Bai 2004).

However, even when external conditions (such as education background, work experience, industry, occupation, geographic location etc.) are identical, income levels still vary due to individual differences. In this chapter, workers with identical external conditions are put into three groups based on their earning ability: "the group with low earning capacity", "the group with medium earning capacity", and "the group with high earning capacity". In order to study the efficiency of education(investment) while maintaining impartiality, this chapter will focus on the impact of education on the income of different social groups.

14.1 Data Description

The data used for statistical and regression analyses in this chapter comes from the Urban Household Survey, conducted by the Organization of Urban Social-Economic Surveys (or Urban Survey Team for short) under China's National Bureau of Statistics. This research includes data from four years: 1991, 1995, 2000, and 2004. The effective sample sizes are respectively 25,905, 25,802, 24,998, and 33,856 (individuals). The data in the first three years comes from 30 provinces, and the data from 2004 is from 12 provinces (Beijing, Liaoning, Zhejiang, Guangdong, Shanxi, Heilongjiang, Anhui, Hubei, Sichuan, Guizhou, Shaanxi, and Gansu).

In this chapter, except for when comparing the income disparities among different years, all the other data used in the analyses is from 2004 alone. The 2004 data includes eight levels of educational attainment: graduate school, undergraduate school, junior college, secondary vocational school, high school, middle school, primary school, and other. The average years of schooling are 18.5 years, 15.5 years, 14.5 years, 11.5 years, 11.5 years, 8.5 years, 5.5 years, and 0 year. The eight types of educational attainment respectively account for 0.6%, 9.2%, 23.5%, 14.1%, 27.0%, 23.3%, 2.2%, and 0.2% of the total number of samples.

The empirical research conducted in this chapter is mainly intended for analyzing the relations between earning and schooling. Therefore, when handling the raw data from 2004, the scope of observation is set to be both currently employed and unemployed individuals between the ages of 16 and 70 with an annual salary above zero.

Table 14.1 The trend in Gini Index of China's urban household income

Item	1991	1995	2000	2004
Gini Index	0.236	0.326	0.351	0.394

Source The numbers are calculated by the author using data from the Urban Household Survey by the Urban Social-Economic Survey Team of the National Bureau of Statistics

14.2 The Gini Index of China's Urban Household Income

14.2.1 The Gini Index of China's Urban Household Income

The Gini index, developed by Italian economist Gini in the early twentieth century based on the Lorenz curve, is a measure of inequality in income distribution. The more equally the income is distributed, the smaller the value of the Gini index is, and vice versa. At the United Nations, a Gini index lower than 0.2 corresponds with perfect income equality; 0.2–0.3 corresponds with relative equality; 0.3–0.4 corresponds with relatively reasonable income gap; 0.4–0.5 corresponds with high income disparity, and a value above 0.6 corresponds with severe income disparity.

In 2004, the Gini index of urban household income in China marked 0.394 (see Table 14.1), just inches away from the 0.4 "red line", which indicates that there is already a disparity in urban household income. The calculation of the Gini index is based on individuals' annual earnings. If non-monetary income and elusive deep pockets are included as well, it is highly likely that the real Gini index has already exceeded 0.4.

The data in Table 14.1 shows a growing gap in China's urban household income. In 1991, the Gini index of urban household income was merely 0.236, which was within the interval of "relative equality". In 1995, 2000, and 2004, the Gini index was still at a "relatively reasonable" level. However, if the Gini index continues to rise at the geometric growth rate between 1991 and 2004, it would reach 4.10 by 2005, entering the realm of "high income disparity".

14.2.2 The Gini Indices of Different Income Groups

To identify the root cause of income gaps and determine if the gap is wider in the group with lower or higher income, the data samples in this chapter are sorted into four groups according to income levels: the low income group, the medium–low income group, the medium–high income group, and the high income group. The Gini indices of all the four groups are then calculated. Since all the samples are already sorted by income, the absolute values of the Gini indices are not necessarily important. However, a comparison of the four Gini indices will reveal which group has the widest income gap and contributes the most to the total income disparity. Data from Table 14.2 suggests that among the four groups, the low-income group

Table 14.2 The income disparities of different groups (2004)

Item	Low income	Medium–Low income	Medium–High income	High income
Gini index	0.235	0.087	0.071	0.222
Education attainment (years)	10.5	11.4	12.2	12.9
Length of employment (years)	18.0	19.8	21.2	22.3

Source The numbers are calculated by the author based on the data from the Urban Household Survey by the Urban Social-Economic Survey Team of the National Bureau of Statistics

has the highest Gini Index, which is 1.06 times that of the high-income group, 2.70 times that of the medium–low income group, and 3.31 times that of the medium–high income group. Since the widening gap in urban household income can be attributed mainly to the income disparity of the low-income group, the most effective way to address income inequality is to increase the earnings of the low-income group.

After sorting all the samples from low to high by income, the first quartile stands at RMB6740, meaning that 25% of the individuals in the dataset have an income lower than that; The second quartile (the median) is at RMB11,521, meaning half of the individuals in the dataset have an income lower than RMB11,521; The third quartile is at RMB17,700, meaning 75% of the individuals have an income below the level of RMB17,700.

One's earnings are positively correlated to both the level of education and their work experience. Namely, individuals with higher income would have both longer years of schooling and longer average length of employment. The individuals with lower income only have 10.5 years of schooling on average, which is respectively 0.9 years, 1.7 years, and 2.4 years shorter than that of the individuals in the medium–low-income group, medium–high-income group, and high-income group. The average years of working for those in the low-income group is 18.0 years, and that is 1.8 years, 3.2 years, and 4.3 years shorter than that of the individuals in medium–low-income group, medium–high-income group, and high-income group. It is safe to say that human capital, which is largely embodied in educational attainment and work experience, plays an important role in the income distribution among China's urban households.

14.2.3 Gini Indices of Different Income Groups Sorted by Education Attainment

Differences in earnings have numerous contributing factors, and education is a crucial one. Table 14.3 displays the Gini indices of different income groups sorted by education attainment. In general, a better-educated group tends to have a narrower income gap. The group that only received primary education has a Gini index of 0.415,

Table 14.3 Income gaps within different groups sorted by education attainment (2004)

Item	Primary school	Middle school	High school	Secondary vocational school	Junior college	College	Graduate school
Gini index	0.415	0.388	0.384	0.372	0.346	0.341	0.291
Average annual income (RMB)	8744	10,269	12,204	13,745	17,290	22,995	37,880

Source The numbers are calculated by the author based on the data from the Urban Household Survey by the Urban Social-Economic Survey Team of the National Bureau of Statistics

showing a severe income disparity. Meanwhile, the groups that finished middle school, high school, secondary vocational school, junior college and undergraduate school all have Gini indices between 0.3 and 0.4, falling in the category of "relatively reasonable income gap". Moreover, the Gini index of the graduate education group was only 0.291, which belongs to the "relatively average" range. This shows that providing access to education for China's urban population and making sure every individual at least finishes middle school helps alleviate income inequality.

Meanwhile, the earnings gap among groups with different education backgrounds is also substantial, proving that education is essential for individuals to raise their income level. In 2004, those who have received primary education have an average annual income of merely RMB8744, which is respectively 85.1%, 71.6%, 63.6%, 50.6%, 38.0%, and 23.1% of the income of those who finished middle school, high school, secondary vocational school, junior college, undergraduate school, and graduate school.

14.3 Comparison of Rates of Return to Education of Different Groups

14.3.1 Regression Analysis

When illustrating the variation in earnings, Mincer (1974) drew on the theories of human capital and stated that in a fully competitive labor market, human capital, which is directly related to one's productivity, is a crucial factor in determining individual income. The productivity is higher when an individual is equipped with more human capital, and more productive workers should receive higher income. Two major forms of human capital are the knowledge obtained from schooling and the experience and capacity gained from employment, knowledge spillover, and on-the-job training. It is hard to quantify the amount of knowledge an individual possesses, but a common recognition is that it is related to how much education he/she receives, which makes education a suitable proxy variable in statistical analyses. Similarly, to quantify someone's capacity is tricky as well. Once an individual joins the workforce, their experience starts to accumulate. However, as they age, their energy declines, their abilities to absorb new knowledge dwindle, and their professional skills and knowledge become outdated with the introduction of more advanced technologies. Therefore, for workers who reach a certain age, their skills or productivity start to go downhill as they become older. In Mincer's earnings function which only includes two explanatory variables: years of schooling and length of employment, the regression is calculated in the following equation:

$$\ln W_i = \beta_0 + \beta_1 SCH_i + \beta_2 EXP_i + \beta_3 EXP_i^2 + u_i \tag{14.1}$$

where, W_i represents a worker's income. SCH_i represents one's years of schooling. EXP_i represents his/her work experience. EXP_i^2 is the length of employment squared (which reflects the non-linear relations between individual earnings and work experience). u_i is the random disturbance, and β_1 represents the return to education, which is the rate of monetary return for each additional year of schooling. The regression coefficient is expected to be positive.

A conventional method for solving the equation above is the ordinary least squares (OLS). The equation's result is an estimation of the conditional expectation of dependent variables when the independent variables are fixed. A hidden requisite of this regression analysis is that the independent variables have the same effect on the dependent variables on different parts of the distribution, which in this case means that the returns to education would be the same for groups with the same education backgrounds and the same lengths of employment. The assumption that the regression coefficient here is constant throughout the conditional distribution of earnings will hamstring the efforts of examining other important characteristics of the income distribution (Buchinsky 1994).

Comparatively, quantile regression is a more well-rounded way of conducting the same estimation. It intends to observe the different effects of the independent variables on different quantiles throughout a distribution. As for the earnings distribution, quantile regression observes the different returns to education on different income quantiles, and the quantile regression in the form of the Mincer equation is:

$$\ln W_i = \beta_{\theta 0} + \beta_{\theta 1} SCH_i + \beta_{\theta 2} EXP_i + \beta_{\theta 3} EXP_i^2 + u_{\theta i} \tag{14.2}$$

To simplify:

$$\ln W_i = X_i \beta_\theta + u_{\theta i} \tag{14.3}$$

where, X_i is the independent variable, β_θ is the parameter, $u_{\theta i}$ is the random disturbance, and $0 < \theta < 1$. The regression coefficient for the θ th quantile is defined as the solution of the following minima problem:

$$\min_{\beta \in R^k} \left\{ \sum_{i:\ln W_i \geq X_i\beta} \theta |\ln W_i - X_i\beta_\theta| + \sum_{i:\ln W_i < X_i\beta} (1-\theta)|\ln W_i - X_i\beta_\theta| \right\} \quad (14.4)$$

The coefficients in quantile regression and the ones in OLS regression can be interpreted similarly. In terms of the regression coefficient of years of schooling (SCH_i), its definition in OLS regression is the coefficient of partial regression of schooling years in an income function generated by a regression of the means of the conditional income distributions. Similarly, in quantile regression, it is the coefficient of partial regression of schooling years in an income function generated by doing a regression using the same quantile in conditional distributions.

From the perspective of economics, the coefficient of quantile regression for the schooling year variable is the returns to education of different income groups. For example, when $\theta = 10\%$, the regression coefficient means an estimation of the return to education for individuals whose income level is in the tenth percentile (ranked from low to high).[1]

14.3.2 The Results of Regression Analyses

Results from OLS (seen in the last column of Table 14.4) show a 12.3% return to education on an individual basis in 2004. According to the research by Ma Xiaoqiang and Ding Hao (2005), such return to education was 2.94% in 1991, 4.7% in 1995, and 8.46% in 2000, demonstrating a rising trend in return to education in urban areas.

The results of quantile regression (see Table 14.4) indicate that in terms of returns to education, the regression coefficient of different quantiles decreases as the quantiles move up. The regression coefficient is the largest at the 10% quantile, standing at 16.0%. Then comes the second to the fifth largest: the ones at 20% quantile, 30% quantile, and 40% quantile, which respectively stand at 13.7%, 12.7%, 11.8%, and 10.8%. The regression coefficients of the four quantiles below the median (the 50% quantile) are all larger than the four above the median, implying a better return to education for "the group with low earning capacity" than for "the group with high earning capacity". The results in this chapter are consistent with those of Ma Xiaoqiang and Ding Xiaohao (2005) who used the data from 1991, 1995, and 2000. However, they differ from the results of Buchinsky and Pereira's. These two scholars worked with data from other countries when analyzing the return to education using quantile regression, and the results demonstrated a higher rate of return for "the group with high earning capacity" (Buchinsky 1994). The quantile regression results generated from China's urban household data are consistent with the data description in earlier sections: Table 14.3 shows that on the one hand, there are significant

[1] In quantile regression, instead of sorting all samples by their values and putting them in different sub-groups, they are all given different weights. Therefore, when = 10%, all samples are included in the quantile regression, but only those under the 10% regression line are given a weight of 0.9. The rest only have a weight of 0.1.

Table 14.4 The regression analysis of return to education on an individual basis

Explanatory variable	Quantile regression									OLS
	10%	20%	30%	40%	50%	60%	70%	80%	90%	
SCH	0.160	0.137	0.127	0.118	0.108	0.101	0.096	0.097	0.105	0.123
EXP	0.072	0.055	0.045	0.039	0.035	0.030	0.025	0.025	0.024	0.031
EXP^2	−0.0013	−0.0009	−0.0007	−0.0006	−0.0005	−0.0003	−0.0002	−0.0002	−0.0002	−0.0003

Note (1) The dependent variable is the natural logarithm of annual income. (2) SCH, EXP and EXP^2 respectively stand for years of schooling, work experience, and work experience squared. (3) Among the 10 regression results, the statistical significance of all regression coefficients reached 1%. The goodness of fit of both quantile regression and OLS regression are within the range of 0.1 and 0.2. (4) The regression equation contains intercept component (constant terms). The estimations are omitted in this table

Source The numbers are calculated by the author based on the data from the Urban Household Survey by the Urban Social-Economic Survey Team of the National Bureau of Statistics

income disparities among those with different education backgrounds (i.e. the annual earnings of college graduates are 1.9 times that of the individuals who only finished high school). The completion of every additional educational level would result in a significant increase in income. On the other hand, the group with better education attainment has a smaller Gini index. Therefore, if the same year of additional schooling is added on top of the same level of education completion, "the group with low earning capacity" would have a bigger increase in their earnings, meaning that the return to education is higher for them.

14.4 Conclusions and Policy Implications

In this chapter, urban household data gathered by the Social Economic Surveys Team of the National Statistics Bureau in 2005 was used to conduct empirical research on income levels of different social groups, disparities in income (measured by the Gini index) and education attainment, and the relations between earning and schooling (by using quantile regression). The findings are as follows:

First, the income gap in China's urban population began to widen in the 1990s. In 2004, the Gini index of urban household income reached 0.394, just inches away from the widely recognized "red line" of 0.4.

Second, the widening gap can be attributed to the severe income inequality in the low-income group. Individuals with low earnings also tend to fall behind both in terms of education attainment and work experience compared to other groups.

Third, when sorting all samples in the dataset by education background, the better educated group has a lower Gini index, meaning that increasing efforts of raising people's education level will help alleviate income inequality.

Fourth, individual return to education for China's urban population has exceeded 10%. The regression coefficient of OLS marks 12.3%, and that of the median marks 10.8%.

Fifth, based on the results of the quantile regression, "the group with low earning capacity" will benefit significantly more than "the group with high earning capacity".

The conclusion drawn from this chapter has positive policy implications: human capital which is measured by education attainment and work experience is an essential explanatory variable for individual earnings, and it also has a great impact on the income disparity in China's urban population. Equality in education will bring about a more even income distribution, and unequal access to education could erode income equality. In particular, the return to education is the highest for "the group with low earning capacity", which makes investing in them a fruitful endeavor. Therefore, for the government which possesses public education resources, safeguarding the access of "the disadvantaged" to education and providing them with necessary resources are a win–win both in terms of social justice and investment efficacy.

References

Ahluwalia, M. (1976). Income Distribution and Development: Some Stylized Facts. *The American Economic Review, 66*(2), 128–135. Papers and Proceedings of the Eighty-Eighth Annual Meeting of the American Economic Association.

Bai, X. (2004). Education and Income Inequality: An Empirical Study on China. *Journal of Management World, 6*, 53–58.

Becker, G. (1975). *Human Capital: A Theoretical and Empirical Analysis, with Special Reference to Education* (2nd edn). National Bureau of Economics Research.

Buchinsky, M. (1994). Changes in the US Wage Structure, 1963–1987: Application of Quantile Regression. *Econometrica, 62*(2), 405–458.

Cai, F. (2003). Urban-Rural Income Gap and Critical Points of Institutional Change. *Social Sciences in China, 5*, 16–25.

Chen, Y., Wang, Z., & Wei, Z. (2004). Wage Inequality and Its Change Among China's Urban Residents in the 1990s. *Economic Science, 6.*

Dong, X. (2004). Understanding the Regional Income Disparity in China: 1952–2002. *Economic Research Journal, 9.*

Guo, X. (2002). Understanding the Kuznets Hypothesis from the Perspective of Development Economics, and the Reasons for Widening Income Gap in China. *Journal of Management World, 3*, 66–73.

Knight, J., & Sabot, R. (1983). Educational Expansion and the Kuznets Effect. *The American Economic Review, 73*(5), 1132–1136.

Li, S. (2003). A Review of Income Inequality in China. *China Economic Quarterly, 1.*

Li, S., & Zhao, R. (1999). A Re-study on Income Distribution in China. *Economic Research Journal, 4.*

Lin, G. (2004). Hierarchy, Market Economy and the Widening Urban-Rural Income Gap. *Journal of Management World, 4*, 30–40.

Ma, X., & Ding, X. (2005). An Empirical Study on the Risks of Urban Residents' Personal Educational Investment in China. *Educational Research, 4*, 25–31.

Mincer, J. (1974). *Schooling, Experience and Earnings.* National Bureau of Economic Research.

Schultz, T. (1960). Capital Formation by Education. *Journal of Political Economy, 68*(6), 571–583.

UNDP. (2005). *China Human Development Report 2005.* China Development Research Foundation.

Chapter 15
Urban Residents' Education and Intergenerational Income Mobility

The relationship between education and income equality is an important issue in education economics. Income equality can be divided into intragenerational income equality and intergenerational income equality. The former refers to a smaller gap between the rich and the poor within the same generation. The latter refers to the fact that the income of offspring is not affected by the predetermined factor of parents' income but rather by the acquired factors of the offspring themselves, such as their ability, education and health. Existing empirical studies on the relationship between education and income equality at home and abroad have paid more attention to the role of education in promoting intragenerational income equality. However, researchers have rarely explored the role of education in promoting intergenerational income equality.

Intergenerational income mobility is an important indicator of intergenerational income equality. In general, the smaller the intergenerational income mobility in a society, the greater the impact of parents' income on their offspring's earnings, and the greater the inequality of intergenerational income. On the contrary, the greater the intergenerational income mobility in a society, the less the impact of parents' income on that of their offspring, the greater the intergenerational income equality is, as the income of offspring is more affected by acquired factors such as education. Therefore, exploring the impact of parents' income and acquired factors such as children's education on children's income can help us better understand the relationship between education and intergenerational income equality.

Since early 2000s, with China's transition from a centrally planned economy to a market economy, the single public ownership is gradually being transformed into "the basic economic system in which public ownership is the mainstay and economic entities of diverse ownership develop together". The indiscriminate egalitarianism in distribution is increasingly being replaced by "distribution according to one's contribution". Accordingly, the original interest pattern among China's urban residents is undergoing profound changes, and income/wealth gaps among different social groups are enlarging (Xu 2004). Widening income gaps allow families with

W. Min, *Educational Input, Resource Allocation and Returns to Human Capital*,
https://doi.org/10.1007/978-981-96-4687-6_15

more economic capital to have access to various means, such as more and better job opportunities, direct financial support, etc., to ensure that their children continue to enjoy higher income and better economic status, and thus carry the intergenerational income inequality to the next generation. Under such circumstances, is education still an important way for disadvantaged groups to rise in social stratum? Does it still have the function of promoting intergenerational income mobility and improving intergenerational income equality? These issues are worthy of attention.

Under the centrally planned economy, China did not have a labor market in the modern sense. The number of working years was the main determinant of a worker's salary, whereas education and ability did not matter. In addition, under the planned economy, the mobility of workers was weaker, and the first assigned job usually became one's lifelong career. All of these greatly limited the function of education in increasing labor income. Since the reform and opening up, China's labor market has become increasingly competitive and mobile, and the human capital value of employees can be fully reflected through competition and mobility in the labor market. Education, as the most important element of human capital, has better functioned in improving labor income. At the same time, with the advancement of technologies and the development of society, some new occupations with higher social status have emerged in early 2000s. These emerging occupations feature higher income and require better education. This means that well-educated children, especially those from low-income families, may have more opportunities in achieving higher income and improving their economic status by entering these emerging sectors, which will further strengthen the role of education in promoting intergenerational income mobility.

The purpose of this chapter is to test the following four hypotheses:

- There is an obvious transmission effect on the intergenerational income of China's urban households.
- Compared with the father's income (the predestined factor), children's education (the acquired factor) has a greater impact on their income.
- More education for children from China's urban families (especially low-income families) helps them enter higher-income groups.
- With the deepening of marketization, a higher level of education for children of urban households has an increasing effect on their entry to the highest income group.

15.1 Literature Review

Intergenerational mobility includes intergenerational urban–rural mobility, occupational mobility, sectoral mobility and income mobility. Prior to the 1990s, foreign studies on intergenerational mobility had focused on intergenerational occupational mobility. Since the 1990s, the focus has shifted from intergenerational occupational mobility to income mobility, as many scholars believed that income, as an important economic resource possessed by members of society, cannot be fully reflected by their occupations for three reasons. First, workers in the same occupation may not have the same earnings. Second, occupation generally reflects a worker's long-term income, which is not necessarily equal to the person's short-term income. Third, even if a pair of father and son have the same occupation, the income of them may be different due to social and economic factors. Therefore, intergenerational occupational mobility of a society may not accord with its intergenerational income mobility, and sometimes may even be completely different.

The research paper *Intergenerational Income Mobility in the United States* by Solon in 1992 is a classic study of intergenerational income mobility. Since its publication, many economists and sociologists have conducted more detailed research on intergenerational income mobility. Table 15.1 summarized the intergenerational income elasticity coefficients[1] of these empirical research.

15.1.1 Country-Specific Studies

Solon (1992) used the intergenerational income data from the US PSID (Panel Study of Income Dynamics) survey to analyze the impact of parental income on children's income by building a regression model of parental income and children's income after controlling for the age factor. There were three models in Solon's research. First, the father's and the son's income in 1967 were used to analyze the impact of the father's income on the son's. Second, the five-year average income of the father and the son from 1967 to 1971 was used to analyze intergenerational income mobility. Third, the father's years of schooling was introduced as the instrumental variable to analyze the relationship between the father's and the son's income. The study found that intergenerational income elasticity coefficients of the three models were 0.386, 0.413 and 0.526, respectively, indicating a strong intergenerational income transmission effect and weak mobility.

Elizabeth's research (1992) results on intergenerational income mobility in the United States are quite different from others. By analyzing relevant variables in the National Longitudinal Surveys (NLS), this research found strong intergenerational income mobility in the US. After controlling for the father's education level, race and other factors, he found that the father's income has a smaller impact on children's income, only 0.228; the logarithm of the father's income can only explain 9%–11% of the change in the logarithm of children's income.

Couch and Lillard (1998) believed that in many studies on intergenerational income mobility, it is unreasonable to exclude samples with zero income. Also using the data from the US PSID survey, they included samples with zero income in the regression model. In addition, they selected the father's one-year income, the son's

[1] The intergenerational income elasticity coefficient measures the degree of influence of the father's income on their offspring's income. The greater the intergenerational income elasticity coefficient, the greater the degree of the influence of the income of the father on that of their offspring. The calculation method of the intergenerational income elasticity will be explained in detail in the methodology section.

Table 15.1 Intergenerational income elasticity coefficients in various countries

Researchers	Sample country	Model	β estimate
Solon (1992)	United States	OLS (father's one-year income)	0.386***
		OLS (father's five-year average income)	0.413***
		IV (father's years of schooling)	0.526***
Elizabeth (1992)	United States	OLS (one-year income)	0.228***
Bjorklund and Jantti (1997)	Sweden	OLS (one-year income)	0.282***
Dearden et al. (1997)	United Kingdom (father and son)	OLS (weekly income)	0.428***
		IV (father's social status)	0.439***
	United Kingdom (father and daughter)	OLS (weekly income)	0.455***
		IV (father's social status)	0.481***
Couch and Lillard (1998)	United States	OLS (father's one-year income and son's four-year average income, including samples with zero income)	0.298***
		OLS (father's one-year income and son's four-year average income, excluding samples with zero income)	0.037***
		OLS (father's annual income and son's annual income, including samples with zero income)	0.511***
		OLS (father's annual income and son's annual income, excluding samples with zero income)	0.037***
Corak and Heisz (1999)	Canada (grouped according to the father's five-year average income)	OLS (average annual income > US$1)	0.228***
		OLS (average annual income > US$100)	0.227***
		OLS (average annual income > US$1000)	0.237***
		OLS (average annual income > US$3000)	0.242***
Aughinbaugh (2000)	United States (compared with Solon's findings)	OLS (one-year income)	0.397***
		OLS (five-year average income)	0.466***

(continued)

Table 15.1 (continued)

Researchers	Sample country	Model	β estimate
Chadwick and Solon (2002)	United States	OLS (father and daughter)	0.429***
		OLS (father and son)	0.535***
Das and Sjogren (2002)	United States	OLS (one-year income, biological son)	0.288***
		OLS (one-year income, adopted son)	−0.244
Levine and Mazumder (2002)	United States	OLS (one-year income, year 1980)	0.217***
		OLS (one-year income, year 1993)	0.414***
Björklund and Chadwick (2003)	Sweden	OLS (one-year income, biological father)	0.24***
		OLS (one-year income, non-biological father)	0.08***

Note *** means the significance level is 0.05

one-year income and four-year average income to measure intergenerational income (Solon, in contrast, using the father's one-year and four-year average income, and the son's one-year income to measure intergenerational income). The results showed that after samples with zero income were included, intergenerational income mobility in the United States has increased significantly, and the impact of parental income on offspring's income has become smaller. In addition, the father's income has a greater impact on the son's short-term income than long-term income. In contrast, Solon found that the father's long-term income has a greater impact on the son's income, compared with the father's short-term income.

Corak and Heisz (1999) believed that the impact of the father's income on children's income may vary greatly among different income groups. They analyzed related data on personal income and tax payment and divided the sample into four groups by using the father's average annual income in five years being US$1, $100, US$1000, and US$3000 as the demarcation points. The results showed that the intergenerational income transmission effect in Canada is not strong in general. The intergenerational income elasticity coefficients of the four groups were slightly higher than 0.2, respectively 0.228, 0.207, 0.237 and 0.242, which indicates the higher the father's annual income the greater its impact on children's income.

Aughinbaugh (2000) used the same methods as Solon with the same data from the PSID survey, also selected the population born from 1951 to 1959, as well as the income of the father from 1967 to 1971. The only difference with Solon is that Aughinbaugh selected son's income in 1989, while Solon selected son's income in 1984. The results showed that the intergenerational income transmission effect in the US has increased significantly. If only the income of 1967 is used to measure the father's income, the intergenerational income elasticity coefficient would have increased from

0.386 in 1984 to 0.397. If the average income from 1967 to 1971 is used to measure the father's income, the intergenerational income elasticity coefficient would have increased from 0.413 in 1984 to 0.466.

15.1.2 International Comparison

Bjorklund and Jantti (1997) used relevant data from the Swedish Level of Living Survey to analyze intergenerational income mobility in Sweden. They used the same model as Solon and compared their results with Solon's. The result showed that parental income has a smaller impact on their offspring's income in Sweden, with the intergenerational income elasticity coefficient being 0.282, significantly smaller than 0.386 in the United States.

Solon (2002) compared existing findings on intergenerational income mobility in various countries, and found that most of the intergenerational income elasticity coefficients calculated in the United States and the United Kingdom were above 0.4, and most of those in Sweden and Canada were below 0.3. Solon therefore concluded that intergenerational income mobility in the United States and the United Kingdom is slightly lower than that in countries such as Canada and Sweden, and thus income distribution in the US and the UK is more unfair.

15.1.3 Gender Comparison

There are not many comparative studies on intergenerational income mobility between men and women. Dearden and Mchin's study on the United Kingdom and Chadwick and Solon's study on the United States are typical, but their empirical results are quite different.

Dearden et al. (1997). used data from the Survey of Research and Development in the UK, by using the father's income in 1974 and children's income in 1991, to build an econometric model to compare the difference in the impact of the father's income on children's income. They found that there is a strong transmission effect of intergenerational income in the UK. The impact of the father's income on children's is slightly different between sons and daughters. The father's income has a smaller impact on the son's income than the daughter's, with the regression coefficients being 0.428 and 0.455 respectively. With the instrumental variable, the father's occupational status, introduced, the coefficients become 0.439 and 0.481 respectively.

Chadwick and Solon (2002) used data from the US PSID survey and selected paired samples with income of fathers and of their sons and daughters who were born in 1968 and had income in 1992. By comparing the impact of the father's income on the son's and the daughter's income, they found that the father's income has a greater impact on the son's income than the daughter's, and the intergenerational income elasticity coefficients are 0.535 and 0.429, respectively.

15.1.4 Historical Comparison

With data from the US National Longitudinal Surveys (NLS) and General Social Survey (GSS), Levine and Mazumder (2002) built an econometric model to compare intergenerational income mobility in 1980 and 1993. They found that the intergenerational income elasticity coefficient was 0.217 in 1980 then rose to 0.414 in 1993. Intergenerational income transmission has increased, and mobility has weakened.

Different from the above-mentioned scholars, Nam (2004) studied intergenerational income mobility in the US by building a binary logistic regression model. He used the survey data of the US PSID and divided the sample population into a high-income group and a low-income group, and also divided the sample population into a 1969-born group and a 1979-born group. A binary logistic regression model was built, with whether the offspring belongs to the high-income group as the dependent variable, and the parents' income group, age, race, children's age group, and the interactive term of the parents' income group and children's age group as independent variables, to compare the trends of intergenerational income mobility of the two age groups. The results showed that in the past ten years, there is still serious income inequality in the US. Children of high-income parents are more likely to have higher income, while those from low-income families face little chance of entering the high-income group.

15.1.5 Comparison Between Biological and Non-Biological Fathers and Sons

Since the twenty-first century, many researchers began to study differences in intergenerational income mobility between biological and non-biological fathers and sons, as represented by Das and Sjogren, and Anders and Chadwick.

Das and Sjogren (2002) analyzed the sample data of 114 families with biological sons and 109 families with adopted sons, and found that the father's income has a significant impact on the biological son's income, with the intergenerational income elasticity coefficient being 0.288, but it has no significant impact on the adopted son's income.

Björklund and Chadwick (2003) mainly studied the difference in intergenerational income mobility between son vs biological father and son vs non-biological father. By using census data of Sweden from 1965 to 1980, they divided the sample into six groups for comparison based on: (a)whether the son and father are biologically related, (b) whether the son lived with the father, and (c) how long the father and son lived together. The results showed that the impact of biological father's income on son's earnings was significantly higher than that of non-biological fathers. The former coefficient was 0.24 and the latter only 0.08. In addition, the research also found that the longer the son lives with his biological father, the greater the impact of the father's income on the son's.

15.1.6 Brief Summary

Based on the above foreign research on intergenerational mobility, we find that most of them studied the impact of parental income on offspring's income, and few explored the relationship between education and intergenerational income mobility, or the role of education in promoting intergenerational income mobility. In addition, these studies mainly focused on developed countries, such as the United States, the United Kingdom, Canada and Sweden, while intergenerational income mobility in developing countries has been rarely analyzed. Empirical research on intergenerational income mobility in these developed countries showed that parental income has a greater impact on offspring's income, and the higher the parental income, the greater its impact on children's income. Comparison of intergenerational income mobility in different countries found that the intergenerational transmission effect of income in the United States and the United Kingdom is greater than that of Canada and Sweden. In other words, compared with Sweden and Canada, the income inequality in the United States and the United Kingdom is more transmitted to next generations.

Comparing empirical research on intergenerational income mobility of different periods in the United States by different scholars, as shown in Table 15.1, and combining the research of Nam, Levine and Mazumder, we can find that the intergenerational income elasticity coefficient in the United States has gradually increased over the years. That is to say, the impact of parental income on children's earnings in the United States is increasing, the intergenerational income mobility is declining, and the inequality in income distribution is increasingly transmitted between generations. Declining intergenerational income mobility also occurs in the United Kingdom. Intergenerational income mobility in the United Kingdom and the United States did not increase with the process of industrialization, but on the contrary, it has gradually weakened. Researchers have only discovered this trend through empirical research, but have not made a reasonable explanation for its causes.

Compared with research on intergenerational mobility by foreign scholars, the existing research on intergenerational mobility by Chinese scholars mainly focused on intergenerational occupational mobility with little attention on intergenerational income mobility. This is mainly because the market economy has not been fully established in China prior to the 1990s. As income gaps among different groups were relatively small, the intergenerational income mobility did not attract the attention of Chinese scholars. Since the 1990s, with the gradual establishment of the market economic system, the gap between the rich and the poor has been widening. The United Nations Development Program (UNDP) statistics in 2005 showed that China's Gini coefficient was 0.45 in 2002 (the international alert value is 0.4), and the poorest 20% of the population accounted for only 4.7% of total income and consumption, while the wealthiest 20% accounted for up to 50% of total income and consumption. Income inequality has become a major constraint on China's future economic development and social stability (UNDP 2005). Under such circumstances, whether income inequality is transmitted to the next generation has attracted more and more attention. On the basis of analyzing the characteristics of China's current intergenerational income mobility, the empirical research part will focus on the function of education in promoting intergenerational income mobility and its changing trend with the improvement of China's marketization level.

15.2 Data Explanation

This chapter examines the relationship between education and intergenerational income mobility in urban China based on the data from the China's Urban Household Education and Employment Survey-2004 by the Institute of Economics of Education, Peking University. The survey samples covered twelve provinces across the country, including Beijing, Zhejiang, Guangdong, Liaoning, Hubei, Anhui, Shanxi, Heilongjiang, Guizhou, Sichuan, Shaanxi and Gansu.

There are 7522 pairs of intergenerational data in this survey. In the survey sample, the average personal income in 2004 was RMB15,196.02, of which the average income of fathers was RMB13,235.62, and the average income of children was RMB15,858.38, higher than that of fathers. The average years of schooling for all samples were 11.04, of which the average years of schooling of fathers were 8.94, and that of children were 11.9.

Since the subsequent empirical analysis will discuss how the role of China's urban residents' education in promoting intergenerational mobility changes with the level of marketization, we divide the years when children were seeking jobs into three time periods according to the feature of China's economic system: 1978 and before (the era of the planned economy), between 1979 and 1991 (the coexistence of the planned economy and the market economy), and after 1992 (the era of the market economy). According to this, our survey samples are divided into three groups of subsamples. As a result, the pre-1979 subsamples have 2,382 pairs of intergenerational data, the 1979–1991 subsamples contain 2422 pairs of intergenerational data, and the post-1992 one has 2718 pairs.

15.3 Methodology

15.3.1 Indicators for Measuring Intergenerational Income Mobility

In addition to indicators such as the intergenerational income inheritance index, intergenerational mobility index, intergenerational income inflow and outflow index, we also introduce the intergenerational income elasticity coefficient to analyze the intergenerational income flow of China's urban residents.

15.3.1.1 Intergenerational Income Mobility and Inheritance Coefficient

The inheritance coefficient measures the level of intergenerational inheritance of income groups, while the mobility coefficient measures the level of intergenerational mobility of income groups. The greater the intergenerational inheritance coefficient of an income group, the more stable the intergenerational inheritance, the smaller the intergenerational mobility, and the stronger the intergenerational transmission effect of the income group is. On the contrary, the greater the mobility coefficient, the more unstable the inheritance between generations, the weaker the intergenerational income transmission effect is.

Assuming there are n income groups, we can build a matrix $A = (a_{ij})n \times n$ that reflects the intergenerational mobility and inheritance of all the income groups. Among them, a_{ij} represents the frequency of the father's income belonging to group i and the child's group j. If the income group to which the father belongs and the income group to which the children belong are independent of each other, the ratio of the observed value of the frequency distribution $a_{ij}\Big/\sum_{i=1}^{n}\sum_{j=1}^{n} a_{ij}$ to its theoretical expected value under the independence assumption $\sum_{i=1}^{n} a_{ij}\sum_{j=1}^{n} a_{ij}\Big/\sum_{i=1}^{n}\sum_{j=1}^{n} a_{ij}\sum_{i=1}^{n}\sum_{j=1}^{n} a_{ij}$ should be close to 1, otherwise the ratio will be far away from 1. We use the ratio of the observed value to the expected value to define the intergenerational mobility coefficient ($i \neq j$) and inheritance coefficient ($i = j$) of an income group:

$$B_{ij} = \left(\frac{a_{ij}}{\sum_{i=1}^{n}\sum_{j=1}^{n} a_{ij}}\Bigg/\frac{\sum_{i=1}^{n} a_{ij}\sum_{j=1}^{n} a_{ij}}{\sum_{i=1}^{n}\sum_{j=1}^{n} a_{ij}\sum_{i=1}^{n}\sum_{j=1}^{n} a_{ij}}\right) = a_{ij}\frac{\sum_{i=1}^{n}\sum_{j=1}^{n} a_{ij}}{\sum_{i=1}^{n} a_{ij}\sum_{j=1}^{n} a_{ij}}$$

If $B_{ij} > 1$, that is, if the observed frequency of the father belonging to income group i and the child group j is greater than its theoretical expected frequency, it means that children whose father belonging to group i is more likely to belong to income group j. And the larger the value B_{ij} is, the more likely it is. Conversely, if $B_{ij} < 1$, in other words, if the observed frequency of the father belonging to income group i and the child group j is smaller than its theoretical expected frequency, it means that children whose father belonging to group i is less likely to belong to income group j. And the smaller the value B_{ij} is, the less likely it is.

15.3.1.2 Intergenerational Inflow and Outflow Coefficient

To further measure the intergenerational mobility of income groups, we also calculate the intergenerational inflow coefficient and outflow coefficient for each income group. The intergenerational income inflow coefficient is defined as $c_j = \frac{\sum_{i \neq j} b_{ij}}{n-1}$, which measures the probability of the father not belonging to income group j but the child belonging to it. In other words, it reflects the level of openness of an income group to children whose fathers do not belong to it. The smaller the intergenerational inflow coefficient of an income group, the smaller the intergenerational mobility of this group, the less likely it is for children whose fathers are not in this group to enter it, the greater the intergenerational transmission effect of the group. Conversely, the larger the intergenerational mobility of an income group, the smaller its intergenerational transmission effect is.

Similarly, the intergenerational income outflow coefficient of an income group is defined as $d_i = \frac{\sum_{j \neq i} b_{ij}}{n-1}$, which measures the probability of the father belonging to income group i and the child not. The greater the outflow coefficient of an income group, the stronger the intergenerational mobility of this group, and the greater the probability that children of this income group enter other income groups, the smaller intergenerational transmission effect of this group is.

15.3.1.3 Intergenerational Income Elasticity Coefficient

The intergenerational income elasticity coefficient measures the degree of impact of the parental income on the income of their offspring. The greater the intergenerational elasticity coefficient, the greater the impact of parental income on offspring's income, and the smaller the entire society's intergenerational income mobility. The smaller the intergenerational elasticity coefficient, the less impact of parental income on offspring's income, the greater the entire society's intergenerational income mobility. This paper selects the intergenerational income mobility model proposed by the Solon (1992) in his classic work *Intergenerational Income Mobility in the United States* to calculate the intergenerational income elasticity coefficient of Chinese urban residents. The model is as follows:

$$y_{sit} = \beta_0 + \rho y_{fit} + \beta_{s1} \exp_{sit} + \beta_{s2} \exp_{sit}^2 + \beta_{f1} \exp_{fit} + \beta_{f2} \exp_{fit}^2 + \varepsilon \tag{15.1}$$

where, y_{sit} is the logarithm of children's income, y_{fit} represents the logarithm of the father's income, $\exp_{sit}$ refers to children's working years, $\exp_{sit}^2$ is the square of children's working years, $\exp_{fit}$ is the father's working years, $\exp_{fit}^2$ is the square of the father's working years, and ρ is the intergenerational income elasticity coefficient.

15.3.2 Path Analysis

Among the factors that affect children's income, which are more important? Ascriptive factors (such as the father's income) or acquired factors (such as children's education)? To answer this question, we introduce path analysis to explore the relationship between education and intergenerational income mobility.

Path analysis is a statistical method to explore the cause-effect relationship of a system, focusing on decomposing the effect coefficient between variables (Guo

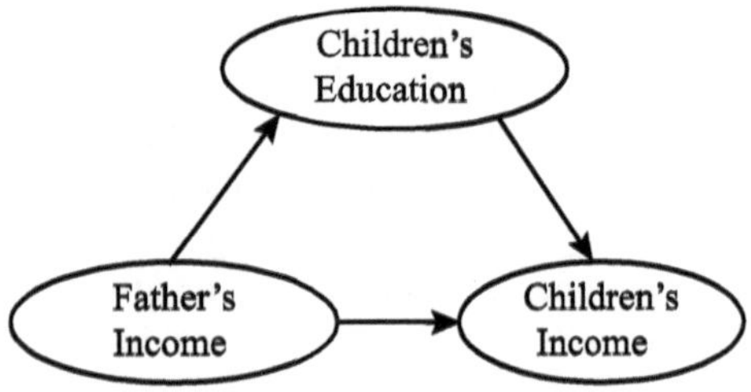

Fig. 15.1 The path diagram

2003). By introducing intermediate variables, path analysis decomposes the total effect of one variable on another variable into direct effect between the two variables and indirect effect through the intermediate variable, and the two types of effects can be compared by standardized regression coefficients. The path model is as follows:

$$z_2 = p_{21}z_1 \tag{15.2}$$

$$z_3 = p_{31}z_1 + p_{32}z_2 \tag{15.3}$$

where, z_1 represents the father's income, z_2 represents children's education, and z_3 represents children's income. p_{21}, p_{31} and p_{32} are the path coefficients in the path model, that is, the standardized regression coefficients of each variable. p_{21} represents the degree of impact of the father's income on children's education, p_{31} represents the degree of influence of the father's income on children's income, and p_{32} represents the degree of influence of children's education on children's income.

Substituting $z_2 = p_{21}z_1$ into the equation $z_3 = p_{31}z_1 + p_{32}z_2$, we can get:

$$z_3 = p_{31}z_1 + p_{32}p_{21}z_1 \tag{15.4}$$

In this equation, the impact of the father's income on children's income is decomposed into two parts. One part is the direct influence of the father's income on children's income, namely p_{31}; the other is the indirect influence of the father's income on children's income by first affecting children's education and then their income, namely $p_{32}p_{21}$.

The path diagram of the above path model is shown in Fig. 15.1:

15.4 Characteristics of Urban Residents' Intergenerational Income Mobility

In order to analyze the characteristics of intergenerational income mobility of Chinese urban residents, we divide the sample into four groups from high to low according to the incomes of fathers and children. Among them, the top 25% are the high-income

Table 15.2 Intergenerational inheritance and mobility coefficient of each income group

Group	Children's income group				
	High income	Upper-middle income	Lower-middle income	Low income	Outflow coefficient
Parental income group					
High income	1.55*	1.04	0.68	0.67	0.8
Upper-middle income	1.04	1.15*	1.02	0.76	0.94
Lower-middle income	0.88	0.95	1.16*	1.05	0.96
Low income	0.54	0.86	1.14	1.52*	0.85
Inflow coefficient	0.82	0.95	0.95	0.83	

Table 15.3 Intergenerational income elasticity coefficient of China's urban residents in 2004

Group	Intergenerational income elasticity coefficient
Overall	0.320
High income group	0.231
Upper-middle income group	0.020
Lower-middle income group	0.024
Low income group	0.378

Note The dependent variable is the logarithm of children's income, and the significance level is 0.01

group, the top 25%-50% the upper-middle income group, the top 50%-75% the lower-middle income group, and the last 25% the low-income group. Intergenerational income mobility of the four groups in 2004 is shown in Table 15.2.

We also substitute the logarithms of the father's and children's income in 2004, years of working, and the square of years of working of the father and children into the model for intergenerational income elasticity, the regression results of which are shown in Table 15.3.

The results in Table 15.2 and Table 15.3 show that the intergenerational income mobility of urban residents in China has the following three characteristics:

First, there is a relatively strong intergenerational transmission of income for urban residents in China. Table 15.2 shows that the intergenerational inheritance coefficient of each income group is significantly greater than 1,[2] and the average

[2] The intergenerational inheritance/mobility coefficient equaling to 1 indicates that intergenerational mobility of a person in an income group is completely unaffected by the economic status of his/her family. The more the intergenerational inheritance coefficient is greater than 1, the more likely it is that the child will stay in the same income group as the father; the more the intergenerational mobility coefficient is greater than 1, the more likely it is that the child will flow to a different income group from the father. The more the intergenerational inflow coefficient of a certain income group is greater than 1, the more likely it is that the offspring of the whole society will flow into

value is 1.35. The intergenerational mobility coefficient of each income group is less than 1, with an average of 0.89. The inflow/outflow coefficient of each income group is less than 1, and the average value is 0.89. This indicates that although there is a certain degree of intergenerational mobility of China's urban residents, the intergenerational transmission effect of income is more powerful.

The results also show that the parental income in urban China has a relatively large impact on their children's income. Table 15.3 shows that the overall intergenerational income elasticity coefficient is 0.32, which means that for every 1% increase in the father's annual income, children's annual income will increase by 0.32%. The regression coefficients of the father's years of working and the children's years of working are both positive, with a significance level less than 0.01, indicating that the increase in the years of working of the father and children helps to increase the income of children.

Second, intergenerational income mobility of the two income groups at both ends is weaker, and that of the middle two groups is relatively stronger. Among the four income groups, the intergenerational inheritance coefficients of the high income and the low income group are 1.55 and 1.52, respectively, greater than 1.15 and 1.16 of the upper-middle and the lower-middle income group respectively. At the same time, the intergenerational inflow coefficients of the upper-middle and the lower-middle income group are both 0.95, significantly greater than the 0.82 of the high income and the 0.83 of the low income group. The intergenerational outflow coefficients of the upper-middle and the lower-middle income group are 0.94 and 0.96, respectively, greater than the 0.8 of the high income and the 0.85 of the low income group. These results show that in urban China, if the father belongs to the high or low income group, his children are more likely to remain in the corresponding income group. But if the father belongs to the upper-middle or lower-middle income group, the possibility of his children moving to other income groups is relatively high.

The intergenerational elasticity coefficients further confirm this feature. Among the four income groups, the intergenerational elasticity coefficient of the low income group to which the father belongs is the largest, reaching 0.378. The high income group follows, with an intergenerational elasticity coefficient of 0.231. The intergenerational elasticity coefficients of the two middle groups to which the parent belongs are smaller, only 0.02 and 0.024. This implies that the impact of the father's income on children's income is particularly pronounced in the income groups at both ends, while in middle income groups, the father's income also has a positive impact on children's income, but smaller than that in the high and low groups. In other words, for children whose parents are in the high income group, their parents' high income can provide more assurance and promotion for their income. For children whose parents are in the low income group, the father's low income may hinder their children from achieving higher income. For children whose parents are in the middle income groups, the father's income has a relatively small impact on their income.

---

this income group; the more the intergenerational outflow coefficient of a certain income group is greater than 1, the more likely it is for offspring to flow into other income groups whose father belongs to this income group.

Third, there is clear segmentation in intergenerational income mobility. Children of the high income group are most likely to stay in the same group as their fathers, and only few of them may move to the upper-middle income group, with very little chance of being in the lower two groups. Children of the upper-middle income group are highly mobile, who can either move upwards to the high income group, or downwards to the lower-middle group, and the possibility of moving upwards is slightly greater than that of moving downwards. In contrast, children of the lower middle and the low income group are more likely to be trapped in lower income groups. Among them, the largest possibility for children of the lower-middle income group is to move downwards to the low income group, and children of the low income group are most likely to stay in the same group as their fathers, with a small possibility of moving up to the lower-middle income group. It is nearly impossible for children of the two lower groups to move up to the two higher groups.

To summarize, there is a strong intergenerational income transmission effect in urban China, and most children remain in the same income group as their fathers. In addition, there is clear segmentation in the scope of intergenerational mobility. Intergenerational mobility between the two higher-income groups is relatively strong, that between the two lower-income groups also relatively strong, but the intergenerational mobility between higher-income and lower-income groups is much weaker. In addition, intergenerational income mobility of the groups at both ends is lacking, and that of the middle income groups is larger.

15.5 Role of Education in Promoting Intergenerational Income Mobility

15.5.1 Factors that May Impact Children's Income

This part discusses the influence of the father's income (an ascriptive factor) and children's education (an acquired factor), on children's income. We build an income path model mainly with the following three variables: the father's income, children's education and children's income. Among them, the father's income is measured by the father's income in 2004, children's education measured by children's education level, and children's income by children's income in 2004. The calculation result of the path coefficients is shown in Table 15.4.

Table 15.4 Path coefficients of children's income

Dependent variable	Independent variable	
	Father's income	Children's education
Children's education	0.129	
Children's income	0.159	0.189

Fig. 15.2 Income path

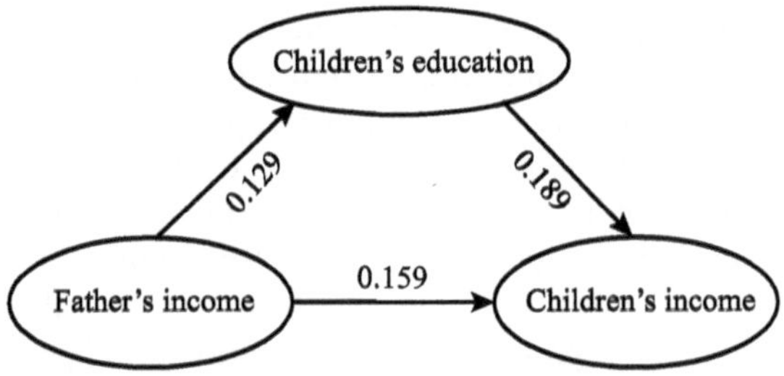

The results show that both the father's income and children's education have a significant impact on children's income, with the path coefficients being 0.159 and 0.189, respectively, which means that children's education has a greater impact on children's income than father's income. Figure 15.2 shows the path diagram.

The influence of the father's income on children's income can be decomposed into the direct influence of the father's income on children's income and the indirect influence of the father's income through first affecting children's education and then children's income. The total impact of the father's income on children's income is the simple regression coefficient of the father's income on children's income, which is 0.183. The direct impact is 0.159, accounting for 86.9% of the total impact. The indirect impact is 0.024, 0.129 multiplied by 0.189, accounting for 13.1% of the total impact. That is to say, the impact of the father's income on children's income is more of a direct impact, and its indirect impact through affecting children's education is much smaller. In other words, children's education plays a role in helping children maintain the economic status of their family, but this role is very limited.

15.5.2 The Role of Education in Helping Children Enter the High-Income Group

To analyze the role of children's education in helping them enter the high-income group, we build a binary logistic regression model:

$$\log it(P) = \beta_0 + \beta_1 X_1 + \beta_2 X_2 + \beta_3 \sum_{i=1}^{n} X_i + \mu \tag{15.5}$$

The dependent variable of the model is a binary variable of "whether the child belongs to the high- income group", with the value 1 if the child does and 0 if he/she does not. The independent variables include the child's years of schooling, the father's years of schooling, and three dummy variables related to the father's income group (the high-income group, the upper-middle-income group and the lower-middle-income group, with the low-income group as the reference variable for the dummy variables).

Results in Table 15.5 indicate that improved education helps children enter the high income group. The β value of children's education is 0.171, and the anti-log of β is 1.186, indicating that for each year increased in children's education, the weighted probability for them to enter the high income group increases by 18.6%. In other words, after controlling for the father's education and income, the increase in the years of schooling for children helps to increase the possibility of children entering the high income group.

Results in Table 15.5 also show that there are large differences in the probability of children of fathers in different income groups entering the high-income group. The Exp(β) for fathers in the high-income group is 3.639, indicating that the children of fathers in this group are 3.6 times as likely to enter the high income group as those of fathers in the low income group. The Exp(β) for fathers in the upper-middle income group is 2.188, indicating that the children of fathers in this group are 2.2 times as likely to enter the high income group as those of the low income group. Similarly, the Exp(β) for fathers in the lower-middle income group is 1.795, indicating that the children of fathers in this group are 1.8 times as likely to enter the high income group as those of the low income group. In other words, children with their fathers in the high income group are much more likely to continue to be in the high income group than those whose parents are in the other three income groups. The probability of children whose parents are in the upper-middle or lower-middle income groups entering the high income group follows, higher than that of children with parents in the low income group. As the most vulnerable group in society, the low income group faces little chance to see their children get beyond the impact of the parents and enter the high income group.

The regression results of the interaction terms for the dummy variables of the father's income group and children's education show that the education received by children of families in different income groups has certain differences in the effect

Table 15.5 Regression results of the binary logistic model of factors affecting children's entry into the high-income group

Item	β value	Significance level	Exp(β)
Children's years of schooling	0.171	0.000	1.186
Father in the high income group	1.292	0.000	3.639
Father in the upper-middle income group	0.783	0.000	2.188
Father in the lower-middle income group	0.585	0.000	1.795
High income group × Children's education	−0.054	0.000	0.947
Upper-middle income group × Children's education	−0.018	0.001	0.982
Lower-middle income group × Children's education	−0.014	0.001	0.986
1979–1991 period × Children's education	0.031	0.000	1.032
Post-1992 period × Children's education	0.050	0.000	1.051
Intercept	−3.989	0.000	0.019

Note The dependent variable is whether the child belongs to the high income group

of helping children enter the high-income group. The regression coefficient of the interaction term for the dummy variable of the father in the high income group and children's education is -0.054, and the anti-log of β is 0.947. The regression coefficient of the interaction term of the dummy variable of the father in the upper-middle income group and children's education is −0.018, and the anti-log of β is 0.982. The regression coefficient of the interaction term of the dummy variable of the father in the lower-middle income group and children's education is -0.014, and the anti-log of β is 0.986. It shows that the effect of education received by children with parents in the low income group on helping them enter the high income group is Exp(0.054), 1.06 times that of the education received by children of parents in the high income group. It is also Exp (0.018) and Exp (0.014), in other words, 1.02 and 1.01 times that of the education received by children of parents in the upper-middle and the lower-middle income group, respectively. That is to say, among the children of parents in the four income groups, education is the most effective factor in helping children move upwards to the high income group for families in the low income group.

In order to further compare the effects of education on children of parents from different income groups enter the high-income group, we run a binary logistic regression for each of the four groups based on the father's income. The dependent variable of the model is whether the child is in the high income group, and the independent variable is the child's years of schooling. The regression results show that the Exp(β) value of the years of schooling of the children for the low income group is the largest, which is 1.226; the Exp(β) value for the two middle income groups are also in the middle, which are 1.150 and 1.162 respectively; the Exp(β) value for the high-income group is the smallest, which is 1.127. The regression results of the four subsamples are completely consistent with those of the interaction terms of the father's income group and children's years of schooling. This means that compared with children of parents in the other three income groups, higher education level of the children of parents in the low income group is more conducive to the children's entry into the high income group.

The results of the income path analysis show that children's education has a greater impact on their income than the father's income. The results of the binary logistic regression model also show that the increase in children's years of schooling helps them enter the high-income group. In comparison, more years of schooling for families in the low-income group have the greatest impact on helping children move up to higher income groups. That is to say, in urban China, although education is replicating the original economic status system to a certain extent, on the whole, education can help children from families with disadvantaged economic status to achieve intergenerational upward income mobility. Education plays a more important role in promoting intergenerational income mobility than replicating the original economic status system.

15.6 Changes in the Role of Education in Promoting Intergenerational Income Mobility

In order to analyze trends in the role of education in promoting intergenerational income mobility with the advancement of marketization in urban China, we construct two interaction terms, one for the dummy variable of the time period from 1979 to 1991 and children's years of schooling, the other for the dummy variable of the period after 1992 and children's years of schooling. The dummy variable of the pre-1978 period serves as the reference variable. The regression results of these two interaction items (see Table 15.5) show that the β value of the former interaction item is 0.031, and the anti-log of β is 1.032; the β value of the latter interaction item is 0.050, the anti-log 1.051. This shows that the effect of children's education on helping children enter the high-income group in the 1979–1991 period is 1.032 times that of the pre-1978 period, and 1.051 times that of the post-1992 period.

In order to compare more detailed differences in the role of education in the three periods in promoting intergenerational income mobility, we run a binary logistic regression for each of the three periods.

The results in Table 15.6 confirm that increase in children's education has a larger effect on their entry into the high-income group as marketization advances. Among them, the Exp(β) value of children's education before 1978 is 1.232, which means that for every additional year of children's education, their weighted chance of entering the high-income group will increase by 23.2%. The Exp(β) value of that in the 1979–1991 period rises slightly to 1.242 and continues to rise to 1.269 after 1992. It indicates that for every additional year of children's education, their weighted chance of entering the highest income class will increase by 24.2% between 1979 and 1991 and 26.9% after 1992.

In order to explore the trend of the effect of education of children, whose parents are in the low-income group, in helping them enter the high-income group during the three periods, we construct an interaction term for the dummy variable of the father

Table 15.6 Comparison of education in helping children enter the high-income group

Item	Pre-1978 Exp(β)	1979–1991 Exp(β)	Post-1992 Exp(β)
Children's education	1.232***	1.242***	1.269***
Father in the high income group	2.865***	2.987***	5.090***
Father in the upper middle income group	1.999***	1.926***	2.642***
Father in the lower-middle income group	1.971***	1.555*	1.875***
Father in the low income group × Children's education	1.049**	1.035	1.069***
Intercept	0.013***	0.017***	0.006***

Note *** indicates the significance level is 0.01, ** indicates the significance level is 0.05, * indicates the significance level is 0.1

in the low-income group and children's years of schooling for each of the three periods. The results in Table 15.6 show that among the three periods, the coefficient of the interaction term before 1978 was 0.048, and that for the 1979–1991 period was 0.034, which failed the significance test. The coefficient of the interaction term after 1992 is 0.067. It shows that before 1978, education received by children of parents in the low-income group has an effect on helping them enter the high-income group Exp (0.048), 1.049 times that of other income groups; there is no significant difference between the two types of income groups from 1979 to 1991; after 1992, the former's advantage over the latter rises slightly to Exp (0.067), which is 1.069 times. This means that the role of education in promoting children from low-income families to move upward to the high-income group has become increasingly larger as marketization advances in urban China.

The above analysis shows that education, as an important mechanism of promoting intergenerational mobility, does play a role in promoting intergenerational income mobility, especially in promoting children from low-income families to achieve a leap in economic status. In addition, as the level of marketization increases, its role shows a rising trend. We try to explain the reasons for this trend as follows:

1. *The advancement of marketization helps increase the revenue of education*

The prerequisite for education as a kind of human capital to increase labor productivity and then increase labor income is that the labor market must be perfectly competitive and fully mobile. Under the traditional planned economy, there was no real labor market in China. The first job assigned to workers usually became their lifelong career, with little chance of change. In addition, years of working rather than education level was the decisive factor of an employee's income in a labor market extremely lacking competition and mobility, therefore the role of education in affecting a person's income cannot be fully realized (Chen 1999). Since the reform and opening up, competitiveness and mobility of the labor market have increased with the overall advancement of marketization in China, the income of workers is more determined by individual abilities rather than working years. This has enabled children who entered the labor market after 1992 to give full play to the education they have received, which helps to increase their income and thus promotes intergenerational income mobility.

2. *High-income emerging occupations and sectors require better-educated workforce*

Emerging occupations with higher social status and new sectors with higher income have emerged one after another with the continuous advancement of marketization and technologies. These emerging occupations and sectors require practitioners to have more knowledge, which allows children who have received a higher level of education, especially those from low-income families, to have more opportunities to enter high income occupations and sectors, thereby smoothly moving upward to higher-income groups.

3. *The role of acquired factors in achieving personal economic success continues to increase with the advancement of marketization*

The society is becoming more and more open with the advancement of marketization in China, while individual acquired factors play a more and more important role in improving one's social and economic status. In addition, a lot of high-income occupations and jobs have been created due to China's one-child policy as well as migrant workers pouring into the urban labor market, along with the cancellation of "succession and replacement"[3] in many high-income occupations. All such jobs prefer well-educated young people, and provide children from low-income families who have received a higher level of education with more opportunities to enter high-income occupations and sectors, thereby helping them achieve an intergenerational leap in economic status.

15.7 Conclusions and Reflections

Using data from the China's Urban Household Education and Employment Survey-2004 by the Institute of Economics of Education, Peking University, this chapter analyzes intergenerational income mobility of China's urban residents with indicators such as the intergenerational inheritance and mobility coefficients of income, and the intergenerational income elasticity coefficient. We also use path analysis and binary logistic regression models to explore the role of education in promoting intergenerational income mobility, as well as the trend of this role with the advancement of marketization in China. Finally, we try to explain the trend with several explanations. The conclusions are summarized as follows:

- There is a strong intergenerational income transmission effect in urban China, and most children remain in the same income group as their father. Further, intergenerational income mobility of the highest and lowest income groups is weaker, and that of the middle-income groups is stronger.
- Children's education, as an acquired factor, has a greater impact on their income than the father's income. In addition, more years of schooling, especially for those from low-income families, effectively help children enter the highest-income group. This means that education in China has a strong function of replicating the original economic status system. Advantageous groups with higher socio-economic status can maintain their economic status by investing in their children's education. At the same time, investing in children's education serves as the most effective way for children of socially disadvantaged groups to achieve a leap in economic status. In other words, in urban China, education, as an important intergenerational mobility mechanism, can help children from families with disadvantaged economic status to move up to higher economic status, and plays an important role in promoting intergenerational mobility.

---

[3] Also known as "succession replacement", means that after parents retire, their children go through the procedures to replace the vacant positions and enter the parents' original workplace to work. This method was an important way of recruiting workers in China in the 1970s and 1980s.

- The role of education in promoting intergenerational income mobility, weakening the intergenerational transmission of income inequality, and improving the overall equality of the entire society is increasing with the advancement of marketization. The reasons may include the following: the advancement of marketization helps increase the revenue of education; high-income emerging occupations and sectors require better educated workforce; the role of acquired factors in achieving personal economic success continues to increase with the advancement of marketization.

China is building a high-standard socialist market economy. During the economic transition period, with the rapid economic growth, the income gap is widening and the social stratum differentiation is becoming more and more serious. These factors are not conducive to China's long-term economic development and long-term social stability, and may further hinder the construction of a harmonious society. The empirical research results of this chapter show that education, as an important intergenerational mobility mechanism, helps to promote intergenerational income mobility, weaken income inequality transmission effect between generations, and promote social equality. In China, education can increase the human capital of children, especially children from lower low-income families, to make up for their competitive disadvantage in congenital factors, have a relatively fair employment platform, and provide them with opportunities to enter the high-income spectrum. This will help to promote the mobility of various income classes in society, facilitate the reconstruction of social relations, maintain the healthy operation of the social system, and help promote the rapid, orderly and healthy development of the social economy and the long-term stability of the country. In view of this, we should pay attention to the social function of education to promote intergenerational income equality while exploring the economic value of education.

References

Aughinbaugh, A. (2000). Reapplication and Extension: Intergenerational Mobility in the United States. *Labor Economics*, *7*(6), 785–796.

Björklund, A., & Chadwick, L. (2003). Intergenerational Income Mobility in Permanent and Separated Families. *Economics Letters, 80*(2), 239–246.

Björklund, A., & Jäntti, M. (1997). Intergenerational Income Mobility in Sweden Compared to the United States. *The American Economic Review*, *87*(5), 1009–1018.

Chadwick, L., & Solon, G. (2002). Intergenerational Income Mobility Among Daughters. *The American Economic Review*, *92*(1), 335–344.

Chen, X. (1999). *Cost Recovery in China's Higher Education.* Doctoral Dissertation, School of Education, Peking University.

Corak, M., & Heisz, A. (1999). The Intergenerational Earnings and Income Mobility of Canadian Men: Evidence from Longitudinal Income Tax Data. *The Journal of Human Resources*, *34*(3), 504–533.

Couch. A., & Lillard, R. (1998). Sample Selection Rules and the Intergenerational Correlation of Earnings. *Labor Economics*, *5*(3), 313–329.

Dearden, L., Machin, S., & Reed, H. (1997). Intergenerational Mobility in Britain. *The Economic Journal, 107*(440), 47–66.
Guo, Z. (2003). *Statistical and Analysis Methods in Social Sciences: SPSS Software Application* (3rd ed.). China Renmin University Press.
Levine, D., & Mazumder, B. (2002). *Choosing the Right Parents: Changes in the Intergenerational Transmission of Inequality Between 1980 and the Early 1990s*. Federal Reserve Bank of Chicago.
Nam, Y. (2004). Is America Becoming More Equal for Children? Changes in the Intergenerational Transmission of Low- and High-Income Status. *Social Science Research, 33*(2), 187–205.
Solon, G. (1992). Intergenerational Income Mobility in the United States. *The American Economic Review, 82*(3), 393–408.
Solon, G. (2002). Cross-Country Differences in Intergenerational Earnings Mobility. *The Journal of Economic Perspectives, 16*(3), 59–66.
Xu, X. (2004). China's Social Structure as Seen from Occupational Prestige and Job Preferences—Appendix A: Index of Socioeconomic Status in China. *Social Stratification in China Today* (1st ed.). Li, Peilin et al. Social Sciences Academic Press (China).

MIX
Papier aus verantwortungsvollen Quellen
Paper from responsible sources
FSC® C105338

If you have any concerns about our products,
you can contact us on
ProductSafety@springernature.com

In case Publisher is established outside the EU,
the EU authorized representative is:
Springer Nature Customer Service Center GmbH
Europaplatz 3, 69115 Heidelberg, Germany

Printed by Libri Plureos GmbH
in Hamburg, Germany